DISCARD

TIME USE:
A Measure of Household Production of Family Goods and Services

by
Kathryn E. Walker
and
Margaret E. Woods

Published by

**Center for the Family
of the
AMERICAN HOME ECONOMICS ASSOCIATION**
2010 Massachusetts Avenue NW
Washington, D.C. 20036

Copyright 1976 by
The American Home Economics Association

Library of Congress Cataloging in Publication Data

Walker, Kathryn E   1917-
    Time use: a measure of household production of family goods and
services.

    Bibliography: p.
    Includes index.
    1. Home economics.   2. Time allocation surveys.
I. Woods. Margaret E., joint author. II. Title.
TX147.W25   658.5'421   75-46524
ISBN 0-8461-0701-5

3M2/76JDL

TABLE OF CONTENTS

Chapter VIII
Marketing and Management

Tables

Preface

The purpose of the research reported in this monograph was to develop a method for measuring household production of goods and services that would be relatively convenient to use and for which data could be easily collected. It has long been recognized that the work within private households of providing food, clothing, shelter, and care for family members is of major significance to the social and economic welfare of a nation. Measuring the amount of work required to produce these household services, however, has been severely limited because of the range, complexity, and service-oriented nature of household work as well as the cost of surveying large numbers of small units.

The present study is the latest phase of a research program on household work that began at Cornell in the 1920's. The time required to produce varying quantities of household work has been the central focus of that research, with the view of measuring household work output in terms of time use. In the study reported here, a clear and direct relationship was found between certain family characteristics and time used to provide the major kinds of household services. Since family characteristics are relatively easy to ascertain, this finding is of major consequence for the further development of a measure of all household production and a step toward the ultimate goal of placing a monetary value on that production.

Although this report represents an advance toward measuring household work loads on a national scale, it does not contain the final answer to the measurement of household work. First, only certain kinds of families were studied: two-parent households with children and two-person husband-wife households. Other kinds of households are known to have patterns of household work different from those in the present study, even when the household size is the same. Second, the data used were from one urban-suburban community in upstate New York; nationwide data from the heterogeneous regions and climates of the United States would be needed before valid generalizations about time use for household work can be made. Third, in the measure of time input, other variables such as knowledge and skill are included only as average inputs, and there is no measure of the quality of goods or services produced.

The major thrust of the report is on measuring the total time used by all workers for all household work and for each separate household work activity. However, complete records of use of time by all family members over age 6 were collected; these provide a measure of the share of the total household work assumed by each type of worker (husband, wife, young children, older children, and others). In addition, there is an extensive amount of descriptive data on each kind of household work, usually in relation to family characteristics. The monograph is viewed as a reference book with a great variety of specific information that can be identified by use of the general table of contents for the volume.

Some readers may be interested in the composite of household work and may find the first three chapters adequate for their interests while others will be more interested in specific activities for which Chapter 2 on the background of the study, Chapter 3 on all household work, plus one chapter on the specific work area of interest might be appropriate. Some will be interested only in the major household work areas, such as all food preparation activities, while others will be interested in specific tasks, such as regular meal preparation or after-meal cleanup. The methodology chapter (Appendix A) may be of the most interest for some researchers.

Some readers may be more interested in time contributions of specific types of workers, e.g., husband compared with wife; others will be more interested in the time of all workers, which was the focus of this research. Some will be interested in specific variables in relation to time use. All tabular presentations are located at the end of chapters.

Each chapter on the separate household work activities has the same organization so that the reader may choose the section that has greatest relevance. The statistical analysis of correlations for the time of all workers or of a particular type of worker with specific variables is summarized and then reported in detail in the first section of each chapter. The differences in hours used for the household work activity by major variables is in the second section, and the characteristics of the work that give increased meaning to the time data are in the third section.

It is hoped that this report of research with

one sample of families in 1967-68 in one area of New York State will stimulate further research into the household production work of all kinds of American families, and it is hoped that data from this report will provide a basis for comparing household work time-use at intervals in the future.

Time-use data combined with other indicators could provide a significant measure of technological, economic, and social change in the household sector of society.

KATHRYN E. WALKER and MARGARET E. WOODS

Acknowledgments

The research reported in this monograph is the result of contributions made over a long period by many individuals, without whom this project would not have been conceived, planned, and carried to completion.

My own interest in time use for household work took shape when I was a graduate student from 1952 to 1955 at Cornell University where I majored in Household Economics and Management in the New York State College of Home Economics. Dr. Jean Warren, who was chairman of my graduate committee, was a pioneer in the development of a tool for measurement of household work load in terms of time. I sincerely appreciate her valuable counsel for development of my study program and for my graduate research, and for contributions as a reviewer of this monograph.

It was Dr. Mabel Rollins, Chairman of the Department of Household Economics and Household Management for 17 of my years at Cornell, who had the greatest impact on the implementation of the research reported in this monograph. Her insight into the potential for use-of-time research and her encouragement for the development of the research proposal were of major importance. Appreciation is expressed to her for her support and for her significant contributions to Chapter I of this report.

For their important roles in obtaining financial support for the project, appreciation is expressed to administrators first in the College of Home Economics and since 1969 in the College of Human Ecology. The major funding came from the State of New York through research money budgeted to the college. I would like to express appreciation to Dr. Ethel Vatter, first as a co-worker in the development of the project and later in a college research administrator position, for her ideas and for her assistance in our efforts to increase the research budget of the college by seeking support of leaders of women's organizations of the state, potential users of time-use facts, and government officials with budget decision-making power. At a later stage in the project, federal funding was provided through programs supported by the United States Department of Agriculture (Agricultural Research Service and Hatch Funds administered through the Cornell Agricultural Experiment Station).

Ideas and plans for a project such as this could not be implemented and carried to completion without valuable contributions of many workers with special skills and abilities. It is difficult to express adequately appreciation to all who did the conscientious and careful work essential for this project. Dr. William Gauger made a significant contribution to the total project as he and his graduate students used the time-use data reported here to put a monetary value on household production. Throughout the monograph recognition is given to specific consultants, colleagues, and graduate students who have played invaluable roles. Appreciation for their various contributions is also expressed to interviewers, secretaries, clerical workers, and programmers, as well as to the community officials and housewives of the Syracuse area who made it possible to obtain the information reported here. Special appreciation is expressed to Mrs. Ruth Schaaf for her exceptional care in typing the manuscript for this report. I also express appreciation to Communication Arts staff members for their valued assistance in development of a graphically illustrated proposal used for obtaining funds, for the production of two half-hour films, for editing of the 1973 bulletin on *The Dollar Value of Household Work*, and for numerous news releases that reported findings.

Special appreciation goes to the research associate for the project, Mrs. Irma Telling, without whom the high standards for quality controls for sampling, data collection, and data handling could not have been maintained. Thanks also is given to the coauthor of this monograph, Margaret Woods, who contributed significantly to the organization and reporting of the vast quantity of data presented. Appreciation is expressed to the reviewers for their constructive suggestions, so useful to the final development of this report. Reviewers for the Center for the Family included: Dr. Margaret Liston, Mrs. Helen Lamale, and Dr. Helen McHugh. Reviewers for selected chapters from the College of Human Ecology included: Dr. Rose Steidl, Dr. Mary Purchase, Dr. Helen Bayer, Dr. Gertrude Armbruster, Dr. Alice Davey, Dr. Jean Warren, and Dr. Mabel Rollins. The editor was Dr. Joan Baird.

And finally, I am indebted to the Center for the Family of the American Home Economics

Association for serving as publisher of this monograph. Home economists have been pioneers in recognizing the problems of household work roles of women. Many other professions are now interested in data on the nonmarket work of the home. Therefore, it is especially pleasing to me that the Center for the Family, whose interdisciplinary programs are planned to assist families and those who work with families, should select this monograph as its first publication.

Acknowledging the contributions of many, I nevertheless accept responsibility for decisions made throughout the years I served as the principal investigator for the research.

KATHRYN E. WALKER, *Principal Investigator*
Professor, Department of Consumer
Economics and Public Policy
New York State College of Human Ecology
Cornell University

Foreword

When Martha Van Rensselaer wrote her first bulletin for farmers' wives, "Saving Steps," in 1902, not only was she giving expression to the ideas that led to the present monograph, but she was starting an educational effort that resulted in the New York State College of Human Ecology. She sought ways to reach the farmer's wife, most isolated, least considered, and most overworked member of society—a position, we might add, that a vast number of the world's women still occupy. The agricultural colleges were developing and disseminating potentially useful information to farmers; why should the same not be done for the farmers' wives? Enthusiastically supported by Dean Liberty Hyde Bailey of the College of Agriculture, the bulletins developed into a reading course, a short course at Cornell University, a department, a school, then a College of Home Economics, and finally the College of Human Ecology.

Household work, especially in farm homes, was so strenuous that detailed measurement seemed unnecessary before trying to make it easier. "Saving Strength" was another of the early bulletins. Attempts to mechanize the heavy tasks or to decrease the time used for the more difficult or disliked tasks led to an interest in both time and energy management.

Miss Van Rensselaer was forced to carry a heavy load of organization and administration, but she did not lose her interest in the problem of the heavy work load that women were carrying. She continued to teach in this area, but she also made great efforts to find and develop staff to expand subject matter in this field as well as in food and nutrition, sanitation and housing, clothing, child development, and other aspects of home economics. Since staff did not come ready-made, a great deal of her effort had to go into finding, inspiring, and pushing promising students into further study. Ella Cushman, Helen Canon, and Jean Warren were all students who had Miss Van Rensselaer's particular interest in the work of the home, and she helped and directed their interest. These three had the most direct influence on the study that resulted in the present monograph.

Ella Cushman combined an almost passionate respect for the job homemakers were doing with study in the emerging field of time and motion analysis. She was a friend of and studied with Lillian Gilbreth, who was an engineer and pioneer in industrial work analysis. Ella Cushman taught part of most of her courses in homes. She constantly pointed out the work simplification techniques that the homemakers themselves had developed and nudged them to make further efforts. She just as constantly impressed on homemakers and students the need for individual modification as work simplification methods were applied to individual homes. She was an innovator both in teaching methods and in subject matter.

Helen Canon's field was economics, particularly as related to the productive contributions, both paid and unpaid, made by women in their homes. Her association with agricultural economists, both as a student and as a faculty member, introduced her to the survey method for the study of small units and to statistics as a necessary component of the analysis of such surveys. It is a telling sidelight that the department of which she was chairman from 1930 to 1952, Economics of the Household and Household Management, and the departments of Agricultural Economics and Rural Sociology, were for many years the sole contributors to the only IBM sorting and tabulating, and later computing, installation on the Cornell University campus. She stressed the usefulness of both surveys and statistics as teaching methods: surveys as a means of introducing students at first hand to the great and surprising variety in the ways people live and view the world in which they live; and statistics as a means of helping in speculations about and developing generalities possibly existing in this area of seemingly infinite variety—the household.

Jean Warren is still participating in innovative research and teaching programs in the area of family economics. Her past professional activities have brought her into contact as a student, co-worker, teacher, or adviser with practically everyone who has studied household work. She has been especially interested in measuring the amount and describing the kinds of work done in homes. In 1928 she was an interviewer on a study which included a listing of the food consumed by farm women. Nancy Morey (1936) used these data to calculate calorie intake. In an effort to check these figures, Morey took the daily time records for New York farm women and estimated the amount of energy required for different household tasks, using data from calorimetry experiments.

Working with Nancy Morey and from her own familiarity with the productive farm work unit used in agriculture, Jean Warren developed an interest in homemaking work units. One of her contributions was to describe household work in units which could be quantified and related to use of time; such as, number of rooms in daily use related to time used for house care, number of pieces of laundry related to time used for washing and ironing. Her research provided the basis for studies made by Wiegand and Walker in the 1950's and for the study reported here.

Maud Wilson's 1929 bulletin on "Use of Time by Oregon Farm Homemakers" furnished ideas for Jean Warren. Miss Wilson's study compared the use of time by farm, village, and city homemakers. Hers was the first real attempt to describe the household work load. In the introduction to this bulletin, Wilson (1929, p. 9) said in part:

> The concern of the home economist is. . . that the homemaker shall find her job as interesting and healthful and stimulating as any other occupation open to her. . . . The homemaker has many advantages that most other workers do not have—an elastic working schedule, . . . variety in her work; and most important of all, personal interest in the product of her labor. Certain unfavorable conditions of labor are common— . . . difficulty of maintaining a work schedule because the desires and needs of various members of the family take precedence over those of the homemaker, and because many operations must be carried on simultaneously; lack of "free" leisure; lack of rest periods at times most needed.

These comments apply as well to the homemaker of today.

Miss Wilson went on to say that while the number of processes done in the home had decreased, the responsibilities had increased partly due to the lack of any help, and to newer knowledge which made homemaking more of a science and less of a tradition. "The effect of changes in the status of women has been to multiply the homemaker's outside interests and to increase possibilities of the productive use of leisure."

Support for the study of household work, intellectually and financially, has always been limited. The small size of the household unit with the consequent high cost of investigating it, the large number of women engaged in homemaking, the individual character and nonmonetary aspect of the work, all combined to handicap interest. Moreover, the household has generally been looked on as an "acted upon" rather than an initiating sector. More interest has been generated in the manipulation of the household as a consuming unit than in study of its functioning.

The close connection between the farm and farm home, however, was perceived early. Thus for many years funding for the study of farm households came from agricultural sources. The breakthrough of this limitation of Agricultural Experiment Station support came in 1952 with Elizabeth Wiegand's comparative study of farm and city households. A great debt is owed to the administrators of the Agricultural Experiment Stations for their vision and support.

Funding for the study that led to the present monograph came from New York State, the Agricultural Research Service, and the New York State Agricultural Experiment Station. These grants permitted the largest sample and greatest depth of analysis of household work that had ever been undertaken at this institution. The earlier work of Warren, Wiegand, and Walker had established a means of classifying a large number of the work activities of households and also the variables within households that were most closely associated with the time spent on these work activities. Thus these earlier studies provided a basis for the selection of the sample of the households and for the analysis of data obtained in the present study.

In this monograph, Kathryn Walker and coworkers have developed a method for measurement of household work in complete family households, an achievement of great use to future research. Of course, investigations of other types of households and other areas of the country are needed, but a way of approaching the problem has been demonstrated. Thus, a long step forward toward the ultimate goal of introducing household production into national indicators has been accomplished. Moreover, the growing realization of the need for prompt information about the *interaction* of households, government, and industry should improve the climate of interest for support of the necessary studies. The indirect, incomplete, and tardy information available about household activities is all too obvious.

For example, in the late 1940's, 1950's, and 1960's households made certain adjustments to the economic climate. Jobs were plentiful and prices of goods and services purchased by the household were relatively low compared to money incomes. Households apparently responded by sending as many members as they could into the paid labor force, and curtailing as much as possible their internal economic activities. Today, households may be engaging in very different actions, but we have little data for determining such a possibility. Jobs are certainly scarcer, and prices of purchased goods and services are certainly rising. Early in the summer of 1975 the increase and popularity of home gardens received an unusual amount of publicity. A little later the failure of industry to provide certain components for the preservation of this homegrown food also attained unusual notice. No notice of an increase in home prepared meals and packed lunches has occurred, but it is possible that such has happened. Unfortunately we have no information in this area. There has, however, been a decrease in many kinds of eating places, from student dormitories to luncheon clubs, with an apparent increase in "fast food" eating establishments and "deli" counters in food stores. Certainly house repair, particularly as it may save heating fuel, has been urged, from the replacement of faucet washers to the addition of insulation and storm windows, with much of the work to be carried on by household labor. How much has occurred, and with what results is not known. How households, the major providers of transportation of people, will respond to the gasoline shortage is still uncertain. Import figures indicate that they seem to prefer small and less-fuel-consuming cars. Forecasts of birth rates have been notably inaccurate. Both the number and age of children in the household have considerable effect, as the present monograph indicates, on the work load in the home. It would appear possible that more information about household work loads could improve our knowledge of the basis of household decisions regarding more children.

Another aspect of current living that seems to call for comparative study of industrial and household work activities is the discontent expressed by a growing number of both industrial employees and housewives with certain aspects of their jobs. Industrial workers complain about the lack of individuality, the concept of bosses, and the stress on monetary evaluation. Housewives are discontented with the female orientation of their job, the complexity of the tasks, and lack of status due to the nonmonetary aspect. As one looks at these discontents, it appears that each group,

housewives and industrial workers, sees desirable aspects in the complaints of the other. Is this situation caused by the nature of the worker or the conditions of the work? If psychologists, sociologists, and economists are to have any solutions for these discontents they are certainly in need of comparative studies of household and industrial work performance and performers. Maud Wilson in 1929 called attention to these same disadvantages, and others, of household work, as well as the advantages. Since then the comparative advantages and disadvantages of the two kinds of work have been very little explored. While the present monograph does not investigate the psychological aspects of household work, it does contain clues as to how such studies might be classified as to tasks, for example, and does contain evaluations by homemakers of the various tasks.

Finally, an increase in the participation of household activities by men has been suggested by a number of persons as a way of improving the present situation, particularly for women. Such participation it is said would relieve women of some of their household work and enable them to engage in gainful employment away from home. In the present study, although the hours the wife spent in household work decreased somewhat as her employment away from home increased, the husband's time spent in household work did not change with her employment. Perhaps sharing of household roles and responsibilities will also offer intrinsic rewards for men.

It has been the purpose of this foreword to point out the way that this monograph has been built on ideas and research that preceded it. It is hoped that this research will serve as usefully in building the next research both at Cornell University and elsewhere.

MABEL A. ROLLINS
and JEAN WARREN

Definitions

Household work or household production—purposeful activities performed in individual households to create the goods and services that make it possible for a family to function as a family.

Household or family—husband-wife households with or without children living at home.

Nonemployed-wife households (NE) or **employed-wife households (E)—**households or families of the nonemployed or employed wives.

Employed wives are those gainfully employed 15 or more hours per week. Conversely, **nonemployed wives** are those not gainfully employed or employed less than 15 hours per week.

Total time—average amount of time used by all workers for the household, i.e., time of wife, husband, children, and adult nonfamily workers.

Time of individual workers—average time of wives, husbands, teenagers, children 6 to 11 years, or nonfamily female and male workers (other workers).

Combined time—time used for all subtasks of a work activity, e.g., time for regular meal preparation plus after-meal cleanup and special food preparation.

Number of children—number of children under 18 living in the households at the time of the study.

Age of youngest child—age by years at last birthday classified as under 1, 1, 2 to 5, 6 to 11, or 12 to 17.

Family type—33 categories that combine number of children and age of youngest ordered from least to most complex, i.e., ordered by increased number of children and decreasing age of youngest within each family size.

Chapter I

The Measurement of Household Production

Household production or household work, as defined in this study, comprises the multiplicity of activities performed in individual households that result in goods and services that enable a family to function as a unit. Over the centuries these activities, though changed in form and content, have continued to make significant contributions to the functioning of the social order.

Some goods and many services used by the family continue to be produced for the family by its members, even though a great variety of goods and services are produced today by industry, and some are provided by the community. Technological and social changes have created demands for new goods and services. Some activities no longer performed in most households, such as carrying water, have been replaced by others; for instance, arranging for maintenance of the mechanical equipment of the house. Some activities formerly of relatively little importance have become major ones; for example, marketing for the household is more time consuming than it once was. Other activities have taken on new dimensions; one example is chauffeuring family members to educational and community functions. Though mechanical equipment is now used for many household work activities, a greater quantity of goods or services is sometimes produced (e.g., more clothes washed), and the quality of products is frequently higher than in earlier periods. More, rather than fewer, resources may be invested today to produce even the basic services of food, clothing, and shelter.

The activities involved in household production of goods and services fit the concept of work as "any conscious, purposeful activity which with satisfaction serves the material and spiritual needs of the individual and community" (Anderson, 1961, p. 25). On the other hand, semantic problems with the word *work* are numerous. *Work* commonly is used to refer to paid employment; it sometimes implies physical labor; and it sometimes carries with it unpleasant connotations. Household work is usually not paid work; many of the activities are not physically laborious; some of the activities are enjoyed by many who do them but are considered unpleasant by others. Many kinds of activities, however, are now called work whether or not they require physical exertion; and all members of the labor force are considered to be working whenever they are engaged in occupational or other obligatory activities (Parker, 1971). Household work is made up of many purposeful activities. Levy (1963, pp. 1-17) makes the point that, although women in the home are commonly considered not to be working in the paid employment sense of the word, they cook, launder, dust, shop, and scrub; and act as purchasing agents, finance officers, processors of raw materials, and public relations counsels. These work activities and work roles, which are shared by wives, husbands, and children, are needed to produce the goods and services required by the family unit.

Need for Measurement of Household Production

The concern of this study was with two measurable aspects of household production: (1) the amount of time spent to keep a household running and (2) the amounts of goods and services resulting from the time spent. The purpose of the research was the development of a measure with which to quantify the nonmarket production of the household.

Although the social contributions of the family to society have been analyzed in numerous studies, the family's economic contribution through household production has received less attention. For many years, economists interested in the measurement of national income have included in their estimates an apology for the omission of household production. In 1930, King wrote:

In this series of income studies, the Bureau [of Economic Research] has naturally been compelled to confine its investigations to types of income translatable into terms of money units. Items upon which no money value can be placed have necessarily been omitted. Furthermore, some items having a definite money value have not been considered because it has proved impossible to estimate their total money value, even roughly. Among such omissions are the value of the services of persons to themselves and to their families. Several critics have urged the inclusion of an estimate of the value of the services of the housewife. If such services are evaluated it is, of course, logical to include also the value of the services of the head of the household when he manages the family business and when he performs such physical labor as building fires, caring for the lawn and shaving himself instead of going to the barber. The value of such home services is tremendous. Furthermore, in estimates like ours, in which the values of such services are not included, every transfer to the factory of work, formerly done at home, as for example, dressmaking and breadmaking, gives an artificial and misleading upward slope to the curve representing estimates of the national income. Yet because the difficulty of correctly evaluating such services is so very great, they have been excluded (p. 35).

In 1969, Fuchs pointed out:

The amount of economic research devoted to services has been far from commensurate with the importance of these industries in the U.S. and other developed economies. Reasons for this neglect in the past are not difficult to find. They include the greater importance of primary and secondary employment at lower levels of real income per capita; the belief of some economists, notably Adam Smith, that only the primary and secondary sectors were "productive"; the difficulty of measuring service output; the difficulty of obtaining data because of the heterogeneity of activity and the small size of most firms in the service sector; the large role of nonprofit organizations in the service sector and the difficulty of analyzing their behavior. Thus a combination of intractable conceptual problems, inadequate statistical coverage, and insufficient empirical analysis has served to limit our understanding of the factors affecting production, employment and productivity in services (pp. 1, 2).

These comments by Fuchs are particularly apt because household production more closely resembles the service sector of production than any other. With the possible exception of those related to nonprofit organizations, all the difficulties that Fuchs listed, as well as additional ones such as the nonmarket aspect, also help to explain the neglect of economic research related to household production.

Indeed, Fabricant (1969, pp. 368-369) commented:

The standard system, and the concept of GNP and the industrial classification embedded in this system, were developed for use in modern industrialized economies. The suitability of the system, even for these economies, is being increasingly questioned, as experience with it teaches us something of its limitations, as the uses to which it is put become more refined, and as change takes place in the structure of the economy and the place of the economic structure in the structure of society as a whole. But there has always been serious doubt about the applicability of the standard system of accounts to economies of a hundred and more years ago, to present-day developing countries, and even to the new crop of 'centrally planned' economies. . . . [The questions] apply with special force, perhaps, to the service industries. The ancient problem raised by the omission of household work in preparing food for consumption, mending and washing clothes, maintaining the home and other buildings, providing health and educational and fire protection services—the list is endless—is just one of these questions. When the service industries are at the center of our attention, and even when we are concerned with them only in order to add services to commodity output to get total national product, we cannot ignore important kinds of household production and their shifts from and back to the household.

The lack of empirical analysis of household production has given rise to widely varying ideas and speculations as to its importance. In their laudatory effort to advance the position of women in the market economy, some members of the women's liberation movement have tended to denigrate household work or production. Friedan (1963, p. 13) referred to the conception of an American housewife as "freed by science and labor-saving appliances from drudgery." Hoffman (1963, p. 26), in speaking of the housekeeping role of women, said ". . . one cannot fail to note the lack of creativity it affords. There is very little skill demanded and very little room for excellence. . . . With the introduction of package mixes, even the skill of literacy is no longer required. . . ."

In the view of another group, the household may well be invading the territory of the service industries. Concerned with the decline in mass transportation, the Census of Transportation in 1965 estimated that ". . . a very substantial portion, probably the major portion, of local transportation between home and work is provided now not by the 'transportation industry' but by the household" (Fabricant, 1969, p. 370).

No matter what one's prejudices or predilections are for employment of women in or outside their households, or for institutional living versus close association with a small group, the lack of information and measurement of household activities hinders rational economic judgment. Moreover, as movement in both directions between household production and the service industries begins to be apparent, the lack of information about household production becomes increasingly serious.

Input/Output Measurement of Household Production

The extent, complexity, and nonmarket quality of household production make its measurement important, difficult, and challenging. Household production varies from household to household, and within households from day to day and from season to season, as well as in other ways, known and unknown. Variety seems to be the "name of the game" in household production; both the activities and the goods and services resulting from these activities are custom made for the needs of the household. Because of this great variety, only studies of households can indicate what is included in the production, and such studies are extremely expensive because of the large number of households required for such a survey and because of the detailed data needed. One of the purposes of the present study has been to simplify problems of sampling and to sharpen the questions necessary to obtain needed information from households.

The definition of household production can be stated in the form of an equation—the time spent on the household work activities (input) equals the goods and services produced (output). The assumption is made, of course, that the labor of the household members is the only factor in the activities (input); no attempt is made to measure capital or other inputs. The equation, implicit in the definition of household production, makes it possible to use known items or quantities on one side of the equation to determine or estimate unknown items or quantities on the other side.

The individual goods and services produced (output) can in many cases be identified, and in a number of cases can be measured or quantified. But such quantification can only be in terms of the individual activities, such as number of meals served or pounds of clothes washed. Thus, it is not possible to obtain a total of the goods and services produced or in any way quantify one item in terms of another. We are faced here with the old problem of adding apples and oranges. Pricing, the common method of economic measurement, is not possible with these nonmarket items.

The time spent on activities (input) presents quite a different problem. Here units of time are available by which the total of the activities can be measured, but the individual activities that make up this total are difficult to untangle and identify. Individual activities in a household, for example, are not uniform, and when started, few can be carried through to completion in one time block. One part of an activity may be started, then interrupted to carry on another activity, and later resumed. Some activities may be performed every day; some much less frequently. The amount of time spent to accomplish household work may vary also according to (1) the age, physical condition, and temperament of the wife; (2) standards of output sought; (3) physical facilities utilized; (4) climate and weather; and (5) work interruptions.

Thus, the activities must be untangled and identified in relation to the output side of the equation, the identifiable goods and services resulting. Since household work has no monetary value set in the marketplace, some resource has to be used on which a value can be placed. In this study, *time* has been the resource used to indicate household work loads, and the use of time has been expressed as the amount of time spent to perform certain household activities. The use of an average amount of work performed in a constant period of time follows standard practice in determining average cost of production, which is frequently expressed as average cost in time or average output per worker (Gage, 1960, p. 61). Household activities can thus be measured in terms of time, and correspondingly the resulting goods and services will also be measured in terms of time. Quantitative comparisons in household production are thus possible.

In this and in all industrialized countries, our public and private living is very much controlled by the clock since time serves as a basis for organization in industry, schools, and business; for transportation to and from these places; and for scheduling social functions. Since time is of major significance, man in the cultural setting of industrialized society is highly conscious of clock time and recognizes the value of time as a resource.

Time as a measure of household production has one limitation that may cause concern. Because household work is variable and discontinuous, it is not economically feasible to record the precise time of beginning and ending work, as can be done in factory production. There is much cultural, social, and psychological variation in the ability to estimate time. However, support for acceptance of ability to estimate time use comes from the French psychologist, Fraisse (1968), who has said that awareness of time is part of our psychological makeup. In commenting on the use of nychthermeral rhythm in orienting time use, he said, "This rhythmic activity turns our organism into a regular clock and gives us points of reference by which we orient ourselves in the time of day. . . [and] man spontaneously makes use of the temporal points of reference provided by his organism. We are conditioned by the rhythm of meals, sleep, and so forth" (p. 28). The sociologist Goody (1968) comments on one's awareness of time by the many cyclical events of living: "Time reckoning begins with the recurrent divisions into night and day that commonly regulate activity . . . . The division of human life into light and dark, movement and rest, waking and sleeping often provides a symbolic framework for many other activities" (p. 32).

Nancy and Richard Ruggles (1970, p. 40) commented on the potential for use of time measures for valuing nonmarket production in discussing the need for redesigning economic accounts:

> The question of productive activity taking place within the household unquestionably needs further study. Time budget studies of how people divide their total time among different activities (including eating, sleeping, and leisure) would be highly informative, and would provide a valuable set of data that could be directly related to the market transactions in the national economic accounts.

Studies of Time Spent on Household Work

Some studies of the amount of time used for household work activities have been conducted over the years in the United States and Europe, but such research has been limited. Studies of farm women in the 1920's and 1930's were sponsored by the Home Economics Bureau of the U.S. Department of Agriculture in numerous agricultural experiment stations, and these have provided excellent though limited historical information. The most frequently quoted of these studies, with a sample of about 500 homemakers, was done in Oregon by Maud Wilson (1929), but many other land-grant institutions conducted similar studies.[1]

Saurio (1947), at the University of Helsinki, collected data from about 400 farm families in 1936, the same year that Warren (1938) collected data from 500 farm families in New York State. Because of the heavy involvement of Finland in World War II, Saurio's data were not analyzed until 1947. A few additional studies of time use for household work were carried on in the United States in land-grant colleges and universities

during the 1940's and 1950's. Samples for these studies were taken primarily from rural areas. Foote (1961) directed a study of time use of husbands and wives in a suburban area for the General Electric Company in the early 1950's, but the results of this study were for company use and have not been published.

In the late 1950's, interest in ways homemakers were using time intensified. This interest may have been spurred by the increased participation of women in the labor force, technological developments that changed household work, and changes in the roles of family members. These developments have made resources of time, energy, and money more and more interchangeable for carrying out the work of homemaking. Interest in time use was also shown by a 1957 study by Boalt (1961; Walker, 1964) of time use of 1,000 homemakers in Sweden and a study by Girard (1958) of about the same number in France. Half of the women in the French study were in the labor force and time use when women combined two roles was emphasized. Employed women in France appeared to have work days that were as long as farm women had had in an earlier period when they worked in the home and on the land.

The most extensive research ever done on use of time was a 1964 multinational study in 12 countries, including the United States. This research was carried out under the leadership of The UNESCO-sponsored European Coordination Center for Research and Documentation in Social Sciences. The same research design, basically the same questions, and the same coding techniques were used in all countries in order that data could be compared. The 1972 publication (Szalai) of the completed study provides a wealth of data for international comparison. While the emphasis of the multinational research was on nonwork time, comparisons were made of time use for paid work, household work, free time, and sleep for employed men and for working and nonworking women (i.e., women not in the labor force). Using time diary techniques similar to those used for the multinational research, data were also collected in Washington, D.C., by Chapin (1974) for analysis of human activity patterns, including homemaking. Although data for the Szalai and Chapin studies were collected at about the same time as those analyzed for this monograph, differences in type of sample and in the unit of study (i.e., the individual versus the household) impose significant restrictions on making comparisons of the household work time reported.

---

[1]An extensive but not necessarily complete listing of studies on time use for household work in the United States is in Appendix C.

Homemaking Work Units

The development of work units for homemaking was the first known attempt to measure household production in terms of the quantity of goods and services produced per unit of time under household working conditions. Work units were developed by Warren (1938 and 1940)[2] in a major pioneering effort to measure household production. She adapted the concept of an agricultural productivity measure, the farm work unit, which scaled amounts of widely different kinds of work output into units of time.

Because of this scaling feature, the work unit seemed to be an answer to the problem of obtaining a measure of all household work as well as each of the diverse household work activities (e.g., care of children and food preparation). Since all the operations related to a work activity take time to perform, the separate segments of time use could be added together to provide a total amount of time spent on a work activity. The relative effects of a number of factors on the total time spent could be examined, and the factors that were most closely related to the time spent could be considered as the factors that determined the amount of work to be accomplished. An average (or other measure of central tendency) could be computed for households having the same characteristics. In this way, the average time would vary only with changes in real output rather than by reason of household differences. The resulting measure is a quantity of output in a household activity by an average worker in a given time unit under certain household conditions.

Warren used farm households exclusively for her research since one significant reason for developing a measure of household work at that time was to determine the major causes for the variability in work loads of farm women. If such causes could be determined, methods might then be devised to lighten these work loads. The earlier studies by the Bureau of Home Economics of the U.S. Department of Agriculture provided guidelines on categories of work activities and clues to factors that influence work loads.

Warren found that the amount of time spent on each household work activity varied according to such factors as number of family members, age of youngest child, or size of dwelling unit. For several household work activities, she was able to distinguish one factor that seemed to be more closely related than others to the time spent. Some of these factors were characteristics of the activity, such as number of articles ironed, while others were family composition variables, such as number of children and age of the youngest child. Once the best time-related variable was found, an average time was computed for the time of all workers who had spent time on the activity. A separate work unit was computed for each variation in the work-related variables; for example, if the distinguishing variable was number of persons in the household, an average time was computed for one-person households, two-person households, and so on. For some household activities, it was not possible to identify a factor that was closely related to time in the activity, and no work units could be computed for these activities.

A major contribution of Warren was to quantify the amount of work in several major activities by isolating the one factor that appeared to have the most effect on the work load in an activity. She was the first researcher to take practical steps to develop a measure of household production, to devise a means of testing such a measure, and to demonstrate that household production could be measured.[3] The work unit showed the average time cost of doing a certain quantity of work. The measure met with wide acceptance and was interpreted as a significant development in home management theory (Gross and Crandall, 1954, pp. 227-228).

Household work loads change in response to extensive changes in technology, broad changes in living patterns, development and use of commercial services, changes in family roles, and re-examination of family values and priorities. Several broad-scale changes were underway at the time of Warren's research (1938); but urban areas were changing more than rural areas. By 1940, for example, about 90% of the urban homes had modern plumbing while only 18% of the farm homes had running water; 56% versus 15% had mechanical refrigeration; and 73% versus 4% used gas for cooking (Wright, 1949, p. 869).

In the early 1950's, steps were taken to further develop the work unit. In 1953, Wiegand

---

[2]This method of measuring household production was developed by Jean Warren as a PhD student in Household Economics and Home Management at Cornell University, in collaboration with Dr. Helen Canon, her faculty adviser.

[3]To increase confidence in the unit of work measurement, additional statistical analysis was done in 1940, under the direction of Helen Canon, by Ruth Remsburg and Rose Smith with results reported in Smith's M.S. thesis (1940).

reported her study of time used for household activities by 250 homemakers in upstate New York. This was the first study on time use for household work activities in New York State that included an urban as well as a farm population. Data on time use by urban homemakers in the labor force also were collected. This study made it clear that changes in life-style, housing, and equipment had affected the total time used for household work and that new work units would be needed. Wiegand's data indicated that the work load in activities varied in accordance with number of family members and age of youngest child. As in Warren's study, the use of time for household activities varied with the standard of work and the equipment as well as with the work load.

By 1954, a major long-term objective was emerging—the development of a measure of household production that could be used by professionals in any field whenever such a measure was called for. The first step in this direction was to further test the concept of the work unit as a measure of household production by computing new work units. Walker (1955) in a reanalysis of Wiegand's data[4] was able to isolate the specific variables that exerted the greatest influences on the amount of time spent on six household tasks. These activities and the variables most closely related to time spent on them were:

Meal preparation	complexity of meals served (number of dishes and degree of manipulation required to prepare them)
Regular house care	presence or absence of children
Physical care of family members	number and ages of children
Washing clothes	number of loads of washing
Ironing clothes	number of pieces ironed
Dishwashing	number of persons in the household

It was estimated that these six work activities accounted for almost four-fifths of household production.[5] In the remaining activities, time

varied with more than one factor, but no one relationship could be identified as dominant.

Walker's work unit was computed by dividing the total time used by households doing the same amount of work by the number of households reporting that quantity of work, just as Warren had done. Also, as in Warren's study, each category of variation within the household work activity had a separate work unit. A major difference in the Warren and Walker work-unit values was the period of time for work measurement. Warren reported amount of work in average minutes per week and Walker reported average hours per day.

Gage (1960) tested the usefulness of the work unit as a means of collecting data for the purpose of placing a monetary value on household work. She demonstrated that the work unit for an activity could be computed by collecting the necessary information for the variables identified in previous research as most closely related to time spent on a work activity. Her study stimulated a further search for a factor or factors for quantification of the amount of work in the remaining household work activities. Her research also pointed up the desirability of having the quantifying variables be those for which data are either readily available or easily collected.

In 1961, a major study on use of all workers' time on household work was begun at Purdue University under the direction of Manning (1968). Aside from the work at Cornell, this is the most complete investigation on time use and work output in household activities that has been done. The research project was initiated to determine work-unit values for households in Indiana for comparison with the ones developed by Walker for New York State in 1955. In the report of the Purdue research, Manning did not use the term "work unit," but the predictors of time cost were essentially the same as the work-unit measures in that they expressed a quantity of work accomplished in a unit of time.

The Purdue sample had approximately equal numbers of urban and rural households in which wives were not employed. Approximately 100 wives kept records for 1 week in each of 4 seasons. As at Cornell, the time spent on the work activities was analyzed in relation to a large number of variables. Manning developed predictors of time costs for the same six household work activities as Walker had; in addition, she identified time costs for packing lunches, special food preparation, food preservation, special house care, upkeep of the house, sewing and mending, financial planning and

---

[4]Jean Warren was faculty adviser for both the Wiegand and Walker research.

[5]In 1961, Suneson, using the same techniques as Warren and Walker, determined that the best predictor for food shopping time was the number of family members eating regularly at home (p. 68).

record keeping, and marketing. The results of this research project were reported in one research bulletin by the project leader and in a group of graduate theses by students who analyzed data for various aspects of the project.[6]

A major thrust of the Purdue research was to obtain quantitative measures of household work and to include quality of performance in the measure. This study highlighted the extensive amount of detail and analytical work required to develop a quantifying variable for each household work activity. For example, observers' records of the performance of one subtask, care of master bedroom, by five respondents under laboratory conditions, clearly indicated that one reason for time variations was that not all women performed the same steps even in this one limited area of housework. Using factor analysis, the Purdue research team found that housekeeping standards accounted for 24% of the time variability among wives in caring for the master bedroom. Other factors were motion economy (number of motions, distance traveled, time used, and storage) and space-purposive activity (room space, free space); these two factors together with housekeeping standards accounted for 60% of the variations in time use. It should be noted that Manning's research, in addition to highlighting the problem of quantifying a household work activity, provided the first measured indication of the effects of homemakers' standards on the time spent.

The Purdue project supported the finding that had become apparent in the Cornell research—for several activities for which work measures were developed, more than one factor was so closely related to time that a different method of determining quantities of work seemed desirable.

Quantifying Variables for Measurement

The kind of measure of household production visualized was a variable that would be common to all or nearly all household work activities. The quantifying variables that had previously been developed had several limitations. One was that a quantifying variable would be needed for each household work activity when all household work was to be measured. Another was the extraordinary amount of detail and analysis required to develop a work unit, as shown by Walker's and

Manning's research. The most important limitation was that the numerous quantifying variables had to be converted to a common unit of measurement for effective use.

Three of the work units developed by Walker in 1955 related time to some quantifiable characteristics of the specific activity—number of loads of washing, number of pieces ironed, and type of meal served. For these three household work activities, certain time-consuming operations have to be performed each time the job is undertaken, and these operations are directly related to the manner in which household materials are processed—the division of household washing into loads for the machine, the separate handling of each piece in ironing, and the varied processing required by different kinds of food. Other household work activities, such as regular house care or special clothing care, require numerous operations that do not necessarily center around a basic core of work. For such tasks quantifiable data are difficult to collect because of the range of possible operations and the mix of operations.

Work measurement based on a quantifiable characteristic of a specific activity does not represent a constant relationship between work accomplished and time spent, because the factors that brought about variations in these two components affect the ratio between time and work as well. A load of washing does not have a constant size and composition for any given worker or average group of workers because of differences in quantity and composition of the load. For example, it was not possible to multiply the average time used to do one piece of ironing by the number of pieces ironed and use that as a measure of a day's work in ironing, without allowing for variations in time spent getting ready and putting away the equipment and the articles ironed. In addition, as Manning demonstrated, the amount of work in an activity can vary according to the types of operations performed with consequent effects on the amount of work accomplished within a given time period.

As a result of the difficulties encountered in quantifying household work by use of task-specific variables, attention was directed to the family composition variables on which the other three work units developed by Walker had been based. Each of these variables was directly related to the time spent on an activity: age of youngest child in the family for physical care of family members, number in household for dishwashing, and presence or absence of children for regular house care. It cannot be said that a child in a

---

[6]See detailed list of time use studies in Appendix C for Purdue reports between 1963 and 1968.

certain age group will require a definite amount of time in the same manner that ironing a piece of clothing requires a definite amount of time. The time varies in accordance with the kind of care needed. It may be 24 hours on 1 day if the child is seriously ill, or less than an hour on another day for routine care. What can be said is that there is a direct relationship between the age of the youngest child and the time spent on child care; as the youngest child in the family grows older, less time is spent on this activity.

Household production changes over time within an individual family. The family is not a static entity but goes through stages of growth and contraction, with each stage requiring a different "mix," quantitatively and qualitatively, of goods and services to meet the needs of family members. The needs of a two-person household are different from those of a six-person household, and the needs of each household vary according to its composition, value system, and priorities.

The direct relationship between family composition and goods and services needed suggested that a family composition variable could have the greatest potential for the development of a measure of all types of household work activities. If time spent on household work varied consistently in response to changes in some one family characteristic, it could then be predicted that any household with the same characteristic (that is, a family with a child in a particular age group) would spend a similar amount of time on a given activity without having to know what specific operations had been performed. Further, since time would vary in relation to changes in this family characteristic, the relationship could be expected to remain relatively constant, in spite of differences in household routines or technological or social change. One deficiency of the work quantifying variables was their susceptibility to technological obsolescence; for example, improvements in equipment could change the number of loads of washing without any real change in the actual work load or in the time spent.

When the conditions of production were defined by a family characteristic, the measure of household production then could be defined as the amount of work accomplished in a given unit of time under certain social and physical conditions. It would express certain relationships between the worker, the work, and the environment. The statistical definition of the measure would be a precise formulation in terms of the average amount of time spent by a group working under similar conditions and could be used to measure the production of any worker under the same conditions.[7] Physiological and psychological characteristics of the worker might still cause an unmeasured amount of variation; such variation could only be assumed to average out over a sample of workers. What was analyzed was not the time of one person but the time of a group of persons. For each individual worker the measure could be the amount of work performed in a given unit of time, and for any given population the measure could be the average time for a certain amount of work.

The establishment of a direct relationship between a family composition variable and time spent on a household work activity means that time spent on the work becomes the measure of production. This measure is not the same as time alone as a measure. The family characteristic is the indicator of the work accomplished in each activity in the time spent; for example, age of youngest child indicates the work accomplished in family care for a designated family in a given period of time. Thus, both time spent and work accomplished are expressed as a unit. The time likely to be used by households with the same family characteristic can be estimated with reasonable accuracy, and any family with the same characteristic can compare its time with the average time.

Expressing a measure of household work in terms of average time for various types of families has several advantages over expressing it in terms of other work-quantifying measures. At the same time, even though measuring the amount of work by a quantifying variable such as number of loads of washing may not be a feasible measure of each type of household production, this type of quantification of household work has value for other reasons. The dimension added by being able to formulate the amount of work in more than one way has marked value in providing deeper insights into the type of household production being carried on in typical households. A measure such as types of meals tells much more about meal preparation practices than does a simple enumeration of number of meals served with no indication of their complexity or the variations in amounts of work required to prepare them.

The advantages of time as a measure of household production are that time varies principally with the amount of work, measures the

---

[7]Medians could be used, but the means (or averages) were used in this study because measures of production developed in past studies were expressed as averages.

work accomplished in each work activity, is additive, is expressible in different units (such as an hour, day, week), and can be developed from data which are relatively easy to collect. Additionally, it may be expressed in units to which wage rates, which are usually computed in units of time, may be applied.

The term "work unit" is not used to describe the present measure, in which work accomplished is expressed in terms of family characteristics directly related to the time spent in doing the work. However, this measure shows the same relationship between time spent and work accomplished as the work unit—a quantity of work accomplished in a given amount of time by an average worker under average household conditions.

Limitations of the Present Study

It should be emphasized that the measure of household production developed by this study is not intended to measure work loads of other than those of complete family households, that is, two-person households made up of husband and wife and two-parent households with children. Work patterns and time spent tend to be different in households of different composition even though the number of persons may be the same as in family households. The majority of households in the United States, it should be pointed out, are made up of parents with children or young or older couples without children. However, additional data on other types of families are needed to expand the usefulness of the measure.

Likewise, it must be emphasized that the measurements determined from data collected from a sample in one city and its suburbs in upstate New York at one point in time cannot be generalized to the entire country. For this, more data from a large national sample would be needed to determine variations in household work patterns related to regional, cultural, or climatic differences. It was the purpose of this research to develop a method for measurement of household production—only one step toward the goal of measurement of household production in families and in the country as a whole.

Research is also needed to determine appropriate methods for incorporating household production into national indicators for economic analysis. One method of attaching monetary value to time used for household work was tested and reported by Walker and Gauger (1973) and by Gauger (1973) as a part of the time-use research project, but neither methodology nor results of that part of the project are reported in this monograph, which focuses on time use as a measure of household production.

Chapter II

Selected Background Data of the Study

Sample Selection and Data Collection

The hypothesis tested in the present study was that family composition, as represented by the number and ages of children in a family, is the principal variable in determining the amount of household work to be done and can be used as the estimator of the total time that will be spent to perform the work. The selection of family composition as the principal variable was based on previous research, which had shown that both number of children and their ages have a marked influence on work time in numerous household activities. If the predicated relationship between family composition and household work time could be verified, one or two variables could be used in the measurement of household production. Since census data regularly report family composition characteristics, this variable could be a convenient one to use for aggregating the value of household production and in measuring its changes.

The design of a study to test the efficacy of family composition as a predictor posed several challenges: (1) the kind of sample that would be needed, (2) the logistics of obtaining a sample with the required characteristics, and (3) the method to be used to collect the data.

The Sample[1]

To determine the time-use effects of variations in family composition and to provide an adequate basis for testing the hypothesis, data were obtained from a sample of 1,296 households selected randomly from households stratified by (1) urban-suburban location and (2) 32 patterns of family composition, defined by number of children and their ages in husband-wife families with children, and by age of wife in households without children. Only husband-wife households with or without children were included in order to have a sample broadly representative of the most typical

families in the population and also to reduce the total number of types of families.

To provide an adequate quantity of data for analysis, 42 households were randomly selected to represent each pattern of family composition. To include seasonal and daily variability, the interviews for each family composition category were equally distributed by day of the week and season of the year.

One major challenge was how to find a sample within an urban-suburban area that would meet the stipulations for controls for families without children and for families with children of varying numbers and ages. The steps that led to the successful achievement of this objective are described in the Methodology, Appendix A. The sample of 1,296 families interviewed in 1967-68 in Syracuse, N.Y., and nine suburbs of the city came from a list of names of over 50,000 husband-wife families stratified by city and suburban residence and by the selected family composition variables.

Method of Data Collection

Several considerations in addition to the control variables were involved in developing instruments and selecting a method to collect the data. The study design called for the collection of data on amounts of time used for all household work activities, descriptive data on the work activities, and data on social and physical variables that could be related to time use or to the major variables. The principal considerations were: the time period the record should cover, the amount of detail needed on household work, and the problems related to the particular method of data collection.

The time reported was distinguished as *primary time* (during which the activity engaged the worker's full attention), and *secondary time* (when some work on an activity was done while work on another activity received primary attention). Time used for travel connected with household work was recorded separately. The time spent on any household work by any type of worker was recorded except that of children under 6 years of

---

[1]All topics related to the design of the study are discussed in detail under Methodology, Appendix A.

age. For this group of children, participation in household activities was considered to be more often play or a learning activity than household production. A complete record of time for the entire 24-hour period for each member of the household over 6 years of age was collected so that the completeness of the time reporting could be checked.

The time record, which was developed after considerable experimentation and testing, listed each type of household work on the vertical axis and time periods in 10-minute intervals on the horizontal axis (Figure 2.1). Time of each type of worker was recorded in the time blocks for each activity. (See Appendix A for instructions for recording time use.) Since the focus of the study was on total work accomplished, the specific operations or tasks performed were not recorded. Time intervals were estimated; that is, approximate rather than precise times of beginning and ending each piece of work were recorded. To increase representativeness, especially for less regularly performed activities, 2 days of records for each family were obtained.

Data were collected by personal interviews with wives and by means of a 1-day time record. The principal advantage of the personal interview as the method of data collection was its potential for obtaining the designated number of complete and usable records for each family type. Other advantages were that the purpose of the survey could be explained and background information provided to encourage the wives' cooperation. Some of the information needed to classify families into the appropriate types was not available from the sample listings; consequently, some type of personal contact with the selected wives was needed. In addition, the requirement of equal numbers in different sample segments meant that the refusal rate and the possibility of incomplete records had to be held to a minimum. That risk was especially high in the present study with the need for a complete record of all use of time for the full 24 hours by each member of the household aged 6 years or older. Personal contact also was considered necessary because of the complexity of the data to be collected and the importance of having the recalled time data complete and accurate.

Insofar as possible, all the questions on the interview schedule were worded to minimize interviewer bias, and the time record chart was designed to remove the possibility of influencing wives by presenting preconceived notions of how household work activities should be conducted.

An initial interview was held, during which the interviewer collected background data and recorded use of time on the previous day by household members as recalled by the wives. The wife was considered to be the person most informed about the household work of all workers in the family. A second time record chart was left with the wives, on which they kept a time record for the day following the interview. They were asked to verify their report of time use of other family members; this method allowed family members to see what the research was about and increased the potential for cooperation. A second interview was held, at which time the interviewer checked the second day's time records for completeness by going over them with the wives. Since wives were asked to complete only one time chart on their own and to record the data soon after instructions had been given, the problem of lost or incomplete time records was minimized.

Interviews were scheduled in such a way that time records were obtained for equal numbers of families in each category on each day of the week and during each season of the year. Data were collected over a year to allow for seasonal variations in each cell. About one-third of the 2,592 record days were reported for each of 3 seasons (862 for winter and early spring, 858 for late spring and summer, and 872 for fall and early winter). A total of 370 days' records were collected for each of 5 days of the week and 371 days' records for each of the other 2 days.

Distribution of the Major Variables

Family Composition

Number and Ages of Children (Tables 2.1, 2.2, and 2.3).[2] Of the 1,296 families in the survey, 1,128 (87%) had children at home. The average number of children in the sample was 2.3 per household. About half of the families had either two or three children; only 6% had five or more (Table 2.1). In over half of the families the youngest child was under school age.

Of the total 2,988 children in the sample, 38% were under age 6, and 62% were age 6 to 17 years (Table 2.2). Of all 1,296 families, 13% had no children, 26% had only preschool age children, 34% had only school age children, and 27% had children of mixed ages.

---

[2]Tabular presentation of data is at end of each chapter. Only measures of central tendency are reported for descriptive analysis of the sample.

FIGURE 2.1—Time chart

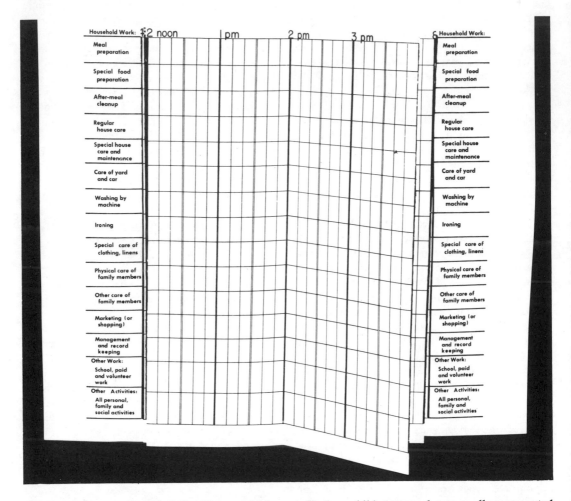

Family Type (Table 2.3). This variable, developed after statistical analysis by rank-order correlations, combined number of children and age of youngest child in each family, and omitted age of oldest child. The purpose was to express the composition of families with children in a simpler form than originally categorized for sample selection. The effects of this conversion were to change a major variable from a control variable to a random variable and to have unequal numbers in the family groups.

Of the 1,296 families, those with no children were equally represented in each of four groups categorized by age of the wives. In one-child families, there was equal representation in each of the five age groups. Families with two children were about equally divided according to age of youngest in age groups of a baby under 1 year and a toddler 1 to 2 years (131 cases), a child 2 to 5 (121 cases), and a child from 6 to 17 years (126 cases). Families

with three children were about equally represented in age groups of youngest child under 2, 2 to 5, and 6 to 11 years, with a smaller proportion of the sample having teenagers as youngest children. More of the families with four children had the youngest child in the 6 to 11 age group than in other age groups. In families with five or more children, the youngest child was most likely to be under school age.

Since employment of wives emerged as a major random variable, the relationship of the family composition variables to time have been analyzed with employment of wives held constant. For family type, this breakdown further decreased the number of cases in some categories, especially the larger and more complex families, in which wives tended not to be employed. Table 2.3 shows the distribution by number of the 979 non-employed-wife families and the 317 employed-wife families into family types. The unequal distribution of numbers created problems in the analysis, which will be discussed in subsequent chapters.

Since employment of wives was so interrelated with the composition of their families, the distribution by family type and employment is discussed in this chapter under "Employment of Wives."

Age of Youngest and Age of Oldest Child (Table 2.4). Though age of oldest child was found not to add to the effectiveness of the family type variable as a predictor, its effects on time use were examined separately by rank correlation analysis.

The largest proportions of families with children of single-age groups were those with both the youngest and oldest children aged 12 to 17 years (13%) and 6 to 11 (15%); 12% of families with children had one or more under 2 years and no older children, and 10% had all children between the ages of 2 and 5. Of the mixed-age groups, the highest single proportions were families with a youngest child 6 to 11 and an oldest child 12 to 17 (11%) and families with the youngest 2 to 5 and the oldest 6 to 11 (10%). In 9% of families the youngest child was 2 to 5 and the oldest 12 to 17. Other combinations were less frequent; the least common were combinations of youngest child age 1 or under with the oldest child 12 to 17 years of age.

Families in which the oldest child was 12 to 17 or 6 to 11 were largely two- or three-child families—these four categories accounted for 44% of all families with children. When the oldest child was 2 to 5, the family typically consisted of two children; when the youngest was 1 year old, it most often consisted of one or two children; and, of course, when the oldest was under 1, that child was usually the only one. Larger families, as expected, were almost completely those in which the oldest child was 12 to 17 or 6 to 11, though 3% of families with an oldest child 2 to 5 were four-child families.

Socioeconomic Status of the Families
(Table 2.5)

Hollingshead's Two Factor Index of Social Position was used to estimate the socioeconomic status of the family (Hollingshead, 1957). This index, based on occupation and education of the head of the household, provides an objective and easily applied means of stratifying a sample into social classes. In Hollingshead's index, the lowest scores have the highest socioeconomic ranking (Table 2.5).

The distribution of the socioeconomic position of sample families is also shown in Table 2.5.

Together, the middle and lower-middle ranges (Classes *3* and *4*) accounted for 68% of the families in the sample. Most husbands in Class *3* had at least some college or training beyond high school and were in managerial positions. At the Class *4* level, husbands more typically had a high school education and were in some type of skilled work or in lower administrative or clerical-sales positions.

Husbands in Classes *1* and *2* were nearly all college graduates, and the principal educational difference between the two groups was the high proportion of men in Class *1* who had graduate degrees. Occupationally, men in Class *1* tended to be in professional occupations while those in Class *2* were mainly managers or administrators.

Husbands at the Class *5* level usually had less than a high school education and for the most part were in semiskilled jobs.

There was no consistent pattern of relationship between family composition or family type with husbands' socioeconomic level.

Employment of Wives

Labor-Force Participation (Table 2.6). Labor-force participation is defined by the U.S. Bureau of Labor Statistics as 1 hour of employment in the previous 7 days. Such a general category was not useful for studying the effects of employment on time used for household work. The variation in amount of time not spent on paid employment was too great between women who were employed only a few hours per week and those who worked for pay 40 hours per week or more. At the same time, the number employed more than 30 hours per week was too small to be used alone. The distribution of time spent on household work by hours of employment of wives was analyzed by using several employment breaks. From this analysis, we saw that wives employed less than 14 hours per week had time patterns similar to those of women who did not work for pay at all. For the major analysis, therefore, *employed women* were categorized as those who worked for pay 15 or more hours per week, and *nonemployed women* as those working less than 14 hours per week. These same categories had been used by Wiegand (1953) and Walker (1955), and their use in the present study would permit comparisons of time use for household work over the years.

By the commonly used definition of employment as working for pay 1 or more hours per week, 34% of the wives in the sample were employed; this percentage was close to the percentage of married women employed nationally (37%) in the year of the study (1967-68) (U.S. Bureau of the Census, 1969, p. 220). The stratification of the sample by family type largely accounts for the small difference between national figures and those of the study.

Two-thirds of the wives in the sample were not employed at all and 9% were employed from 1 to 14 hours per week; thus, the category of non-employed wives comprised 75% of wives in the sample and the category of employed wives comprised 25%.

Employment Status of Wives (Table 2.6). Most of the wives employed 15 or more hours per week worked for others (85%) rather than being self-employed. None of the wives classified as employed was on vacation at the time of the interview; 11 employed wives on vacation were classified as nonemployed because their work patterns were assumed to be similar to the nonemployed wives for the 7 days preceding the interview. None of the wives in the sample was classed as student or retired.

Length of Wives' Employment Week (Table 2.6). The hours of wives' employment ranged from 1 to over 70 per week, with 9% of the total sample employed 40 or more hours. The same proportion (9%) of all wives were employed 1 to 14 hours as were employed 15 to 29 hours per week. Of those employed 15 or more hours per week, most had employment workweeks of 15 to 29, 30 to 39, and 40 to 49 hours in about equal proportions (one-third each). Thus, the proportion employed 30 or more hours per week was twice as high as the proportion employed 15 to 29 hours.

Occupations of Employed Wives (Table 2.6). Almost half of the wives employed 15 or more hours per week (44%) were in clerical occupations; one-third were in professional or management or administrative positions; and a quarter were doing semiskilled or unskilled work.

Family Composition and Employment of Wives (Tables 2.7 and 2.8). Employment of wives for 15 or more hours per week was associated with number of children in the family, age of youngest child, and family type.

The proportion of wives who were employed 15 or more hours per week decreased progressively as the number of children in the family increased, from 42% in families with no children to 10% in those with seven to nine children (Table 2.7).

Age of the youngest child was also associated with employment of wives. The proportion of wives who worked for pay 15 or more hours per week was much higher in families with teenage children (43%) than in those with younger children. When there was a baby under 1 year in the family, only 8% of the wives were employed, and this percentage increased to 20% when the youngest child was in the 2 to 5 age group.

The combined effects of these two variables—number of children and age of youngest child—can be seen when the relationship between family type and employment of wives is examined (Table 2.8). As the type of family became more complex, employment of wives 15 or more hours a week declined. Only 2 of the 21 wives with seven to nine children were employed. In families with five or six children only 9 of the 56 wives were employed. When there were children in the home, employed wives outnumbered the nonemployed in only 1 of the 29 family types (four-child families with youngest child 12 to 17). In two other categories wives were almost as likely to be employed as not to be employed—when there was one child in the household and the child's age was between either 6 and 11 or 12 and 17.

Wives tended not to be employed when they had children 1 year old or younger, and this tendency was not affected by the number of children in the family. When the youngest child was 2 to 5, wives were employed to some extent in one-child families (38%), but less so as the number of children increased. A similar trend was observed in families with the youngest child 6 to 11, except that the differences were smaller and less consistent as the number of children increased. With any number of children, more mothers were employed when their youngest child was of school age than when the youngest child was of preschool age.

Wives in the sample tended not to be employed when: (1) the youngest child was of preschool age, except in households with one child between 2 and 5 years; (2) they had five or more children; and (3) they had two, three, or four children unless the youngest was between 6 and 17. Four-fifths of all children 6 to 11 and two-thirds of all those 12 to 17 were in homes of nonemployed mothers.

Age of Wives and Employment (Tables 2.9 and 2.10). Employment of wives was related linearly to their ages. The same proportions (30%) of wives under 25 years and of wives 40 to 54 were employed 15 or more hours a week, while wives in the age levels of 25 to 39 and 55 and older were less likely to be employed that many hours (Table 2.9).

The age groups of children according to age of wife followed the expected pattern in the sample (Table 2.10). When wives with children were under 25, most (86%) had only one or two children; in all cases the youngest child was under age 6, and most often was 1 year or less (86%). Wives 25 to 39 were likely to have two or more children in a greater variety of age groups than did younger wives—for 70% the youngest child was under school age, 26% had a youngest child between 6 and 11, and 4% had only teenage children. When the wife was 40 to 54, older children (6 to 17 years) predominated; but about a fifth had children 2 to 5 and 6% had children 1 year or less. In only 6 families with wives aged 55 and older were there children at home, and these children were all teenagers.

When families without children were considered, the age of the wives tended to relate to being employed 15 or more hours per week (Table 2.9). When they had no children, younger wives were more likely to be employed than older ones— 62% of those under 25 years and 55% of those 25 to 39 compared with 29% and 24%, respectively, for the age groups of 40 to 54 and 55 or older.

In each age group of wives, the percentage employed 15 or more hours per week increased as the youngest child was older. When the wife was 40 to 54 years of age and had only teenage children, the proportion employed (43%) was higher than the proportion employed of this age group with no children (29%). This supports the observed trend of middle-aged women to return to the labor force, especially when their children are teenagers and there are typically increased expenditures.

Wives' Education and Employment (Table 2.11). About one-fifth (240) of the total number of wives were college graduates and 5% (58) had graduate degrees. All except about 11% were high school graduates and 30% had had some college work.

There were some minor differences in employment status by education of wives. About one-third of those with graduate level education and one-third of those with junior high school or less were employed as compared with about one-fourth for each of the other levels of education.

Socioeconomic Level and Employment of Wives (Tables 2.11 and 2.12). Socioeconomic level of husbands was somewhat associated with employment of wives in that employment of wives for 15 or more hours per week increased slightly as the families' socioeconomic level declined (Table 2.11). Only 15% of the wives at the top socioeconomic level were employed, compared with 23% to 29% employment of other classes. Since education of the wives and the husbands' socio-

economic status were interrelated, it is difficult to determine which of these factors was more closely associated with the employment of wives. Almost half of the wives whose husbands were in the highest two classes were college graduates or had graduate training, and about one-third more had some college education (Table 2.12). Wives whose husbands were in the third and fourth levels tended to be high school graduates or to have some college, while those whose husbands were at the lowest socioeconomic level tended to be either high school graduates (44%) or to have less than a high school education (52%). At all socioeconomic levels of husbands, most of the wives were at least high school graduates.

Wives whose husbands were at the highest socioeconomic level tended to be employed proportionately less than others, whether or not they had children. On the other hand, at the two lowest levels wives were likely to be employed to a greater extent than other classes when they had children.

In summary, employed wives in the sample generally had small families and older children, with some modifications according to the family's socioeconomic level.

House Type (Table 2.13)

Most of the families in the sample lived in one-family houses (75%), and most of the remainder lived in apartments (13%) or two-family dwellings (11%). Only seven families lived in mobile homes and three in "other" housing.[3]

The families that lived in apartments had the typical characteristics associated with that type of housing—no children and younger wives (under age 40), or only one or two children who were generally young, 1 year old or less (Table 2.13). These characteristics were apparent in employed-wife households as well as in all households.

Living in either apartments or one-family houses tended to be associated with the age of the wife if there were no children, or with age of the youngest child; the proportion living in an apartment declined from 67% of young families without children to 23% of those with the youngest under 1, and 2% with a teenager as the youngest child. The proportion living in a one-family house was lowest in families with no children but was four-fifths or more of families with two or more children.

---

[3]Details of the housing characteristics are reported in Chapter 6.

Location of Residence (Table 2.14)

Fifty-two percent of the families lived in the suburbs and 48% in the city. Typically, living in the suburbs is associated with living in a one-family house, and living in the city is associated with living in an apartment. Of the various house types in the sample in Syracuse, N.Y. in 1967-68, the majority of apartments (74%) and two-family houses (86%) were in the city and the highest proportion of one-family houses (62%) were in the suburbs. Also in line with typical housing patterns, the majority of families in the suburbs lived in one-family houses (89%). This type of house predominated whether or not the wives were employed.

Location of residence showed no clear-cut association with any family composition variable. While number of children and age of youngest child tended to relate to the type of house, location of the house in city or suburb was less strongly associated with family composition. Compared with other families, however, more of the older families without children and more of those with only one child lived in the city.

Characteristics of Husbands (Table 2.15)

Ages of husbands in the sample were similar to those of wives; the average age of husbands was 38 years, about 2 years older than wives.

Also, like the wives, husbands tended to be either high school graduates (28%) or to have some college or training beyond high school (24%). A higher proportion of husbands (32%) than of wives were college graduates or had graduate degrees; but also, a higher proportion of husbands (16%) than wives had less than high school education. As with wives, the educational level of husbands was somewhat above the national level.

Employment of Husbands. Only 15% of husbands in the sample worked less than 40 hours per week. The most prevalent workweek for husbands was from 40 to 49 hours (52%). One-third had longer workweeks, and 15% worked 60 or more hours per week.

At the time of the study only 10% of the husbands were self-employed; 3% were on vacation, retired, or enrolled as students.

Three-fifths of husbands were at three occupational levels (one-fifth each): administrative, clerical, and skilled. About one-quarter were in management or professional occupations. Husbands in professional occupations were less likely than husbands in most other occupations to have employed wives (7%). Of the 12 husbands doing unskilled work, only 1 had a wife who was employed.

TABLE 2.1—Distribution of families, by number of children and age of youngest child under 18 years living at home
(1,296 husband–wife households, Syracuse, N.Y., 1967-68)

Number of children	Percent of families	Age of youngest child	Percent of families
None	13	No children	13
1	16	Under 1 year	15
2	29	1 year	14
3	23	2-5 years	24
4	13	6-11 years	23
5-6	4	12-17 years	11
7-9	2		

TABLE 2.2—Distribution of age categories of children in sample
(1,128 husband–wife families with children, Syracuse, N.Y., 1967-68)

Age of child	Percent of children
	(N = 2,988)
Under 1 year	7
1 year	8
2-5 years	23
6-11 years	37
12-17 years	25

TABLE 2.3—Number of families, by family type
(1,296 husband–wife households, Syracuse, N.Y., 1967-68)

Family type	Number of families	Number of cases by family type	
		Nonemployed wives	Employed wives
		(N = 979)	(N = 317)
No-child households by age of wives	168		
under 25 years	42	16	26
25–39	42	19	23
40–54	42	30	12
55 and over	42	32	10
Number of children by age of youngest child			
1 child	210		
12–17 years	42	22	20
6–11	42	23	19
2–5	42	26	16
1	42	37	5
under 1	42	41	1
2 children	378		
12–17 years	42	27	15
6–11	84	60	24
2–5	121	93	28
1	59	50	9
under 1	72	65	7
3 children	294		
12–17 years	42	26	16
6–11	84	58	26
2–5	83	70	13
1	50	48	2
under 1	35	31	4
4 children	169		
12–17 years	14	5	9
6–11	66	51	15
2–5	33	32	1
1	22	19	3
under 1	34	32	2
5–6 children	56		
12–17 years	1	--	1
6–11	18	16	2
2–5	20	17	3
1	7	6	1
under 1	10	8	2
7–9 children	21		
6–11 years	2	2	--
2–5	12	10	2
1	3	3	--
under 1	4	4	--

TABLE 2.4—Distribution of ages of youngest and oldest child in families with children
(1,128 husband–wife families with children, Syracuse, N.Y., 1967-68)

Youngest child	Oldest child	Percent of families with children
12-17 years	12-17 years	13
6-11	12-17	11
6-11	6-11	15
2-5	12-17	9
2-5	6-11	10
2-5	2-5	10
1	12-17	2
1	6-11	5
1	2-5	4
1	1	4
Under 1	12-17	1
Under 1	6-11	2
Under 1	2-5	5
Under 1	1	3
Under 1	Under 1	5

TABLE 2.5—Socioeconomic status[a] scoring and sample distribution

Occupational levels		Graduate work	4-year college degree	Post-high school study	High school graduate	Some high school (10th or 11th grade)	8th or 9th grade	Less than 7th grade
		1	2	3	4	5	6	7
					Scores			
Executive and major professional	1	11	15	19	23	27	31	35
Management and professional	2	18	22	26	30	34	38	42
Administrative personnel and small business owners	3	25	29	33	37	41	45	49
Clerical and technical workers	4	32	36	40	44	48	52	56
Skilled manual workers	5	39	43	47	51	55	59	63
Semiskilled workers	6	46	50	54	58	62	66	70
Unskilled workers	7	53	57	61	65	69	73	77

aBased on Hollingshead's (1957, p. 10) two factor index, occupation of husbands was weighted 7 and education 4 as follows:

SES level	Percent of sample N = 1,296	Score	
1 (high)	13	11 — 17	(Occupational level 1 x 7 + educational level of 1 or 2 x 4)
2	13	18 — 27	(Occupational level 1 to 3 x 7 + educational level of 1 to 5 x 4)
3	31	28 — 43	(Occupational level 2 to 5 x 7 + educational level of 1 to 7 x 4)
4	37	44 — 60	(Occupational level 3 to 7 x 7 + educational level of 1 to 7 x 4)
5	6	61 — 77	(Occupational level 5 to 7 x 7 + educational level of 3 to 7 x 4)

TABLE 2.6—Employment characteristics of wives
(1,296 husband-wife households, Syracuse, N.Y., 1967-68)

| | Percentage distribution of wives | | |
	All	Nonemployed	Employed
	(N = 1,296)	(N = 979)	(N = 317)
Employment status			
Not in labor force	65	87	--
Self-employed	6	3	15
Employed by others	28	9	85
On vacation	1	1	--
Hours per week of paid work			
0	66	87	--
1-14	9	13	--
15-29	9	--	35
30-39	7	--	31
40-49	8	--	31
50+	1	--	3
Occupation			
Professional/Technical			2
Business/Managerial			18
Administrative			10
Clerical			44
Skilled			2
Semiskilled			10
Unskilled			14

TABLE 2.7—Percentage of wives employed, by number of children and age of youngest child
(1,296 husband-wife households, Syracuse, N.Y., 1967-68)

| | | Row[a] percent of wives | |
Variable	Number	Nonemployed	Employed
Number of children			
0	168	58	42
1	210	71	29
2	378	78	22
3	294	79	21
4	169	82	18
5-6	56	84	16
7-9	21	90	10
Age of youngest child			
12-17 years	141	57	43
6-11	296	71	29
2-5	311	80	20
1	183	89	11
under 1	197	92	8

[a]Percent of total wives in each category—nonemployed and employed.

TABLE 2.8—Percentage of wives in each family type not employed or employed 15 or more hours per week
(*1,296 husband–wife households, Syracuse, N.Y., 1967-68*)

Family type	Number	Row[a] percent of wives in each family type	
		Nonemployed	Employed
No-child households by age of wives			
under 25 years	42	38	62
25–39	42	45	55
40–54	42	71	29
55 and over	42	76	24
Number of children by age of youngest child			
1 child			
12–17 years	42	52	48
6–11	42	55	45
2–5	42	62	38
1	42	88	12
under 1	42	98	2
2 children			
12–17 years	42	64	36
6–11	84	71	29
2–5	121	77	23
1	59	85	15
under 1	72	90	10
3 children			
12–17 years	42	62	38
6–11	84	69	31
2–5	83	84	16
1	50	96	4
under 1	35	89	11
4 children			
12–17 years	14	36	64
6–11	66	77	23
2–5	33	97	3
1	22	86	14
under 1	34	94	6
5-6 children			
12–17 years	1	--	<1
6–11	18	89	11
2–5	20	85	15
1	7	86	14
under 1	10	80	20
7-9 children			
6–11 years	2	<1	--
2–5	12	83	17
1	3	100	--
under 1	4	100	--

[a]Percent of wives in each category—nonemployed and employed.

TABLE 2.9—Percentage of wives employed 15 or more hours per week, by age of wife, presence of children, and age of youngest child
(*1,296 husband–wife households, Syracuse, N.Y., 1967-68*)

Age of wives in years	Age of youngest child	Number wives	Row[a] percent of wives Nonemployed	Employed
Under 25		153	70	30
	2–5 years	16	50	50
	1 year	37	86	14
	Under 1 year	58	90	10
	No children	42	38	62
25–39		774	79	21
	12–17 years	28	54	46
	6–11 years	194	71	29
	2–5 years	239	80	20
	1 year	137	89	11
	Under 1 year	130	94	6
	No children	42	45	55
40–54		325	70	30
	12–17 years	107	57	43
	6–11 years	102	51	29
	2–5 years	56	86	14
	1 year or less	18	89	11
	No children	42	71	29
55 and over		48	75	25
	12–17 years	6	67	33
	No children	42	76	24

[a]Percent of wives in each category—nonemployed and employed.

TABLE 2.10—Number and ages of children in families with children, by age of wife
(*1,128 husband–wife families with children, Syracuse, N.Y., 1967-68*)

Variable	Total	Age of wife under 25	25–39	40–54	55 and over
	(N = 1,128)	(N = 111)	(N = 728)	(N = 283)	(N = 6)
Number of children					
1	18	51	13	19	66
2	34	35	33	34	a
3	26	5	29	26	a
4–6	20	9	23	18	--
7	2	--	2	3	--
Age of youngest child					
12–17 years	13	--	4	38	100
6–11	26	--	26	36	---
2–5	28	14	33	20	---
1	16	34	19	3	---
under 1	17	52	18	3	---

[a]Only one case.

TABLE 2.11—Percentage of wives nonemployed and employed, by wives' education and husbands' socioeconomic level
(1,296 husband-wife households, Syracuse, N.Y., 1967-68)

Variable	Number	Row[a] percent of wives Nonemployed	Employed
Education of wives			
Graduate degree	58	66	34
4-year college graduate	182	75	25
Partial college or post h.s.	387	78	22
High school graduate	526	76	24
Partial high school	105	74	26
Junior high school or less	38	69	31
Husbands' socioeconomic level[b]			
Class 1 (highest)	163	85	15
Class 2	163	77	23
Class 3	402	76	24
Class 4	483	71	29
Class 5	85	71	29

[a]Percent of wives in each category—nonemployed and employed.
[b]Based on Hollingshead's (1957) two-factor index.

TABLE 2.12—Education of wives, by husbands' socioeconomic level
(1,296 husband-wife households, Syracuse, N.Y., 1967-68)

Wives' education	All	Husbands' socioeconomic level[a] High 1	2	3	4	Low 5
	N = (1,128)	(163)	(163)	(402)	(483)	(85)
		Percent				
Graduate degree	4	13	14	3	*	--
4-year college graduate	14	34	36	13	3	--
Partial college	30	38	31	39	24	5
High school graduate	41	14	17	40	58	44
Partial high school	8	1	1	5	12	33
Junior high school or less	3	--	--	1	4	19

[a]Based on Hollingshead's (1957) two-factor index.

TABLE 2.13—Type of housing, by family composition
(1,296 husband-wife households, Syracuse, N.Y., 1967-68)

Variable	Number	1-family house	Apart-ment	2-family house	Mobile home or "other"
		Row[a] percent			
Age of wives in families without children					
Under 25 years	42	19	67	12	2
25–39	42	48	45	7	--
40–54	42	83	7	10	--
55 and over	42	74	14	12	--
Number of children					
1	210	61	23	16	<1
2	378	78	11	10	1
3	294	82	5	13	<1
4	169	89	2	7	2
5–6	56	80	4	14	2
7–9	21	95	--	5	--
Age of youngest child					
12–17 years	141	87	2	10	1
6–11	296	88	4	7	<1
2–5	311	79	6	14	1
1	183	69	16	14	1
under 1	197	63	23	12	2
Socioeconomic status					
Class 1 (highest)	163	81	14	5	--
Class 2	163	71	20	9	--
Class 3	402	80	11	9	--
Class 4	483	74	12	14	1
Class 5 (lowest)	85	61	12	25	2

[a]Percent of wives in each category—nonemployed and employed.

TABLE 2.14—Location of residence, by family composition
  (1,296 husband–wife households, Syracuse, N.Y.,1967-68)

Variable	Number	Row[a] percent by location City	Suburbs
All families	1,296	48	52
Number of children			
0	168	52	48
1	210	59	41
2	378	45	55
3	294	48	52
4	169	34	66
5-6	56	52	48
7-9	21	52	48
Age of youngest child			
12-17 years	141	54	46
6-11	296	49	51
2-5	311	49	51
1	183	40	60
under 1	197	44	56
Age of wives in families without children			
under 40 years	84	45	55
40 years and over	84	60	40

[a]Percent of each category in city and suburbs.

TABLE 2.15—Employment characteristics of husbands and wives, by employment of wives

(1,296 husband–wife households, Syracuse, N.Y., 1967-68)

Characteristics	Percent of families		Percent of husbands with wives[a]	
	Wives	Husbands	Nonemployed	Employed
	(N = 1,296)		(N = 979)	(N = 317)
Age in years				
Under 25	12	6	6	6
25–39	59	56	59	49
40–54	25	32	30	36
55 and over	4	6	5	9
Education				
Graduate professional	4	11	12	7
4-year college	14	21	22	19
Partial college	30	24	24	23
High school graduate	41	28	28	30
Partial high school	8	10	9	13
Junior high school or less	3	6	5	8
Employment status				
Not in labor force	65	1	1	1
Self employed	6	10	10	10
Employed by others	28	86	86	86
On vacation	1	1	1	1
Retired	--	1	1	2
Student	--	1	2	<1
Occupation				
Professional	1	13	15	7
Business	6	12	13	11
Administrative	4	21	21	22
Clerical	15	20	19	23
Skilled	1	20	20	22
Semiskilled	3	12	12	14
Unskilled	6	1	1	<1
Hours per week employment				
0	66	4	4	3
1–14	9	2	1	2
15–29	9	3	3	3
30–39	7	6	6	6
40–49	8	52	51	53
50–59	1	18	18	18
60–69	--	10	10	8
70 and over	--	5	5	6

[a]Percent of wives nonemployed and wives employed.

Chapter III

All Household Work

This chapter presents a discussion of the relationships between time spent on all household work and the major variables. Time for all household work is that time used for work related to meeting the specific needs of the family for food, clothing, shelter, nurture, and the fulfillment of family goals. Relationships of variables to time spent on each kind of household work will be discussed separately in subsequent chapters, but some of the implications for total household work of the varying frequencies and varying amounts of time spent on different household work activities are discussed in this chapter.

Household work programs are somewhat flexible and can be tailored to meet special family situations. Some of the services are provided daily for all or almost all families, while others are irregularly provided. The time spent on household work also varies according to personal preferences and differences in health, efficiency, or other personal factors.

Sources of time variability were reduced as much as possible in the present study by sample and data collection controls. Records of time spent on household work were collected for 2,592 record days spread evenly over the days of the week and over a 1-year period. This period was long enough to permit the kinds of household work not performed daily to be represented. Perhaps more important, the daily average time reported includes the daily and seasonal variations in household work and differences in time spent caused by typical family pressures and situations. When the average time is based on a large enough number of families, these kinds of variability are reduced in importance. The average times reported, therefore, represent the amount of time that would be spent on 1 day if all household work were distributed evenly over every day of the year.

The focus of the present study was on the total time spent by all workers on household work. This total household work time and total time spent on each activity was made up of the separate times of all the workers over 6 years of age who spent 5 minutes or more on a work activity on the 2 record days. In the sample, other workers in addition to

the wives were husbands, children 12 to 17 and 6 to 11, and, to a lesser extent, other female and male workers who were not regular members of the household.

Since the relationships between the variables and total time of all workers would be affected by the relationships between the variables and the time of individual workers, the time use of the three most important groups of workers (wives, husbands, and teenagers) was analyzed separately. Like the total average time of all workers, the average time for each group of workers represented an average of the time spent by the entire group, including those who spent much, little, or no time. No rank correlations were determined for the time of children 6 to 11 or for the time of adult workers other than wives and husbands because their average daily time was too low or too variable for valid relationships to be found.

The hypothesized relationship between changes in time and corresponding changes in the family life cycle is depicted in Figure 3.1. Household production time of all workers in the family rises as the number of children increases and as the children reach school age, then drops abruptly as children enter the teen years. Time continues to decline as the children leave home, but more slowly. The time level for older couples whose children have all left home remains higher than that of the young married couple, since the older couple frequently continues to live in the more complex physical and social environment, which usually evolves during the child-rearing years.

Statistical Analysis

A rank correlation technique was used to identify the variable or variables most closely related to the daily time spent on household work. The statistical technique used for determining correlation was Kendall's rank correlation coefficient (Kendall Tau), a nonparametric measure of association.[1]

---

[1] See Methodology section (Appendix A) for further discussion of choice of measure used.

FIGURE 3.1—Hypothesized relationship between time use and family composition

This type of analysis shows whether an association exists between variables; for instance, that more time is spent when family size is larger than when it is smaller. The relationship indicated between the two variables is not necessarily causal; that is, it cannot be said that a certain number of children causes a certain amount of time to be spent on household work.

The measure does not show how great the increase or decrease in time is, but it indicates whether there is or is not some consistency in direction of change. For meaningful interpretations, the Tau values must be looked at with average time use to see the extent of change. For example, in all food preparation activities there is a statistically significant and positive association between time contributed by husbands and employment of wives, but husbands' time increase when wives were employed averaged only 6 minutes per day. Although the increase in time use reported for husbands was not a by-chance increase in our sample, the statistical significance alone does not show the extent of change or answer the question of the relative importance of a 6-minute increase in time use.

All Tau values reported in tabular form or referred to in the text were significant at the .001 level unless otherwise stated. Although correlation coefficients were determined for all major variables, only significant relationships are reported in tables and only the correlations strong enough to change the amount of time used daily are discussed to any extent. The values of correlation coefficients required to show significant associations varied according to the amount of average daily time spent on the work. For all household work, for example, a correlation value of $\pm .15$ was high enough for a change in daily average time to be perceptible.

In all of the correlation analyses, time spent was ranked by minutes per day. The reason for this ranking was to determine whether or not any relationship could be found with a particular variable and to test the strength of the relationship. To eliminate the effect of varying numbers, only the time spent by the 1,260 families in the original 30 complete cells was used.[2] In the analysis of time, time was averaged to the nearest .1 of an hour, since data were collected by 5- or 10-minute intervals and this unit of reporting

---

[2] Eliminated from this analysis were the 21 families with seven to nine children and the 15 families with four to six children with all in the 12- to 17-year age group.

reflects the approximation of the time reported. The records of all 1,296 families were used to determine average daily time use.

To obtain an average of time spent on all household work and in each household work activity, the time reported for each type of worker was totaled and averaged over the entire sample. Since all families in the sample were husband-wife families, all wives and husbands had an equal chance to contribute time to household production in all families. Each family in the sample also was considered to have had an equal chance to utilize paid or unpaid workers from outside the household.

The time spent by children 12 to 17 and 6 to 11 also was averaged over the entire sample in order to have an average total time of all workers for all household work and for each work activity. However, since all families did not have children of these ages, this overall average time spent by children was too distorted to serve as a measure of the contributions of children to household work. Therefore, the average time spent by children 12 to 17 and 6 to 11 on household work is shown in the tables and discussed as an average of time only for the number of families with children in each of the two groups.

Distribution of household work among several workers may result in more time spent on an activity than would be used if the job were done by one person. For example, shopping by two may double the time spent without adding to productivity. However, as long as the work is a part of useful household production or the practice of skills for future production, the increased time, if any, was judged to be a legitimate part of household work time. Over a sample of 1,296 families, minor variations in reported time caused by different levels of skill and varying personal choices could be expected to average out to insignificant proportions of total time.

At some point in the analysis, all the important variables identified in previous research were examined for their effects on household time use. The variables found to have the closest association with time spent on all household work or with some major kind of household work were: (1) *number of children*, (2) *family type*, (3) *employment of wives*, and (4) *age of youngest child*. For these four major variables, average time use is reported throughout this monograph for all household work, for each separate activity, and for groups of activities.

Family type, as defined for this study, was a combination of two variables—number of children

and age of youngest child. Types of families as defined by these two characteristics were ranked according to a theoretical progression from least complex (families with no children at home) to most complex (families with several children, some of whom were under age 2). As explained in the Methodology (Appendix A), age of the oldest child was used in sample selection but not in defining the family types.

The effects of ages of children other than the youngest on household work time could not, of course, be completely eliminated. Therefore, age of oldest child was analyzed as a separate variable in the rank correlations. The rank correlation values between time use and several other tested variables are also reported when statistically significant because such variables are frequently considered to have some effect on household work time. These additional major variables are: house type, location of residence, socioeconomic status, education of wives, education of husbands, and husbands' hours of employment.

Employment of wives was a major characteristic differentiating time use among households. In general, however, employed wives in the sample had fewer children at home, older children, and less complex families. (See Chapter 2.) These characteristics tended to decrease household work time. In order to separate the effects of family composition from those of employment for the analysis of time, households with the same number of children, age of youngest child, and family type were differentiated according to households with employed or nonemployed wives. As will be seen, some of the differences in time use between employed- and nonemployed-wife households in these matched cases were negligible while others were substantial.

The nature of the variables used in this study caused some problems in ranking for the correlation analysis. The order of ranking for the variables is discussed in the methodology but, to clarify the interpretations of the correlation coefficients in the subsequent pages, the meaning of the correlation signs for each major variable is given below:

Variable	Correlation Meaning
Number of children	A positive correlation signifies an increase in time use as number of children increases.
Age of youngest child	Age groups of children were ranked from oldest (12 to 17) to youngest (under 1 year). A positive correlation indicates an increase in time use as age of youngest child declines.

Family type	A positive correlation indicates an increase in use of time as family type increases in complexity.
Employment of wives	A negative correlation indicates a decrease in time use when wives are employed.
Husbands' hours of employment	A positive correlation signifies an increase in use of time as hours of husbands' employment increase.
House type	A positive correlation indicates an increase in time use from apartments to one-family houses.
Location of residence	A positive correlation signifies an increase in time use in suburban areas.
Socioeconomic level, education of wives and husbands	For use in determining socioeconomic position (Hollingshead, 1957), these variables were ranked from highest to lowest class and highest to lowest educational level. A negative correlation, therefore, signifies an increase in use of time as socioeconomic or educational level increases and a positive correlation indicates an increase in time use as either level declines.

Partial rank correlations were determined for the major variables that showed effective relationships with time use. The purpose was to determine the strength of the relationships, particularly those for the variables that were known to be interrelated. The constants used in these partial rank correlations indicate the relationship between the two variables.

The interrelationships between variables were as expected from the descriptive data of the sample discussed in Chapter 2. For example, the negative relationship between number of children and employment of wives (-.16) indicated that as family size increased, fewer wives were employed (Table 3.1). Because age groups of youngest child were ranked from oldest to youngest, the negative relationship between that variable and employment of wives (-.22) indicated that more wives were employed as the youngest child became older. Both age of the youngest and the number of children were interrelated with house type; when the type of house was more complex (that is, two- or one-family houses), the youngest child tended to be older and family size larger. The highest interrelationship was between house type and residential location; as more one-family houses were occupied, residential location was increasingly suburban (.33).

Rank Correlations of Total Time Used by All Workers and Major Variables

Total Time of All Workers (Table 3.2). The time spent by all workers on all household work was most closely related to the number of children in the household (.37) and family type (.36). Time on all household work increased as the number of children in the family increased and as family composition became more complex. The third variable of importance in relation to time spent by all workers on all household work was employment of wives; time decreased significantly when wives were employed (-.23).

Although statistically significant, the correlations of other variables with total time use were weaker than the correlations of number of children, family type, and wives' employment. More time was spent on all household work in single conventional houses than in apartments or other types of housing (.14), in households with younger children (.13), and in suburban areas (.08).

In the partial rank correlation analysis, the values for number of children and family type changed only slightly when other major variables were held constant. The correlation of number of children and time use did not change when age of the youngest child was held constant; more time was spent on household work as family size increased without regard to age of the youngest child. The effects of number of children and family type were associated only slightly with employment of wives or house type; time increased with the number of children and complexity of the family in households in which the wives were employed as well as those in which they were not, and in any type of house.

Employment of wives was somewhat interrelated with family type and number of children as shown by the decline in correlation value from -.23 to -.19 or -.18 when number of children or family type was held constant. Employment was, however, a stronger variable than age of youngest child, as shown by the almost complete lack of change in correlation value when the latter variable was held constant; employment of wives operated to reduce time on all household work at any age of youngest child.

The correlation value for age of youngest child with total time use on all household work remained the same when number of children was held constant, a confirmation of the lack of relationship between the effects of these two variables on total time. Some of the effects of age of youngest child, however, were interrelated with wives' employment. The already low correlation (.13) became weaker when employment was held constant (.08); the increase in time spent in households with younger children was somewhat less when wives were employed. The correlation of age of youngest child with time use increased slightly when house type was held constant (from .13 to .16). This increase, though small, indicated that total time spent on all household work increased in households with younger children in any type of house.

Some of the effect of house type on time spent by all workers resulted from influence of number of children or family type; the correlation value declined from .14 to .07 and .09, respectively, when the latter variables were held constant. The correlation value between house type and total time increased slightly when age of youngest child was held constant, from .14 to .17; and this change, though relatively small, suggested that more time would be spent on all household work in one-family houses than in other types whether children were older or younger.

Residential location was related to house type; the low but significant correlation (.08) declined to .04 when house type was held constant. Apparently, there was no measurable difference in time spent on all household work between families living in the city and those living in the suburbs if they lived in the same type of housing.

Rank Correlations of Time Used by Individual Workers and Major Variables (Table 3.2)

Wives were the principal workers and their time accounted for the highest proportion of total time on all household work and in nearly all of the separate activities. A correlation value of ±.15 was required for any change in wives' time spent on all household work to be apparent. The time spent by husbands and teenagers was highly variable and, for this reason, the indicated relationships between their household work time and the variables had only a slight, and not always consistent, effect on their average time use.

The rank correlations for the time of individual workers to major variables differed considerably from those for time of all workers. The major variable that had the closest relationship with the time wives spent on all household work was employment (-.36); wives' time on all household work decreased when they were employed.

Other moderately strong relationships were those between wives' time use and number of children (.27), family type (.30), and age of youngest child (.30); the husbands' hours of

employment variable was only weakly related to wives' time use for all household work (.08).

The interrelationship between employment of the wives and age of the youngest child is shown by the marked increase in the correlations for each of these variables when the other was held constant, from -.36 to -.46 for employment of wives, and from .30 to .42 for age of youngest child. It was apparent that: (1) wives, employed or not, spent considerably more time on all household work when their children were younger than when they were older; and (2) employed wives spent considerably less time on all household work than nonemployed wives whether they had younger or older children in the family.

Husbands' time use for all household work was related only to husbands' hours of employment (-.15); as their hours of paid work increased husbands spent less time on all household work.

The time spent by teenagers on all household work (in families with teenagers) was related to number of children (.21), and to a lesser extent to family type (.15).

Amount of Household Work Time

Comparison of Wives' Time with Some Historical Data (Table 3.3)

Contrary to the opinion of many, average time used by wives for household work has not been drastically reduced because of technological developments in automatic equipment such as dishwashers, washers, and garbage disposers. Much of the work of the family cannot be automated. Some activities are easier to do because of new equipment and sometimes more is done because changes in technology have made the work easier to do. For other activities, such as child care, time use has increased for chauffeuring children to educational and social functions.

No one will deny that the physical demands of many tasks have been reduced, but the time demands of some activities have increased while others have decreased. Unfortunately, relatively little historical data are available, except for farm families, on changes in time use for household work, and most of those studies were limited to homemakers' time. However, data from a 1926-27 study of urban homemakers in Oregon (Wilson, 1929) and from one in 1952 in New York State (Wiegand, 1954) can be compared with homemakers' time use in the current study.

The average amount of time used by

nonemployed wives for household work was remarkably similar in 1967-68 in New York State to time used in the urban sample in Oregon in 1926-27. There has been a decrease of 30 minutes in the homemakers' average time per day since 1927 in food preparation and after-meal cleanup, but since that time there has been an increase of more than half an hour for marketing, record keeping, and management. Possibly the time "saved" in food preparation and after-meal cleanup went into selecting and buying the convenience foods. The increased time use reported for family care may reflect a real change, or it may be that the average figures have been affected by varying proportions of families with children in the studies.

Even after discounting variations in methodology and sampling, wives' household work time has not decreased. If such work time were to be aggregated for the entire country, however, one would expect to find decreases in total household work time because of changes in average number of children in households and number of wives employed in the labor force.

Amount of Household Work Time by Family Characteristics

Since all households require goods and services related to food, clothing, shelter, and some type of family care, the types of household work that produce the goods and services for a family are similar in all households. The amount of time spent on this work, however, varies among families. In this study, the average total time of all workers on all household work was 8 hours or less on 24% of the record days, between 8 and 12 hours on 35%, from 12 to 16 hours on 27%, and more than 16 hours on 15%. Over the entire sample of 1,296 families, the average total time of all workers spent on all household work was 10.5 hours a day.

An overall figure of average time of 10.5 hours a day is interesting but meaningless in itself. An average time for a group of households of different characteristics may be computed for convenience in showing overall trends. However, the meaningful averages of time use that express a quantity of household work are those for households with the same family composition characteristics, e.g., households with the same number of children or a youngest child in the same age group.

Table 3.4 and Figures 3.2 and 3.3 show the effects of number of children and age of the youngest child combined with employment of wives on the household work time of all workers and of individual workers. The wide variations in average daily time use with changes in these variables show clearly the importance of differences in family characteristics in defining household work loads.

Number of Children and Age of Youngest Child

Total Time of All Workers (Table 3.4 and Figures 3.2 and 3.3). The effect of number of children on total time is very clear. In nonemployed-wife households the average time used by all workers for all household work increased progressively by number of children, from 7.2 hours per day if there were no children to 9.7 hours in families with one child up to 17.4 hours a day in households with seven to nine children. Similarly, when wives were employed, the average hours per day increased from 5.0 hours if there were no children to 7.7 hours in one-child households and to 13.0 hours in families with five or six children. Although the time use increased with each increase in number of children, the size of each increase varied.

Number of children exercised a more consistent effect on time use than age of the youngest child. Age of the youngest child had the strongest effect on time used on household work when children were very young, while the effect of number of children was spread out over the range of family size.

Calculated by age of the youngest child, the greatest amount of average time used for all household work was in families in which the youngest child was a baby (13.2 hours per day when wives were employed and 12.4 in nonemployed-wife households; as indicated in the figure and table, the higher time use when wives were employed was the result of a greater use of paid or unpaid assistance). The effect of a baby on increasing household work time can be seen by the large decline in time between households with a baby under 1 year and those with a child 1 year old as the youngest, over an hour a day whether wives were employed or not. There was no consistent decline in all household work time between the other groups by age of youngest. When the wives were not employed, the least total time was used in households with the youngest child a teenager (10.8 hours per day); when the wives were

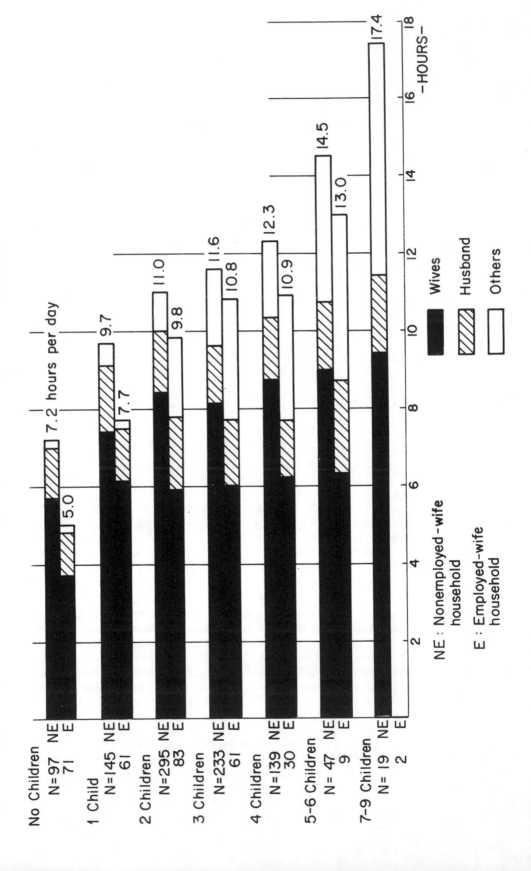

FIGURE 3.2—Total time of all workers for all household work by number of children and employment of wives

Figure 3.3—Total time of all workers for all household work by age of youngest child and employment of wives

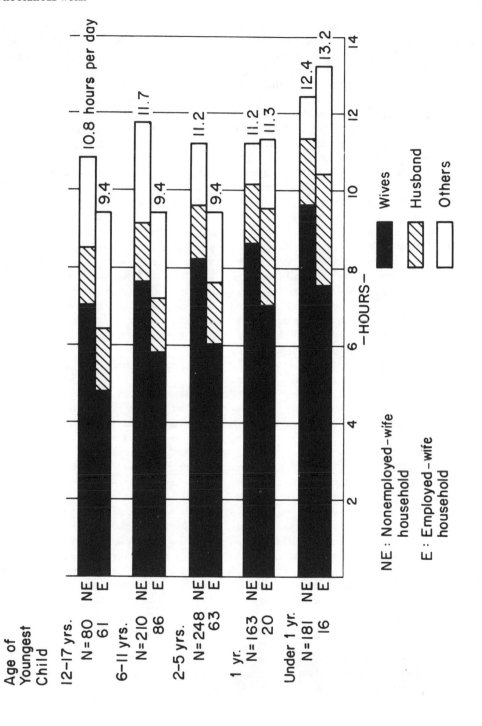

Age of
Youngest
Child

NE : Nonemployed–wife
      household

E : Employed–wife
     household

employed, the lowest average amount of time (9.4 hours per day) was used whether the youngest child was 12 to 17, 6 to 11, or 2 to 5 years.

The effect of employment of wives on total household work time was distinct from the effects of either the number of children or age of the youngest child. With the exception of households in which the youngest child was under 1 year, employment of wives operated to reduce all workers' time use. Total amount of time used for all household work declined by about 2 hours a day in families with no children and in those with one child. The decrease in time was approximately 1 hour per day with two or three children and 1.5 hours in larger families.

Wives' Time (Table 3.4 and Figures 3.2 and 3.3). Age of the youngest child was more closely associated with wives' time use on all household work than with all workers' time. Whether or not employed, wives' average time on all household work decreased consistently as the age of the youngest child increased. When not employed, wives' time declined from an average of 9.6 hours a day in households with a child under 1 year to 7.0 hours in households with the youngest a teenager; the decline was greater when wives were employed (from 7.5 hours to 4.8 hours per day).

Wives' household work time increased as the number of children in the family increased. The time of employed wives increased regularly by number of children, as did the time of non-employed wives except between two and three children. (This exception probably results from the mix of ages of children in the two groups.) Wives' time increased appreciably between families with no children and those with one child (from 5.7 to 7.4 hours for nonemployed and from 3.7 to 5.1 hours for employed wives). The highest time use of nonemployed wives was in families with seven to nine children (an average of 9.4 hours a day).

When wives were employed, the increase in their daily time between families with no children and those with five or six children was 2.6 hours, and employed wives spent the highest average time on all household work in these larger families (6.3 hours per day). The effect of employment on wives' use of time for household work is shown by the decrease of 2 hours or more per day in the time used by employed wives in all family sizes.

Husbands' Time (Table 3.4 and Figures 3.2 and 3.3). Husbands spent an average of 1.6 hours a day on all household work, whether or not wives were employed. Only in employed-wife families with a baby or a toddler as the youngest child did husbands' time average over 2 hours a day. Husbands' time for all household work did not vary consistently by number of children, age of youngest child, or employment of wives.

Other Workers' Time (Table 3.4). The average time contributions of workers other than family members to all household work was less than half an hour per day. Whether wives were employed or not, the time of female workers from outside the household did not vary by number of children, but they tended to spend somewhat more time in some of the households in which there were children 1 year or younger, especially when wives were employed. The small amount of time used by nonfamily male workers did not vary by number of children but did vary slightly by employment of wives in families with young children.

Time of Children (Table 3.4). In the 413[3] families with teenage children, the accumulated contributions of teenagers added up to a sizable amount of household work time, whether or not their mothers were employed. Their average time was 2.0 hours a day in households with non-employed wives and a little more when wives were employed (2.2 hours). This time varied with number of children. Average daily household work time of teenagers whose mothers were not employed ranged from 1.2 hours in one-child families to 3.4 hours in seven-to-nine-children families. For those families with employed mothers, teenagers' average time varied from 1.1 hours (one-child households) to 3.6 hours (five- or six-children households). There was no consistent change in teenagers' household work time among age of youngest child groups.

The accumulated time of children 6 to 11 years (in the 588 families with children in that age group) did not consistently vary with number of children. In nonemployed-wife families, the time use of this age group increased by number of children from .4 hour in one-child families to 2.6 hours a day in families of seven to nine children; in employed-wife households, the changes in time use of 6- to 11-year-old children were erratic. On the average, children 6 to 11 spent about the same amount of time whether or not their mothers were employed (1.1 hours per day when nonemployed and 1.0 when employed).

---

[3]Note that this number differs from the 375 used for the correlation analysis from which two cells with less than 42 families had been eliminated. All households are included in reporting of time use.

Family Type

The combined effects of number of children and age of youngest child are reflected in the family type variable. Each of these component variables was associated to a different extent with total time used by all workers and by individual workers. Because the effects of number of children and age of youngest child were not of equal strength, the effects of family type tended to be similar to those of the stronger variable. Number of children had the stronger relationship to all household work time, and in general, the effects of family type followed the same pattern as those of number of children.

Table 2.3 shows that some categories of family type had few cases. Most of these were in the more complex families, i.e., in large families with young children, which are uncommon types of families in the general population, especially in households in which the wife is employed. The number of cases for several family types was too low to show the normal variability of daily household work. The average daily time shown for these categories cannot be considered as reliable estimates. Consequently, the variability is not discussed if there were fewer than 10 families. If there were 3 or more families, however, averages are presented in the tables because these figures may provide clues for further study.

Total Time of All Workers (Table 3.5). There was no regular progression in increased total time spent on household work as family type became more complex, i.e., as families increased in size and decreased in age of youngest child. The higher time use in the most complex family types, whether the wives were employed or not, reflects the effects of both number of children and age of youngest child. The most household work is likely when the different mixes of goods and services for each age group of children are all needed in a particular household.

The strength of number of children as a predictor of household work time was clearly apparent in the families with the youngest children under teenage. When wives were not employed, time increased by more than 1.5 hours between one- and two-child households and there was a varying size increase with each number of children at each age of youngest except teenage. Total time of all workers in employed-wife households was not closely associated with number of children at all ages of youngest child, but the differences in time by number of children were frequently greater than in nonemployed-wife households.

The effects of age of youngest child were somewhat mixed. When wives were not employed, total time did not increase or decrease regularly by age of youngest in all family sizes.

Less time was spent in households of employed than of nonemployed wives in most family types. The effect of employment was greater in the family types with older children than in those with younger children, in which the average times spent were similar whether or not wives were employed. In families without children, total time spent varied inconsistently by age of wives, but less time was spent when wives were employed in all age groups.

Several of the differences in total household work time by family type seemed inconsistent with the hypothesis that such time varies principally with family composition. For one thing, the total time was averaged over smaller portions of the sample. Also, the time on the separate activities that make up the household work load was averaged over varying numbers of families. Particularly in employed-wife households, some of the abnormally high time values are due to sample variations and the small number of cases. They do, however, serve to express some of the discrepant variations in total time and suggest a need for further study with larger samples in some categories.

Some of the extensive variations in total time shown in Table 3.5 resulted from changes in the content of household work in response to combined changes in family composition and employment of wives. In a few family types more total time was spent by all workers when wives were employed than when they were not. In other family types much less total time was used in employed-wife than in nonemployed-wife households. Most of these variations resulted from differences in the way physical and nonphysical care of family members was given in a relatively small number of employed-wife households. When other female workers cared for the children in the home, they spent a large amount of time, and their time was averaged over a small number of cases. When employed mothers took a preschool-age child to be looked after away from home, time used was likely to drop sharply because only time spent on family care at home was considered in the study.

Other erratic variations in total time used on all household work were caused by some nonroutine events, such as an unusually large amount of time given to a less frequent but time-consuming activity. The effects of unusual amounts of time on some record days are evident in the family type tables for time used on the individual activities.

Wives' Time (Table 3.5). In all but one family type (those with four teenage children) employed wives used much less time for all household work than nonemployed wives (from over 1 hour to as much as 3½ hours per day less). Employed wives quite consistently spent about 2 hours less time than nonemployed wives on all household work in one-child families when children were over age 2 and in two-child families at all ages of youngest.

Only when the youngest child was 6 to 11 or under 1 year old was there a fairly regular increase in the time of nonemployed wives with increased family size. There was no regular increase with family size in the time spent by employed wives at any age of youngest. The effect of age of youngest child on wives' time was stronger when the wives were not employed than when they were. The time of nonemployed wives declined as the youngest child became older in most family sizes. The time of employed wives, on the other hand, declined less consistently when the youngest child was older.

An examination of Tables 3.5 and 3.6 indicates that some of the differences in the time use of nonemployed and employed wives were related to the presence of other workers in the household. In families with more than one teenager, the lower time of employed wives may have been the result of the increased contributions of teenagers in some families. In families with younger children, and especially those with babies, husbands usually spent slightly more time than in families with older children when wives were employed. The time of nonfamily female workers also was higher in families with preschool children, especially when wives were employed.

Time of Children 12 to 17 (Table 3.6). Greater amounts of teenagers' time usually were spent in the larger families with the youngest child a teenager than in other types of families. The average time per teenage child was 1.2 hours per day, varying little whether or not the mother was employed.

An increased time of teenagers with an increased number of children does not reflect an increase in time per teenager, but teenagers' combined times made a sizable contribution—particularly when there were several teenagers in the family. It seems probable that these contributions from teenage children made it possible for many wives with older children to enter or return to the labor force (Walker, 1970, pp. 13-15).

Time of Children 6 to 11 (Table 3.6). In families with children 6 to 11, the average time per child 6 to 11 on all household work was .6 hour a day, varying little whether or not the mother was employed. Like teenagers, children 6 to 11 generally spent about this average time per child in most households, regardless of the number of children, age of youngest child, or family type.

Characteristics and Content of Household Work

The total time spent on all household work in 1 day is the sum of the time spent on the separate activities that make up household work. For the purposes of this study, these activities have been classified into 13 specific kinds of work. All of these activities meet Reid's (1934, p. 11) definition of measurable household work as:

> . . . unpaid activities which are carried on, by and for the members, which activities might be replaced by market goods, or paid services, if circumstances such as income, market conditions, and personal inclinations permit the service being delegated to someone outside the household group.[4]

These 13 specific activities were then grouped into the 5 major categories of activities, which defined the services provided by household work—

Group Categories	Individual Activities
All food preparation	Regular meal preparation After-meal cleanup Special food preparation
All house care	Regular house care Special house care Yard and car care
All family care	Physical care Nonphysical care
All clothing care	Washing Ironing Special clothing care
Marketing and management	Marketing or shopping Management and record keeping

---

[4]Although Reid's definition specifies "unpaid activities," in this study there was no separation of unpaid and paid work. Very little of the household work was done by nonfamily members, and there was no attempt to identify these workers—whether they were grandparents, neighbors, or paid workers. Likewise, no attempt was made to determine if children were paid for their participation in household work.

The classifications of special house care, yard and car care, and special clothing care were largely residual categories and were, therefore, made up of a variety of subtasks. These activities were expected to have large variations in time reported.

In reporting data that describe the content and characteristics of all household work combined and of individual activities, only measures of central tendency are used.[5]

Frequency of Household Work Activities and the Proportion of Total Time in Each
(Tables 3.7 and 3.8)

In the sample families, from 7 to 10 household activities were performed on two-thirds of the record days; 9 activities, the number most commonly performed, took place on 20% of the record days (Table 3.7). On only 20% of the record days were fewer than 7 activities carried on, and at least 3 activities were performed on nearly all of the record days. In contrast, on only 12% of the record days were more than 10 activities performed, and all 13 activities included in the study were carried on during fewer than one-half of 1% of the days.

Each of the 13 work activities produces a good or service for the family or its individual members. More time is needed to complete some activities because they are more complex than others. Some work activities may be repeated several times a day, others are not performed daily unless by choice, and still others are infrequently performed by any household. Variations in both time spent and frequency of occurrence also can be brought about by decisions within a household or by unusual circumstances that demand time. In nearly all of the activities, but in some more than others, both work and time may be reduced by choices made with respect to standards, materials, supplies, equipment, organization, and delegation of the work.

Essentially, the repetitiveness of any household work activity is determined by the type of service the activity provides, by the family's need for that service, and by the standards accepted for such service. The frequency of the 13 individual work activities varied from daily or almost daily (94% to 100% of days) to once or twice a week

(Table 3.8). In households with either nonemployed or employed wives the most and least frequent activities were the same; e.g., regular meal preparation on almost all of the record days and special food preparation on less than a quarter of the days.

In at least 9 of every 10 households of employed and nonemployed wives, time was spent daily on three highly repetitive activities—regular meal preparation, after-meal cleanup, and regular house care. Physical and nonphysical care of family members was done on from two-thirds to three-fourths of all record days (when performance was averaged over the entire sample). These family care activities, of course, were daily activities in certain types of households. Marketing and washing by machine were not daily activities but were performed frequently.

Six of the work activities studied accounted for seven-tenths of all household work time in both employed- and nonemployed-wife households. When wives were not employed, these activities were: regular meal preparation (15%); regular house care, marketing, nonphysical and physical care of family members (12% each); and after-meal cleanup (9%). The largest difference between nonemployed- and employed-wife households was the lower proportion of time spent in the latter households on physical care of family members (6% versus 12% of total daily time, respectively). Washing by machine, though a frequent activity, accounted for only 5% of total household work time.

Of the seven activities frequently performed, three were both frequent and time consuming in households of both nonemployed and employed wives: (1) regular meal preparation, (2) regular house care, and (3) marketing. Both regular meal preparation and regular house care may be performed several times a day and the time used can vary with the frequency and complexity of the operations performed. Marketing, on the other hand, is not usually a daily activity but is one that may take a considerable amount of time when it is performed.

Two other regular activities, after-meal cleanup and washing by machine, accounted for less time than their high frequency would suggest, whether the wives were employed or not.

Among the less frequently performed activities, small differences in proportionate shares of total time also occurred between households with nonemployed and employed wives. Special house care represented 6% and 8%, respectively, for nonemployed- and employed-wife households,

---

[5]Other statistical measures (e.g., chi-square) were used to identify significant associations between major variables of the study and characteristics of the activities, but statistical results of these analyses are not reported in this monograph.

while none of the other five less frequent activities represented more than 5% of total work time. Although any of the less frequently performed activities may take considerable time when they are performed, special house care was the only infrequent activity to have a relatively high average time expenditure—almost three-fourths hour a day, on the average, in households with either nonemployed or employed wives.

Effects of Family Composition and Employment of Wives (Table 3.8)

In spite of the similarities in the patterns of household work whether or not wives were employed, employed-wife households spent a substantially lower amount of average time on household work than those with nonemployed wives (almost 2½ hours a day less). Some of this substantial difference in time use related to the interrelationship of family composition and employment of wives.

By wives' employment, the greatest variation in the total work load and the sharpest decline in average time spent on all household work activity was in physical care of family members (an average of 48 minutes less a day in households with employed wives). As shown in Chapter 5, physical care was predominately care of preschool-age children; and, as pointed out earlier, preschool-age children were concentrated in households in which the wives were not employed. The extraordinary decline in the work load made by a difference in this one family characteristic can be seen in the large drop in the frequency of physical care, from 75% of record days when wives were not employed to 48% when they were, and the reduction in average time from 1.3 hours per day to one-half hour. Although time spent on non-physical care in households with employed wives was less by only .3 hour a day, the lower amount of time spent on family care accounted for almost half (1.1 hours) of the 2.4 hours difference in total household work time between the two types of households.

However, the difference in family composition and other characteristics of households with employed wives had implications beyond those related to family care. Less time was spent on each work activity when the wives were employed, and each work activity was performed a little less frequently. The remaining difference in time used between households of nonemployed and employed wives was made up of the small decreases in time spent on the other work activities—on the

average, about 18 minutes a day less on regular meal preparation; 12 minutes less on after-meal cleanup, washing, and yard and car care; and 6 minutes a day less on regular house care and marketing and the less regular activities of ironing, special clothing care, and management. As shown in Table 3.5, the lower time use in employed-wife households was accentuated in certain family types, those with no children or those with only teenage children.

Distribution of Household Work Time

This study concentrated on the total time spent on household work by all workers in the household. The contributions of the various household workers to household work were not distributed evenly over all of the household work activities; instead, they varied in amount, frequency, and kinds of work performed. The distributions of total time among the household workers is discussed in this section, together with some of the factors that affected their availability for household work.

The assuming of household work roles relates to a variety of cultural, social, and economic factors; and many generalizations are often made about the effects of changes in these factors on work roles of men and women, boys and girls. The time records of individual workers collected for the study showed how much the work loads of urban-suburban households were shared and by which family members.

Number of Daily Activities by Each Worker (Table 3.9)

The number of daily activities by household workers provides an overview of how the household work load was distributed. Wives seldom worked in fewer than 4 to 6 of the 13 work activities and most usually (on 54% of the record days) did some work in 7 to 9. When work in more than 9 activities was performed, it was done chiefly by wives. Husbands tended to perform from 1 to 3 activities, though on about a fifth of the record days they did none, and on another fifth they did from 4 to 6.

On 88% of the record days, teenagers did some work in 1 or more household activities in the families that had teenagers. Over half of the families with teenagers reported work by them in from 1 to 3 activities and another quarter reported work in 4 to 6 activities. A few teenagers had done some work in 10 activities. In the families with children 6 to 11, children in this age group worked in from 1 to 3 activities (on 57% of the record days), but 12% worked in from 4 to 6.

Few families in the sample had female or male workers other than family members. Usually, other female workers were involved in from 1 to 3 activities (88% of the days on which they worked), and typically in only 1 activity. Other male workers likewise were engaged in from 1 to 3 activities only and typically in only 1 activity.

Contributions of Individual Workers
(Tables 3.10 and 3.11)

Most of the time spent on household work, whether or not wives were employed, was by family members. Wives, employed or not, were the principal workers and spent the most time; on the average, 72% of total household work time was the wives' time when they were not employed and 62% when they were (Table 3.10). The next highest proportion of time input was by husbands, but it was considerably lower (14% when wives were not employed and 18% when they were). When averaged over the 1,296 families, the time of older children accounted for 5% of total work time when the wife was not employed, and 10% when she was. The time inputs of younger children varied little by mothers' employment (5% and 4%). The average amount of total time spent on household work in the 1,296 families by nonfamily female workers represented 5% of total time in employed-wife households and 3% in those with non-employed wives. Other male workers accounted for 1% of all time whether or not the wife was employed.

Although the percentage of the total time contributed by other family members increased with employment of the wife, it is important to keep in mind that the drop in wives' time rather than an increase in time of others is largely responsible for this change in proportionate times. The interrelationship between wives' employment and the age of the youngest child also had an effect. Percentages reported here, however, point up overall time relationships.

Since the purpose of this study was to develop a measure of household production, no attempt has been made to determine whether or not the time of other workers substituted for wives' time or complemented it; that is, whether other workers "saved" the wives' time or whether wives spent as much or more time when others contributed. In any case, the time figures indicate that wives had

the principal responsibility for conducting the work of the home and apparently turned some of it over to others to a limited degree. Primary responsibility was accepted by others in only a few activities.

In the types of activities on which the greatest average amount of time was spent, wives' time accounted for at least half the total time and usually for substantially more. Whether employed or not, wives were the principal workers in five of the regular and time-consuming activities: (1) regular meal preparation, (2) regular house care, (3) physical care of family members, (4) after-meal cleanup, and (5) marketing. The time of nonemployed wives accounted for four-fifths or more of total time on four of the most frequent activities and that of employed wives for three-fifths or more.

Over half of the total time spent on marketing was contributed by wives, whether employed or not. Almost no one but wives did washing by machine; their time was over nine-tenths of total time. Among the less regular activities, wives' time was less than half of total time in only two, special house care and yard and car care. In only one of the more time-consuming activities, nonphysical care of family members, was there much change in the wife's share of the work time when she was employed.

Though the proportion of days on which workers other than wives did some household work was fairly substantial, the largest portions of their work were selectively concentrated in a relatively few activities (Table 3.11). Of the more time-consuming activities, whether the wives were employed or not, marketing and nonphysical care of family members were the principal ones in which workers other than wives spent any appreciable amount of time. The erratic contributions of time by workers other than the wife indicated some flexibility in assigning or sharing parts of the work load when the wives were employed. Some wives turned the work over to nonfamily female workers; others, to husbands, teenage children, or elementary school-age children; or to some combination of them. Aside from those related to family care, most of the activities that employed wives performed less frequently were activities that offered considerable choice as to frequency of performance and delegation of work.

Other workers may have reduced time and effort for the principal workers in ways not reported because time was not recorded if less than five minutes was spent on an activity at any one time. Wives may assume the more time-consuming parts of household work because other family members do not have the time available in large blocks, or, again, it may represent a preference of wives. And, it may be that some family members do not fully appreciate the extensiveness and complexity of household work and do not recognize the need for sharing it.

Principal Activities of Various Household Workers (Table 3.12)

When wives were not employed, 4 of the 13 activities accounted for over half of wives' daily average time: regular meal preparation (17%), regular house care (14%), physical care (14%), and after-meal cleanup (10%). The other 2 time-consuming activities, marketing and non-physical care of family members, represented 9% each of nonemployed wives' total time. Of nonemployed wives' daily average time 7% was spent in washing by machine, 5% on ironing, and 4% on special clothing care. The only differences in the ordering of these activities when wives were employed were the much smaller proportions of their time spent on the two family care activities and the somewhat higher proportion of time spent on marketing.

The activities in which husbands were engaged most frequently were two regular ones (marketing and nonphysical care of family members) and two less regular ones (yard and car care and special house care). On the average, each of these represented 14% to 20% of husbands' total time. Their activity pattern did not vary to any extent when wives were employed.

It seemed clear from the records that children performed some household operations regularly. One or more teenagers (in those families with teenagers) did some household work on about nine-tenths of the record days (Table 3.11). The four activities in which they worked most frequently were regular ones—regular meal preparation, after-meal cleanup, regular house care, and marketing. These activities represented 60% of their total time in households of nonemployed mothers and 72% when mothers were employed (Table 3.12).

Like teenagers, younger children (6 to 11) in the families with children in that age group, most frequently did some work in regular house care, marketing, after-meal cleanup, and regular meal preparation. They contributed time less frequently than teenagers; in some activities, they worked less frequently when their mothers were employed.

Their time was more diffused among the activities than that of teenagers, with regular house care being the most important, followed by marketing and after-meal cleanup.

Since the focus was on total time of all household workers, data for time spent by children were not analyzed by sex of the child for the 1,296 families in this report. However, some information on the difference in time contributions by sex of children in the two age groups is available from three other studies related to the overall project. They all have shown that, in general, girls spend more time than boys and tend to do more regular activities on inside household work, while boys do more of the outside work (Hoppen, 1966; Walker and Nordenstedt, 1966, and Lynch, 1975).

Lynch analyzed data from a subsample of the present study, which was made up of 419 school-age boys and 387 school-age girls from one-, two-, and three-child households, to determine sex and age differences in children's participation in household work. At ages 6 to 8 years, boys and girls spent the same average amount of time per day (.3 hour). By age 9 to 11, the differences in their time were clear (.8 hour for girls versus .5 hour for boys). By age 12 to 14, girls were contributing about twice as much time as boys (1.1 hours versus .6 hour) and this continued at the 15- to 17-year level (1.3 for girls versus .6 for boys). The activities that were done more by girls than boys were meal preparation, after-meal cleanup, and regular house care; while the ones in which boys participated more often were lawn and car care.

Hours Family Members Were at Home on Record Days

The amount of time household members are able to spend on household work can be assessed to some extent from the time they have available at home, free from other time commitments such as school attendance or paid employment. Analysis of time at home on the record days does not show when the time blocks occurred or how each was used, but it does provide an overview of the availability of potential household workers; the regularity of work routines and leisure time provides general information on the periods of the day when wives and husbands who were employed and children who attended school were likely to be at home continuously. The variations in presence of husbands and school-age children at home also may account for some of the variations in time spent on household work activities.

Wives' Time at Home or Away (Table 3.13). Wives, whether employed or not, spent the most time at home of any family members. In fact, when not employed, over half the wives in the sample spent from 22 to 24 hours of the record days at home and another 29% spent 19 to 21 hours at home. Less than one-half of 1% of non-employed wives spent fewer than 10 hours in their homes. On the record days about one-fifth spent time on volunteer work.

It was apparent that, except for their time for paid employment, employed wives also spent most of their time at home; 53% spent from 13 to 18 hours at home and 21% spent 22 to 24 hours at home. Another 18% were at home for 19 to 21 hours. A high proportion of employed women were not away from home for paid employment on the record days (45%); this is probably accounted for by the inclusion of weekends and vacation days in the total number of days. On the record days the usual number of hours of paid employment was 7 to 9 (30%). A somewhat smaller proportion of employed than of nonemployed wives spent time on volunteer work (15%), but the difference is small when the lower availability of time for employed wives is considered.[6]

Husbands' Time at Home or Away (Table 3.13). The typical time of husbands at home was from 10 to 15 hours, whether the wives were employed or not; only about 10% had spent less than that many hours at home, and only a fifth of the husbands had spent 19 or more hours at home on the record days.

Like wives, the principal reason for husbands' being away from home was paid employment—almost three-fourths of husbands had spent some time at paid work on the record days, usually from 7 to 12 hours. Husbands not away from home on paid employment included retired men, those on vacation, and those whose record days were reports of weekends.

Whether or not the wives were employed, about the same proportion of husbands (12%) had spent time on volunteer work on the 2 record days. The proportion of husbands who did such work was lower than those of either employed or nonemployed wives who had done volunteer work.

Children's Time at Home or Away (Table 3.13). The employment of mothers related, to some extent, to hours that children were at home.

---

[6]In response to a question in another section of the interview, more nonemployed wives (62%) than employed wives (44%) reported that they did some volunteer work.

A somewhat larger percentage of school-age children spent 16 to 24 hours at home when the mothers were not employed than when they were employed (84% of days compared with 79% for 6- to 11-year-olds, and 64% compared with 58% for those 12 to 17 years). On the other hand, a larger percentage of children of employed mothers were at home 7 to 15 hours (20% of 6- to 11-year-olds in households with an employed mother, compared with 16% in those with nonemployed mothers; and 40% of 12- to 17-year olds with employed mothers, compared with 32% with nonemployed mothers).

Hours of Employment of Wives, Husbands, and Children

Wives' Hours of Employment (Table 3.14). As discussed in the preceding section, total time of all workers and time of individual workers spent on all household work varied in relation to paid employment of wives. For the most part, employment of wives 30 or more hours per week had more effect on time use than employment for fewer hours a week. Of the wives who worked 15 or more hours a week, two-thirds worked 30 or more hours a week and one-third worked from 1 to 29 hours. Only 9% of the wives had worked for pay 40 hours or more in the week previous to the interviews.

The time per day used for all household work by all workers and by wives decreased considerably as the length of wives' employment increased. All workers' time declined consistently from 11.1 hours per day when wives were not employed to 8.0 hours when wives were employed 30 or more hours per week. Wives who were not employed used an average of 8.1 hours per day in household work, while those who were employed 30 or more hours per week used 4.8 hours per day.

In households in which wives were employed 30 or more hours a week (compared with those in which they were employed fewer hours), less time was spent on several of the more time-consuming activities by wives and by all workers. Food preparation activities continued to be the ones on which the most time was spent, but the total time of all workers was one-half hour less in households in which the wife was employed 30 or more hours per week than it was in those in which wives were not employed at all. When compared with non-employed wives, employed wives' average time use on food preparation was three-quarters of an hour less. Wives' time use on physical and nonphysical care declined regularly as their hours of employment increased, and dropped sharply when the employment week was 30 hours or more.

Husbands' time and pattern of activities remained about the same regardless of wives' hours of employment. Large amounts of time may have been spent by some husbands, but their time was not sufficient to raise the average time and apparently was not a typical situation. The time used for any kind of household work by children 12 to 17 or 6 to 11 (in families with children in those age groups) did not change consistently as their mothers were employed longer hours.

Husbands' Hours of Employment (Tables 3.15 and 3.16). Of all variables studied, husbands' time contribution to the household work was most closely related to their employment work time, i.e., their primary productive time, which most often is basic for the purchasing of goods and services the family uses. The average household work times varied from 2.1 hours for husbands employed less than 40 hours per week to 1.2 hours for those employed 50 or more hours per week (Table 3.15).

The relationships between husbands' hours of employment and time of wives, husbands, and all workers on all household work were somewhat modified by employment of wives. When the wives were not employed, total time on all household work increased regularly as husbands' hours of employment increased but did not increase when the wives were employed (Table 3.16). Husbands who were employed less than 40 hours a week spent the most time on all household work (an average of over 2 hours a day), but whether the wives were employed or not, husbands' time declined relatively rapidly as they worked longer hours. The increase in wives' time as husbands' hours of employment increased was more marked when wives were not employed; the time of employed wives increased only by small increments as husbands' work hours increased.

Since over half of the husbands in the sample were employed 40 to 49 hours a week and another third worked for pay 50 or more hours, the relationship between husbands' weekly employment time and their daily household work time partly explains the relatively low contribution of husbands to total household work time.

Total Workweek of Husbands and Wives (Table 3.17 and Figure 3.4). The average hours per day that wives used in work other than household work ranged from one-half hour to 5.3 hours. The "other work" category combined paid work with unpaid, volunteer work. This category averaged 1.7 hours per day for wives in the sample and 7.6 hours per day for husbands, the reverse of household work time averages of 7.3 hours for

wives and 1.6 for husbands.

When all work time was combined, i.e., time for employment work, household work, and volunteer work, men and women in the Syracuse sample fit the picture of a work-oriented society. Because each day of the week was equally represented in the data, it is appropriate to multiply the average daily figures by seven for a picture of the total workweek. The average workweek for the 1,296 wives was 63 hours and for husbands it was 64 hours. All women and men worked, on the average, about 9 hours per day.

When the women were employed for 15 or more hours per week, however, their total work time was about 10 hours per day. The work time of husbands of women employed 15 to 29 hours per week was about 9 hours per day, and for husbands of women employed 30 hours or more it was about 8 hours per day. Husbands' total work time did not increase or decrease consistently with wives' employment.

Children's Hours of Paid Work. Children between the ages of 6 and 17 spent some of their time outside school in paid work. As might be expected, teenagers had paid jobs more often than younger children did. About the same proportion of teenagers was employed whether the mothers were employed or not (47% and 45%, respectively) and both groups worked about 12 hours a week, on the average. In most of the families only one teenager was employed.

Of the households with children 6 to 11, 7% of those with nonemployed mothers and 6% of those with employed mothers reported children 6 to 11 doing some paid work. In most households the amount of time these young children worked for pay was 1 to 4 hours per week. Usually, only one child in that age group worked for pay when the mother was employed.

Wives' Attitudes Toward Household Work (Tables 3.18 and 3.19)

Wives' attitudes toward the various kinds of household work are assumed to affect the amount of time spent on some activities. Therefore, data on attitudes of wives toward household work and each work activity were collected as part of the present study. These data were analyzed by Jarmon (1972) in relation to several demographic and situational variables.

Attitudes of wives were expressed on a 6-position ordinal scale, which ranged from "dislike very much" (numbered *1*) to "like very

FIGURE 3.4—Average hours per day used by wives and husbands for all household work and other work by wives' hours per week of paid employment

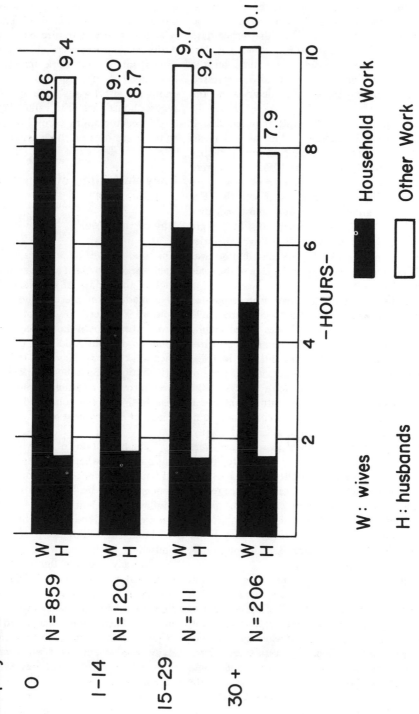

much" (numbered 6). The number of cases varied by the specific activities. Only homemakers who had spent time on an activity on the record days were asked to express an attitude toward it, but some others who had not spent time on the particular day of the record also expressed attitudes. All responses were included in the analysis.

Each position on the scale required that a specific attitude be expressed. Median and mean attitudes of wives toward household work activities (and also toward volunteer and paid work) were then computed. Median attitudes of wives were determined for 17 specific kinds of activities. For part of the analyses, the two most negative categories ("dislike very much, dislike") were combined, as were the two most positive categories ("like very much, like"). The distribution was heavily skewed toward the positive side of the scale (Table 3.18).

For the most part, the wives who responded expressed favorable attitudes toward household work activities. However, attitudes varied among the work activities, which suggested that wives tended to like household work but still had less positive attitudes toward some activities or parts of activities. According to Jarmon's analysis, the work activities with a median attitude rank of 5.0 or more were special food preparation, non-physical care of family, physical care of family, and meal preparation. Almost as well liked were washing by machine (4.9), yard care (4.9), management (4.8), and marketing (4.8). Less well liked but nevertheless somewhat liked were record keeping (4.3), regular house care (4.3), special clothing care (4.1), and special house care (4.0). None of the activities had a median rating below 3.0; least liked were car care (3.6), ironing (3.5), and after-meal cleanup (3.1).

Wives' attitudes were examined by Jarmon in relation to a number of variables by use of Kendall rank correlation coefficients including: number of children; age of youngest child; employment, education, occupation, and age of wife and husband; time use; and location of residence. Other variables, such as number of rooms and house type, were analyzed in relation to some of the specific activities. Of the 250 rank correlations tested, only 3 were stronger than ±.15. About one-fourth of the relationships tested were statistically significant but were not strong in correlation values (54 were less than ±.10 and 11 were between ±.10 and ±.15).

Number of children and time use were related to wives' attitudes toward more activities than other variables; residential location, wives' occupation, and hours of wives' employment were related to attitudes toward only one activity each. Attitudes of wives were slightly related to their time spent on nine work activities (Table 3.19), but only two of these relationships were strong enough to affect wives' time use. Wives who liked regular house care (Tau value .12) and those who liked special clothing care (Tau value .17) tended to use more time on these activities.

Daily Variability of Household Work
(Table 3.20)

Day of the Week

The total time of all workers and of each household worker represent averages of their time use on each of the 7 days of the week. No attempt has been made in the present study to analyze household work patterns by day of the week since this distribution would not affect either total time spent on all household work or the time spent on each work activity. However, the somewhat uneven distribution of household work over the days of the week provides additional information about the distribution of the household work load and the effects of employment of wives on household work time.

The busiest day of the week in all households was Saturday, when the highest time was spent on all household work—12.6 hours by all workers in nonemployed-wife households and 11.1 hours in employed-wife households. On each day of the week except Sunday (when the average time was 8.7 hours for all families), less time was spent on household work when wives were employed.

Sunday was the lightest workday for non-employed wives (5.5 hours); from 2 to 3 hours less was spent than on other days. Saturday also was a lighter workday than weekdays for these wives (7.5 hours). Their time tended to increase fairly regularly from Monday to Friday; in contrast, the daily time of employed wives varied among the days and reached a weekday peak on Thursday (5.7 hours compared with 6.4 on Saturday).

The similarity in average time used by all workers on Sunday points to a difference between the nonemployed- and employed-wife households. In employed-wife households total time spent on Sunday was equal to time spent on Friday and higher than the time spent on other days except Saturday. The average of 6.4 hours spent on all household work by employed wives was more time than they spent on any other day, and an hour and a half more than they spent on Sunday (4.9 hours). The time employed wives spent on Saturday and Sunday, though still lower, was much closer to the time spent by nonemployed wives than was their time on other days.

In both nonemployed- and employed-wife households, the most time of husbands was spent on Saturday and Sunday, an average of at least 2 hours; and when the wives were not employed, this average was close to 3 hours on Saturday. This distribution is typical, since husbands' largest blocks of time free from employment normally are on weekends. On other days, their time was less than their average time of 1.6 hours a day, whether the wives were employed or not, except on Friday in employed-wife households.

Teenagers spent some time daily on household work and, in general, their time (in families with teenagers) increased throughout the week and was highest on Saturday—about 3½ hours when their mothers were not employed and almost 4 hours when they were. This distribution, like that of husbands, appeared typical, since Saturday would be the day when teenagers would have time most free from school work. Since teenagers worked principally in regular and time-consuming activities, their weekly distribution of time paralleled their mothers'. When their mothers were not employed, teenagers spent the least time on household work on Sunday (1.5 hours); in households with employed mothers, teenagers' workdays were heavier both on Sundays (2.6 hours) and Saturdays (3.8 hours) than on weekdays.

Children 6 to 11, like teenagers, spent some time daily on household tasks. The major difference by employment of mothers in time contributed by children 6 to 11 in families with children in that age group was in their higher time on Saturday, 1.5 hours, when their mothers were not employed. The additional time use of this age group on Saturday when their mothers were not employed, and the lack of change in their time use on Saturday when their mothers were employed, possibly indicated more time available to nonemployed mothers to work with these children when they had free time.

Saturday was the day on which nonfamily female workers most frequently spent time on household work, an average of one-half hour in nonemployed-wife households and three-quarters in employed-wife households. In employed-wife households, these workers spent more time than in nonemployed-wife households on Tuesdays and Fridays, while on the other 4 days the time spent was similar in both types of households (from .2 to .3 hour a day). Nonfamily male workers spent the same average time on each day (.1 hour).

Unusual Conditions on the Record Days (Table 3.21)

Unusual circumstances affecting the family or the home environment upset normal routines and bring about atypical patterns of household work. In general, the occurrence of unusual conditions of any kind was relatively low in the sample. Among sample households, about 18% reported unusual health conditions on the record days and 22% reported such conditions during the previous 7 days. Many of the unusual health conditions were the result of minor illnesses in the family on the record days (8%) or of a mentally or physically handicapped family member (7%).

Most of the other unusual conditions for both time periods were conditions that affected inside work, such as broken major appliances (1% on the record days) or remodeling (2% on the record days and 4% during the previous 7). On only 1% of the days was a condition reported that would affect work outside the house. For the most part, weather conditions were reported as normal for the season.

Unusual family conditions had a somewhat higher incidence than other types of unusual conditions; 40% of families reported effects of such conditions during the previous 7 days and 24% reported them on the record days. By far the largest proportion of these (17%) were due to the special occurrences related to family life, such as visiting or entertaining, planning for special events, or added work caused by higher-than-normal chauffeuring demands or extra hours of paid work.

TABLE 3.1—Rank correlation coefficients between major variables
(1,260 husband–wife households, Syracuse, N.Y., 1967-68)

	Age of youngest child	Employment of wives	House type	Location of residence
Number of children		-.16	.20	
Age of youngest child[a]	-.004	-.22	-.21	
Family type		-.19	.16	
House type				.33

[a]Coefficients were computed for 1,260 households except for the variable, age of youngest child, for which only households with children were used (1,092).

TABLE 3.2—Rank and partial rank correlation coefficients between major variables and all household work time of all workers, wives, husbands, and teenagers
(1,260 husband–wife households, Syracuse, N.Y., 1967-68)

Variable	Kendall Tau[a]	Partial rank correlation[b] with major variables held constant					
		Number of children	Age of youngest	Family type	Empl. of wives	House type	Location of residence
All workers' time[c] correlated with:							
Family composition variables							
Number of children	.37		.37		.35	.35	
Age of youngest child[c]	.13	.14			.08	.16	
Family type	.36				.33	.35	
Employment							
Wives	-.23	-.19	-.21	-.18			
Husbands' hours	.044						

Housing							
House type	.14	.07	.17	.09			.12
Location of residence	.08					.04	
Wives' time[c] correlated with:							
Family composition variables							
Number of children	.27	.31	.28		.23		
Age of youngest child[c]	.30				.42		
Family type	.30				.25		
Employment							
Wives	-.36	-.33	-.46	-.32			
Husbands' hours	.08						
Husbands' time[c] correlated with:							
Family composition variables							
Age of youngest child[c]	.05*						
Employment							
Husbands' hours	-.15						
Education							
Husbands	-.03≠						
Teenagers' time[d] correlated with:							
Family composition variables							
Number of children	.21		.22		.22		
Age of youngest child	-.07**						
Family type	.15				.16		
Employment							
Husbands' hours	-.06≠						

[a] All Tau values reported were significant at the .001 level unless otherwise indicated as: * = .005, ** = .01 or .02, and ≠ = .03 to .05. For discussion of effects of ranking of variables on positive and negative values see Chapter III, Statistical Analysis (pp. 30-31).

[b] Partial rank correlation values are reported only for major variables at the .001 level of significance.

[c] Tau values were computed on the basis of 1,260 households except for the variable age of youngest child, for which only households with children were used (1,092).

[d] Tau values computed on basis of 378 families with teenagers.

TABLE 3.3—Time used for household work by urban wives at

Household work activities	Oregon[b] 1926-27	Auburn, N.Y.[c] 1952 NE[d]	E
Number	154	102	53
		Average hours	
All homemaking work	7.3	7.4	4.1
All food activities	2.8	2.6	1.9
Care of house	1.3	1.6	.8
Care of clothes	1.6	1.6	.8
Care of family members	1.2	1.1	.3
Marketing and record keeping	.4	.5	.3

TABLE 3.4—Total household work time of all workers and individual workers, by (*1,296 husband-wife households, Syracuse, N.Y., 1967-68*)

Number of children	Number of households NE[a]	E	All workers NE	E	Wives NE	E	Husbands NE	E	Other workers Females NE	E	Males NE	E
						Average hours per day[b]						
0	97	71	7.2	5.0	5.7	3.7	1.4	1.2	.1			
1	149	61	9.7	7.7	7.4	5.1	1.7	1.4	.2	.5	.1	.1
2	295	83	11.0	9.8	8.4	5.9	1.6	1.9	.3	.7	.1	.2
3	233	61	11.6	10.8	8.1	6.0	1.5	1.7	.4	.4	.1	
4	139	30	12.3	10.9	8.7	6.2	1.6	1.5	.3	.5	.1	
5-6	47	9	14.5	13.0	9.0	6.3	1.7	2.4	.2	.8	.2	
7-9	19	2	17.4		9.4		2.0		.2			
Average	979	317	11.1	8.7	8.0	5.3	1.6	1.6	.3	.4	.1	.1
Age of youngest child												
12-17	80	61	10.8	9.4	7.0	4.8	1.5	1.6	.1	.3	.1	
6-11	210	86	11.7	9.4	7.6	5.8	1.6	1.3	.2	.4	.1	
2-5	248	63	11.2	9.4	8.2	6.0	1.6	1.7	.3	.7	.1	.2
1	163	20	11.2	11.3	8.6	7.0	1.7	2.5	.3	1.0	.1	.1
Under 1	181	16	12.4	13.2	9.6	7.5	1.7	2.9	.5	1.5	.1	.3
Total number	882	246	11.5	9.8	8.3	5.8	1.6	1.7	.3	.6	.1	.1

[a]NE and E indicate households with nonemployed or employed wives.

[b]Time reported only if there were three or more families and if average time was 3 minutes or more.

three points in time[a]

Syracuse, N.Y. 1967–68	
NE	E
979	317
per day	
8.0	5.3
2.3	1.6
1.6	1.2
1.3	.9
1.8	.8
1.0	.8

[a]Data previously published in *Journal of Home Economics* (Walker, 1969, p. 622).
[b]Data from Wilson (1929).
[c]Data from Wiegand (1954).
[d]NE and E indicate nonemployed or employed wives.

number of children, age of youngest child, and employment of wives

Number of households with children 12-17 years		Time for households with children 12-17 years		Number of households with children 6-11 years		Time for households with children 6-11 years	
NE	E	NE	E	NE	E	NE	E
		Average hours per day[b]				Average hours per day[b]	
22	20	1.2	1.1	23	19	.4	.6
82	44	1.1	1.6	128	40	.6	.6
91	35	2.2	2.9	156	38	1.0	1.5
43	19	2.2	3.2	91	18	1.5	1.0
31	6	2.8	3.6	46	8	1.6	1.1
18	2	3.4		19	2	2.6	
287	126	2.0	2.2	463	125	1.1	1.0
80	61	2.1	2.7				
87	41	2.0	1.7	210	86	1.3	1.0
85	17	1.6	1.7	133	24	.8	.7
20	5	2.2	1.4	77	9	.8	.9
15	2	2.6		43	6	1.4	1.2
287	126	2.0	2.2	463	125	1.1	1.0

TABLE 3.5—Total household work time of all workers and individual workers by family type and employment of wives
(1,296 husband–wife households, Syracuse, N.Y., 1967-68)

Family type	Number of households		All household workers		Wives		Husbands		Other workers			
									Females		Males	
	NE[a]	E	NE	E	NE	E	NE	E	NE	E	NE	E
			Average hours per day[b]									
No-child households by age of wives												
under 25 years	16	26	6.2	4.9	5.1	3.5	.9	1.4		.2		
25–39	19	23	7.2	5.1	5.9	3.8	1.2	1.4				
40–54	30	12	7.6	4.9	6.1	4.1	1.4	.8				
55 and over	32	10	7.3	5.2	5.3	4.1	1.8	1.0	.2			.1
Number of children by age of youngest child												
1 child												
12–17 years	22	20	10.5	7.9	7.0	4.7	2.0	1.7	.1	.3	.1	
6–11	23	19	9.0	7.9	7.0	5.7	1.4	1.2	.1	.3		
2–5	26	16	9.0	7.3	6.7	4.5	1.8	1.5	.2	.9	.3	.5
1	37	5	9.3	8.2	7.5	6.8	1.7	.6	.1	.9		
under 1	41	1	10.4		8.3		1.6		.6			
2 children												
12–17 years	27	15	11.0	9.9	7.4	5.1	1.7	1.8	.2	.5	.1	
6–11	60	24	10.5	8.8	7.4	5.4	1.6	1.5	.1	.4	.1	
2–5	93	28	10.6	9.2	8.3	6.2	1.6	1.8	.2	.6	.1	.2
1	50	9	11.2	12.1	8.9	6.3	1.7	3.7	.3	1.1	.1	.2
under 1	65	7	11.7	12.1	9.6	7.7	1.5	1.6	.5	2.1		.6

	NE[a]	E[a]	NE	E	NE	E	NE	E	NE	E	NE
3 children											
12–17 years	26	16	11.0	8.8	6.7	3.9	1.1	1.5	.1	.2	.1
6–11	58	26	11.9	11.2	7.4	6.3	1.6	1.5	.3	.3	.1
2–5	70	13	11.2	11.3	8.0	7.6	1.4	2.1	.5	.8	
1	48	2	11.5		8.9		1.6		.3		
under 1	31	4	12.6	10.9	10.1	6.6	1.4	2.1	.5	.1	.1
4 children											
12–17 years	5	9	9.8	12.9	6.2	6.1	.9	1.1	.2	.2	.1
6–11	51	15	12.3	9.0	8.0	5.7	1.4	1.0	.5	.4	.2
2–5	32	1	11.9		9.1		1.4		.5		.6
1	19	3	12.6	10.8	9.3	7.7	2.0	2.1	.1	.6	.1
under 1	32	2	14.6		10.6		2.2		.5		.3
5–6 children											
12–17 years	0	1									
6–11	16	2	15.8	11.2	8.6	6.0	2.0	1.8	.1	.5	.2
2–5	17	3	13.4		9.0		1.5		.8		.9
1	6	1	12.3		7.5		1.1		.3		
under 1	8	2	16.1		10.5		2.2		.3		
7–9 children											
6–11 years	2	0									
2–5	10	2	15.9		8.8		2.1				
1	3	0	21.4		10.4		1.4		1.0		
under 1	4	0	18.4		11.7		2.0				

[a] NE and E indicate households with nonemployed or employed wives.

[b] Time reported only if there were three or more families and if average time was 3 minutes or more.

TABLE 3.6—Total household work time of children 12-17 and 6-11 by employment of
(413 husband-wife households with teenagers and 588 households with

Family type	Number households with children 12-17 years NE[a]	E	Total number of teenagers NE	E	Average hours per day[b] Per family with 12-17 NE	E	Per teenager NE	E
Number of children by age of youngest child								
1 child								
12-17 years	22	20	22	20	1.2	1.1	1.2	1.1
6-11								
2 children								
12-17 years	27	15	54	30	1.8	2.5	.9	1.3
6-11	26	16	26	16	.8	1.0	.8	1.0
2-5	26	11	26	11	.8	1.2	.8	1.2
1	2	2	2	2				
under 1	1	0	1	0				
3 children								
12-17 years	26	16	78	48	3.1	3.2	1.0	1.1
6-11	27	15	39	28	2.0	2.6	1.4	1.4
2-5	29	2	37	4	1.5		1.2	
1	6	1	9	1	2.9		1.9	
under 1	3	1	3	1	1.5		1.5	
4 children								
12-17 years	5	9	20	36	2.5	5.4	.6	1.4
6-11	20	8	39	18	2.1	1.5	1.1	.7
2-5	9	1	16	3	1.5		.8	
1	6	1	7	1	1.2		1.0	
under 1	3	0	5	0	5.4		3.2	
5-6 children								
12-17 years	0	1	0	5				
6-11	12	2	34	6	4.0		1.4	
2-5	11	1	24	1	2.2		1.0	
1	3	1	4	2	1.7		1.3	
under 1	5	1	9	3	2.2		1.2	
7-9 children								
6-11 years	2	0	8	0				
2-5	10	2	26	5	3.2		1.2	
1	3	0	5	0	4.1		2.5	
Under 1	3	0	5	0	1.9		1.1	
N =	287	126	499	241				
Average time					2.0	2.2	1.2	1.2

[a]NE and E indicate households with nonemployed or employed wives.

[b]Time reported only if there were three or more families and if average time was 3 minutes or more.

mothers and family type
children 6-11 years, Syracuse, N.Y., 1967-68)

Number of households with children 6-11 years		Total number 6-11 year olds		Average hours per day[b]			
				Per family with 6-11		Per 6-11 year olds	
NE	E	NE	E	NE	E	NE	E
23	19	23	19	.4	.6	.4	.6
60	24	94	32	.9	.6	.6	.5
32	10	32	10	.3	.3	.3	.3
23	5	23	5	.4	.9	.4	.9
13	1	13	1	.3		.3	
58	26	135	50	1.5	1.7	.6	.9
53	9	79	16	.8	.6	.5	.3
31	1	42	1	.5		.4	
14	2	19	3	.9		.7	
51	15	165	42	1.8	1.1	.6	.4
21	0	39	0	.7		.4	
14	2	22	4	1.0		.6	
5	1	8	1	3.4		2.1	
16	2	50	4	2.0		.6	
17	3	42	10	1.3	1.4	.5	.4
6	1	17	1	1.2		.4	
7	2	20	3	2.0		.7	
2	0	8	0				
10	2	33	6	1.8		.5	
3	0	9	0	4.3		1.4	
4	0	15	0	3.3		.9	
463	125	888	208				
				1.1	1.0	.6	.6

TABLE 3.7—Percentage of record days on which various numbers of household work activities were performed by all workers
(*1,296 husband–wife households, Syracuse, N.Y., 1967-68*)

Number of individual activities	Number of record days	Percent of record days
0	2	<1
1	2	<1
2	6	<1
3	28	1
4	75	3
5	146	6
6	247	9
7	390	15
8	486	19
9	514	20
10	380	15
11	223	8
12	84	3
13	9	< 1

Total record days   2,592

Mean = 8.2 activities per day

TABLE 3.8—Frequency of performing 13 household work activities, average daily time for each, and percentage of each in total household work time, by employment of wives
(*1,296 husband-wife households, Syracuse, N.Y., 1967-68*)

	Percent of days activity performed[a]		Average hours per day		Percent of total household work time	
	NE	E	NE	E	NE	E
All household work	100	100	11.1	8.7		
More frequent activities						
Regular meal preparation	100	99	1.6	1.3	15	15
After-meal cleanup	98	97	1.0	.8	9	9
Regular house care	97	94	1.3	1.2	12	14
Nonphysical care of family members	77	72	1.3	1.0	12	12
Physical care of family members	75	48	1.3	.5	12	6
Marketing	68	68	1.3	1.2	12	14
Washing by machine	66	56	.6	.4	5	5
Less frequent activities						
Special clothing care	51	47	.4	.3	5	3
Management	49	41	.4	.3	4	3
Yard and car care	49	42	.6	.4	5	5
Ironing	43	42	.4	.3	4	3
Special house care	43	33	.7	.7	6	8
Special food preparation	23	22	.1	.1	<1	<1
Total number of record days	1,958	634				

[a]NE and E indicate households with nonemployed or employed wives.

TABLE 3.9—Percentage of record days on which various numbers of household work activities were performed by individual workers
(*1,296 husband-wife households, Syracuse, N.Y., 1967-68*)

Household worker	Number of record days	Number of household activities				
		None	1-3	4-6	7-9	10-13
		Percent of record days				
Wives	2,592	<1	3	30	54	13
Husbands	2,592	19	61	18	2	--
Children - 12-17 years	826	12	57	27	4	<1
Children - 6-11 years	1,176	31	57	12	1	--
Other workers - females	2,592	90	9	1	<1	--
(Days reported)	(276)	(--	88	11	1	--)
Other workers - males	2,592	97	3	<1	--	--
(Days reported)	(89)	(--	98	2	--	--)

TABLE 3.10—Distribution among individual workers of total time used in each of 13 household work activities, by employment of wives

(1,296 husband–wife households, Syracuse, N.Y., 1967-68)

	Wives[a]		Husbands		Children 12-17		Children 6-11		Other workers Females		Males	
	NE	E	NE	E	NE	E	NE	E	NE	E	NE	E
	Row percent of total time											
All household work	72	62	14	18	5	10	5	4	3	5	1	1
More frequent activities[b]												
Regular meal preparation	86	75	5	10	4	10	4	3	1	2	—	—
After-meal cleanup	80	67	4	7	8	16	7	7	1	3	—	<1
Regular house care	83	70	1	4	6	14	8	9	2	3	—	—
Nonphysical care of family	55	38	22	25	3	5	4	4	14	24	2	4
Physical care of family	88	76	9	15	1	1	1	1	1	7	<1	—
Marketing	58	53	24	24	9	15	8	6	1	2	<1	—
Washing	96	92	2	4	1	2	<1	<1	1	1	—	—
Less frequent activities												
Special clothing care	87	77	2	3	8	16	2	1	1	3	—	—
Yard and car care	26	20	48	61	11	10	12	9	1	<1	2	<1
Management	62	59	35	37	2	3	<1	<1	<1	—	—	—
Ironing	95	87	<1	1	3	7	<1	2	1	3	—	—
Special house care	44	32	41	51	5	7	3	3	1	2	6	5
Special food preparation	84	60	6	29	4	10	3	<1	3	1	—	—

[a] NE and E indicate households with nonemployed or employed wives.

[b] Activities ordered by frequency of performance by all workers on record days (see Table 3.8).

TABLE 3.11—Frequency of individual workers' performance of 13 household work activities, by employment of wives
(1,296 husband-wife households, Syracuse, N.Y., 1967-68)

	All Workers		Wives		Husbands		Children 12-17		Children 6-11		Other workers Females		Other workers Males	
	NE[a]	E	NE	E	NE	E	NE	E	NE	E	NE	F	NE	E
Number	1,958	634												
					Percent of record days									
Any household work	100	100	100	99	81	81	87	90	69	70	10	12	3	3
More frequent activities[b]														
Regular meal preparation	100	99	99	96	31	42	54	61	32	30	3	5	1	<1
After-meal cleanup	98	97	96	90	11	17	48	54	29	26	3	4	--	<1
Regular house care	97	94	95	87	5	10	47	60	40	40	1	2	--	--
Nonphysical care of family	77	72	68	57	35	34	19	16	14	17	6	7	1	1
Physical care of family	75	48	74	45	21	13	7	5	5	2	3	3	<1	1
Marketing	68	68	51	54	32	32	27	32	14	14	1	2	<1	--
Washing	66	56	65	53	2	3	3	7	2	2	<1	1	--	--
Less frequent activities														
Special clothing care	51	47	48	43	3	3	10	13	2	2	1	1	--	--
Yard and car care	49	42	22	13	28	27	22	17	17	14	<1	<1	1	<1
Management	49	41	43	34	21	19	5	5	2	1	<1	--	<1	<1
Ironing	43	42	41	39	<1	1	8	10	1	2	<1	1	--	--
Special house care	43	33	30	20	19	17	10	8	5	3	<1	1	2	2
Special food preparation	23	22	22	19	2	2	4	8	2	1	<1	<1	--	--

[a]NE and E indicate households with nonemployed or employed wives.

[b]Activities ordered by frequency of performance by all workers on record days (see Table 3.8).

TABLE 3.12—Distribution of individual workers' household work time among the 13 household work activities, by employment of wives

(1,296 husband–wife households, Syracuse, N.Y., 1967-68)

| | Wives | | Husbands | | Children 12-17 | | Children 6-11 | | Other Workers | | | |
| | | | | | | | | | Females | | Males | |
	NE[a]	E	NE	E	NE	E	NE	E	NE	E	NE	E
N =	979	317	979	317	287	126	463	125	979	317	979	317
						Percent						
All household work	100	100	100	100	100	100	100	100	99	100	100	100
More frequent activities												
Regular meal preparation	17	19	5	8	12	16	11	11	4	5	1	--
After-meal cleanup	10	11	2	4	15	16	15	16	5	5	--	1
Regular house care	14	16	1	3	13	20	22	28	9	9	--	--
Nonphysical care of family	9	8	18	16	8	6	9	10	63	59	24	57
Physical care of family	14	7	7	4	2	1	2	1	5	8	1	--
Marketing	9	12	19	18	20	20	18	18	4	5	4	--
Washing by machine	7	7	1	1	<1	1	--	--	1	1	--	--
Less frequent activities												
Special clothing care	4	5	1	1	6	6	1	1	1	3	--	--
Yard and car care	2	1	17	14	10	4	14	8	1	<1	14	1
Management	3	3	9	7	2	1	1	2	<1	--	2	1
Ironing	5	5	<1	<1	3	2	--	1	2	2	--	--
Special house care	4	4	19	20	7	5	5	4	3	3	53	40
Special food preparation	2	2	1	4	2	2	1	--	1	<1	--	--

[a]NE and E indicate households with nonemployed or employed wives.

TABLE 3.13—Number of hours parents and school-age children were at home and away from home on record days, by employment of wives
(1,296 husband-wife households, Syracuse, N.Y., 1967-68)

Household member	Number of record days NE[a]	Number of record days E	0 NE	0 E	1-3 NE	1-3 E	4-6 NE	4-6 E	7-9 NE	7-9 E	10-12 NE	10-12 E	13-15 NE	13-15 E	16-18 NE	16-18 E	19-21 NE	19-21 E	22-24 NE	22-24 E
								Row percent[b] of days											
Wives	1,958	634																		
At home			<1	1	<1	<1	<1	<1	<1	1	1	7	4	29	13	24	29	18	52	21
Paid employment - away			98	45	1	3	1	17	1	30	<1	5	--	<1	--	--	--	--	--	--
Paid employment - at home			95	85	5	9	<1	2	<1	3	--	1	--	--	--	--	--	--	--	--
Volunteer work			79	85	17	13	2	3	1	--	<1	<1	--	--	--	<1	--	--	--	--
Husbands	1,958	634																		
At home			2	2	1	1	2	1	7	7	23	25	34	35	11	9	10	10	10	10
Paid employment - away			26	29	3	3	5	5	27	30	31	26	5	6	2	1	<1	<1	2	1
Paid employment - at home			91	93	7	4	1	1	1	1	<1	<1	<1	--	--	--	<1	<1	--	--
Volunteer work			88	88	9	7	3	4	1	1	<1	<1	<1	<1	--	--	--	--	<1	--
Children 12-17 years	574	252																		
At home			2	1	<1	1	1	<1	1	2	6	9	25	29	32	31	15	14	17	13
Children 6-11 years	926	250																		
At home			1	<1	<1	<1	<1	<1	1	<1	2	2	13	18	44	46	16	13	24	20

[a] NE and E indicate households of nonemployed or employed wives.
[b] Percentages may not add to 100 due to rounding.

TABLE 3.14—Average hours per day used by all workers and individual workers for household work activities, by hours of wives' employment
(1,296 husband–wife households, Syracuse, N.Y., 1967-68)

Hours per week of wives' employment	Number of households	All household work	All meal preparation	All house care	All clothing care	All family care	Marketing & management
		All workers' average hours per day					
0	859	11.1	2.7	2.7	1.4	2.6	1.7
1-14	120	10.6	2.7	2.6	1.4	2.1	1.7
15-29	111	9.9	2.5	2.4	1.3	2.1	1.6
30+	206	8.0	2.2	2.2	.9	1.2	1.5
		Wives' average hours per day					
0	859	8.1	2.3	1.6	1.3	1.9	1.0
1-14	120	7.3	2.2	1.4	1.3	1.4	1.0
15-29	111	6.3	1.9	1.3	1.1	1.1	.9
30+	206	4.8	1.5	1.1	.8	.6	.8
		Husbands' average hours per day					
0	859	1.6	.1	.6	<.1	.4	.4
1-14	120	1.7	.1	.7	<.1	.3	.4
15-29	111	1.6	.2	.6	<.1	.4	.4
30+	206	1.6	.2	.6	<.1	.3	.4
	Number of Households with 12-17 year olds	12-17 Year olds' average hours per day per family					
0	248	1.9	.5	.6	.2	.2	.4
1-14	39	2.2	.7	.8	.1	.2	.6
15-29	51	1.7	.5	.4	.1	.1	.5
30+	75	2.6	.9	.8	.2	.2	.5
	Number of Children 12-17 years	12-17 Year olds' average hours per day per child					
0	428	1.1	.3	.4	.1	.1	.2
1-14	72	1.2	.4	.3	.1	.1	.3
15-29	92	.9	.3	.2	.1	.1	.3
30+	149	1.3	.4	.4	.1	.1	.2
	Number of Households with 6-11 year olds	6-11 Year olds' average hours per day per family					
0	408	1.1	.3	.5	<.1	.1	.2
1-14	55	1.0	.3	.4	.1	.2	.2
15-29	57	.9	.3	.3	<.1	.1	.2
30+	68	1.0	.2	.5	<.1	.1	.2
	Number of Children 6-11 years	6-11 Year olds' average hours per day per child					
0	779	.6	.2	.2	<.1	.1	.1
1-14	107	.5	.1	.2	<.1	.1	.1
15-29	91	.6	.2	.2	<.1	.1	.1
30+	117	.6	.1	.3	<.1	.1	.1

TABLE 3.15—Average hours per day used by husbands for household work activities, by husbands' hours of employment
(1,296 husband–wife households, Syracuse, N.Y., 1967-68)

Hours per week of husbands' employment	Number	Grouped household work activities					
		All household work	All food preparation	All house care	All clothing care	All family care	Marketing and management
		Average hours per day					
Under 40	190	2.1	.3	.8	.1	.5	.6
40–49	672	1.7	.2	.7	<.1	.4	.5
50 and over	434	1.2	.1	.4	<.1	.3	.3
All husbands	1,296	1.6	.2	.6	<.1	.4	.4

TABLE 3.16—Total household work time of all workers, wives, and husbands, by husbands' hours of paid work and employment of wives
(1,296 husband–wife households, Syracuse, N.Y., 1967-68)

Hours per week of husbands' employment	Number of households		All workers		Wives		Husbands		Others	
	NE[a]	E	NE	E	NE	E	NE	E	NE	E
	Average hours per day									
Under 40 hours	143	47	10.8	8.9	7.3	5.1	2.1	2.2	1.4	1.6
40–49 hours	503	169	11.0	8.5	8.1	5.3	1.7	1.6	1.2	1.6
50+	333	101	11.3	8.9	8.4	5.5	1.2	1.3	1.7	2.1
All households	979	317	11.1	8.7	8.1	5.3	1.6	1.6	1.4	1.8

[a]NE and E indicate households of nonemployed or employed wives.

TABLE 3.17—Average hours per day used by wives and husbands for all household work, paid and volunteer, and total work, by hours of wives' employment
(1,296 husband–wife households, Syracuse, N.Y., 1967-68)

Hours per week of wives' employment	Number of households	All workers	Wives	Husbands	Others
		Average hours per day in household work			
0	859	11.1	8.1	1.6	1.4
1-14	120	10.6	7.3	1.7	1.6
15-29	111	9.9	6.3	1.6	2.0
30+	206	8.0	4.8	1.6	1.6
All households	1,296	10.5	7.3	1.6	1.6
		Average hours per day in paid and volunteer work			
0			.5	7.8	
1-14			1.7	7.0	
15-29			3.4	7.6	
30+			5.3	6.3	
All households			1.7	7.6	
		Average hours per day in total work			
0			8.6	9.4	
1-14			9.0	8.7	
15-29			9.7	9.2	
30+			10.1	7.9	
All households			9.0	9.2	

TABLE 3.18—Attitude[a] of wives toward 17 household work activities
(*1,296 husband-wife households, Syracuse, N.Y., 1967-68*)

Task	N[b]	Attitude scale			Median	Mean
		Dislike (1-2)	(3-4)	Like (5-6)		
			Percent			
Meal preparation	1,295	3	26	71	5.0	4.8
Special food preparation	1,040	4	17	79	5.3	5.1
After-meal cleanup	1,295	35	55	11	3.1	3.0
Regular house care	1,296	9	50	41	4.3	4.2
Special house care	1,129	23	41	37	4.0	3.8
Yard care	727	11	23	66	4.9	4.6
Car care	328	32	40	27	3.6	3.4
Washing	1,286	2	25	72	4.9	4.8
Ironing	1,267	36	36	28	3.5	3.3
Other clothing care	1,251	20	40	40	4.1	3.9
Physical family care	1,125	1	16	83	5.1	5.1
Nonphysical family care	1,180	1	11	88	5.2	5.2
Marketing	1,274	11	28	61	4.8	4.5
Management	1,260	6	31	63	4.8	4.6
Record keeping	975	12	36	52	4.3	4.5
Volunteer work	614	4	18	78	5.1	5.1
Paid work	496	2	13	85	5.4	5.2

[a]Data previously reported by Jarmon (1972, Table 3, p. 39).

[b]Number of cases varied by number of wives who expressed an attitude toward each household work activity. Those who had used time for an activity were asked to indicate how much they liked it or disliked it, but some who had not used time on the record days but sometimes do the work also reported their attitudes.

TABLE 3.19—Rank correlation coefficients for time use and wives' attitude[a] toward household work activities
(1,296 husband–wife households, Syracuse, N.Y., 1967-68)

Work activity	Number[b] reporting	Kendall[c] Tau
Meal preparation	1,295	.08
Regular house care	1,296	.12
Nonphysical care of family members	1,180	-.05
Marketing	1,274	.04
Special clothing care	1,251	.17
Washing by machine	1,286	.03
Ironing	1,267	.08
Management (except record keeping)	1,260	.06
Special food preparation	1,040	.06

[a]Data previously reported by Jarmon (1972, Table 7, p. 45).
[b]Number of cases varied by number of wives who expressed an attitude toward each work activity.
[c]All of Jarmon's reported rank correlation coefficients had significance levels of .05 or better.

TABLE 3.20—Total household work time of all workers and individual workers, by day of week and employment of wives
(1,296 husband-wife households, Syracuse, N.Y., 1967-68)

Day of week	Number of records NE[a]	Number of records E	All workers NE	All workers E	Wives NE	Wives E	Husbands NE	Husbands E	Children 12-17 NE	Children 12-17 E	Children 6-11 NE	Children 6-11 E	Other workers Females NE	Other workers Females E	Other workers Males NE	Other workers Males E
						Average hours per day[b]										
Sunday	274	97	8.7	8.7	5.5	4.9	2.0	2.1	1.5	2.6	1.0	.8	.2	.3	.1	.1
Monday	277	93	10.9	7.6	8.5	5.2	1.2	1.2	1.6	1.6	1.0	1.2	.2	.3	.1	<.1
Tuesday	281	89	11.0	7.9	8.5	4.8	1.2	1.2	1.7	1.7	1.0	.9	.2	.6	.1	.1
Wednesday	288	82	11.2	8.1	8.6	5.4	1.3	1.3	1.8	1.9	1.0	1.2	.2	.2	.1	.1
Thursday	288	82	11.5	8.5	8.8	5.7	1.2	1.4	1.8	1.8	1.1	.9	.3	.2	.1	.1
Friday	274	97	11.7	8.7	8.9	5.1	1.4	1.7	2.1	2.0	1.1	1.1	.3	.5	.1	.1
Saturday	276	94	12.6	11.1	7.5	6.4	2.8	2.1	3.4	3.8	1.5	1.0	.5	.8	.1	<.1

[a] NE and E indicate households of nonemployed or employed wives.
[b] Time cannot be added across because averages for children are based upon number of families with children of these ages rather than all families.

TABLE 3.21—Circumstances reported as unusual for record days and for previous 7 days
(1,296 husband-wife households, Syracuse, N.Y., 1967-68)

	Percent of record days	Percent of families reporting for previous 7 days
Unusual health conditions		
None	82	78
Minor illness of wife	2	3
Minor illness of husband or child	6	9
Pre- or post-natal period	3	3
Physical handicap of wife	2	2
Physical handicap of husband or child	4	4
Psychological problem	1	1
Unusual physical problems of house		
None	95	91
Problems related to transportation	1	1
Miscellaneous -- outside house	1	1
Miscellaneous -- inside house	3	7
Unusual weather conditions		
Nothing unusual	51	42
Clear, fair	11	12
Hot	4	4
Cold	14	14
Rain	12	16
Snow	9	12
Unusual family situation		
Visitors or guests	4	9
Absence of 1 or more family members	4	7
Family outing	4	5
Preparation for special event	3	8
Added work for miscellaneous reasons	4	4
Husband wife on vacation at home	2	2
Trip to doctor	2	4
Death or illness	1	1

Chapter IV

Food Preparation

All food preparation was made up of three activities, two of which, regular meal preparation and after-meal cleanup, were regularly performed and time consuming. The third activity, special food preparation, was of minor importance in frequency and in average total work time. The proportions of total food preparation time spent on these activities were: 57% on meal preparation, 37% on after-meal cleanup, and 6% on special food preparation.

Regular meal preparation was defined in this study as the preparation and serving of food for meals eaten at home by any family member on the record days. In addition to the preparation of food for morning, midday, and evening meals the category included the preparation of food for snacks; packed lunches; and food for babies, young children, and invalids. All of these were considered to be regular meals, although they may not have been prepared and served at regular times each day. Packed lunches, though not eaten at home, take preparation time and are often a regular part of food preparation. Time spent on menu planning was included under management, and shopping for food was included with other kinds of shopping under marketing.

To have clearly and easily distinguished categories, routine operations had to be separated from nonroutine ones in the activities that combined regular and special types of work. Therefore, to avoid the possibility of excessive variability in the time spent on regular food preparation, data on special kinds of food preparation were collected and analyzed separately.

Special food preparation included nonroutine food preparation activities such as holiday meals or food for other special occasions, parties, and community or group functions. Special food preparation also included food preservation. Although food preservation by canning or freezing in quantity was not expected to be as important in contemporary urban households as it had been in previous studies that included rural households, some advance preparation of foods such as soups, casseroles, and desserts for use in a few days or weeks was expected. Other kinds of work included in the classification were considered to be "special" in that they were assumed to be uncommon, seasonally related, or special occasion types of food preparation. Though a seasonal or sporadic activity, some kinds of special food preparation (such as preparing a holiday meal) can consume a considerable amount of time, while other kinds (baking a cake for a bake sale) may take little extra time if combined with other food preparation work.

Time spent on after-meal cleanup included time for after-meal care of table, dishes, leftovers, kitchen equipment, and refuse; and returning clean equipment, dishes, and utensils to storage. The time spent loading and unloading dishwashers and placing material in garbage disposers was included, but the time dishwashers were in operation was not. As explained under regular meal preparation, cleanup operations during the food preparation process were classified as part of that activity.

Rank Correlations of Time Used for Food Preparation Activities [1,2]

Summary of Rank Correlations
(Tables 4.1, 4.2, and 4.3)

Number of children was the variable most closely related to time of all workers for all food preparation (correlation .33), meal preparation (.31), and after-meal cleanup (.28). Family type was a much more complex variable than number of children; when family type was correlated with time use for

---

[1]All Tau values reported in tabular form or referred to in the text were significant at the .001 level unless otherwise stated. Although correlation coefficients were determined for all major variables, only significant relationships are reported in tables and only the correlations strong enough to change the amount of time used daily are discussed to any extent.

[2]For an explanation of meaning of positive and negative correlation values as related to the different variables, see pages 30-31.

meal preparation and after-meal cleanup the correlation values were .28 and .25. For special food preparation, the correlation values were generally low.

Relationships of number of children and family type with the time of the two principal workers (wives and teenagers) in food related activities were both positive; together they accounted for the relatively strong effects of these two variables on the total time of all workers. Employment of wives, on the other hand, had a lesser effect on all workers' time than on wives' time—the increased time of other workers, probably teenagers, offset the decline in wives' time with employment to some extent.

Age of the youngest child was negatively and weakly related to total time, although it was positively and somewhat more closely related to wives' time (especially when their employment was held constant). We found a considerably closer relationship between age of oldest child than age of youngest child and all workers' time spent on all food preparation (-.18 versus -.08), regular meal preparation (-.16 versus -.06), and after-meal cleanup (-.12 versus -.07). This result could be expected when more time was spent on regular and time-consuming activities as children in the family were older.

Employment of wives was negatively correlated (-.19 or -.18) with total time used by all workers in food preparation. Interrelationships were evident between employment of wives and all three variables of family composition, as determined by partial rank correlation values holding the family composition variables constant while examining employment, and by holding employment constant while examining family composition.

In examining the time use of individual workers, number of children correlated with time of wives and teenagers in all food preparation (.21 each), in regular meal preparation (.22 and .17), and in after-meal cleanup (.14 and .15). The number of children and time of husbands correlated for after-meal cleanup but with a low negative value (-.08). Correlation values between time for individual workers and family type were similar to those for number of children.

Employment of wives correlated negatively with wives' time in the two major areas (-.26 for regular meal preparation and -.27 for after-meal cleanup). For husbands' time use for food preparation, the highest correlation values were with wives' employment and husbands' hours of employment (.12, .13, and .10 for wives' employment and -.12, -.11, and -.10 for husbands' hours of employment for all food preparation, regular meal preparation, and after-meal cleanup, respectively).

Because of their levels of correlation and practicality of multiple applications, the variables selected as the most effective time estimators in the areas of food preparation were (1) number of children and (2) employment of wives.

Rank Correlations of Total Time Used by All Workers and Major Variables

Number of Children (Table 4.1). Number of children had the highest correlation with time used for all work related to food preparation activities (.33), regular meal preparation (.31), and after-meal cleanup (.28). More time was spent on this group of activities and on the two major components when there were more children in the family.

The relationship between number of children and time for all food preparation, regular meal preparation, and after-meal cleanup remained relatively strong when other variables were held constant. The effects of number of children on time use for all food preparation were somewhat interrelated with those of employment of wives. The correlation value for each of these variables with total food preparation time declined when the other variable was held constant (from .33 to .30 for number of children with employment held constant, and from -.19 to -.15 for employment of wives with number of children held constant).

More time was spent on regular meal preparation as family size increased, whether wives were employed or not, as shown by the negligible change in the correlation value for number of children with all food preparation time when employment of wives was held constant (from .31 to .29). Number of children and employment of wives were somewhat interrelated in their effects on total time spent on after-meal cleanup, as shown by the decline in value of each correlation when the other variable was held constant. This decline was negligible for number of children (from .28 to .26) but sufficiently strong for employment of wives (from -.18 to -.14) to indicate that the latter variable had less effect than family size on time used for after-meal cleanup.

When house type was held constant, the very small changes in correlation values between number of children and time spent on all food preparation, regular meal preparation, and after-meal cleanup likewise indicated that, of these two variables, the effect of number of children was stronger. Time spent on food preparation work increased with an increase in family size in any type of house. No interrelationship effects were evident between number of children and age of the youngest child on the time spent on any food preparation activity.

The relative strength of number of children as a predictor of time use for after-meal cleanup agrees with findings in earlier research. Wiegand (1954) found a relationship between number of people served and time spent on this activity. Of the variables in Walker's 1955 research, the number of persons for whom dishes were washed was most closely related to time spent on cleaning up. In the Purdue project daFonseca (1964) used number in family, alone or combined with variables such as number of meals eaten or meal class, as time predictors for dishwashing.

Ages of Youngest and Oldest Child (Table 4.1). Ages of children had much less effect than number of children on time used by all workers for food preparation work. The correlation values for age of youngest child as related to these activities were low: -.08 for all food preparation and -.07 for after-meal cleanup.

Age of oldest child had closer relationships with time spent on food preparation than age of youngest child. The correlation values with age of oldest child were: -.18, all food preparation; -.16, regular meal preparation; -.12, after-meal cleanup; and -.07, special food preparation. These somewhat higher correlation values for age of oldest child with all workers' time were indicative of the stronger effect of age of oldest child than age of youngest child in increasing time spent on food preparation.

The correlations between age of youngest child and time spent on all food preparation and after-meal cleanup were closer when employment of wives was held constant (from -.08 to -.13 for all food preparation, and from -.07 to -.11 for after-meal cleanup). These relationships indicated that somewhat more time was spent on these activities in families with older children, whether or not the wives were employed.

Family Type (Table 4.1). Family type was almost as closely related as number of children to total time spent on all food preparation work (.28), regular meal preparation (.28), and after-meal cleanup (.25). Time spent on this group of activities, and on each separate activity, increased as family composition became more complex.

The effects of family type on total time used for all food preparation, regular meal preparation,

and after-meal cleanup were only slightly interrelated with those of employment of wives. The respective declines in the correlation values for the family type variable when employment of wives was held constant were: from .28 to .26, from .28 to .25, and from .25 to .22. These small changes indicated only slight decreases in food preparation time in more complex families when the homemaker was employed.

The relative strength of the family type relationship to time use for food preparation work was largely the effect of number of children.

Employment of Wives (Table 4.1). The correlation values for employment of wives and time use by all workers for all food preparation activities (-.19), regular meal preparation (-.19), and after-meal cleanup (-.18) were considerably weaker than those for number of children or family type, and became somewhat weaker when either of those variables was held constant (from -.19 to -.15 and from -.18 to -.14). Thus, the effect of employment of wives in decreasing food preparation time was modified somewhat by both family size and family type. The decrease in total time spent on food preparation in employed-wife households was likely to be less in larger and more complex families than in smaller and less complex ones.

Employment of wives had more effect than age of youngest child on time used for all food preparation, regular meal preparation, and after-meal cleanup. Employment effects on food preparation time were independent of the effects of age of youngest child, as shown by the larger values for employment of wives when age of youngest child was held constant. These relationships indicated that less time would be spent on food preparation work at any age of youngest child when wives were employed.

House Type (Table 4.1). House type showed some relationship with total time spent on all food preparation (.13), regular meal preparation (.15), and after-meal cleanup (.11). The direction of the relationship indicated an increase in food preparation time between families living in apartments and those living in one-family houses. Much of the effect of house type, however, on time for food preparation activities was the effect of number of children or type of family, as shown by the substantial declines in the correlation values for house type and food preparation time when number of children or family type was held constant.

Socioeconomic Status (Table 4.1). Socioeconomic status had a slight relationship with time spent on after-meal cleanup (.07). The positive relationship indicated that a little more time was spent on this activity by families at lower socio-economic levels, but this difference in time was only a few minutes a day.

Education of Wives and Husbands (Table 4.1). The correlation values for education of wives and education of husbands (.10 and .07, respectively, for total time spent by all workers on after-meal cleanup) were similar to the values for socioeconomic level.

Meal Types. Types of meals prepared expressed output of work in food preparation and was closely related to time use (.46). Because this variable was a very complex one for both data collection and analysis, its use in measurement of meal preparation was abandoned. It is discussed, however, in the last section of this chapter.

Rank Correlations of Time Used by Individual Workers and Major Variables

Individual Workers' Share in Food Preparation. Food preparation activities included some sharing by others, principally husbands and teenagers, but wives were the primary workers. When not employed, wives' time accounted for 86% of all time for meal preparation, 80% of after-meal cleanup, and 84% of special food preparation. When employed, their time in these areas accounted for 75%, 67%, and 60%, respectively (Table 3.10). Husbands' share of time in these activities was 5%, 4%, and 6%, respectively, when the wives were not employed and 10%, 7%, and 29% when they were. Although husbands' share of all workers' time used in special food preparation appears to change dramatically with wives' employment (from 6% to 29%), it must be remembered that there was relatively little time used in this activity. Of all time reported, the teenagers' share was 4% of meal preparation, 8% of after-meal cleanup, and 4% of special food preparation when mothers were not employed, but 10%, 16%, and 10%, respectively, when they were.

Wives did some regular meal preparation on 99% of the days when they were not employed and on 96% when they were (Table 3.11). Husbands contributed some time (at least 5 minutes a day) on about one-third of the days, while teenagers contributed some time on more than half of the days in households with teenagers. Likewise, wives did some after-meal cleanup on 96% or 90% of the days, while husbands did some on 11% of the days if wives were not employed and on 17% if they were. Older children, in families with teen-

agers, did after-meal cleanup on about half of the days and younger children, in families with children 6 to 11 years, on about a quarter of the days.

Number of Children (Tables 4.2 and 4.3). Wives' time spent on food preparation work was related to number of children, with correlation values of .21 for all food preparation, .22 for regular meal preparation, and .14 for after-meal cleanup (Table 4.2).

The effects of number of children on wives' time use for major food preparation work were interrelated with those of employment of wives; when employment was held constant, the correlation value for number of children and wives' time spent on all food preparation work declined from .21 to .17. Similar declines in value can be noted for the correlations between number of children and wives' use of time on both regular meal preparation and after-meal cleanup.

The correlations between number of children and total time spent by all workers on food preparation were largely the result of the relationship of number of children to wives' time and, to some extent, to teenagers' time. Husbands' time spent on all food preparation work (-.07) and after-meal cleanup (-.08) was negatively related to number of children (Table 4.3); as family size increased husbands spent a little less time on food preparation work.

The best relationship between teenagers' time use for food preparation activities was with number of children (Table 4.3). The correlation values were .21, .17, and .15, respectively, for teenagers' time spent on all food preparation, regular meal preparation, and after-meal cleanup. These relationships were independent of the effects of employment of wives or age of youngest child, as shown by the lack of change in the values for number of children when either wives' employment or age of youngest child was held constant.

Age of Youngest Child (Tables 4.2 and 4.3). Age of the youngest child was only weakly related to wives' food preparation time. The highest correlation value (.11) was with wives' time spent on after-meal cleanup followed by a value of .07 for all food preparation (Table 4.2). The values for age of youngest child and wives' food preparation time increased considerably when employment of wives was held constant; increases were from .07 to .14 for time use for all food preparation and from .11 to .19 for after-meal cleanup.

The positive relationships between wives' food preparation time and age of the youngest child indicated that, employed or not, wives spent a little more time on food preparation work when children in the family were younger than when children were older. This change in direction of the correlation values for age of youngest child between all workers' time and wives' time was related to the effect of time contributions by teenagers on total time. All of the relationships between age of the youngest child and teenagers' time were negative and indicated a higher use of time in families with older children: -.13 for all food preparation, -.14 for regular meal preparation, -.11 for after-meal cleanup, and -.09 for special food preparation (Table 4.3). These relationships of age of youngest child with teenagers' time were not interrelated with those of other variables.

Family Type (Tables 4.2 and 4.3). Wives' time use for food preparation work was related to family type about as closely as to number of children. This similarity would be expected because of the much stronger effect of family size than of age of the youngest child on food preparation time. The correlation values were .20, .21, and .15 with wives' time spent on all food preparation, regular meal preparation, and after-meal cleanup, respectively. Family type, however, had less effect in increasing wives' time use on food preparation when employment was held constant.

The correlations between husbands' time use on food preparation and family type were all negative; the highest value, -.07, was with their time spent on after-meal cleanup (Table 4.3).

Family type was related to teenagers' time use only for all food preparation, with a correlation value of .12.

Employment of Wives (Tables 4.2 and 4.3). This variable had the highest relationship of any of the variables with the wives' time use for all food preparation, regular meal preparation, and after-meal cleanup, with correlation values of -.29, -.26, and -.27, respectively. Employment effects on wives' time for the individual food-related activities were stronger than the effects of any of the family composition variables (Table 4.2).

Some correlation was evident between employment of wives and husbands' time spent on food preparation— .12, .13, and .10 for all food preparation, regular meal preparation, and after-meal cleanup, respectively (Table 4.3). These positive correlations indicated a slightly greater use of time by husbands for food preparation when their wives were employed. When these correlation values are examined in conjunction with time use (Tables 4.4, 4.5, and 4.6), the effect of employment of wives on husbands' time is evident. Although

the increase in average time was only about 6 minutes per day, it was consistently an increase. There was practically no interrelationship between family composition variables and employment of wives in their effects on husbands' time spent on food preparation activities.

Husbands' Hours of Employment (Table 4.3). The relationships of husbands' hours of employment with their food preparation time (-.12 for all food preparation, -.11 for regular meal preparation, and -.10 for after-meal cleanup) were stronger than those of the family composition variables and were comparable to the effects of wives' employment. Husbands' hours of employment was the only variable related to husbands' time spent on special food preparation (-.06).

Teenagers' time use for after-meal cleanup was weakly related to their fathers' hours of employment (-.10). Teenagers tended to spend a little less time on this work when their fathers worked longer hours.

Education of Wives and Husbands (Tables 4.2 and 4.3). Wives' education was weakly related to their time use for after-meal cleanup (.06); wives with less education used a few minutes more time per day. Husbands' food preparation time had some small relationships with wives' education, -.06 between wives' education and husbands' time spent on all food preparation and regular meal preparation. Husbands whose wives had more education spent a little more time on this type of work.

Time Used for Food Preparation Activities

Total Time of All Workers

Number of Children and Employment of Wives (Table 4.4). As the number of children increased in both nonemployed- and employed-wife households, larger amounts of the total time of all workers were spent on major food preparation tasks.

When the wives were not employed, total time spent on all food preparation activities increased from an average of 2.3 hours a day in one-child families to 4.1 hours a day in families with five and six children. When wives were employed, time use increased between these family sizes, but the amount of increase was less (from 2.0 to 3.3 hours a day). Daily time for regular meal preparation was about 1½ hours more in the largest families than in one-child families when the wives were not employed and was about an hour a day more when wives were employed. For after-meal cleanup, all workers' time use was about twice as high in households with five and six children as in those with no children (.8 to 1.6 hours per day, wife employed; .5 to 1.2 hours, wife not employed). Less time was spent on both regular meal preparation and after-meal cleanup in most family sizes when wives were employed; employed-wife households, on the average, used about half an hour less per day on all food preparation work than those with nonemployed wives.

Age of Youngest Child and Employment of Wives (Table 4.5). The total time spent on food preparation activities was not closely related to age of the youngest child, but, in nonemployed-wife households, more time was spent in families with older children. The low relationship with age of the youngest child was more variable when wives were employed.

Family Type and Employment of Wives (Table 4.6). The somewhat opposing relationships of number of children and age of the youngest child with total time use for food preparation are apparent. Within each age group of children, whether the wives were employed or not, the tendency was for more time to be used for all food preparation as family size increased. Age of the youngest child had less effect than number of children, but more time tended to be used for all food preparation when children in the family were of school age.

The same trends were apparent in time used for each food preparation activity separately but were more consistent in nonemployed-wife than in employed-wife households. Whether or not the wives were employed, however, it was apparent that, as family type became more complex, more time was spent on food preparation activities.

In families without children, when the wives were not employed, total time use for all food preparation increased as age of wives increased.

Time Spent by Individual Workers

Number of Children and Employment of Wives (Table 4.4). Whether or not wives were employed, their average use of time on all food preparation increased as the number of children advanced; further, as family size increased, more time was used on both regular food preparation and after-meal cleanup. Wives' time use for special food preparation was low, with averages the same or varying only by about 6 minutes a day from small to large families. Although wives' time use

was related to family size, their food preparation time was more affected by their employment than was the time of all workers.

The relatively strong effect of employment on wives' food preparation time was evident in the substantially smaller amount of time used by employed wives in almost all family sizes. The average decline in the time use when wives were employed was 36 minutes a day for all food preparation activities—24 minutes a day on regular meal preparation and 12 minutes a day on after-meal cleanup.

Husbands' use of time for any food preparation work was only weakly related to number of children; on the average they spent about the same amount of time in most large families as in small ones. The relationships between husbands' time for food preparation activities and employment of the wives also were weak, but it was apparent that husbands fairly consistently averaged 6 minutes more time per day on food preparation work when their wives were employed.

Teenage children spent more time on all food preparation as family size increased. In families with teenage children, the increase between small and large families was substantial (over an hour a day more in families with seven to nine children than in those with one child when the mothers were not employed and over half an hour a day more in families with five and six children than in one-child families when the mothers were employed). Teenagers' time use on both regular food preparation and after-meal cleanup was in irregular increments by family size, especially when the mothers were employed, but the relationship with time use for the combined activities indicated that teenagers did increase their time use for one or both of these activities as family size increased. Teenagers' average time spent on regular meal preparation increased about 6 minutes a day when the mothers were employed.

The time use of children 6 to 11 for all food preparation increased fairly steadily as the number of children increased, whether or not the mothers were employed. In the separate activities, the time spent by this age group was less related to family size, although these children in larger families did tend to spend a little more time on regular meal preparation and after-meal cleanup.

Female workers other than family members spent only small amounts of time on any of the food preparation activities singly, and their time on all food preparation was very low. Since one of the major activities of these workers was child care, it was probable that their reported time in employed-wife households was largely spent preparing or clearing away after some simple meals or snacks.

Age of Youngest Child and Employment of Wives (Table 4.5). Although wives' time varied somewhat by age of youngest child, both nonemployed and employed wives spent a little more time when their children were younger than when they had teenage children. Employed wives spent less time than nonemployed wives on all food preparation, regular meal preparation, and after-meal cleanup at all ages of youngest child.

The relationship between teenagers' food preparation time and age of the youngest child was low, and their time varied inconsistently in relation to the age of youngest child variable. The slightly higher time use indicated by the correlation of teenagers' time with employment of mothers was evident mostly in the families with all teenage children.

Family Type and Employment of Wives (Tables 4.6 and 4.7). In general, nonemployed wives spent a little more time on any kind of food preparation work in larger and more complex families. Also, their time use for food preparation tended to increase more consistently with increases in family size when children in the family were all preschool age. The time use of employed wives for all food preparation activities and after-meal cleanup varied inconsistently among family types, although their time spent on regular meal preparation tended to increase in the larger and more complex families. Wives' time use for most food preparation work showed a more consistent relationship with their employment than with family composition.

In families without children, wives' time use for after-meal cleanup increased with their age, whether or not they were employed. Wives' time use for regular meal preparation was not related to age.

The effects of family type on husbands' time use for all food preparation and after-meal cleanup were too weak to affect their average daily time. The relationships between employment of wives and husbands' food preparation time also were low. Table 4.6 shows that the slightly higher time spent by husbands on all food preparation and regular meal preparation tended to be mostly in smaller families.

Whether or not the mothers were employed, teenagers tended to spend a little more time on all food preparation in the smaller families when younger children were school age (6 to 17 years) than when children were younger (Table 4.7) and

to spend the most time on regular meal preparation in families with all teenage children. Children 6 to 11 tended to spend more time on all food preparation when the youngest child was 6 to 11, whether the mothers were employed or not.

Characteristics and Content of the Work in Food Preparation

Characteristics of the Work

Food Preparation. In the present study, as in past studies, regular meal preparation was the most consistently performed household work activity. On only 8 of the 2,592 record days was no time reported for such work. It also received more time, on the average, than any other household work activity; 1.6 hours a day was spent when the wives were not employed and 1.3 hours a day when they were, or 15% of the total time spent on all household work (Table 3.8).

One of the reasons for a high expenditure of time on regular meal preparation is its repetitiveness, which is frequently "a stable element around which we can fix other events" (Steidl and Bratton, 1968, p. 83). Meals are prepared at certain times in response to outside events, such as the relatively fixed time for leaving to go to work or school in the morning and the time of return in the evening. However, improvements in products and processing equipment do bring about changes in type and amount of output from the worker. Further, some flexibility as to the time required to prepare food may be introduced through choice of foods, complexity of meals, types of processing, and kinds of mechanical equipment and utensils used.

Whether or not wives were employed, special food preparation was the least frequent of all household work activities and was performed on fewer than one-quarter of the record days; the total time spent on this kind of work was less than 1% of total household work time.

After-meal Cleanup. In the present study, after-meal cleanup was usually a daily activity; it was performed on about 98% of the record days in both nonemployed- and employed-wife households. It was also one of the time-consuming activities, averaging 1.0 hour a day when the wives were not employed and .8 hour a day when they were (Table 3.8).

After-meal cleanup, as Steidl and Bratton (1968, p. 250) point out, is a supportive task for food preparation and, although output in each of these activities is measured separately, they are closely interrelated. Wiegand (1954, p. 17) reported that food preparation and dishwashing were of major importance in total household work time; whether the wives were employed or not, the largest portion of total household work time was used on these two activities together.

Kitchen Work Space and Equipment

In the present research, house and kitchen design and equipment were designated random variables, features of which would occur in the sample to the extent that they were represented in the population. In general, it was assumed that the results of kitchen research over the years had permeated many homes and that appliances that had been on the market for a relatively long time would be commonly found in the sample households, while those that were comparatively new would be in less general use.

Work Space and Storage Space (Table 4.8). The indicators of kitchen design included in the interview schedule were related to the adequacy of storage and counter space in terms of location near major work centers and the amount of storage and counter space available (see Steidl and Bratton, 1968, Chapter 13).

Almost all (92%) of the wives in the sample had at least 36 inches of counter space and about 7 out of 10 had 72 inches of counter space. The majority (77%) had work space at both the right and left of the sink; some had space at only one side (15%) and a small percentage (6%) had no work space at either side of the sink. A large proportion had counter space by both the range and oven (66%); a small proportion had space only beside the surface units, and one-fourth had no work space beside their cooking equipment. Less than half (41%) had work space adjacent to the latch side of the refrigerator. Somewhat fewer employed than nonemployed wives had 72 inches of counter space (63% versus 71%).

Almost all of the wives (about 9 out of 10) had 72 inches or more of wall and base cabinet frontage for kitchen storage space. Nearly all (94%) had storage space by the sink, 78% near the range, and 63% by the refrigerator. Over half (55%) had storage space at all three of these work centers and three-quarters had such space beside the two most frequently used kitchen centers, the range and sink centers.

Available work and storage spaces were not related to the number of children, or, among wives without children at home, to the age of wives.

Although kitchen work space did not vary consistently by socioeconomic level, smaller proportions of the two lowest levels than of the three highest met the standards for work space, storage, and facilities. To some extent, socioeconomic level reflected a difference between the groups in the types of housing occupied.

Equipment Owned (Table 4.9). As expected, all of the families in the sample had ovens and broilers and nearly all of them had an electric mixer or blender (98%). Over four-fifths of the wives had a 0° freezer or freezer unit, an electric frypan or grill, and an outdoor grill or fireplace. Of the less standard kitchen equipment, about one-half had kitchen exhaust fans and two-fifths had pressure cookers. Dishwashers, on the other hand, were available to only 30% of the families, and only about one-quarter had a disposer or indoor incinerator.

In general, the only real difference between employed- and nonemployed-wife households in ownership of kitchen equipment was that only one-quarter of those households having employed wives had dishwashers in contrast with almost a third of those with nonemployed wives. Ownership of kitchen equipment was not related to the number of children, except for dishwashers, for which the proportion owning increased fairly regularly by number of children. Having a 0° freezer or freezer unit increased with age of wives in families without children, and ownership of pressure cookers was more common among wives over age 40. Ownership of most of the equipment items was not closely related to socioeconomic level except for dishwashers and disposers, for which ownership declined by socioeconomic level from 60% and 45% of the families at the highest level to 5% of those at the lowest. Differences in percentages also indicated a slight tendency for possession of such equipment as kitchen exhaust fans, electric grills, and outdoor fireplaces to be less at the lowest socioeconomic level.

Satisfaction with Kitchens (Table 4.10). On a 6-point scale, most of the respondents (83%) rated their kitchens 4 or above, that is, as satisfactory for regular meal preparation; 42% reported them as being very satisfactory. Only 17% found their kitchens unsatisfactory for regular food preparation activities; only 6% rated their kitchens as very unsatisfactory (Scale 1).

Only a few differences in level of satisfaction with kitchens for regular meal preparation by size were found. The principal differences among the groups were in the proportions who rated their kitchens as very satisfactory. Employed wives were a little less inclined (38%) than nonemployed ones (43%) to rate their kitchens as very satisfactory for regular food preparation. In families without children, the proportion who found their kitchens very satisfactory increased with age of wives from 31% to 52%. The proportion of women in the lowest socioeconomic group who rated their kitchens as very satisfactory was lower than at other socioeconomic levels.

Almost nine-tenths of the wives, whether employed or not, were mainly satisfied (rating of *4* or above) with their kitchens for after-meal clean-up work; about two-fifths found them very satisfactory. There was no evident relationship of satisfaction with kitchens for this work with number of children or, in families without children, age of wives. There was a tendency for wives at the lowest socioeconomic level to be less satisfied with kitchens for after-meal cleanup than were those at other levels.

Use of Selected Kitchen Equipment on the Record Days and During Previous 7 Days (Tables 4.11 and 4.12). Almost three-fifths of the households, whether the wives were employed or not, used the oven on the record days. Although differences in use of equipment were minor between nonemployed- and employed-wife households, the general tendency was for a slightly lighter use of all items of equipment when the wives were employed.

In the previous 7 days freezers and ovens received the most use, followed by electric mixers or blenders and kitchen exhaust fans (Table 4.12). Electric cooking equipment was used only a little more frequently than broilers; seasonal equipment, such as outdoor grills and fireplaces had a low frequency of use.

Ovens, electric mixers, and dishwashers were used more often as the number of children increased. In families with five or more children the oven was used an average of almost 5 days in the previous 7, compared with about 3½ days by families with no children or only one child. Likewise, families with five or more children used an electric mixer or a dishwasher about twice as frequently as families with no children. Uses of electric cooking equipment and food from a 0° freezer were only slightly related to family size; both were used a little more often in larger families than in smaller ones. Except for the use of food from the freezer, no relationship was evident in the use of kitchen equipment by age of wife in households that had no children. The use of most kitchen equipment tended to decline slightly with socioeconomic level.

Meal Preparation

As with other household work activities, the two principal factors affecting the amount of time used on regular meal preparation were the size of the job and the definition of the task. Warren (1938) found that the number of persons served was more closely related to time spent on meal preparation than were other variables; number of persons also was closely associated with the second important variable, number of meals. Wiegand (1953) found that less time was spent on meal preparation by employed than by nonemployed wives, by smaller than by larger families, and by families with all adult members or older children than by families with at least one child under 10.

In the Wiegand (1953) research, meals were classified from simple to complex by the amount of preparation required. Using Wiegand's data, Walker (1957, p. 12) found that the type of meal prepared was the most important predictor of time used for regular food preparation and, further, "Although the larger households tended to have the more complex meals, size of household itself was not closely related to the amount of time used in meal preparation." Manning (1968, pp. 9-10), using a modification of Walker's meal classification, found that 40% of the variation in time spent on meal preparation was explained by differences in types of meals prepared. Also in that research, complexity of the meal preparation increased with the number of people to whom the meal was served.

Meal Types (Table 4.13).[3] Not all of the meals served in any household are of the same complexity although they may be served to the same number of people. Even menus for the most complex meal of the day vary within the same household. Because of the extensive variations in daily menus among the families in her sample, Warren (1938) used a weekly measure to estimate time devoted to regular meal preparation.

Wide variations are possible in the complexity of meal preparation even though resulting menus may be similar; therefore, Wiegand (1953) used the amount of handling required to prepare and process the food from its original to its finished state. She then classified the levels of complexity

[3]Another variable, meal patterns, which combined number of meals with types of meals, was constructed for the present study. When this variable was related to family composition and time spent, the findings were in line with Walker's finding that larger households prepared more complex meals and hence used more time.

as defined by the number of operations used in preparing the food into 7 major meal types with 53 subtypes. She found these types to be related to the total time used for regular meal preparation.

Walker (1955) used both the amount of handling required to process the food and the time taken to prepare the meal in an attempt to simplify the meal-type classifications. On this basis, she defined four categories of meal types, which she classified as *Types 1, 2, 3,* and *4,* from least to highest complexity.

In the present study, the objective was to simplify measurement of types of meals insofar as possible and to discover whether any better relationship could be found between family composition and types of meals prepared in a sample of urban and suburban households. Building on the previous studies by Wiegand (1953) and Walker (1955), detailed data were collected for the classification of meal types.[4] The method used to type meals was similar to the one used by Walker.

In order to develop a measure of types of meals, only those prepared by wives were used in the analysis. This decision reduced variability in operations and time use that might be caused by including the time of less frequent workers whose skills probably would vary more widely than those of the wives.

Data on meals were collected in the order in which meals were served rather than by the commonly used classification of breakfast, lunch, and dinner, to eliminate bias that might be caused by preconceived ideas of what ought to be served during a particular part of the day. For example, when one breakfast menu was prepared and eaten by one person and a second by a second person these became meals *1* and *2;* when a member of the family was "late" for the family meal his meal became a second meal if some operations, such as heating, were involved before serving it. Snacks, baby meals, and packed lunches were also designated as meals.

The total number of meals prepared on the 2 record days was 10,796 and about 78% of them were prepared by wives working alone. Seven percent were prepared by husbands alone and the remaining 15% by children, outside help, or several family members working together.

Each meal prepared by the wives was classified by the time used and the number of operations

or amount of handling involved in preparing the food items. Cooking and noncooking operations were first analyzed separately in relation to time use; however, it was found that the time spent by wives on meal preparation was more closely related to the total number of operations.

The five types of meals, as defined by number of operations and average preparation time, are shown in Table 4.13. The very simple meals that required almost no preparation (3 or fewer cooking or noncooking operations) were all in *Type 1.* Meals that required easy cooking operations, such as heating or toasting and/or limited noncooking operations (a total of 4 to 7 operations) were *Type 2.* More complex meals *(Types 3, 4,* and *5)* involved both cooking and noncooking operations varying in number from 8 to 14, 15 to 24, and 25 and over, respectively.

The mean and median time for each type of meal was the same or varied by only .1 hour, indicating that the differences in time devoted by households to each type tended to be limited. Among the five different types of meals, the time varied from .2 hour for *Type 1* meals to .5 hour for *Type 3* and 1.5 hours for *Type 5;* thus the range of time used by the wives increased with the complexity of the meal. Almost three-quarters of *Type 1* meals required between 5 and 10 minutes to prepare and 79% of *Type 2* meals took from 5 to 20 minutes. Three-quarters of *Type 3* meals varied from 15 to 50 minutes, 75% of *Type 4* meals took from 35 to 100 minutes, and 81% of *Type 5* meals had a preparation time of at least 55 minutes.

The variable of meal types furnished an excellent example of a work-load measure and illustrates the kinds of complex data needed to evolve such a measure. The type of meal was defined by the entire number of both cooking and noncooking operations used to prepare it. As indicated earlier, the large amount of data required to construct the meal-type variable severely restricts its usefulness.

Number and Types of Meals (Tables 4.14, 4.15, and 4.16). For the sample as a whole, 4.2 meals were served per record day. About half of the households served either three or four meals per day, whether or not the wives were employed. Since the total number of meals prepared included snacks and special meals for babies as well as morning, noon, and evening meals, a substantial proportion of the total sample (38%) prepared five or more meals on the record days (Table 4.14). On the average, fewer meals were prepared in employed-wife households than in those of nonemployed wives (3.6 versus 4.4 meals).

---

[4]Meal preparation time as defined in the present study was the same as used in both the Wiegand and Walker studies.

Employed-wife households, more frequently than others, prepared fewer than three meals (25% versus 9%). Further, nonemployed-wife households more than others prepared five or more meals (42% versus 26%).

When families had children, whether or not wives were employed, increases in the average number of meals by family size were mostly between families with one child and those with four or more children. The effect of employment of wives was more consistent; at any number of children, employed-wife households prepared a lower average number of meals.

The relationship between total number of meals prepared and age of the youngest child indicated very clearly the effect of young children on increasing the number of meals. Whether the wives were or were not employed, the average number of meals was appreciably larger when the youngest child was under 2 years of age. Households with employed wives served fewer meals on the average than households with nonemployed wives when youngest children were over age 2, but when the youngest child was under 2 years, the average number of meals prepared was the same in both nonemployed- and employed-wife households.

A meal at least as complex as *Type 3* was served by approximately three-fourths of the households in the sample (Table 4.15). One-third prepared a *Type 4* or *Type 5* meal and 23% prepared nothing more complex than *Type 2*.

In addition to analysis of number and types of meals, data were coded for analysis of conventional meals (breakfasts, lunches, and dinners) according to the time of day at which meals were served. Second and third meals at any time of the day tended to be either very simple or simple; only a small scattering of these meals were of greater complexity (Table 4.16). The proportion of families who had served a fourth meal of any kind was very low (2% of the total sample) and almost all of these meals were *Type 1*.

Number and Types of Breakfasts (Tables 4.16, 4.17 and 4.18). One breakfast was the most common number prepared. Simple (*Type 2*) breakfasts were most prevalent; less than a third of the total sample served the more simple *Type 1* meal as a first breakfast[5] and only one-fifth or less served *Type 3* or more complex meals in the morning (Table 4.16). Relatively few households had no breakfasts prepared, but the percentage of employed-wife households with no breakfast prepared was generally greater than in other households of the same size. Families

with two or more children were somewhat more likely to serve more than one breakfast than those with no children or only one child, whether or not wives were employed (Table 4.17).

Although the number of breakfasts served was not closely related to the age of the youngest child, families with children of school-age rather than those with preschool age children tended to serve two or more breakfasts (both nonemployed- and employed-wife households). In families with no children, most households typically served one breakfast, but more of the young employed-wife than older employed-wife households had not prepared breakfast.

Variations from the pattern of relatively simple breakfasts were not related to number of children, age of the youngest child, or, in families without children, age of wives (Table 4.18). Relatively elaborate breakfasts (*Type 4*) were infrequently prepared, and then only in families with children in which wives were not employed.

Number and Types of Lunches[6] (Tables 4.16, 4.17, and 4.18). Lunches usually were even less complex than breakfasts; two-fifths of the first lunches were *Type 1* and only about 10% were of higher complexity than *Type 2* (Table 4.16). There was a strong tendency for only one lunch to be prepared in both nonemployed- and employed-wife households, but the number of lunches prepared varied somewhat by increases in family size. When wives were not employed, the proportion serving two or more lunches increased regularly as the number of children increased. When wives were employed, the proportion serving three lunches tended to increase as the number of children increased (Table 4.17). The proportion of employed-wife households having no lunch prepared was consistently higher than nonemployed-wife households at nearly all family sizes. In families without children, employment of wives was more of a factor in the number of lunches prepared than was age of wives. In families with employed wives the proportion preparing no lunch increased with the age of the youngest child (from 10% in families with a 1-year-old to 31% with the youngest a teenager). When wives were not employed, two or more lunches were served

---

[5]Because second, third, and fourth meals served at any time of day were predominantly *Type 1* or *Type 2*, only the first meal served at a particular time of day is discussed in relation to family composition variables.

[6]Lunches included evening meals if they were lighter in type than the main meal of the day. Typically, the lighter meal was at noon except on Sundays.

somewhat more frequently when the youngest child was older than 2 years (about one-fourth compared with 15 to 20%).

Types of first lunches varied by age of the youngest child somewhat differently when wives were employed than when they were not, though in neither case were they closely related to age of the youngest child (Table 4.18). In both types of households, the proportion of *Type 1* lunches was largest when children under 2 were the youngest. In nonemployed-wife families without children, the proportion of *Type 2* or higher first lunches increased with age of wives. There was no relationship between age of wives and complexity of first lunch prepared when wives were employed— nearly all of the first noon meals served were *Type 1* or *Type 2*.

Number and Types of Dinners (Tables 4.16, 4.17, and 4.18). Dinners were typically more complex than other meals; over three-fifths of the total sample had prepared meals of *Type 3* or higher as the first dinner. At the same time, when a *Type 3* meal was not prepared as the first evening meal, the meal served was as likely to be less complex as to be more complex. *Type 5* meals, in particular, were seldom prepared and probably reflected special family occasions or entertaining.

About four-fifths of the households served one dinner, whether or not the wife was employed, but the number prepared was somewhat related to the number of children; the proportion of families in which dinner was not served declined between smaller and larger families and the proportion serving two or more dinners tended to increase as family size increased (Table 4.17). These decreases and increases were less consistent by number of children when wives were employed. In some sizes of family, employed-wife households were somewhat more likely to serve two or more dinners than those with nonemployed wives.

The effect of age of youngest child was evident only in the proportion of both nonemployed- and employed-wife households in which no dinner was served; this proportion was lower when children in the households were over age 2. In families without children, the number of separate dinners prepared was not related to age of either nonemployed or employed wives.

The first dinners prepared were most frequently of intermediate complexity, without regard to number of children, age of the youngest child, or, in families without children, age of wives. None of the deviations from this general pattern were consistently related to any of the three variables (Table 4.18).

Age of youngest child had some effect on complexity of dinners prepared. When all children in the family were teenagers, whether or not the wives were employed, meals of greater complexity than *Type 3* were prepared more frequently than meals of lower complexity. When the youngest child was under 1 year and mothers were employed, the proportion of *Type 1* meals as first evening meals increased somewhat (Table 4.18). In general, fewer complex dinners were prepared when the wives were employed.

When they did not prepare the typical *Type 3* dinner, households without children were more likely to prepare dinners of higher than of lower complexity, in all age groups of wives, whether or not the wives were employed. More dinners of *Types 4* and *5* were prepared in all age groups of wives when the wife was not employed than when she was.

Baby Meals and Snacks (Table 4.19). As would be expected, the greatest variation in total number of meals served in a day was in those for babies. The extent of repetitiveness of baby meals in households in which the youngest child was under age 2 is clear.

Snacks were not typically a part of meal patterns in the sample. Since activities which took less than 3 minutes were not included in the data, there was no record of the simple snack assumed to be part of the current eating patterns. Only about one-quarter of the sample households had prepared one snack and about 6% had prepared two or more. These proportions were slightly lower in employed-wife households.

Perhaps surprisingly, the number of snacks reported on the record days was not related to either the number of children or age of youngest child. Usually, only one snack was prepared, regardless of family size or employment of wife; the highest proportion preparing two snacks (11%) were families with seven to nine children and nonemployed wives. In families without children, fewer households with employed wives in all age groups prepared snacks than did those with nonemployed ones.

TABLE 4.1—Rank and partial rank correlation coefficients for food preparation time of all workers and major variables

(1,260 husband–wife households, Syracuse, N.Y., 1967-68)

Total time of all workers in:	Kendall Tau[a]	Partial rank correlation[b] with variables held constant				
		Number of children	Age of youngest	Family type	Empl. of wives	House type
ALL FOOD PREPARATION ACTIVITIES						
Family composition variables						
Number of children	.33		.33		.30	.31
Age of youngest child	-.08	-.09			-.13	-.06
Age of oldest child	-.18					
Family type	.28				.26	.27
Employment						
Wives	-.19	-.15	-.22	-.15		
Socioeconomic level	.04**					
Wives' education	.05*					
Husbands' education	.05**					
Housing						
House type	.13	.07	.12	.09		
REGULAR MEAL PREPARATION						
Family composition variables						
Number of children	.31		.31		.29	.29
Age of youngest child	-.06*					
Age of oldest child	-.16					
Family type	.28				.25	.26
Employment						
Wives	-.19	-.15	-.21	-.15		
Husbands' hours	.04≠					
Housing						
House type	.15	.09	.14	.11		
Location of residence	.04**					
AFTER-MEAL CLEANUP						
Family composition variables						
Number of children	.28		.28		.26	.27
Age of youngest child	-.07	-.07			-.11	-.05
Age of oldest child	-.12					
Family type	.25				.22	.23
Employment						
Wives	-.18	-.14	-.20	-.14		
Socioeconomic level	.07					
Wives' education	.10					
Husbands' education	.07					
Housing						
House type	.11	.06	.10	.07		
SPECIAL FOOD PREPARATION						
Family composition variables						
Number of children	.06*					
Age of youngest child	-.05*					
Age of oldest child	-.07					
Family type	.04**					

[a]All Tau values reported were significant at the .001 level unless otherwise indicated as: * = .005, ** = .01 or .02, and ≠ = .03 to .05. For discussion of effects of ranking of variables on positive and negative values, see pp. 30-31. Correlation coefficients were based on 1,260 households, except for age of youngest child for which only families with children were used (1,092).

[b]Partial rank correlation values reported only for major variables at the .001 level of significance.

TABLE 4.2—Rank and partial rank correlation coefficients for food preparation time of wives and major variables
(1,260 husband–wife households, Syracuse, N.Y., 1967-68)

Wives' time in:	Kendall Tau[a]	Partial rank correlation[b] with variables held constant			
		Number of children	Age of youngest	Family type	Empl. of wives
ALL FOOD PREPARATION ACTIVITIES					
Family composition variables					
Number of children	.21		.21		.17
Age of youngest child	.07	.07			.14
Family type	.20				.16
Employment					
Wives	-.29	-.26	-.31	-.26	
Husbands' hours	.05*				
Education					
Wives	.04≠				
REGULAR MEAL PREPARATION					
Family composition variables					
Number of children	.22		.22		.19
Age of youngest child	.04**				
Family type	.21				.17
Employment					
Wives	-.26	-.24	-.28	-.23	
Husbands' hours	.06*				
AFTER–MEAL CLEANUP					
Family composition variables					
Number of children	.14		.14		.10
Age of youngest child	.11	.11			.19
Family type	.15				.11
Employment					
Wives	-.27	-.26	-.31	-.25	
Husbands' hours	.03≠				
Education					
Wives	.06				
SPECIAL FOOD PREPARATION					
Family composition variables					
Number of children	.04≠				
Age of youngest	-.04**				
Employment					
Wives	-.04≠				

[a]All Tau values reported were significant at the .001 level unless otherwise indicated as: * = .005, ** = .01 or .02, and ≠ = .03 to .05. For discussion of effects of ranking of variables on positive and negative values, see pp. 30-31. Correlation coefficients were based on 1,260 households, except for age of youngest child for which only families with children were used (1,092).

[b]Partial rank correlation values reported only for major variables at the .001 level of significance.

TABLE 4.3—Rank and partial rank correlation coefficients for food preparation time of husbands and teenagers and major variables *(1,260 husband-wife households, Syracuse, N.Y., 1967-68)*

Time in:	Husbands' time[c]					Teenagers' timed[d]			
	Kendall Tau[a]	Partial rank correlation[b] with variables held constant				Kendall Tau[a]	Partial rank correlation[b] with variables held constant		
		Number of children	Age of youngest	Family type	Empl. of wives		Number of children	Age of youngest	Empl. of wives
ALL FOOD PREPARATION ACTIVITIES									
Family composition variables									
Number of children	-.07					.21		.21	.22
Age of youngest child	-.06				-.05	-.13	-.14		-.15
Family type	.12				-.04	.12			
Employment									
Wives	-.12	.11		.11		.07≠			
Husbands' hours						.09*			
Education									
Wives	-.06								
Husbands	-.04≠								
REGULAR MEAL PREPARATION									
Family composition variables									
Number of children	-.04**					.17		.17	.18
Age of youngest child	-.04≠					-.14	-.14		-.16
Family type	.13	.13	.13			.09*			
Employment									
Wives	-.11					.06≠			
Husbands' hours						-.07≠			
Education									
Wives	-.06								
AFTER-MEAL CLEANUP									
Family composition variables									
Number of children	-.08		-.08			.15		.15	.16
Age of youngest child	-.07				-.07	-.11	-.11		-.13
Family type	.10		.11		-.06	.09**			
Employment									
Wives	-.10	.09		.09		.07≠			
Husbands' hours						-.10			
Education									
Wives	-.03≠					.09*			
Husbands	-.04**								
SPECIAL FOOD PREPARATION									
Family composition variables									
Age of youngest child						-.09			
Employment									
Wives						.10*			
Husbands' hours									
Education									
Wives	-.06					-.08**			

[a] All Tau values reported were significant at the .001 level unless otherwise indicated as * = .005, ** = .01 or .02, and ≠ = .03 to .05. For discussion of effects of ranking of variables on positive and negative values, see pp. 30-31.

[b] Partial rank correlation values reported only for major variables at the .001 level of significance.

[c] Correlation coefficients were based on 1,260 households, except for age of youngest child for which only families with children were used (1,092).

[d] Tau values computed on basis of 378 families with teenagers.

TABLE 4.4—Food preparation time of all workers and individual workers, by number of
(1,296 husband–wife households, Syracuse, N.Y., 1967-68)

Activity	Number of children	Total number of families NE[a]	E	All workers (Total)[c] NE	E	Wives NE	E	Husbands NE	E	Other workers Females NE	E	Males NE	E
								Average hours per day[b]					
All food preparation	0	97	71	2.3	1.5	2.0	1.3	.2	.2				
	1	149	61	2.3	2.0	2.1	1.6	.1	.1	.1			
	2	295	83	2.6	2.4	2.3	1.8	.1	.2	.1			
	3	233	61	2.9	2.8	2.3	1.8	.1	.2	.1			
	4	139	30	2.9	3.0	2.3	1.9	.1	.2	.1			
	5-6	47	9	4.1	3.3	2.7	1.9	.2	.2	.1			
	7-9	19	2	4.7		2.6		.1					
	Average	979	317	2.8	2.3	2.3	1.7	.1	.2				
Regular meal preparation	0			1.2	.9	1.1	.8	.1	.2				
	1			1.3	1.2	1.2	.9	.1	.2				
	2			1.5	1.4	1.4	1.1	.1	.1				
	3			1.7	1.5	1.4	1.0	.1	.1				
	4			1.8	1.9	1.6	1.2	.1	.1				
	5-6			2.2	1.9	1.7	1.3	.1	.1	.1			
	7-9			2.7		1.8		.1					
	Average			1.6	1.3	1.4	1.0	.1	.1				
After-meal cleanup	0			.8	.5	.7	.4	.1					
	1			.9	.7	.8	.5	.1	.1				
	2			.9	.9	.8	.6		.1				
	3			1.0	1.1	.8	.6						
	4			1.2	1.0	.9	.6			.1			
	5-6			1.6	1.2	.8	.6	.1	.1				
	7-9			2.2		.9							
	Average			1.0	.8	.8	.6		.1				
Special food preparation	0			.2	.1	.2	.1						
	1			.1	.1	.1	.1						
	2			.1	.1	.1	.1						
	3			.1	.2	.1	.1						
	4			.2	.2	.2	.1						
	5-6			.2	.2	.2							
	7-9			.2		.2							
	Average			.2	.1	.1	.1						

[a]NE and E indicate households with nonemployed or employed wives.

[b]Time is reported only if there were three or more families and if average time was 3 minutes or more.

[c]Sum of average time for individual workers may not equal total time of all workers because of rounding and because averages of children's time include only households with children of specified ages.

children and employment of wives

Number households with children 12-17 years NE	E	Time of children 12-17 NE	E	Number households with children 6-11 years NE	E	Time of children 6-11 NE	E
		Av. hrs. per day[b]				Av. hrs. per day[b]	
22	20	.2	.4	23	19	.1	.1
82	44	.3	.4	128	40	.1	.1
91	35	.6	1.0	156	38	.3	.3
43	19	.6	1.1	91	18	.3	.4
31	6	.9	1.1	46	8	.6	.4
18	2	1.3		19	2	.9	
287	126	.6	.7	463	125	.3	.3
		.1	.1				
		.1	.2			.1	
		.3	.4			.1	.1
		.3	.7			.1	.2
		.3	.4			.2	.2
		.6				.3	
		.2	.3			.1	.1
		.1	.2			.2	.1
		.2	.2			.1	.1
		.3	.5			.1	.2
		.3	.4			.2	.2
		.5	.4			.4	.2
		.7				.6	
		.3	.3			.2	.2
			.1				
			.1				
			.3				

TABLE 4.5—Food preparation time of all workers and individual workers, by age of youngest
(1,128 husband–wife households, Syracuse, N.Y., 1967-68)

Activity	Age of youngest child (years)	Number of families NE[a]		All workers (Total)[c] NE	E	Wives NE	E	Husbands NE	E	Other workers Females NE	E	Males NE	E
							Average hours per day[b]						
All food preparation	12-17	80	61	2.9	2.8	2.2	1.5	.1	.2	.1			
	6-11	210	86	3.2	2.5	2.4	1.8	.1	.2				
	2-5	248	63	2.9	2.4	2.5	1.9	.1	.2	.1			
	1	163	20	2.7	2.2	2.4	1.8	.1	.2	.1			
	Under 1	181	16	2.6	2.5	2.3	1.8	.1	.3	.1			
	Average	882	246	2.9	2.5	2.4	1.8	.1	.2	.1			
Regular meal preparation	12-17			1.7	1.6	1.3	.9	.1	.2				
	6-11			1.8	1.4	1.5	1.1	.1	.1				
	2-5			1.7	1.3	1.5	1.1	.1	.1				
	1			1.6	1.3	1.4	1.1	.1	.1	.1			
	Under 1			1.6	1.4	1.4	1.1	.1	.2				
	Average			1.7	1.4	1.4	1.1	.1	.1				
After-meal cleanup	12-17			1.0	.9	.7	.4		.1				
	6-11			1.2	1.0	.8	.6		.1				
	2-5			1.1	.9	.9	.7		.1				
	1			1.0	.8	.9	.6		.1	.1			
	Under 1			1.0	.8	.8	.5		.1				
	Average			1.1	.9	.8	.6		.1				
Special food preparation	12-17			.2	.2	.2	.1						
	6-11			.2	.1	.1	.1						
	2-5			.2	.1	.1	.1						
	1			.1	.1	.1	.1						
	Under 1			.1	.3	.1	.2						
	Average			.2	.2	.1	.1						

[a]NE and E indicate households with nonemployed or employed wives.

[b]Time is reported only if there were three or more families and if average time was 3 minutes or more.

[c]Sum of average time for individual workers may not equal total time of all workers because of rounding and because averages of children's time include only households with children of specified ages.

child and employment of wives

Number of households with children 12-17 years		Time of children 12-17		Number of households with children 6-11 years		Time of children 6-11	
NE	E	NE	E	NE	E	NE	E
		Av. hrs. per day[b]				Av. hrs. per day[b]	
80	61	.1	1.0				
87	41	.6	.5	210	86	.4	.3
85	17	.4	.4	133	24	.2	.3
20	5	.6	.1	77	9	.2	.1
15	2	.7	<.1	43	6	.4	.1
287	126	.6	.7	463	125	.3	.3
		.3	.5				
		.3	.2			.1	.1
		.2	.2			.1	.1
		.2	.1			.1	
		.2	<.1			.1	.1
		.2	.3			.1	.1
		.3	.4				
		.3	.3			.2	.2
		.2	.2			.1	.2
		.3				.1	.1
		.4	<.1			.2	.1
		.3	.3			.2	.2
			.1				
			<.1				

TABLE 4.6—Food preparation time of all workers, wives,
(1,296 husband–wife households, Syracuse,

			All workers' time[c]						
						After-meal			
	Number		All food prep.		Reg. meal prep.		cleanup		Spec. food prep.
Family type	NE[a]	E	NE	E	NE	E	NE	E	NE	E
			Average hours per day[b]							
No-child households by age of wives										
under 25 years	16	26	2.0	1.5	1.1	.9	.6	.4	.3	.1
25-39	19	23	2.1	1.4	1.2	.9	.7	.5	.2	.1
40-54	30	12	2.3	1.5	1.3	1.0	.8	.5	.2	
55 and over	32	10	2.5	1.9	1.2	.9	.9	.6	.3	.3
Number of children by age of youngest child										
1 child										
12-17 years	22	20	2.8	2.3	1.4	1.3	1.1	.8	.2	.2
6-11	23	19	2.4	2.2	1.3	1.4	.9	.8	.1	.1
2-5	26	16	2.4	1.6	1.3	.9	.9	.6	.2	.1
1	37	5	2.2	1.8	1.2	1.0	.9	.7	.1	.1
under 1	41	1	2.2		1.3		.8		.1	
2 children										
12-17 years	27	15	2.8	2.8	1.7	1.5	.9	1.1	.2	.2
6-11	60	24	2.8	2.3	1.7	1.2	1.0	.9	.1	.1
2-5	93	28	2.6	2.4	1.5	1.4	1.0	.9	.1	.1
1	50	9	2.7	2.1	1.6	1.2	1.0	.8	.2	.1
under 1	65	7	2.3	2.2	1.4	1.5	.8	.6	.1	.1
3 children										
12-17 years	26	16	3.1	2.9	1.8	1.6	1.1	1.0	.2	.3
6-11	58	26	3.1	2.9	1.8	1.5	1.1	1.3	.2	.1
2-5	70	13	2.7	2.6	1.6	1.3	1.0	1.1	.1	.2
1	48	2	2.9		1.8		1.0		.1	
under 1	31	4	2.8	1.9	1.8	1.3	1.0	.6	.1	
4 children										
12-17 years	5	9	3.6	3.6	2.2	2.3	1.2	1.1	.1	.2
6-11	51	15	3.5	2.7	2.0	1.7	1.2	1.0	.3	.1
2-5	32	1	3.1		1.8		1.1		.2	
1	19	3	3.1	2.6	1.6	1.7	1.3	1.0	.2	
under 1	32	2	2.9		1.7		1.0		.2	
5-6 children										
12-17 years	0	1								
6-11	16	2	4.3		2.2		1.8		.3	
2-5	17	3	4.1	3.4	2.3	2.1	1.5	1.2	.2	.1
1	6	1	3.2		1.8		1.3		.2	
under 1	8	2	4.2		2.4		1.8			
7-9 children										
6-11 years	2	0								
2-5	10	2	5.2		2.8		2.1		.2	
1	3	0	5.2		2.6		2.6			
under 1	4	0	4.4		2.1		2.1		.2	

[a]NE and E indicate households with nonemployed or employed wives.

[b]Time is reported only if there were three or more families and if average time was 3 minutes or more.

[c]Sum of average time for individual workers may not equal total time of all workers because of rounding and because averages of children's time include only households with children of specified ages.

husbands, and nonfamily female workers, by family type and employment of wives N.Y., 1967-68)

Wives' time								Husbands' time								Non-family female workers' time
All food prep.		Reg. meal prep.		After-meal cleanup		Spec. food prep.		All food prep.		Reg. meal prep.		After-meal cleanup		Spec. food prep.		All food prep.
NE	E	NE	E	NE	E	NE	E	NE	E	NE	E	NE	E	NE	E	NE E

Average hours per day[b]

1.9	1.2	1.0	.7	.6	.4	.3	.1		.2		.2					.1
1.9	1.2	1.1	.7	.6	.4	.2	.1	.2	.2	.1	.1	.1				
2.1	1.3	1.2	.8	.7	.5	.2		.1	.2	.1	.2					
2.1	1.6	1.1	.8	.8	.5	.2	.3	.4	.2	.1	.1	.2	.1	.1		
2.4	1.6	1.3	1.0	.9	.5	.2	.1	.2	.2	.1	.2	.1	.1			.1
2.2	1.8	1.3	1.1	.8	.6	.1	.1	.1	.3	.1	.2		.1			
2.1	1.3	1.2	.8	.8	.6	.1	.1	.2	.2	.1	.1					.1
2.0	1.7	1.1	1.0	.8	.7	.1	.1	.1		.1		.1				.1
2.0		1.2		.7		.1		.1		.1		.1				.1
2.3	1.6	1.4	1.0	.6	.5	.2	.2	.1	.4	.1	.2		.1			.1
2.4	1.8	1.5	1.1	.8	.6	.1	.1	.1	.2	.1	.1		.1			
2.4	2.1	1.4	1.2	.9	.7	.1	.1	.1	.2	.1	.1	.1	.1			
2.5	1.5	1.4	.8	.9	.6	.1	.1	.1	.3	.1	.2		.1			.2
2.2	1.7	1.3	1.2	.8	.5	.1	.1	.1	.3	.1	.3		.1			.1
2.0	1.4	1.2	.8	.7	.4	.1	.2	.1	.2	.1	.1			.1		
2.2	1.8	1.4	1.1	.8	.6	.1	.1	.1	.1	.1	.1					
2.3	2.1	1.4	1.1	.8	.9	.1	.1	.1	.2	.1	.1		.1			.1
2.6		1.5		.9		.1		.1		.1						
2.5	1.4	1.5	.9	.9	.5	.1		.1	.3	.1	.1		.1			.2
1.9	1.4	1.2	1.0	.6	.4	.1		.1	.1	.1	.1					.1
2.6	1.8	1.6	1.2	.8	.6	.2	.1	.2	.1	.1	.1					.1
2.9		1.7		1.0		.2		.1								
2.8	2.3	1.5	1.6	1.1	.8	.2		.1	.3	.1	.1		.2			
2.6		1.5		.9		.2		.2		.1						
2.5		1.5		.7		.3		.2		.1		.1				
3.0	2.4	1.9	1.6	.9	.8	.2	.1	.1	.2	.1	.2					
2.2		1.3		.9		.1										.1
2.9		1.9		.9				.1		.1						
3.0		1.8		1.0		.2		.1		.1						
2.7		2.1		.6				.1		.1						
2.8		1.8		.8		.2										

TABLE 4.7— Food preparation time of children 12 to 17 and 6 to 11 years, by family
(413 husband–wife households with teenagers and 588 households with

Family type	Number		All food prep.		Reg. meal prep.		After-meal cleanup		Spec. food prep.	
	NE[a]	E	NE	E	NE	E	NE	E	NE	E
					Average hours per day[b]					
Number of children by age of youngest child										
1 child										
12-17 years	22	20	.2	.4	.1	.1	.1	.2		
6-11										
2 children										
12-17	27	15	.5	.7	.2	.3	.3	.3		
6-11	26	16	.3	.2	.1	.1	.2	.2		
2-5	26	11	.1	.4	.1	.2		.2		
1	2	2								
Under 1	1	0								
3 children										
12-17	26	16	.9	1.3	.4	.7	.4	.6	.1	.1
6-11	27	15	.7	.9	.3	.3	.3	.6	.1	
2-5	29	2	.3		.1		.2			
1	6	1	.6		.3		.2			
Under 1	3	1	.5		.2		.3			
4 children										
12-17 years	5	9	1.5	1.9	.9	1.2	.6	.6		.1
6-11	20	8	.4	.5	.2	.3	.2	.2		
2-5	9	1	.3		.1		.2			
1	6	1	.3		.1		.2			
Under 1	3	0	1.0		.3		.5		.2	
5-6 children										
12-17 years	0	1								
6-11	12	2	1.3		.5		.7		.1	
2-5	11	1	.6		.3		.4			
1	3	1	.5		.2		.2		.1	
Under 1	5	1	.9		.2		.6			
7-9 children										
6-11	2	0								
2-5	10	2	1.4		.7		.7			
1	3	0	1.2		.2		1.0			
Under 1	3	0	.6		.2		.4			

[a]NE and E indicate households with nonemployed or employed wives.

[b]Time is reported only if there were three or more families and if average time was 3 minutes or more.

type and employment of mothers
children 6-11 years, Syracuse, N.Y., 1967-68)

		All food prep.		Reg. meal prep.		After-meal cleanup		Spec. food prep.	
			Time of children 6-11 years						
Number									
NE	E	NE	E	NE	E	NE	E	NE	E
				Average hours per day[b]					
23	19	.1	.1			.1	.1		
60	24	.2	.2	.1	.1	.1	.1		
32	10		.1			.1			
23	5	.1	.1			.1			
13	1	.1				.1			
58	26	.4	.4	.2	.1	.2	.2		
53	9	.1	.2	.1	.1	.1	.2		
31	1	.1		.1					
14	2	.3		.2		.1			
51	15	.5	.5	.2	.3	.3	.2		
21	0	.1		.1		.1			
14	2	.1				.1			
5	1	.4		.1		.1		.2	
16	2	.6		.3		.3			
17	3	.5	.7	.1	.3	.4			
6	1	.7		.3		.3			
7	2	.7		.3		.4			
2	0								
10	2	.7		.3		.4			
3	0	1.1		.2		.9			
4	0	1.1		.2		.9			

TABLE 4.8—Work and storage spaces available in kitchens, by selected variables
(*1,296 husband–wife households, Syracuse, N.Y., 1967-68*)

Households	Number	Work Spaces Available						
		36 in. or more of counter space	72 in. or more of counter space	At right of sink	At left of sink	Beside surface unit of range	Beside oven	Adjacent to latch side of refrig.
				Percent				
Total group	1,296	92	69	86	87	75	67	41
Nonemployed wives	979	93	71	86	87	75	68	42
Employed wives	317	88	63	88	88	73	64	38
Socioeconomic level								
Class 1 (highest)	163	95	80	91	95	83	76	53
Class 2	163	94	70	88	90	76	68	39
Class 3	402	94	73	90	89	81	71	44
Class 4	483	89	64	80	84	68	62	38
Class 5	85	87	56	82	76	60	54	26

	Storage Spaces Available				
	72 in. or more of wall cabinet storage	72 in. or more of base cabinet storage	Beside range	Beside sink	Beside refrigerator
			Percent		
Total group	89	88	78	94	63
Nonemployed wives	90	89	79	94	64
Employed wives	87	85	78	95	61
Socioeconomic level					
Class 1 (highest)	94	94	86	97	72
Class 2	91	84	75	98	66
Class 3	90	91	84	96	66
Class 4	86	85	74	92	59
Class 5	78	86	71	89	45

TABLE 4.9—Equipment available for food preparation and after-meal cleanup, by selected variables
(1,296 husband–wife households, Syracuse, N.Y., 1967-68)

Households	Number	Equipment available						
		0-degree freezer or freezer unit	Outdoor fireplace or grill	Electric frypan or grill	Kitchen exhaust fan	Pressure cooker	Dishwasher	Disposer
		Percent						
Total group	1,296	86	85	85	52	43	30	24
Nonemployed wives	979	87	85	85	53	40	32	24
Employed wives	317	84	84	85	49	51	25	22
Number of children								
0	168	82	71	85	57	53	25	31
1	210	85	83	88	51	37	26	24
2	378	88	87	87	51	42	24	20
3	294	85	89	83	56	43	36	24
4	169	88	88	82	48	41	37	24
5 or more	77	86	87	74	44	42	44	27
Age of wives in families without children								
Under 25	42	69	74	86	50	38	17	36
25-39	42	81	79	86	60	38	21	29
40-54	42	88	71	81	67	71	40	40
55 and over	42	90	62	88	50	64	21	19
Socioeconomic level								
Class 1 (highest)	163	91	85	86	63	44	60	45
Class 2	163	84	89	85	57	41	35	32
Class 3	402	88	88	85	60	46	38	28
Class 4	483	84	83	86	45	39	16	14
Class 5	85	81	75	72	28	45	5	5

TABLE 4.10—Extent of satisfaction with kitchens for food preparation and after-meal cleanup, by selected variables
(1,296 husband-wife households, Syracuse, N.Y., 1967-68)

Households	Number	Food preparation satisfaction scale						After-meal cleanup satisfaction scale					
		Very unsatis-factory (1)	(2)	(3)	(4)	(5)	Very satis-factory (6)	Very unsatis-factory (1)	(2)	(3)	(4)	(5)	Very satis-factory (6)
		Percent						Percent					
Total group	1,296	6	5	6	20	22	42	4	4	5	26	21	40
Nonemployed wives	979	6	5	6	21	21	43	4	3	5	27	20	41
Employed wives	317	8	4	8	18	24	38	4	5	4	25	25	38
Age of wives in families without children													
Under 25	42	2	5	2	29	31	31	2	5		21	31	40
25-39	42	10		2	19	38	33	5	5	2	21	31	36
40-54	42	5	2	2	14	26	50	5			24	12	60
55 and over	42	2		2	26	19	52		2		33	21	43
Socioeconomic level													
Class 1 (highest)	163	4	3	9	15	24	44	3	3	9	19	20	46
Class 2	163	7	6	6	18	24	39	5	6	6	22	24	37
Class 3	402	5	4	4	17	21	48	4	3	2	25	20	44
Class 4	483	7	5	6	23	21	38	4	4	4	29	21	39
Class 5	85	7	6	14	29	13	31	5	4	6	38	21	27

TABLE 4.11—Percentage of all households using selected kitchen equipment on the record days, by employment of wives
(1,296 husband–wife households, Syracuse, N.Y., 1967-68)

Selected kitchen equipment	All households	Nonemployed-wife households	Employed-wife households
Number	1,296	979	317
	Percent		
Oven	59	60	55
Kitchen exhaust fan	30	31	26
Electric mixer, blender	28	30	25
Disposer	22	23	20
Electric fry pan, griddle, fryer	18	20	15
Broiler	16	16	15

TABLE 4.12—Frequency of use of selected kitchen equipment in the previous 7 days, by selected variables
(1,296 husband–wife households, Syracuse, N.Y., 1967-68)

Households	Number	Food from 0° freezer	Oven	Electric mixer/ blender	Kitchen exhaust fan	Dish- washer	Disposer	Electric frypan, griddle, fryer	Broiler	Outdoor fireplace	Pressure cooker
					Average days of use						
Total group	1,296	5.0	3.9	2.2	2.2	1.8	1.5	1.5	1.4	.3	.2
Nonemployed wives	979	5.0	3.9	2.3	2.3	1.9	1.6	1.6	1.5	.4	.2
Employed wives	317	4.7	3.6	2.1	2.0	1.3	1.4	1.3	1.3	.3	.2
Number of children											
0	168	3.9	3.5	1.7	1.8	1.2	1.8	1.2	1.3	.2	.3
1	210	4.8	3.6	2.0	2.2	1.4	1.6	1.6	1.5	.4	.2
2	378	5.2	3.8	2.3	2.3	1.4	1.3	1.5	1.5	.4	.2
3	294	5.0	3.9	2.3	2.5	2.2	1.5	1.5	1.4	.4	.2
4	169	5.5	4.1	2.4	1.9	2.4	1.6	1.7	1.3	.4	.1
5 or more	77	5.0	4.8	3.2	1.9	2.8	1.8	1.8	1.3	.4	.3
Age of wives in families without children											
Under 25	42	3.2	3.8	1.7				1.1	1.3	.4	
25–39	42	3.6	3.5	2.0				1.3	1.5	.2	
40–54	42	4.0	3.0	1.6				.8	1.8	<.1	
55 and over	42	5.0	3.7	1.5				1.5	.7	<.1	
Socioeconomic level											
Class 1 (highest)	163	5.4	4.3	2.5	2.5	3.7	2.9	1.5	1.9	.4	.2
Class 2	163	4.9	4.3	2.3	2.2	2.0	2.1	1.6	1.5	.4	.2
Class 3	402	5.0	3.9	2.2	2.5	2.3	1.9	1.5	1.5	.4	.2
Class 4	483	4.8	3.5	2.1	2.1	.9	.9	1.5	1.2	.3	.1
Class 5	85	4.7	3.5	1.9	1.0	.2	.1	1.3	1.0	.2	.2

TABLE 4.13—Meal types by number of operations and preparation time
(1,296 husband–wife households, Syracuse, N.Y., 1967-68)

Type	Description	Number of operations	Average time used to prepare	
			Median	Mean
			Average hours	
1	Very Simple Meals			
	Easily prepared foods (babies' bottles or meals; snacks of already prepared food; some sandwiches); noncooking or cooking operations only, or combined simple cooking and noncooking operations.	0-3	.2	.2
2	Simple Meals			
	Quickly prepared foods requiring somewhat more handling than those in Type 1 meals (leftovers warmed up; buttered toast and coffee); noncooking operations only or combined cooking and noncooking operations.	4-7	.3	.3
3	Intermediate[a] Meals			
	Partially prepared foods (salad and sandwich; packed lunches); largely combined cooking and noncooking operations.	8-14	.5	.6
4	Moderate-complex Meals			
	Meals with 1 or 2 menu items that require some preparation at home; practically all combined cooking and noncooking operations.	15-24	.9	.9
5	Complex Meals			
	Meals containing at least one totally home-prepared dish, such as a pie or cake or consisting of a complex menu with several items requiring home preparation; all a combination of noncooking and cooking operations.	25 or more	1.4	1.5

[a]Corresponds to moderate complexity in Walker's 1955 study.

TABLE 4.14—Number of meals prepared on the record days, by selected variables
(1,296 husband–wife households, Syracuse, N.Y., 1967-68)

Variables	All households	Total number of meals Nonemployed–wife households	Employed–wife households
Number of record days	2,592	1,958	634
		Percent	
Total number of meals			
0	<1	<1	1
1	3	2	6
2	10	7	18
3	27	26	29
4	23	23	21
5	17	18	14
6	11	12	7
7 or more	10	12	5
Average number served	4.2	4.4	3.6
		Average number of meals prepared	
Number of children			
0		3.2	2.6
1		4.3	3.4
2		4.6	4.1
3		4.4	3.8
4		4.8	4.7
5–6		4.6	4.1
7–9		5.1	a
Age of youngest child			
12–17		4.2	4.0
6–11		4.2	3.7
2–5		4.2	3.6
1		4.4	4.4
Under 1		5.6	5.6
Age of wives in families without children			
Under 25		2.7	2.5
25–39		3.2	2.5
40–54		3.6	2.9
55 and over		3.2	2.8

[a]Fewer than three households.

TABLE 4.15—Types of meals prepared on the record days, by meal of highest complexity
(1,296 husband–wife households, Syracuse, N.Y., 1967-68)

Highest complexity of meal prepared	Number of record days	Total
		Percent
5	171	7
4	699	27
3	1,100	43
2	550	21
1	64	2
Total	2,584[a]	100

[a]Does not include 8 record days on which no meals were served.

TABLE 4.16—Complexity of meals prepared on the record days, by employment of wives
(1,296 husband–wife households, Syracuse, N.Y., 1967-68)

| | Type of meal served | | | | | | | | | | | |
| | None | | 1 | | 2 | | 3 | | 4 | | 5 | |
	NE[a]	E	NE	E	NE	E	NE	E	NE	E	NE	E
					Percent							
1st breakfast	2	5	28	30	50	51	20	14	<1			
2nd breakfast	65	68	17	16	15	14	2	2				
3rd breakfast	92	92	4	4	3	3	<1	<1				
1st lunch	13	30	42	36	33	24	8	8	3	2	1	1
2nd lunch	76	84	14	10	8	6	1	<1	<1	<1		
3rd lunch	97	98	2	2	1	1	<1				<1	
1st dinner	9	13	8	8	18	19	35	34	24	22	7	4
2nd dinner	92	92	4	5	3	2	1	1	<1		<1	
3rd dinner	99	99	<1	<1	<1		<1					
All 4th or later meals including snacks	98	98	1	1	<1	1	<1					

[a]NE and E indicate households with nonemployed or employed wives.

TABLE 4.17—Number of breakfasts, lunches, and dinners prepared on the record days, by employment of wives and other selected variables

(1,296 husband–wife households, Syracuse, N.Y., 1967-68)

Percent

	Record Days NE[a]	Record Days E	Bf None NE	Bf None E	Bf 1 NE	Bf 1 E	Bf 2 NE	Bf 2 E	Bf 3 NE	Bf 3 E	Bf 4 NE	Bf 4 E	Ln None NE	Ln None E	Ln 1 NE	Ln 1 E	Ln 2 NE	Ln 2 E	Ln 3 NE	Ln 3 E	Din None NE	Din None E	Din 1 NE	Din 1 E	Din 2 NE	Din 2 E	Din 3 NE	Din 3 E
Number of children																												
0	194	142	3	9	76	77	20	14	<1				25	53	65	39	10	8	1	1	17	24	81	75	2	1		
1	298	122	6	11	70	63	22	22	2	4	1	1	21	28	64	59	14	12	1	1	14	13	81	74	4	12	1	1
2	590	166	2	<1	62	55	27	36	8	5	2	<1	11	23	65	57	22	19	3	2	8	7	85	88	6	5	<1	<1
3	466	122	1	<1	56	67	33	20	7	8	<1	2	13	25	62	50	21	11	4	3	7	11	81	81	11	7	<1	<1
4	278	60		<1	58	47	32	25	8	22	<1	<1	6	18	62	50	26	27	5	5	4	3	86	77	10	18	1	1
5–6	94	18			54	61	32	28	11	<1	<1	<1	10	11	55	78	31	11	4	5	5	6	79	78	15	17	1	1
7–9	38	4	<1		63	<1	13	<1	21		<1	<1	3		37	<1	42	<1	16	<1			82	<1	16	<1	3	2
Age of youngest child																												
12–17	160	122	1	5	49	42	32	31	12	16	6	7	16	31	58	48	23	18	4	3	7	9	81	75	10	14	1	2
6–11	420	172	1	2	55	67	32	25	10	6	2	1	13	24	58	58	27	15	2	2	5	7	85	84	9	9	<1	
2–5	496	126	1	2	59	70	32	25	8	3	1		10	21	61	63	23	13	6	2	7	9	83	82	9	10	<1	
1	326	40	5	18	64	50	26	22	4	10	<1		10	10	67	53	20	25	3	3	10	12	82	88	8	8	<1	
Under 1	362	32	4	9	73	53	20	31	3	3		3	15	16	68	59	15	16	2		11	19	82	72	6	9	1	
Age of wives in families without children																												
Under 25	32	52	9	10	75	83	16	8					44	48	50	46	6	6			25	27	75	71		2		
25–39	38	46	13	13	97	74	3	13					21	54	66	35	13	11			8	26	89	72		2		
40–54	60	24	2	8	60	63	37	29	2				25	50	65	46	10	4			17	17	80	83		3		
55 and over	64	20	3		80	85	17	15					17	65	72	20	9	15	2		19	20	81	81		3		

[a]NE and E indicate households with nonemployed or employed wives.

[b]Lunches include evening meals if most complex meal of the day was prepared at noon.

TABLE 4.18—Types of breakfasts, lunches, and dinners served
(1,296 husband–wife households, Syracuse, N.Y.,

| | Number of record days | | Type of first [a] breakfast | | | | | |
| | NE [b] | E | 1 | | 2 | | 3 | |
			NE	E	NE	E	NE	E
					Percent			
Number of children								
0	194	142	20	28	56	51	21	11
1	298	122	26	29	54	44	14	16
2	590	166	29	32	49	48	19	18
3	466	122	28	26	49	57	21	14
4	278	60	33	37	47	57	19	5
5–6	94	18	23	44	45	44	29	11
7–9	38	4	29	<1	37	<1	32	
Age of youngest child								
12–17	160	122	30	30	52	49	18	16
6–11	420	172	29	27	50	52	20	19
2–5	496	126	26	38	50	52	22	9
1	326	40	27	22	47	50	21	10
Under 1	362	32	32	38	48	41	16	13
Age of wives in families without children								
Under 25	32	52	22	37	44	38	25	15
25–39	38	46	29	20	50	57	21	11
40–54	60	24	22	33	58	54	18	4
55 and over	64	20	13	20	63	70	22	10

[a]Only first meals are reported as to type because additional ones were almost
with the youngest child 6 to 11 and 2 to 5, and about 2% of the same type wives

[b]NE and E indicate households with nonemployed or employed wives.

on the record days, by employment of wives and other selected variables *1967-68*)

	Type of first lunch or supper										Type of first dinner									
	1		2		3		4		5		1		2		3		4		5	
	NE	E	NE	E	NE	E	NE	E	NE	E	NE	E	NE	E	NE	E	NE	E	NE	E
	Percent										Percent									
	33	27	31	17	10	3	1	1			5	4	14	13	28	32	26	23	9	4
	46	35	26	25	5	9	1	2	1	1	8	13	16	20	37	32	22	18	3	3
	43	42	34	24	9	9	4	2	<1		9	8	18	17	34	35	24	28	7	4
	43	41	32	25	8	9	3		1	1	7	6	20	23	36	36	22	19	7	4
	42	30	36	35	11	10	4	7	1	2	10	10	19	30	38	35	23	17	6	5
	39	28	41	28	4	22	2	6	3	6	6	22	12	22	36	44	30	6	11	
	34	<1	47	<1	13		3				5		16		34		34	<1	11	
	37	34	36	22	8	10	4	3			9	7	20	16	28	32	27	33	9	4
	44	38	33	24	7	9	2	2	<1	2	8	10	16	26	41	35	22	16	7	6
	38	33	38	29	9	13	3	2	1	1	6	10	18	20	34	34	26	24	8	3
	47	50	29	35	10	3	3	3	1		9	10	18	12	36	48	23	18	5	
	47	56	28	22	7	6	2		1		10	16	19	28	36	28	21	9	4	
	28	27	19	19	6	4	3	2			13	8	3	13	28	23	22	21	9	8
	39	30	32	13	8	2						2	18	17	42	30	32	22		2
	28	17	35	29	12	4					7		12	4	20	50	28	29	17	
	36	30	34	5	13						3		20	15	27	40	23	20	8	5

always Type 1. Type 4 breakfast served only in 1% of nonemployed-wife households with three children and with five or more children.

TABLE 4.19—Number of separate baby meals and snacks prepared on the record (*1,296 husband–wife households, Syracuse, N.Y., 1967-68*)

| | Number of record days[a] | | Number of snacks | | | | | | | | | |
| | | | None | | 1 | | 2 | | 3 | | 4 | |
	NE	E	NE	E	NE	E	NE	E	NE	E	NE	E
							Percent					
Number of children												
0	194	142	70	82	26	16	3	1	1	1	1	
1	298	122	73	83	21	13	5	4	1			
2	590	166	71	68	22	23	5	8	2			1
3	466	122	74	70	20	27	6	3			<1	
4	278	60	67	70	28	27	4	2	1	2	<1	
5-6	94	18	66	83	29	17	5					
7-9	38	4	63	<1	26	<1	11					
Age of youngest child												
12-17	160	122	75	80	21	18	4	2				
6-11	420	172	67	69	25	26	6	4	1	1	<1	1
2-5	496	126	70	74	23	20	5	6	1			
1	326	40	70	65	21	25	7	10	1		<1	
Under 1	362	32	76	78	19	19	4	3	1			
Age of wives in families without children												
Under 25	32	52	78	85	22	15						
25-39	38	46	71	83	26	17	3					
40-54	60	24	65	79	25	17	5		3	4	2	
55 and over	64	20	70	75	28	15	2	10				

[a]NE and E indicate households with nonemployed or employed wives.

days, by employment of wives and other selected variables

No baby meals		1		2		3		4		5 or more	
NE	E	NE	E	NE	E	NE	E	NE	E	NE	E
					Percent						
63	95	11	2	8	1	11	2	3		2	
77	89	6	4	4	4	7	2	3	<1	2	1
84	93	6	2	5	2	3	2	1		1	2
78	95	9	2	4		7	3	1		1	
89	83	3	11	6		1	6				
97	<1	3									
100	100	<1		<1							
99	98	<1	2	<1							
70	63	20	23	6	10	3	5	1		1	
22	31	17	13	18	16	28	25	9	3	7	13

Chapter V

Care of Family Members

Family care activities were made up of two regular and time-consuming activities, physical and non-physical care. Nonphysical care accounted for a little more than half (53%) of all time reported for family care, and physical care for a little less than half (47%). Physical care of family members was reported on about three-fourths of the record days in households in which the wife was not employed and on about half of the days when she was (Table 3.11). Nonphysical care of family members was given in about three-fourths of the families, whether or not wives were employed.

In many earlier studies, the work related to care of family members was classified as child care. In the present study, although it was expected that most of this work would be child care, it was considered advisable to expand the category of family care to include care of temporary or chronic invalids or mentally or physically incapacitated family members cared for at home.

Physical care included such activities as bathing, feeding, or dressing any family member; giving bedside care or first aid; and taking family members to the dentist, physician, or beauty shop.

Nonphysical care of family members included all activities related to their social and educational development. Activities classified as nonphysical included helping children with lessons, reading to children or other family members, chauffeuring children or adults for any purpose except physical care, and taking care of the family's pets. Though much of pet care is physical in nature, it was defined as nonphysical care, because families tend to have pets for their educational, psychological, and social contributions.

It was recognized that the area of nonphysical care would be subject to varying interpretations; for example, playing with a baby or young child was likely to be looked upon by many as nonwork. In developing the category, it was decided that only the mother could classify the activity accurately and that there would be some variations in the classification. When the mother thought the particular activity engaged in was intended for the education or socialization of a child, it was classified as nonphysical care; when it was considered a purely pleasurable activity engaged in as a family social activity, it was classified under the general heading used for activities other than work.

Time recorded as used for either physical care or nonphysical care included only the time spent on these activities at home or by family members outside the home. For example, the time of a person employed in the home for family care purposes was included, but when an employed mother took her child to a day-care center, only her travel time was reported.

When family care activities were concurrent with other activities in which the worker was primarily engaged, they were classified as secondary. One can wash dishes and watch children playing in the back yard; one can iron and discuss a school assignment or a problem with a child. Much of the time of parents that went into being present in case of need or for interaction was recorded as secondary time. In no other area of household work was there as much of such time reported as in family care. For nonphysical care, not only was a large amount of total secondary time used, but the amount remained high until all children in the family reached teenage. No attempt has been made to combine primary and secondary time because such double reporting of time spent would produce data suggesting days of more than 24 hours. However, many individuals feel that care of young children is a full 24-hour-a-day activity if one considers all of the time when someone in the household is responsible for the care and safety of children. They would say that time use reported only as primary or secondary time blocks seriously underestimates the actual amount of work and responsibility that goes with family care.

Rank Correlations of Time Used for Care of Family Members

Summary of Rank Correlation Coefficients

The closest relationship found in the entire study between time used for any household activity and any major variable was between time used for physical care of family members and age of the youngest child (.70 for both time of all workers and for time of wives). The correlation coefficients between time use for nonphysical care and age of youngest child were considerably lower (.23 and .18, respectively, for all workers and wives).[1,2]

When times used for physical care and nonphysical care were combined as all family care, the correlation coefficients between time use and age of the youngest child were .56 for all workers and .60 for wives. The strong effects of age of the youngest child on physical care combined with the large share of physical care in all family care largely accounted for these high correlation coefficients.

Although the correlation coefficients were considerably lower between age of youngest child and time used in physical care by husbands and teenagers (.35 and .22) than by all workers and wives (.70), all correlations showed a strong inverse relationship between time use for physical care and age of youngest child.

For nonphysical care time used by all workers and by wives, the number of children had a slightly higher coefficient than age of the youngest child (.27 versus .23 for all workers' and .25 versus .18 for wives' time). For husbands' and teenagers' time used in nonphysical care the correlations with number of children were slightly lower than with age of the youngest child.

Family type, a variable that combines number of children with age of the youngest child, was closely associated with all workers' and wives' time use in all family care (.36 for both), in physical care (.35 for both) and nonphysical care (.28 for all workers and .26 for wives). The closer correlation between time use and family type compared to time use and number of children resulted from the effects of the two components of the variable (number of children and age of youngest) having similar effects on increasing time use for family care in more complex families.

Employment of wives correlated with all workers' time use with a coefficient of -.24 for physical care and -.10 for nonphysical care. When age of youngest child was held constant, these

values were reduced to -.12 and -.05, respectively. For wives' time use related to their employment the coefficients were -.26 for physical care and -.16 for nonphysical care; when age of the youngest was held constant, the correlation values between employment and physical care increased dramatically from -.26 to -.60, and for nonphysical care the increase was -.16 to -.21. Wives' employment related only weakly and negatively with husbands' time use for physical care (-.08).

Education of wives and husbands did not correlate significantly with time use of all workers or of wives for physical care of family members. The strongest correlation coefficients between time use for nonphysical care and education were in households in which the youngest child was 6 to 11 years (-.18 for wives' education with husbands' time use, and -.14 for husbands' education with husbands' time use).

Rank Correlations of Total Time Used by All Workers and Major Variables

Age of Youngest and Oldest Child (Table 5.1). Age of youngest child was the variable most closely related to total time use of all workers on physical care (Kendall Tau value .70) and all family care (.56). Age of youngest child also was related to total time spent on nonphysical care (.23). All of these relationships remained practically unchanged when other major variables were held constant. The correlation between age of the youngest child and total time use on *physical care* was the closest relationship found in this study between any variable and time spent on any household work activity. The relationship was strong; total time use on physical care increased as age of the youngest child was lower, regardless of number of children, employment of wives, or type of house occupied.

Age of oldest child had relatively close relationships with time use of all workers on physical care (.46) and on all family care (.40); it was much less closely related to total time use on nonphysical care (.16). These relationships indicate that whether families were ranked by age of oldest or youngest child, more time was used when children in the family were younger.

Number of Children (Table 5.1). Number of children was related to total time used by all workers for all family care (.29), physical care (.25), and nonphysical care (.27). Number of children had the closest relationship of any major variable except family type with total time use on nonphysical care, and the effects of number of

---

[1]All Tau values reported in tabular form or referred to in the text were significant at the .001 level unless otherwise stated. Although correlation coefficients were determined for all major variables, only significant relationships are reported in tables and only the correlations strong enough to change the amount of time used daily are discussed to any extent.

[2]For an explanation of meaning of positive and negative correlation values as related to the different variables, see pages 30-31.

children on nonphysical care time were not interrelated with those of other major variables.

The correlation values for number of children and all workers' time used for physical care and all family care increased substantially when age of the youngest child was held constant, from .25 to .35 and .29 to .35 respectively. Considerably more time was spent on physical and all family care at any age of youngest child as the number of children increased. The effects of number of children on total time use on all family care were not interrelated with those of employment of wives or house type. However, for physical care time, there was some interrelationship between number of children and wives' employment, as shown by the slight decline in the correlation value for number of children (from .25 to .22) when wives' employment was held constant.

Family Type (Table 5.1). The correlation between time spent on physical care and family type (.35) was much lower than that with either of the age variables but was stronger than the correlations between the family type variable and time use on most of the other household work activities. This relatively strong association resulted from the positive relationships of its two components with physical care time. Since both decreasing the age of the youngest child and/or increasing the number of children increased the time used, more time was spent on physical care in more complex families; that is, families with younger children or more children or both.

The effects of family type on total time used on physical care were independent of the effects of house type but were weakly interrelated with the effects of employment of wives. When employment of wives was held constant, the decline in the correlation value between family type and time for physical care from .35 to .32 indicated that increasing family complexity was a little less related to increased time use when mothers were employed.

The correlation value for family type in relation to time used for nonphysical care (.28) was about the same as that for number of children (.27). This value remained almost unchanged when either employment of wives or house type was held constant.

Family type was almost equal in association with total time used by all workers for all family care (.36) and with their time used for physical care (.35). This relationship was stronger than that for time use and number of children (.29), principally because of the strong effect of age of youngest child. When tested by partial rank

correlation, the relationship was not affected by either employment of wives or house type.

Employment of Wives (Table 5.1). Much of the effect of employment of wives on total time used by all workers for family care was the effect of family composition. The correlation value for wives' employment and total time spent on physical care (-.24) declined when age of the youngest child, number of children, or family type was held constant, to -.12, -.21, and -.19, respectively. Similarly, the correlation value for employment of wives and all family care time declined from -.19 to -.08, -.13, and -.15 respectively, when age of youngest, family type, or number of children was held constant.

The association of time use of all workers for nonphysical care and employment of wives was weak (-.10). This correlation value declined to -.06, -.05, and -.05, when number of children, family type, or age of youngest child was held constant. These declines indicated that a large part of the effect of employment of wives in reducing total time used for family care was the result of having older children in the household or having smaller and less complex families.

House Type (Table 5.1). The relationship between house type and total time spent on physical care was weak (-.07), but the correlation value increased somewhat when number of children, age of the youngest child, or family type was held constant (to -.12, .11[3], and -.13, respectively). The correlation value of house type with all workers' time for physical care also increased slightly (from -.07 to -.10) when location of residence was held constant. In general, a few minutes more per day were used for physical care in apartments than in one-family houses.

The relationship between house type and total time spent on nonphysical care also was weak (.08), and just the opposite of its direction of relationship with total time use for physical care. When number of children or family type was held constant the correlation value for house type and time use declined sharply (from .08 to .02 and .03, respectively). In contrast, the correlation value for house type and nonphysical care time increased (from .08 to .13) when age of youngest child was held constant; a little more time was spent on nonphysical care of family members at any age of

---

[3]The change from negative to positive for house type when age of youngest child was held constant is further evidence of the strong effect of age of youngest child on time use for physical care.

youngest child in one-family houses than in other dwellings.

Location of Residence (Table 5.1). Residential location was weakly associated with all workers' time used for physical care (.07), nonphysical care (.07), and all family care (.08). These weak correlations changed very slightly when house type was held constant; residential location could have had only a small effect on the average daily time spent on physical and nonphysical care of family members. The only other household work activity for which the correlation between time use and residential location was statistically significant was care of yard and car.

Education of Wives and Husbands (Table 5.1). The only statistically significant relationship between the total time use of all workers (in the 1,260 families) for family care and either education variable was a weak relationship for total time spent on nonphysical care and husbands' education (-.06).

When only the data from the 1,092 families with children were used in the rank correlations, a number of relationships were found, although most of them were weak. The correlation values for wives' education and all workers' time used for all family care and nonphysical care in all families with children were -.10 and -.09, respectively. The values for husbands' education and all family care and nonphysical care time (-.10 each) were similar to those for wives' education.

When rank correlations were determined for specific age groups of children, all workers' time for all family care was related to wives' education when the youngest child was 6 to 11 (-.14) or 2 to 5 (-.14). The closest correlation between wives' education and time was with all workers' time spent on nonphysical care when the youngest child was 6 to 11 (-.17). When the youngest child was in that age group, households in which wives had a higher educational level spent somewhat more time on nonphysical care than did households in which wives had a lower educational level.

Husbands' education was related to the time spent by all workers on all family care in families with children when the youngest child was 6 to 11 (-.12) or 2 to 5 (-.13). Husbands' education also was related to total time used for nonphysical care when the youngest child was 6 to 11 (-.14). These relationships were in the same direction as those for wives' education and indicated a slightly greater time use for some kinds of family care by households as the educational level of husbands increased.

Number of Children Under Age 6. The strong effect of preschool-age children in increasing all workers' time used for physical care suggested that the relationship of number of children might be stronger when all or some children were preschool age than when all children were 6 or over. Consequently, another variable, number of children under age 6, was examined in relation to time use on physical care. That relationship had a correlation value of .66, almost as strong as the correlation value for age of youngest child alone. No further analysis was made using the variable of number of children under age 6 for this study; the finding is presented, however, as a suggestion for future research.

Rank Correlations of Time Used by Individual Workers and Major Variables

Individual Workers' Share in Family Care. Of the total time reported for physical care, most was contributed by wives, whether or not employed (88% of all time reported for this activity was the time of nonemployed wives and 76% was the time of employed wives) (Table 3.10). Only a small average amount of time was spent on physical care by any other worker; when there was another worker, it was usually the husband. The fact that husbands did physical care work less frequently when the wives were employed, on 13% of record days, compared with 21% when not employed (Table 3.11), no doubt reflects the relationship of wives' employment to age of the youngest child. However, the proportionate share of husbands' time in total time spent increased from 9% to 15% (Table 3.10), reflecting some increase in time use when wives were employed if there were small children. The time of other female workers also rose in employed-wife households, from 1% to 7% of total time for physical care. Other female workers were probably important workers in some households, but, on the average for the 1,296 households, their time contribution was small. About 1% of all time reported for physical care was time of older children in the 12- to 17-year age group and about 1% was time of children 6 to 11.

Nonphysical care of family members was shared by husbands and adult female workers other than the wives to a greater extent than physical care. Although wives did nonphysical care work more frequently than any other worker, their time accounted for only a little over half of the total time of the household spent when wives were not employed and a little less than two-fifths when they were (Table 3.10). Husbands were the principal workers other than wives when wives were not employed. In these households, husbands' time accounted for 22% of total time spent on nonphysical care. When wives were employed, husbands' time represented 25% of total time spent on nonphysical care. In employed-wife households other female workers used almost as much time as husbands and accounted for 24% of the total time spent. As an activity, however, nonphysical care of family members represented a relatively high proportion of husbands' total household work time; it was 18% in nonemployed-wife households and 16% in employed-wife households (Table 3.12). Time of teenagers accounted for 3% of all time for nonphysical care when wives were not employed and 5% when they were (Table 3.10). Nonphysical care was the household work activity on which adult female workers other than wives spent the most time; it represented about three-fifths of their total time spent on household work (Table 3.12). Adult male workers other than husbands spent some time on nonphysical care; when the wives were not employed, that time represented 2% of total time spent on the activity (Table 3.11). When wives were employed, the time of other male workers represented 4% of total time.

Age of Youngest Child (Tables 5.2 and 5.3). The strongest correlation between time use on physical care by wives, husbands, and teenagers was with age of youngest child; the time spent on physical care by each type of worker increased as the age of the youngest child was lower. The correlation value with wives' time was the highest and the same as that for total time (.70); the correlation with husbands' time had a relatively high value (.35), while that for teenagers' time was considerably lower (.22).

The effect of age of the youngest child on wives' time use for physical care remained practically unchanged when the number of children was held constant but increased substantially (from .70 to .81) when employment of wives was held constant. This increase in the correlation value of wives' time indicated the strong effect of age of the youngest child on the physical care time of wives whether or not they were employed. The correlation value for husbands' time use for physical care increased slightly when wives' employment was held constant (from .35 to .38).

In contrast to their time use for physical care, wives' time use for nonphysical care was no more closely related to the age of the youngest child than to other major variables. This correlation value (.18) increased somewhat (to .22) when wives' employment was held constant; wives, employed or not, spent more time on nonphysical care when children were younger than when they were older.

The age of the youngest child correlated with husbands' time use on nonphysical care slightly more than did the other major variables; this weak relationship (.12) remained stable when other variables were held constant. Husbands spent only slightly more time on nonphysical care when children in the family were younger than when children were older. The relationship between age of the youngest child and teenagers' nonphysical care time (.19) was closer than that with husbands' time; this value remained essentially unchanged when other variables were held constant (Table 5.3).

For wives' time used for all family care in relation to age of the youngest child, the correlation value was strong (.60). This correlation coefficient increased slightly (to .63) when the number of children was held constant. This change was low in relation to the size of the correlation and emphasized the strong and independent effect of age of the youngest child on family care. The relationship of age of youngest with wives' time use for all family care (.60) was somewhat lower than for physical care (.70) and markedly greater than the relationship with their time use on nonphysical care (.18); this emphasized the greater use of time for physical than nonphysical care in families with younger children. Husbands' time and teenagers' time spent on all family care also were more closely related to the age of the youngest child than to the other variables (.23 and .21, respectively).

Number of Children (Tables 5.2 and 5.3). Wives' time used for physical care was related to number of children (.25); this relationship increased markedly (to .34) when the age of the youngest child was held constant. Wives spent more time on physical care as family size increased whether children were younger or older. The effects of number of children were slightly interrelated with those of wives' employment, as shown by the decline in correlation value (from .25 to .22) when the latter variable was held constant. A very small part of the decline in wives' time spent on physical care in larger families was the result of being employed. Husbands' time use and teenagers' time use for physical care also were related to number of children; the correlation values (.14 and .15, respectively) did not change substantially when employment of wives was held constant.

Number of children correlated with wives' use of time for nonphysical care at the same level (.25) as with their time use for physical care. Number of children and employment of wives were slightly interrelated in their effects on wives' time use for nonphysical care. The time spent by both husbands and teenagers on nonphysical care was somewhat related to number of children (.08 and .13). These values remained more or less unchanged when other variables were held constant.

Number of children was related to wives', husbands', and teenagers' time use for all family care (correlation values of .28, .12, and .16, respectively). The correlation value for number of children and wives' family care time, when age of youngest child was held constant, increased from .28 to .35; mothers spent more time on all family care as family size increased at all ages of youngest child.

Family Type (Tables 5.2 and 5.3). The time use of wives, husbands, and teenagers for physical care was somewhat more closely related to family type than to number of children. The correlation values were .35, .19, and .18, respectively. These relationships reflected the strong effect of age of the youngest child on the time spent by these workers on physical care. For wives' physical care time, the effects of family type were slightly interrelated with the effects of their employment.

Family type had about the same relationship with wives' time spent on nonphysical care (.26) as did number of children. The effect of family type was only slightly interrelated with the effect of wives' employment; employed as well as non-employed mothers spent more time on nonphysical care as family complexity increased.

Though weaker, the relationships between family type and husbands' time (.09) and family type and teenagers' time for nonphysical care (.15) were in the same direction as the relationship between family type and wives' time. Each of these groups of workers spent more time, in varying amounts, on nonphysical care when families were more complex.

The correlation values for family type with the time spent by wives and husbands on all family care (.36 and .15, respectively) were similar to the values for their time use on physical care. The correlation value for teenagers' all family care time was .17, about the same as the correlations with their time use for each separate activity.

Employment of Wives (Table 5.2). The closest relationship between wives' employment and time used for physical care was with wives' time (-.26); husbands' time spent on physical care was only weakly related to wives' employment (-.08).

The most striking change in the partial rank correlations in this study (from -.26 to -.60) was that for employment of wives in relation to their time use on physical care when age of the youngest child was held constant. Though employed as well as nonemployed mothers spent more time on physical care when children in the family were younger, employed mothers themselves spent much less time on this activity than nonemployed ones at all ages of youngest child. Since the relationship between employment of wives and total time of all workers was weak when age of the youngest child was held constant, this sharp decline in wives' time use on physical care with employment was made up by increased time from other workers. This distribution of time indicated the necessary and nondeferrable nature of much physical care.

The weak correlation value between employment of wives and time use by husbands for physical care also increased considerably when the age of the youngest child was held constant, from -.08 to -.18. It was clear that husbands, like wives, spent less time on physical care when the wives were employed.

Of the time spent on nonphysical care by the individual workers, only wives' time was related to their employment (-.16). The decline in the correlation value for wives' time and their employment (from -.16 to -.12 and -.11 when either family type or number of children was held constant) indicated that some of the decline in employed mothers' time use for nonphysical care was the result of smaller or less complex families. On the other hand, the value for employment of wives increased when age of the youngest child was held constant (from -.16 to -.21), as did the value for age of youngest child when employment was held constant. These changes indicated that (1) when employed, wives spent less time on nonphysical care at all ages of youngest child, and (2) whether employed or not, wives spent more time when children were younger than when they were older.

Employment of wives had the same correlation value for wives' time use on all family care (-.26) as for their time spent on physical care and a higher correlation than that with their time spent on nonphysical care (-.16). The decline in this correlation value when either number of children or family type was held constant indicated a lesser effect of employment in reducing mothers' family care time in larger or more complex families. When age of the youngest child was held constant, the substantial increase in the correlation value for employment of wives in relation to their combined time on all family care activities (from -.26 to -.50) was the result of the same change in relation to wives' time used on physical care.

Education of Wives and Husbands (Table 5.2). When education of wives and husbands was analyzed in all families with children, time spent by both increased slightly with increased education of either wives or husbands for all family care and nonphysical care (Tau values ranging from -.07 to -.11). For physical care, husbands' time but not wives' time increased slightly with husbands' education (-.07). When specific age groups were examined separately, it was in families with the youngest child in the 6- to 11-year age group that the Kendall Tau values showed significant relationships between husbands' time use on nonphysical care and both husbands' education and wives' education (values ranging from -.14 to -.18).

When the youngest child was 6 to 11, husbands' all family care time was related to wives' education (-.14) but not to their own. In families with the youngest child under 1 year, husbands' education and husbands' time use for all family care and nonphysical care were also somewhat related (-.16 and -.15, respectively).

Husbands' Hours of Employment (Table 5.2). Wives' and husbands' time spent on family care had weak relationships with husbands' hours of employment (none higher than .06) and indicated that any change in average daily time of either wives or husbands as husbands' hours of employment increased would be negligible.

Time Used for Family Care

Total Time of All Workers

Age of Youngest Child and Employment of Wives (Table 5.4). Whether or not the wives were employed, total time spent on any kind of family care was greatest in households in which the youngest child was under 1 and declined as the age of the youngest child increased. An average of about 3 hours a day was spent on physical care in families with a baby under 1, while only a negligible amount of time was used in households with teenagers as youngest. Employed-wife households generally spent less time on physical care than did nonemployed-wife households. The differences by employment in the time use of all workers were greatest in families with a baby under 1 year of age; an average of about half an hour a day less was used when the wives were employed.

More time was spent on nonphysical care than on physical care when the youngest child was age 2 or over. Time used for nonphysical care decreased as the youngest child became older; children in households with the youngest child a teenager received this care an average of about half an hour a day, for example, while those with the youngest child 2 to 5 received about an hour and a half. As much or more time was spent for nonphysical care when the wives were employed than when they were not. The exceptionally high average time use for nonphysical care of 3.1 hours a day in employed-wife households when the youngest child was a baby was the result of a large amount of time use reported by a few families averaged over a small number of cases.

The difference in all family care time between families with a teenager as the youngest child and those with a baby was great; about 4½ hours more a day was used in the latter families when the wives were not employed, and over 5 hours more a day when they were. The low effect of employment of wives on total time used on all family care can be seen in the greater amount of all workers' time spent in employed- than in nonemployed-wife households when the youngest child was under 2 and in the small decreases in all workers' total time in employed-wife households with school-age children. In families with preschool-age children as youngest, the large amount of family care time resulted from more time on both physical and nonphysical care, while in families with school-age children, most of the family care time was spent on nonphysical care.

Number of Children and Employment of Wives (Table 5.5). There was no consistent increase in all workers' time spent on physical care with an increase in number of children, whether or not wives were employed. When wives were not employed, an average of over an hour a day was spent on physical care in all family sizes. Time varied more when wives were employed, but the most time was spent in families with five or six children. The decline in physical care time with the employment of wives was sharp—an average of over 40 minutes a day less when wives were employed.

Total time used on nonphysical care also did not increase regularly as the number of children increased; but, both when wives were employed and when they were not, the greatest amount of time was spent in the largest families (an average of almost 3 hours a day). As would be expected from the weak relationship of employment of wives with all workers' time, the decline in time when wives were employed was not consistent and was mostly in a few family sizes. On the average, however, employed-wife households spent a little less time on nonphysical care than nonemployed-wife households (1.1 hours compared with 1.3 hours a day).

All workers' time spent on all family care averaged an hour more per day in households of nonemployed than in those of employed wives (2.5 versus 1.5 hours). The time spent in both types of households varied somewhat inconsistently in relation to number of children, with much more time spent in the largest families than in any of the smaller ones, whether or not wives were employed.

Family Type and Employment of Wives (Table 5.6). Whether wives were employed or not, total time use for physical care declined as the age of the youngest child increased in each family size. A difference of about 2 hours can be seen between families with a child under 1 and a child 2 to 5. Though the effect of number of children was somewhat erratic, more time was spent on physical care in the more complex families. In two family types in which the youngest child was under age 2 the decrease in time spent on physical care in employed- as compared with nonemployed-wife households was an average of half an hour per day. The possible explanation for these declines is a greater use of child-care services away from home by some of the employed wives. In several of the comparable family types, a little less time was spent on physical care when wives were employed, while in others as much or more time was used.

In nearly all family sizes, amounts of time spent on nonphysical care tended to increase when the age of the youngest child was lower. This general trend was apparent whether wives were employed or not but was somewhat less consistent in employed-wife households. When wives were not employed, at all ages of youngest children there was a noticeable tendency for total time of all workers to increase with family size. There was no consistent increase with number of children or complexity of family when wives were employed.

The effects of employment of wives on total time of all workers for nonphysical care were not consistent. At some combinations of age of youngest child and number of children, much more time was spent when wives were employed without any apparent relation to family type. For example, in households where the only child was 2 to 5, twice as much total time was spent on nonphysical care (2.0 hours) when the wives were employed as when they were not. Also, in two-child households in which the youngest was under 1 year, over twice as much time was spent (3.5 hours) by employed as by nonemployed wives (1.7 hours). Probably these differences in time reflect varied methods of providing essential care to small children. After children reached school age, differences in all workers' time between households in which wives were employed versus those in which they were not were less marked, and the all workers' times tended to be similar.

Total time used on all family care showed the same relationships with family type as total time spent on the separate activities. The increased time used in all family care in families with babies over time for families with children of school age provided some idea of the time requirements for care of young children even in small families. For example, in families with one to three children, whether wives were employed or not, time increased between families with only teenagers and those with a baby by an average of 4 hours or more.

Time Spent by Individual Workers

Age of Youngest Child and Employment of Wives (Table 5.4). Wives' time spent on physical care was greatest when children in the family were under age 2 and declined regularly as age of youngest child advanced. When the youngest child was under 1 year, wives' average time use for physical care was about 3 hours a day when not employed and over 2 hours a day when they were. When the youngest child was 1 year old, wives' time averaged over an hour a day, whether or not employed.

Table 5.4 shows that the sharp decline in wives' physical care time when employed (indicated by the partial correlation value for employment of wives when age of youngest was held constant) was in families in which the youngest child was under age 2.

Wives, when not employed, tended to spend more time on nonphysical care in families with preschool-age children than in those with older children; their time use for nonphysical care was not consistently related to the age of the youngest child, however. Whether employed or not, the principal difference in wives' time by age of youngest was the increased time in families in which children were under teenage. At all ages of youngest child, except teenage, employed wives spent less time on nonphysical care than nonemployed ones.

Wives' time spent on all family care increased by an average of almost 3½ hours a day between families with only teenagers and those in which the youngest child was a baby, when they were not employed, and by an average of almost 2½ hours a day between the same kinds of families when they were. When there was a baby in the household, the average time per day spent on all family care was 4 hours for nonemployed wives and close to 3 hours for those employed.

The strong effect of employment on wives' time use for all family care is clearly evident in Table 5.4. Employed wives spent less time on all family care than nonemployed wives at each age of youngest child. The differences in time use in families with only teenagers was only 6 minutes a day less when wives were employed; this difference increased regularly as the age of the youngest child declined until, in families with babies, employed wives were spending an average of over an hour a day less on all family care. Since more total time was spent by all workers on these activities in families with babies when wives were employed than when they were not, it was apparent that the lower time of employed wives was compensated for by a higher time contribution from other workers. Most of the reduced time of employed wives came from reduced time use for physical care (an average of .7 hour a day less); in addition, they also spent less time on nonphysical care (an average of .3 hour a day less).

Husbands' time use on physical care was greatest when the youngest child was under 1 year, whether wives were employed or not, and the husbands' time declined as children in the family were older. Regardless of wives' employment, children and other workers also tended to spend a little more time on physical care when the youngest child was under age 2.

The time spent by each worker other than wives on nonphysical care tended to increase as age of the youngest was lower, especially when wives were not employed. Most of the individual workers other than wives spent more time when wives were employed than when they were not, at least in families with children under age 2. Amounts of change in the time of household workers (other than wives) were not very marked when wives were not employed but were fairly substantial between households with older and households with younger children when wives were employed. When wives were employed, other female workers were relatively important contributors to nonphysical care in families with a baby. The extensive sharing of nonphysical care work in the families with preschool-age children reflects the nature of this activity, which consists of both active participation with the child and custodial care. It also suggests the ongoing nature of this work, in which the more or less constant presence of a worker is a prerequisite.

Husbands' time spent on all family care declined as the youngest child was older, whether wives were employed or not. Like wives, all of the other household workers also spent most of their time on all family care when the youngest child was under age 2.

Number of Children and Employment of Wives (Table 5.5). The time spent by both employed and nonemployed wives for physical care varied inconsistently by family size, and the same inconsistent variations were apparent in wives' time use for all family care. On nonphysical care, wives, employed or not, tended to spend more time in larger than in smaller families and their time tended to increase fairly regularly as family size increased. Employed wives consistently spent less time than nonemployed wives on any family care work, and their lower time use was especially marked for physical care (an average of .7 hour a day less). On the average, employed wives spent only a little more than half as much time (.4 hour a day) on nonphysical care as nonemployed wives (.7 hour a day). Employed wives spent less time than nonemployed wives on all family care in all family sizes except those with no children. In these families very little time was used.

At each family size, husbands spent about the same amount of time on any kind of family care whether or not their wives were employed. On nonphysical care, they spent an average of 18 minutes a day, except in the largest families in which they spent about twice as much time. The increase in their time use for all family care as the number of children increased was mostly a result of the time used for nonphysical care.

Teenagers' time spent on any kind of family care tended to be a little greater in larger than in smaller families but did not consistently increase as the number of children increased. Children 6 to 11 tended to spend about the same amount of time in all family sizes on either physical or nonphysical care. Most of the time use of this age group for all family care was spent on nonphysical care.

Family Type and Employment of Wives (Tables 5.6 and 5.7). Wives' use of time on all family care in relation to family type followed the same pattern as time of all workers, i.e., an increase in time for each family size when age of youngest child was lower. For wives, this increase was apparent when they were employed as well as when they were not. With larger numbers of children, wives' time for family care did not increase consistently at each age of youngest child, regardless of employment; also, there was no strong tendency for the time of either employed or nonemployed wives to increase in larger families, except in those with children under age 2. Employed wives spent less time than nonemployed wives on family care in most family types.

In most family sizes, husbands' time use on family care also tended to increase as age of youngest child was lower, usually whether or not wives were employed. At any age of youngest child there was no consistent tendency for husbands' time to increase with increments in family size.

Teenagers' time spent on family care (in families with teenagers) varied among family types and was usually low, whether their mothers were employed or not (Table 5.7). However, in some family types (those with three or more children, youngest child under age 2, and nonemployed mothers) teenagers spent an average time of over half an hour a day on family care.

When their mothers were not employed, the time children 6 to 11 spent on family care (in families with children in this age group) tended to be low in small families and to increase in larger families when the age of youngest child was lower. If their mothers were employed, time use by children 6 to 11 for family care was consistently low in all family types.

In several family types in which wives were employed, adult female workers other than wives spent as much time on nonphysical care as did wives; when the youngest child was under 1 year, they spent more (Table 5.6).

Time for Physical and Nonphysical Care Compared

Proportionally, more of the care for babies was physical in nature, while much more care time was nonphysical in families with children 2 to 5 years, and most of the care time was nonphysical when children were all of school age. Both physical care and nonphysical care were daily activities in families with young children but were less frequent in families with the youngest child of school age.

The amount of time used by all workers for physical care shifted from about 3 hours per day in families with a baby to about 2 hours in families with a toddler, and about 1 hour in those with the youngest child 2 to 5 (Table 5.4). On the other hand, time used for nonphysical care was between 1½ to 2 hours in households with nonemployed wives before children were in school, about 1 hour

per day when the youngest child was 6 to 11, and a half-hour per day in families in which all the children were 12 to 17. For employed-wife households, the pattern by age of youngest child was more varied.

A substantial amount of time spent on physical care, but not all of it, was accounted for by the combined time of wives and husbands. On the average, the time contributions to physical care by workers other than the parents were limited, as can be seen by the relatively small differences between parents' time and all workers' time. In small families, the difference was usually the time of another adult female worker, while in families with teenagers, the difference was usually accounted for by the time contributions of children in that age group, particularly in very large families (Tables 5.6 and 5.7). Relatively few families, however, had both teenagers and babies in the same family, and only a few had an adult come into the house to care for children.

Time contributions of wives and husbands accounted for a large portion of time used in nonphysical care of family members, but it was in this area, more than in physical care, that other members of the family and workers from outside the family did account for some of the time reported.

Secondary Time for Physical and Nonphysical Care

Time of All Workers, Wives, and Husbands

Age of Youngest Child (Table 5.8). Secondary time was reported for all household work activities, but the largest amount, by far, was used for family care. Secondary time used for family care activities was principally for nonphysical care of family members. Not only was a large amount of secondary time of all workers used for this activity, but also the amount remained high until all children in the family had reached teenage. Secondary time used for nonphysical care of preschool age children varied by age of the youngest child. The greatest amount of time (7.3 hours per day) was used when the youngest was 1 year, a somewhat smaller amount (6.9 hours) when the youngest was 2 to 5, and a little less (6.6 hours) when the youngest was under 1 year. In families with the youngest child 6 to 11, the total secondary time contributed was about 4 hours a day; when the youngest was a teenager, a little more than an hour was used.

In all ages of children through elementary school age, less secondary time was spent in households in which wives were employed than in those in which they were not; when the youngest child was under 1, total secondary time used was about 5 hours, compared with over 6½ hours spent in households with nonemployed wives. The secondary time spent by all workers when wives were employed was .6 hour less when the youngest child was 1 year, over an hour less when the youngest was 2 to 5, and almost an hour less when the youngest child was 6 to 11. When all children were teenagers, there was little difference in the amount of secondary time used. The differences in total secondary time among age groups of children (except the 12 to 17 group) were larger when wives were employed. For example, when wives were not employed, the secondary time spent by all workers was only .4 hour less when the youngest child was 2 to 5 (6.9 hours) than when the youngest was 1 year (7.3 hours); when wives were employed it was 1.1 hours less for the older age group.

Considering that nonphysical care is a major responsibility of wives, it was not surprising that the largest proportion of all secondary time was that of wives. The pattern of wives' time was the same as that for all workers' time. Wives spent less secondary time when the youngest child was 6 to 11, but still a substantial amount (2.9 hours per day, on the average, when not employed and 2 hours per day when employed). Likewise, whether wives were employed or not, almost the entire hour a day of secondary time used for nonphysical care of teenagers was wives' time.

Employed wives spent considerably less secondary time than nonemployed wives in all age groups of children. When the youngest child was under 1 year or 2 to 5 years, employed wives spent about 1½ hours less secondary time than nonemployed wives and almost an hour less when the youngest child was 1 year or of elementary school age.

The principal difference in husbands' secondary time use was between households with the youngest child of preschool age and those with school-age children. Husbands spent an hour or more of secondary time for nonphysical care when the youngest child was of preschool age, whether wives were employed or not. This figure dropped to .7 hour per day when the youngest child was 6 to 11 in both nonemployed- and employed-wife households, and dropped again to half an hour or less in households with all teenage children.

A relatively small amount of secondary time was reported for physical care. This situation is understandable since physical care usually requires the performing of some specific action that demands full attention, although some short duration actions may be combined with other activities, such as bandaging a finger, while primary attention is directed toward completing preparations for a meal. The amounts of secondary time reported for physical care were small (not more than an average of .2 hour per day) and were contributed principally by wives. At any age of youngest child, employed wives spent a little less secondary time on physical care than nonemployed wives.

Except in households with only teenage children, husbands' and wives' time together did not fully account for total secondary time. The remaining portion was small, no more than 12 minutes a day on the average, and more frequently only an average of 6 minutes. These small amounts represent the secondary time of other family members and workers other than family members.

Characteristics and Content of Work in Family Care

Family care is a highly repetitive activity on which variable amounts of time, from only a few minutes to several hours, may be spent during any one time period. Some of the work has to meet relatively inflexible circumstances. Unexpected illnesses or injuries must be dealt with when they happen. Even the routine actions such as visits to doctors or dentists or going to educational or social events must meet schedules that are not set by the household. Though children require varying amounts of care at different ages, regular care usually has to be given at certain intervals or certain times of day.

By analysis of time use records collected in Sweden, Walker (1964, p. 15) found that periods of half an hour or an hour or more were the most common time periods devoted to child care when the one child in the family was a baby, and that periods were of lesser duration (one-quarter to one-half hour) as children became older or when there was more than one child.

Family care activities differ from most other household work activities in their direct relationship to the age of the youngest child. In addition, these activities differ from many others in that they have no one work setting or room. Much of the work related to them may be done anywhere in or around the house whenever the need arises, and some of the work requires time for transportation to points away from home.

In the present study the description of kinds of family care is limited to quantitative measures of performance of physical or nonphysical care on the record days and during the previous 7 days. Chauffeuring patterns of the family are also described.

Care Away from Home (Table 5.9)

When wives were not employed, family care was basically done by the family at home, especially when children were young. On the record days, less than one-fifth of children under 2 years of age and less than one-third of children 2 to 5 were under the supervision of a nonfamily member away from home. In most cases, the length of time for care by others was relatively short when wives were not employed. On 9% of the record days babies were under the supervision of others from 1 to 3 hours, and this increased to 17% for preschool-age children. Less than 2% of children under 1 year were away from home under someone else's supervision for more than 9 hours on the record days.

When wives were employed, a much higher proportion of preschool-age children were under the supervision of others, and somewhat higher proportions of each age group were under non-family supervision away from home for more than 3 hours. On almost half of the record days, children under 1 were supervised away from home; on 13% of the days, children in this age group were cared for by nonfamily members from 4 to 6 hours, and on 9% from 7 to 9 hours. On a third of the record days, children 1 year old were cared for away from home, usually from 1 to 3 hours (12%) or 7 to 9 hours (12%). On about half of the record days children 2 to 5 whose mothers were employed were under supervision of a nonfamily member, and on about one-fifth they had been given such supervision for periods of 7 hours or more.

Children of school age were typically supervised by someone outside the home some of the time, whether their mothers were employed or not. On about two-fifths each of the record days in nonemployed-wife households, children of elementary-school age and teenage were away from home under the supervision of someone other than a family member for 7 to 9 hours a day; these proportions were higher when the mothers were employed, 52% and 45%. Much of this time undoubtedly was time related to hours of school and school-related activities. (See Table 3.13 for total time of school-age children at home.)

Physical Care on the Record Days and Previous 7 Days (Table 5.10)

Physical care of family members was a regular part of household work activities if children under school age were in the household. Whether wives were employed or not, all except one family with a child under 2 gave physical care on the record days and almost all of the families with children 2 to 5 (98%) spent some time for physical care. This proportion dropped when children were elementary school age but still remained high (66% of all families with children in the age group). Though much less physical care was provided when children were teenagers, it still was more than when only adults were in the household (16% compared with 1%). About the only difference in the proportions of families providing physical care when mothers were and were not employed was when children were 6 to 11 (60% with employed mothers and 68% with nonemployed mothers). While most of the time used for physical care of family members was for routine types of care, some of this care was related to illness. However, illness requiring bed care was reported on the record days for only 1% of all-adult households and 2% of families with children in any of the age groups.

The pattern of physical care provided over the previous 7 days was similar to the pattern for the record days (Table 5.10). Practically all families with a child under 2, and most families with a child 2 to 5, provided some kind of physical care on each of the 7 preceding days. Practically all families with a child under 2, and most families with a child 2 to 5, provided some kind of physical care on each of the 7 preceding days. About half of the families with children of elementary school age had contributed physical care on all 7 days, while only 5% of families with teenage children had done so. Physical care was irregularly provided in families with children of elementary school age, but only 11% of these families had not provided physical care on at least 1 of the previous 7 days. When children were teenagers, physical care was typically not provided at all (over half of the families) or on only 1 or 2 days (about 30% of the families).

Nonphysical Care on the Record Days and Previous 7 Days (Table 5.10)

Nonphysical care, like physical care, was a regular household activity for most families with pre-school-age children. On the record days, whether or not wives were employed, over 90% of families with preschool-age children had given some kind of nonphysical care. Nonphysical care was a much more frequent activity on the record days when physical care in families with school-age children. Almost nine-tenths of the households had given nonphysical care to children 6 to 11 and over three-fifths had provided some kind of nonphysical care to teenagers. Employment of wives made little difference in the percentage of record days in which children were given care.

As with physical care, the performance of nonphysical care over the previous week substantiated its position as a regular household activity. When preschool-age children were in the household, nonphysical care activities were performed daily only a little less often than those related to physical care. Whether or not wives were employed, nine-tenths of the families with children under 2 provided some kind of nonphysical care on all 7 days and over four-fifths of those with children 2 to 5 provided some nonphysical care every day. This latter proportion was somewhat higher when wives were not employed (88%) than when they were (83%).

The provision of nonphysical care, especially on a daily basis, declined considerably as children moved out of elementary school age. Three-quarters of the households with children 6 to 11 provided nonphysical care on all 7 days, and this proportion was only a little lower in employed-wife households (72%). In only about 2% of the households was no nonphysical care provided for children 6 to 11 on at least 1 day. Whether wives were employed or not, over two-fifths of families with teenagers had given some kind of nonphysical care every day during the past week, and about the same proportion had provided such care within the week, but not daily.

Care of Pets (Table 5.10)

Almost half of the families in the sample had one or more cats or dogs (the only kinds of pets considered likely to take time in an urban environment). Having at least one cat or dog was related to family size in that larger families tended to have at least one pet.

About two-fifths of all families reported some care of pets on the record days and almost 90% of the families that had pets reported care for them on the record days. As with time on other activities, no time reported does not necessarily mean that no care was given but may mean that the time spent was less than 3 minutes. Practically

all of this was routine care; only 6% of families reported spending extra time on the record days for such activities as caring for sick animals or training pets. Over the previous 7 days, more than four-fifths of the families that had pets reported care for them every day.

Chauffeuring Family Members on the Record Days and the Previous 7 Days (Tables 5.11 and 5.12)

One major part of nonphysical care frequently cited as highly time consuming is the chauffeuring of family members, especially children, for various purposes. Data were collected on chauffeuring in five categories for the present study—taking family members shopping, to school or work, to or from social and educational functions, and for physical care. The fifth category was transporting helpers from outside the household, since this service is sometimes provided by families.

Though a small proportion of the families may have done more than one kind, chauffeuring was not widespread on the record days. Of the time spent on all family care by all workers, wives, and husbands, only .2, .1, and .1 hour, respectively, was travel time (Table 6.26). Less than one-fifth of the families had chauffeured family members for any purpose. The most prevalent purpose was chauffeuring family members to or from educational or social activities or transporting them to school or work (Table 5.11). In employed-wife families, the proportion chauffeuring some family members to school or work was substantially higher (24%) than in those families in which wives were not employed (14%). The amount of chauffeuring for other purposes was about the same in both nonemployed- and employed-wife households. Most of the chauffeuring was done by wives or husbands, with husbands doing a higher proportion of chauffeuring for school or work in families in which wives were employed (14%).

Although not a daily activity for the majority of the families, chauffeuring was nevertheless a frequent activity over the course of a week. Of the sample, 40% reported chauffeuring a family member to school or work on 1 or more of the previous 7 days; 51% had taken a family member to social or educational activities. About 25% of the nonemployed- and 18% of the employed-wife households had chauffeured for physical care (Table 5.12).

The largest difference in chauffeuring fre-

quencies over the previous week due to employment status of the wives was in the higher proportion that chauffeured a family member to school or
work (51%) of employed- versus 36% for
nonemployed-wife households). This type of
chauffeuring had been provided on 5 or more of
the preceding 7 days by 18% of employed-wife
families. Nearly all kinds of chauffeuring in the
previous 7 days, except that for shopping, tended
to increase with increases in family size.
Chauffeuring family members to school or work
and to educational or social functions, in particu-

lar, was considerably more frequent in larger
families than in smaller ones.

As would be expected, chauffeuring family
members to school or work declined in families
without children as age of wives increased; to a
slight extent, chauffeuring helpers also decreased
in frequency. The frequency of transporting
helpers declined as socioeconomic level declined.
With decreased socioeconomic level, chauffeuring
family members to shop increased while trips to
work or school decreased somewhat.

TABLE 5.1—Rank and partial rank correlation coefficients for family care time of all workers and major variables
(1,260 husband–wife households, Syracuse, N.Y., 1967-68)

Total time of all workers in:	Kendall Tau[a]	Partial rank correlations[b] with major variables held constant					
		Number of children	Age of youngest child	Family type	Empl. of wives	House type	Location of residence
ALL FAMILY CARE ACTIVITIES							
Family composition variables							
Number of children	.29		.35		.27	.30	
Age of youngest child	.56	.58			.54	.57	
Age of oldest child	.40						
Family type	.36			-.13	.34	.37	
Employment							
Wives (N = 1,092)	-.19	-.15	-.08				
Husbands' hours	.05**						
Education							
Wives (N = 1,092)	-.10						
Youngest child 6-11 (N = 294)	-.14						
Youngest child 2-5 (N = 299)	-.14						
Husbands (N = 1,260)	-.05*						
Husbands (N = 1,092)	-.10						
Youngest child 6-11 (N = 294)	-.12						
Youngest child 2-5 (N = 299)	-.13						
Youngest child 1 (N = 180)	-.09ƒ						
Housing							
Location of residence	.08					.09	
PHYSICAL CARE							
Family composition variables							
Number of children	.25		.35		.22	.27	
Age of youngest child	.70	.72			.68	.70	
Age of oldest child	.46						
Family type	.35				.32	.36	

Employment					
Wives	-.24	-.21	-.12	-.19	
Husbands' hours	.04†				
Education					
Wives (N = 1,092)	-.05†				
Youngest child 2-5 (N = 299)	-.07†				
Youngest child <1 (N = 193)	-.08†				
Husbands (N = 1,092)	-.05**				
Youngest child 2-5 (N = 299)	-.10*				
Youngest child 1 (N = 180)	-.10†				
Housing					
House type	-.07	-.12	.11	-.13	
Location of residence	.07			.10	-.10
NONPHYSICAL CARE					
Family composition variables					
Number of children	.27		.28	.26	.26
Age of youngest child	.23	.24		.21	.25
Age of oldest child	.16				
Family type	.28		.27		.28
Employment					
Wives	-.10	-.06	-.05		
Husbands' hours	.05*				
Socioeconomic level	-.04**				
Wives' education (N = 1,260)	-.03†				
Wives' education (N = 1,092)	-.09				
Youngest child 6-11 (N = 294)	-.17				
Youngest child 2-5 (N = 299)	-.11*				
Husbands' education (N = 1,260)	-.06				
Husbands' education (N = 1,092)	-.10				
Youngest child 12-17 (N = 126)	-.11†				
Youngest child 6-11 (N = 294)	-.14				
Youngest child 2-5 (N = 299)	-.10*				
Housing					
House type	.08	.02	.13	.03	.05
Location of residence	.07				.05

[a]All Tau values reported were significant at the .001 level unless otherwise indicated as: * = .005, ** = .01 or .02, and † = .03 to .05. For discussion of effects of ranking of variables on positive and negative values, see pp. 30-31. Correlation coefficients were based on 1,260 households except for age of youngest child, for which only families with children were used (1,092).

[b]Partial rank correlation values are reported only for major variables at the .001 level of significance.

TABLE 5.2—Rank and partial rank correlation coefficients for family care time of wives and (*1,260 husband–wife households, Syracuse, N.Y., 1967-68*)

Total time of _wives_ in:	Kendall Tau[a]	Wives' time Partial rank correlations[b] with major variables held constant			
		Number of children	Age of youngest child	Family type	Empl. of wives
ALL FAMILY CARE ACTIVITIES					
Family composition variables					
Number of children	.28		.35		.25
Age of youngest child	.60	.63			.70
Family type	.36				.33
Employment					
Wives	-.26	-.22	-.50	-.21	
Husbands' hours	.06				
Education					
Wives (N = 1,092)	-.07				
Youngest child 2-5 (N = 299)	-.10**				
Youngest child 1 (N = 180)	-.13*				
Husbands (N = 1,092)	-.08				
Youngest child 6-11 (N = 294)	-.11*				
Youngest child 2-5 (N = 299)	-.09⧸				
Youngest child 1 (N = 180)	-.15*				
PHYSICAL CARE					
Family composition variables					
Number of children	.25		.34		.22
Age of youngest child	.70	.72			.81
Family type	.35				.32
Employment					
Wives	-.26	-.23	-.60	-.21	
Husbands' hours	-.04**				
Education					
Wives (N = 1,092)	-.05⧸				
Husbands (N = 1,092)	-.05*				
Youngest child 2-5 (N = 299)	-.07⧸				
Youngest child 1 (N = 180)	-.08⧸				
NONPHYSICAL CARE					
Family composition variables					
Number of children	.25		.25		.23
Age of youngest child	.18	.18			.22
Family type	.26				.24
Employment					
Wives	-.16	-.12	-.21	-.11	
Husbands' hours	.06				
Education					
Wives (N = 1,092)	-.07				
Youngest child 2-5 (N = 299)	-.09**				
Youngest child 1 (N = 180)	-.14*				
Husbands (N = 1,092)	-.09				
Youngest child 6-11 (N = 294)	-.10**				
Youngest child 2-5 (N = 299)	-.09**				
Youngest child 1 (N = 180)	-.13*				

[a]All Tau values reported were significant at the .001 level unless otherwise indicated as: * = .005, ** = .01 or .02, pp. 30-31. Correlation coefficients were based on 1,260 households except for age of youngest child, for which

[b]Partial rank correlation values are reported only for major variables at the .001 level of significance.

husbands and major variables

| | | Husbands' time | | | |
| | | Partial rank correlations[b] with major variables held constant | | | |
Total time of husbands in:	Kendall Tau[a]	Number of children	Age of youngest child	Family type	Empl. of wives
ALL FAMILY CARE ACTIVITIES					
Family composition variables					
Number of children	.12		.12		.12
Age of youngest child	.23	.23			.25
Family type	.15				.14
Employment					
Wives	-.05**				
Husbands' hours	-.06				
Education					
Wives (N = 1,092)	-.09				
Youngest child 6-11 (N = 294)	-.14				
Youngest child <1 (N = 193)	-.13*				
Husbands (N = 1,092)	-.11				
Youngest child 6-11 (N = 294)	-.11^A				
Youngest child 2-5 (N = 299)	-.10*				
Youngest child <1 (N = 193)	-.16				
PHYSICAL CARE					
Family composition variables					
Number of children	.14		.14		.12
Age of youngest child	.35	.35			.38
Family type	.19				.17
Employment					
Wives	-.08	.06	-.18	.05	
Husbands' hours	-.06				
Education					
Wives (N = 1,092)	-.06*				
Youngest child <1 (N = 193)	-.09⧸				
Husbands (N = 1,092)	-.07				
Youngest child 2-5 (N = 299)	-.08⧸				
Youngest child 1 (N = 180)	-.08⧸				
Youngest child <1 (N = 193)	-.11⧸				
NONPHYSICAL CARE					
Family composition variables					
Number of children	.08		.08		.08
Age of youngest child	.12	.12			.13
Family type	.09				.09
Employment					
Husbands' hours	-.05*				
Education					
Wives (N = 1,092)	-.09				
Youngest child 6-11 (N = 294)	-.18				
Youngest child 2-5 (N = 299)	-.07⧸				
Youngest child <1 (N = 193)	-.11**				
Husbands (N = 1,092)	-.11				
Youngest child 6-11 (N = 294)	-.14				
Youngest child 2-5 (N = 299)	-.10*				
Youngest child <1 (N = 193)	-.15				

and ⧸ = .03 to .05. For discussion of effects of ranking of variables on positive and negative values, see only families with children were used (1,092).

TABLE 5.3—Rank and partial rank correlation coefficients
(1,260 husband–wife households, Syracuse,

Total time of <u>teenagers</u>[c] in:	Kendall Tau[a]
ALL FAMILY CARE ACTIVITIES	
Family composition variables	
Number of children	.16
Age of youngest child	.21
Family type	.17
PHYSICAL CARE	
Family composition variables	
Number of children	.15
Age of youngest child	.22
Family type	.18
NONPHYSICAL CARE	
Family composition variables	
Number of children	.13
Age of youngest child	.19
Family type	.15

[a]All Tau values reported were significant at the .001 level unless otherwise indicated as: * = .005, ** = .01 or .02, and ≠ = .03 to .05. For discussion of effects of ranking of variables on positive and negative values, see pp. 30-31.

[b]Partial rank correlation values reported only for major variables at the .001 level of significance.

[c]Tau values computed on basis of 378 families with teenagers.

for family care time of teenagers and major variables
N.Y., 1967-68)

	Partial rank correlations[b] with variables held constant		
Number of children	Age of youngest child	Family type	Empl. of wives
	.16		.16
.21			.22
			.17
	.16		.15
.22			.22
			.18
	.14		.13
.19			.20
			.14

TABLE 5.4—Family care time of all workers and individual workers, by age of (1,128 husband–wife households, Syracuse, N.Y., 1967-68)

Activity	Age of youngest child (years)	Number of families NE[a]		All workers (Total)[b] NE	E	Wives NE	E	Husbands NE	E	Other workers Females NE	E	Males NE	E
			E										
				Average hours per day[c]									
All family care	12-17	80	61	.7	.6	.4	.3	.2	.2				
	6-11	210	86	1.5	1.3	1.0	.7	.3	.3	.1	.2		
	2-5	248	63	2.5	2.5	1.7	1.2	.4	.5	.2	.5		.1
	1	163	20	3.4	3.8	2.5	1.9	.5	.8	.2	.7		.1
	Under 1	181	16	5.1	5.8	3.8	2.7	.7	1.0	.4	1.3		.3
	Average	882	246	2.8	1.9	2.0	1.0	.4	.4				.1
Physical care	12-17			.1	.1	.1	.1						
	6-11			.4	.2	.3	.2						
	2-5			1.0	.8	.9	.6	.1	.1				
	1			1.8	1.9	1.6	1.2	.2	.3		.3		
	Under 1			3.2	2.7	2.9	2.2	.3	.4	.1			
	Average			1.4	.6	1.2	.5	.1	.1				
Nonphysical care	12-17			.5	.5	.3	.3	.1	.2				
	6-11			1.1	1.1	.7	.5	.3	.2	.1	.2		
	2-5			1.5	1.7	.9	.5	.3	.4	.2	.5		.1
	1			1.5	1.9	.8	.7	.3	.5	.2	.4		.1
	Under 1			1.8	3.1	.9	.5	.4	.7	.3	1.3		.3
	Average			1.4	1.3	.8	.5	.3	.3	.2	.3		.1

TABLE 5.5—Family care time of all workers and individual workers, by number of (1,296 husband–wife households, Syracuse, N.Y., 1967-68)

Activity	Number of children	Total number of families NE[a]	E	All workers (Total)[b] NE	E	Wives NE	E	Husbands NE	E	Other workers Females NE	E	Males NE	E
				Average hours per day[c]									
All family care	0	97	71	.2	.3	.1	.1	.1	.1				
	1	149	61	2.4	1.5	1.8	.7	.4	.3	.2	.3		.1
	2	295	83	2.8	2.2	2.1	1.1	.4	.4	.2	.5		.1
	3	233	61	2.5	1.8	1.8	.9	.4	.4	.2	.3		
	4	139	30	3.3	1.6	2.3	1.0	.5	.4	.3	.2	.1	
	5-6	47	9	2.9	4.0	1.8	1.4	.5	.9	.1	.7	.1	
	7-9	19	2	4.5		2.7		.7		.2			
	Average	979	317	2.5	1.5	1.8	.8	.4	.3	.2	.3		
Physical care	0												
	1			1.3	.4	1.2	.3	.1			.1		
	2			1.5	.7	1.4	.6	.1	.1		.1		
	3			1.2	7	1.0	.5	.1	.1				
	4			1.6	.5	1.4	.4	.2	.1				
	5-6			1.3	1.1	1.1	.8	.1	.2				
	7-9			1.5		1.2		.1					
	Average			1.2	.5	1.1	.4	.1	.1				
Nonphysical care	0			.1	.2	.1	.1		.1				
	1			1.1	1.1	.6	.4	.3	.3	.1	.2		.1
	2			1.3	1.4	.7	.5	.3	.3	.2	.5		.1
	3			1.4	1.1	.8	.4	.3	.3	.2	.3		
	4			1.7	1.1	.9	.6	.3	.3	.3	.2	.1	
	5-6			1.6	2.9	.8	.6	.4	.7	.1	.7	.1	
	7-9			3.0		1.5		.6		.2			
	Average			1.3	1.1	.7	.4	.3	.3	.2	.3		

youngest child and employment of wives

Number of households with children 12-17 years		Time of children 12-17		Number of households with children 6-11 years		Time of children 6-11	
NE	E	NE	E	NE	E	NE	E
		Av. hrs. per day[c]				Av. hrs. per day[c]	
80	61	.1	.1				
87	41	.1		210	86	.1	.1
85	17	.2	.4	133	24	.1	.1
20	5	.5	.8	77	9	.2	.2
15	2	.5		43	6	.3	.5
287	126	.2	.2	463	125	.1	.1
		.2					
		.2	.1			.1	
		.1					
		.1				.1	.1
		.2	.4			.1	.1
		.3	.8			.2	.2
		.3				.2	.4
		.1	.1			.1	.1

[a]NE and E indicate households with non-employed or employed wives.

[b]Sum of average time for individual workers may not equal total time of all workers because of rounding and because averages of children's time include only households with children of specified ages.

[c]Time is reported only if there were three or more families and if average time was 3 minutes or more.

children and employment of wives

Number of households with children 12-17 years		Time of children 12-17		Number of households with children 6-11 years		Time of children 6-11	
NE	E	NE	E	NE	E	NE	E
		Av. hrs. per day[c]				Av. hrs. per day[c]	
22	20			23	19	.1	.1
82	44	.1	.1	128	40	.1	.1
91	35	.2	.2	156	38	1	.2
43	19	.1		91	18	.2	.1
31	6	.3	1.4	46	8	.1	.1
18	2	.7		19	2	.3	
287	126	.2	.2	463	125	.1	.1
		.1	.1			.1	
		.2					
						.1	
		.1	.1				.1
		.2	.2			.1	.1
		.1				.2	.1
		.2	1.3			.1	.1
		.5				.2	
		.1	.1			.1	.1

[a]NE and E indicate households with non-employed or employed wives.

[b]Sum of average time of individual workers may not equal total time of all workers because of rounding and because averages of children's time include only households with children of specified ages.

[c]Time is reported only if there were three or more families and if average time was 3 minutes or more.

TABLE 5.6—Family care time of all workers, wives, husbands, and nonfamily female
(1,296 husband-wife households, Syracuse, N.Y., 1967-68)

Family type	Number NE[a]	E	All workers' time[b] All family care NE	E	Physical care NE	E	Non-physical care NE	E	Wives' time All family care NE	E	Physical care NE	E	Non-physical care NE	E
						Average hours per day[c]								
No-child households by age of wives														
under 25 years	16	26	.2	.2	.1		.1	.2	.1	.1	.1		.1	.1
25-39	19	23	.2	.4	.1		.2	.3	.2	.2			.2	.2
40-54	30	12	.2	.2			.2	.2	.1	.1			.1	.1
55 and over	32	10	.1	.2			.1	.2	.1	.1			.1	.1
Number of children by age of youngest child														
1 child														
12-17 years	22	20	.5	.5	.1	.1	.5	.5	.4	.3	.1		.3	.3
6-11	23	19	1.1	1.2	.3	.2	.9	1.0	.7	.6	.2	.1	.4	.4
2-5	26	16	1.6	2.7	.6	.7	1.0	2.0	1.2	1.1	.5	.5	.6	.6
1	37	5	2.9	3.0	1.6	1.9	1.3	1.1	2.3	1.9	1.5	1.3	.8	.6
under 1	41	1	4.3		2.7		1.6		3.1		2.3		.8	
2 children														
12-17 years	27	15	.7	.7	.1	.2	.6	.6	.4	.4	.1		.3	.3
6-11	60	24	1.4	1.4	.4	.2	1.0	1.2	.9	.8	.3	.2	.6	.6
2-5	93	28	2.4	2.2	1.1	.7	1.3	1.5	1.8	1.1	1.0	.6	.8	.5
1	50	9	3.3	3.6	1.8	1.7	1.5	1.9	2.4	1.7	1.7	1.0	.8	.7
under 1	65	7	5.2	6.3	3.5	2.9	1.7	3.5	4.2	3.1	3.2	2.5	1.0	.6
3 children														
12-17 years	26	16	.8	.6	.2	.2	.6	.4	.5	.3	.2	.1	.3	.2
6-11	58	26	1.6	1.3	.3	.2	1.2	1.0	.9	.6	.3	.2	.7	.4
2-5	70	13	2.5	2.6	.9	1.1	1.6	1.5	1.6	1.4	.8	.9	.9	.5
1	48	2	3.4		1.8		1.5		2.5		1.6		.9	
under 1	31	4	4.6	5.7	3.2	3.4	1.4	2.2	3.6	3.0	2.8	2.6	.8	.5
4 children														
12-17 years	5	9	.2	.8		.1	.2	.6	.2	.4		.1	.2	.3
6-11	51	15	1.6	1.3	.4	.2	1.2	1.1	1.1	.9	.3	.2	.8	.7
2-5	32	1	3.1		1.2		1.9		2.2		1.0		1.1	
1	19	3	3.8	3.9	2.3	1.8	1.5	2.1	2.8	2.3	2.0	1.4	.8	.9
under 1	32	2	6.3		3.8		2.5		4.4		3.3		1.1	
5-6 children														
12-17 years	0	1												
6-11	16	2	1.8		.6		1.2		1.3		.5		.8	
2-5	17	3	2.5	4.5	1.2	1.2	1.3	3.3	1.7	1.7	1.0	1.0	.7	.7
1	6	1	3.9		1.5		2.4		2.0		1.3		.6	
under 1	8	2	5.0		2.8		2.2		3.1		2.2		1.0	
7-9 children														
6-11 years	2	0												
2-5	10	2	3.9		1.0		2.9		2.2		.8		1.4	
1	3	0	6.4		2.6		3.8		3.0		1.7		1.4	
under 1	4	0	5.4		2.6		2.9		4.3		2.4		1.9	

[a]NE and E indicate households with nonemployed or employed wives.

[b]Sum of average time for individual workers may not equal total time of all workers because of rounding and because averages of children's time include only households with children of specified ages.

[c]Time is reported only if there were three or more families and if average time was 3 minutes or more.

workers, by family type and employment of wives

Husbands' time						Nonfamily female workers' time					
All family care		Physical care		Non-physical care		All family care		Physical care		Non-physical care	
NE	E	NE	E	NE	E	NE	E	NE	E	NE	E
						Average hours per day[c]					
	.1				.1						
.1	.2				.2						
	.1				.1						
.1	.1			.1	.1						
.1	.2			.1	.2	.1	.1			.1	.1
.3	.4		.1	.3	.3		.7		.1		.7
.4	.4	.1	.1	.3	.3	.1	.8		.5	.1	.3
.5	.2	.1		.3	.2	.4		.1		.4	
.7		.3		.4							
.2	.2			.2	.2		.1	.1			
.3	.2			.3	.2	.1	.3			.1	.3
.4	.5	.1	.1	.3	.4	.2	.5			.2	.5
.5	.6	.1	.3	.4	.3	.3	.8		.4	.2	.4
.6	.6	.2	.3	.4	.3	.4	2.0	.1	.1	.4	1.9
.1	.1			.1	.1						
.3	.2			.2	.2	.1	.3			.1	.3
.4	.5	.1	.1	.3	.4	.3	.5			.3	.5
.5		.2		.3		.3				.3	
.5	1.1	.2	.8	.3	.3	.4	.6	.1		.3	.6
	.3		.1		.3						
.3	.2	.1		.2	.2	.1	.1			.1	.1
.3		.1		.2		.4				.4	
.5	.9	.2	.4	.3	.5	.1	.6			.1	.6
1.0		.5		.5		.5				.4	
.3				.3							
.3	.9	.1	.2	.2	.7	.1	.5			.1	.5
.6				.6		.2				.2	
1.1		.2		.9		.2				.2	
1.0		.1		.8							
.8		.3		.5		1.0				1.0	
.2				.2							

TABLE 5.7—Family care time of children 12 to 17 and 6 to 11 years, by family type and
(413 husband–wife households with teenagers and 588 households with

	Number		All family care		Physical care		Nonphysical care	
	Time of children 12–17 years							
Family type	NE[a]	E	NE	E	NE	E	NE	E

Average hours per day[b]

Number of children by age of youngest								
1 child								
12–17 years	22	20						
6–11								
2 children								
12–17 years	27	15	.1	.1		.1	.1	
6–11	26	16						
2–5	26	11	.2	.2			.2	.2
1	2	2						
Under 1	1	0						
3 children								
12–17 years	26	16	.2	.1			.2	.1
6–11	27	15	.2	.1			.2	
2–5	29	2	.1				.1	
1	6	1	.3		.1		.2	
Under 1	3	1	.7		.2		.4	
4 children								
12–17 years	5	9		.1				.1
6–11	20	8	.1				.1	
2–5	9	1						
1	6	1	.3		.1		.2	
Under 1	3	0	.6		.1		.5	
5–6 children								
12–17 years	0	1						
6–11	12	2	.1					
2–5	11	1	.4		.1		.3	
1	3	1	.8		.1		.7	
Under 1	5	1	.3		.3			
7–9 children								
6–11 years	2	0						
2–5	10	2	.7				.6	
1	3	0	.9		.6		.3	
Under 1	3	0	.5		.2		.3	

[a]NE and E indicate households with nonemployed or employed wives.

[b]Time is reported only if there were three or more families and if average time was 3 minutes or more.

employment of wives
children 6-11 years, Syracuse, N.Y., 1967-68)

Number		All family care		Physical care		Nonphysical care	
NE	E	NE	E	NE	E	NE	E

Average hours per day[b]

Number		All family care		Physical care		Nonphysical care	
23	19	.1	.1			.1	
60	24						
32	10						
23	5	.2	..3			.2	.3
13	1						
58	26	.1	.1			.1	.1
53	9	.1				.1	
31	1	.1				.1	
14	2	.1				.1	
51	15	.1				.1	
21	0	.2				.2	
14	2	.3		.1		.2	
5	1	.9				.9	
16	2						
17	3	.1	.2			.1	.2
6	1	.3				.2	
7	2	.4		.2		.1	
2	0						
10	2	.1				.1	
3	0	.7		.1		.6	
4	0	.6		.1		.5	

TABLE 5.8—Primary and secondary time for physical and
(1,128 husband–wife households, Syracuse,

Activity	Age of youngest child	Number NE[a]	E
Physical care	12–17 years	80	61
	6–11	210	86
	2–5	248	63
	1	163	20
	Under 1	181	16
Nonphysical care	12–17 years		
	6–11		
	2–5		
	1		
	Under 1		

[a]NE and E indicate households with nonemployed or employed wives.

[b]Sum of average time for wives and husbands will not equal total time of all workers.

[c]Time is reported only if there were three or more families and if average time was 3 minutes or more.

nonphysical care of family members, by age of youngest child and employment of wives
N.Y., 1967-68)

Primary time of:						Secondary time of:					
All workers[b]		Wives		Husbands		All workers		Wives		Husbands	
NE	E	NE	E	NE	E	NE	E	NE	E	NE	E
				Average hours per day[c]							
.1	.1	.1	.1								
.4	.2	.3	.2	.1		.1		.1			
1.0	.8	.9	.6	.1	.1	.1		.1			
1.8	1.9	1.6	1.2	.2	.3	.2	.1	.2	.1		
3.3	2.7	2.9	2.2	.3	.4	.2	.1	.2	.1		
.5	.5	.3	.3	.2	.2	1.2	1.3	.9	.8	.3	.5
1.1	1.1	.7	.5	.3	.2	3.7	2.9	2.9	2.0	.7	.7
1.5	1.7	.9	.5	.3	.4	6.9	5.6	5.6	4.2	1.1	1.2
1.5	1.2	.8	.7	.3	.5	7.3	6.7	6.1	5.2	1.1	1.3
1.8	3.1	.9	.5	.4	.7	6.6	5.1	5.5	3.9	1.0	1.0

TABLE 5.9—Time spent by children under supervision of persons other than family members away from home on the record days, by employment of wives

(1,128 husband–wife households, Syracuse, N.Y., 1967-68)

Age of child in years	Number of children in category		Hours per day away from home — Percent of record days																	
	NEa	E	0		1-3		4-6		7-9		10-12		13-15		16-18		19-21		22-24	
			NE	E	NE	E	NE	E	NE	E	NE	E	NE	E	NE	E	NE	E	NE	E
Under 1	194	16	85	53	9	19	4	13	1	9	1	6								1
1	216	25	84	66	9	12	5	8	1	12		2		<1		<1		<1		<1
2-5	599	102	69	51	17	17	10	13	3	14	<1	5		<1		<1		<1		1
6-11	887	208	30	21	12	8	14	16	40	52	3	3	1		<1	<1	<1			1
12-17	500	241	29	28	9	6	10	6	39	45	8	10	2	2	1	1	1	1		2

aNE and E indicate households with nonemployed or employed wives.

TABLE 5.10—Physical and nonphysical care of family members on record days and on previous 7 days, by employment of wives
(1,296 husband–wife households, Syracuse, N.Y., 1967-68)

Ages of children	Number of families		On record days		0		1-2		3-4		5-6		7	
	NE[a]	E	NE	E	NE	E	NE	E	NE	E	NE	E	NE	E
							Percent of families giving physical care							
Children under 2	344	36	100	100									100	100
Children 2-5	397	75	98	94			1	1	1	3	3	7	96	89
Children 6-11	463	125	68	60	10	14	18	18	8	13	11	11	52	45
Children 12-17	287	126	16	15	55	56	30	29	7	6	2	5	6	4
Adults	979	317	1	<1	88	87	9	10	2	1	1	1	1	<1
							Percent of families giving nonphysical care							
Children under 2	344	36	94	97	1		3	3	1	1	4	6	90	92
Children 2-5	397	75	95	91	<1		2	4	5	5	5	8	88	83
Children 6-11	463	125	89	87	2	3	5	8	7	6	10	11	76	72
Children 12-17	287	126	63	66	14	11	17	17	14	15	11	13	44	43
Adults	979	317	3	5	91	88	6	7	2	2	1	2	1	2
Pets	442	167	87	86	7	8	5	4	3	2	4	3	81	82

[a]NE and E indicate households with nonemployed or employed wives.

TABLE 5.11—Chauffeuring on the record days, by employment of wives
(1,296 husband–wife households, Syracuse, N.Y., 1967-68)

Purpose	Total chauffeuring		By whom: Wives		Husbands		Teenagers		Others	
	NE[a]	E	NE	E	NE	E	NE	E	NE	E
					Percent					
Take family members shopping	9	9	3	2	5	5		1	1	1
Take family members to school or work	14	24	9	7	4	14	<1	<1	1	2
Take family members to or from social or educational functions	18	20	7	8	9	9	<1	<1	1	3
Take family members for physical care	5	5	3	2	2	2			<1	<1
Transport helpers to or from home to residence	3	3	1	2	2	2	<1			

[a]NE and E indicate households with nonemployed or employed wives.

TABLE 5.12—Chauffeuring during previous 7 days, by selected variables
(1,296 husband–wife households, Syracuse, N.Y., 1967-68)

Households	Number	Chauffeuring family members:				
		For shopping	To school or work	To or from social or educational functions	For physical care	Transporting helpers
		Percent of families who chauffeured on 1 or more days				
Total group	1,296	35	40	51	23	11
Nonemployed wives	979	35	36	50	24	11
Employed wives	317	34	51	54	18	11
Number of children						
0	168	24	28	23	6	4
1	210	36	33	41	16	10
2	378	36	42	54	23	12
3	294	40	40	60	28	14
4	169	32	47	59	32	12
5 or more	77	40	53	66	35	10
Age of wives in families without children						
Under 25	42	19	43	21	2	7
25–39	42	26	31	29	10	5
40–54	42	24	24	21	2	2
55 and over	42	26	14	21	12	
Socioeconomic level						
Class 1 (highest)	163	33	42	52	24	17
Class 2	163	29	45	50	18	14
Class 3	402	36	40	52	26	11
Class 4	483	35	37	48	20	9
Class 5	85	41	34	54	25	2

Chapter VI

Care of the House

The three activities that made up house care work were regular house care, special house care, and yard and car care. Regular house care was a frequently performed and time-consuming work activity. Over nine-tenths of the families had performed some regular house care work on the record days (Table 3.10). Special house care was one of the less frequently performed activities (on 43% and 33% of the record days in nonemployed- and employed-wife households, respectively), but the average daily time spent on it was the highest of any time spent on a less frequent activity. Yard and car care was infrequently performed (on 49% and 42% of the record days in nonemployed- and employed-wife households) and had a relatively low average daily time input. Time spent on regular house care made up the largest portion (52%) of all workers' time for all house care work, substantially more than either of the other two activities. Special house care time was 28% of total time on the combined activities, and yard and car care was only 20%.

Regular house care, as defined for this study, consisted of two classifications of house care work: (1) cleaning the house (mopping, dusting, vacuuming) and (2) keeping it at a certain level of cleanliness and order (making beds, putting rooms in order, caring for house plants or flowers). The term "regular" was defined broadly to include all the house care work usually performed at fairly uniform and relatively frequent intervals (daily, semiweekly, weekly, or biweekly) as determined by the standards and routines of particular households.

Special house care included time spent on two types of work: (1) occasional or seasonal home care activities, such as washing windows, cleaning closets, waxing floors, defrosting and cleaning freezers, cleaning ovens; and (2) repair and upkeep of the house, appliances, and furnishings (including such activities as painting and papering, repairing furniture or equipment, reupholstering, and redecorating). House maintenance work was included in special house care because home maintenance is seldom carried on at regularly scheduled intervals. All work classified as special house care is usually carried on at a period of the year most convenient for the family; most of the work takes a considerable amount of time, frequently a period of several days. The variability in the work load and time used in special house care has made it practically impossible to develop a means of measuring it. It is made up of several subtasks, few of which are performed frequently enough to be studied as separate entities.

The problem of measurement of work activities has been increased by the expansion of the work in house care to include the lot on which the dwelling is located and the family car as a "second house" in which family members spend a great deal of time. To keep this work separate from the other two classifications, a new category was set up for this study, yard and car care. This category included daily and seasonal work related to care of the family car(s), the yard, and the equipment used for such outside work. It included seasonal work such as lawn cutting, snow shoveling, caring for gardens and grounds, as well as regular tasks such as preparing garbage and trash for pickup. This last type of work differs from the disposal of refuse as part of after-meal cleanup in that it involves the collection of refuse and trash from outside the house and the handling of garbage after it has been placed in a container for disposal.

The kinds of work included under yard and car care are distinguishable from those included under special house care in that they are all activities performed outside the dwelling unit and many of them are seasonal in nature. Many of the subtasks related to this type of house care are performed with varying degrees of frequency because of seasonal variations as well as family preferences and standards.

Rank Correlations of Time Used for House Care

Summary of Rank Correlation Coefficients

In this category the closest correlations were between regular house care time used by all workers and number of children (.26) and family type (.22); for time use in all house care activities combined, these values were slightly lower (.20 .16, respectively).[1,2]

Number of children correlated positively as closely as wives' employment correlated negatively with wives' time use in regular house care (.16 and -.16, respectively). When all house care activities were combined, wives' time correlated less closely with number of children (.11) than with wives' employment (-.18). Teenagers' time use was more closely related to number of children than to any other variable (.15 for regular house care and .12 for all house care).

Wives' employment correlated negatively with their time use in each house care activity (-.18, -.16, -.12, and -.11 for all, regular, and special house care; and care of yard and car, respectively). Wives' employment correlated positively with husbands' and teenagers' time use in regular house care (.12 and .11, respectively).

House type was correlated with all workers' time for each of the house care activities with coefficients of from .09 to .13 and .18 for all house care activities combined.

For special house care no correlation coefficients between time use of any or all workers and the major variables were as high as .10, except for employment of wives in relation to their time use, which had a correlation coefficient of -.12.

Rank Correlations of Total Time of All Workers and Major Variables

Number of Children (Table 6.1). This variable had the closest correlation of any of the variables with total time spent on all house care (.20) and regular house care (.26). The correlation of number of children with total time spent on the less regularly performed activity of yard and car care was much weaker (.08). The effects of number of children on total time used on house care activities were not interrelated with those of any other variable except house type. Total time used on these house care activities increased with increasing family size, whether or not wives were employed. The decline in the correlation value for all house care time and number of children from .20 to .17 when house type was held constant, and similar small declines in the values for regular house care and yard and car care, indicated that a little of the effect of larger families in increasing time was the effect of living in more complex kinds of housing.

Ages of Youngest and Oldest Child (Table 6.1). Age of the youngest child had a lower correlation coefficient with total time spent on all house care (-.15) and regular house care (-.10) than age of the oldest child (-.17 and -.16) and a slightly higher correlation with total time spent on yard and car care (-.12 and -.09). All of these correlations indicated the relatively stronger effect of older than of younger children on time used for these activities.

The correlation coefficients for age of the youngest child and all house care time increased slightly when employment of wives was held constant; more time was spent on house care work, whether wives were employed or not, when children in the family were older than when they were younger. The effects of age of youngest child, however, were slightly interrelated with those of house type, as shown by the decline in correlation values when house type was held constant (to -.11, -.08, and -.09 for time used on all house care, regular house care, and yard and car care, respectively). This interrelationship would be expected since small families with young children tended to be the ones living in apartments.

Family Type (Table 6.1). This variable had a slightly lower relationship than number of children with total time spent on all house care (.16), regular house care (.22), and yard and car care (.06). The effects of family type on all workers' time used for house care activities were, like those of number of children and age of youngest child, somewhat interrelated with the effects of house type. A limited interrelationship also was evident between family type and employment of wives in their effects on total time spent on all house care; a little less time was spent in more complex families when wives were employed than when they were not.

Employment of Wives (Table 6.1). This variable had relatively weak relationships with all workers' time spent on most house care work; correlation values were -.11, -.08, and -.09, for all house care, regular house care, and special house

---

[1] All Tau values reported in tabular form or referred to in the text were significant at the .001 level unless otherwise stated. Although correlation coefficients were determined for all major variables, only significant relationships are reported in tables and only the correlations strong enough to change the amount of time used daily are discussed to any extent.

[2] For an explanation of meaning of positive and negative correlation values as related to the different variables, see pages 30-31.

care, respectively. Although slight, the relationship between employment of wives˙ and special house care was closer than that of any other variable except house type.

These correlation values for employment of wives were somewhat higher when age of the youngest child was held constant, a change from -.11 to -.15 and from -.08 to -.11 for total time used by all workers for all house care and regular house care, respectively. Employment of wives, however, had less effect when both family type and number of children were held constant; a large part of the decline in time spent on house care with employment was the result of the smaller or less complex families in employed-wife households.

House Type (Table 6.1). The correlation value of .18 for house type with time use for all house care activities combined was the strongest correlation between house type and time spent on any group of household work activities. This relationship is not surprising since time use for any kind of house care would be expected to be greater in one-family houses than in apartments. Correlations of house type with the separate work activities were lower than for all combined (.12 for regular house care, .09 for special house care, and .13 for yard and car care).

Though not strong, the correlation coefficient between house type and all workers' time use for yard and car care was higher than that of any other variable, and the correlation of house type with time use for special house care was one of the two highest. These two relationships remained relatively stable when the family composition variables were held constant, except for a small decline in the correlation between house type and yard and car care time when age of the youngest child was held constant (from .13 to .11). House type, therefore, was a stronger variable than family composition in relation to time spent on the two less regularly performed activities. Weak relationships with family composition and time for special house care and yard and car care would be expected since scheduling of these two kinds of work is usually determined by a number of other factors in addition to family composition.

The correlation values for house type and total time use for regular house care declined when family composition variables were held constant (from .12 to .08 for family type, .07 for number of children, and .10 for age of youngest child). A small part of the increased time on regular house care in more complex houses was the effect of the more complex or larger families that lived in them and, to a slight extent, the presence of older

children. A similar pattern of interrelationships was evident for total time spent on all house care. These several interrelationships emphasize the relatively strong influence of family size and complexity on the type of house occupied by a family and all workers' time use on house care.

The effects of house type on total time spent on regular, special, or all house care were not interrelated with those of location of residence. A slight interaction was indicated between these two variables in relation to time used on yard and car care, for which the correlation value for house type declined from .13 to .11, when residential location was held constant. A small part of the effect of house type resulted from the suburban location of a high proportion of the one-family houses.

Location of Residence (Table 6.1). The only relationship between location of residence and house care time was with all workers' time spent on yard and car care (.08). Residential location was a much weaker variable than house type, as shown by the decline in its correlation value when house type was held constant.

Socioeconomic Status (Table 6.1). This variable had a very weak relationship with total time input on regular house care (.06).

Education of Wives and Husbands (Table 6.1). Total time spent on all house care (.08) and regular house care (.13) was related to education of wives; husbands' education was weakly related to all workers' time used on regular house care (.07). The positive correlation values indicated that total time increased slightly as educational level was lower.

For regular house care, the relationship between total time use and wives' education was slightly greater than the relationship with employment of wives, but was too weak to affect the average daily time used.

Husbands' Hours of Employment (Table 6.1). The only relationship between total time and this variable was the weak one for regular house care (.09).

Rank Correlations of Time Used by Individual Workers and Major Variables

Individual Workers' Share in House Care. Whether or not wives were employed, they did most of the regular house care work (Tables 3.10 and 3.11). Regular house care involved wives on 95% of the record days when not employed, and on about 90% of the days when employed. Nonemployed- and employed-wives' time accounted for 83% and 70% of total time, respectively. The decline in wives' time was balanced by increased participation by teenagers (from 47% to 60% of the record days). Teenagers were second to mothers in amount of time input when their mothers were employed—their portion increased from 6% to 14% of total time. Husbands also did some regular house care slightly more frequently when the wives were employed (on 10% of record days), but their portion of total time spent was less than 5%, regardless of wives' employment.

Special house care was done more frequently by wives, employed and nonemployed, than by any other worker, with husbands the second most frequent workers (Table 3.11). When wives were not employed, their time and their husbands' time were each about two-fifths of total work time and the time of other male workers (6%) and children (8%) made up the remainder. When the wives were employed, their proportion of time on special house care declined to a third; the remainder of time came from husbands (51%), children (10%), and other workers (7%).

Husbands were the principal workers in yard and car care with some time given on 27% of the record days (Table 3.11). Teenagers and children 6 to 11 also worked relatively frequently in this activity. The husbands' time was almost half of all workers' time when their wives were not employed and three-fifths of the total time when wives were employed (Table 3.10). Wives' time was about a quarter of total time when they were not employed and only a fifth when they were. The remaining time was children's, about 10% for each age group.

Number of Children (Tables 6.2 and 6.3). Number of children was related to wives' time use for regular house care (correlation value of .16) and was weakly related to their time use for yard and car care (.07) and all house care (.11). Some of the effect of number of children resulted from the wives' employment status; when employment of wives was held constant, correlation values for number of children and time use by wives for all house care, regular house care, and yard and car care each declined (from .11 to .08, from .16 to .14, and from .07 to .05, respectively).

Number of children was weakly related to husbands' time use for regular house care (-.06). Teenagers' time use for all house care and regular house care correlated positively with number of children (Tau values of .12 and .15, respectively). Each of these associations with number of children was stronger than those with other variables. When employment of wives was held constant, the

correlation value for number of children and teenagers' time use for regular house care increased slightly. Teenagers tended to spend some time on this work whether or not their mothers were employed.

Age of Youngest Child (Table 6.2). Age of the youngest child was related only to wives' time spent on yard and car care (-.09). The effects of age of youngest on wives' time use were slightly interrelated with those of wives' employment, as shown by the decline in this value to -.07 when employment was held constant.

Family Type (Table 6.2). The relationships between this variable and wives' time were similar to those for number of children (correlation values of .10 with time use on all house care and .15 with time use on regular house care). These values were lower than the ones of time use with wives' employment and were interrelated with the effects of employment. In more complex families, wives spent a little less time on house care work when they were employed than when they were not.

Employment of Wives (Tables 6.2 and 6.3). The relationship between wives' time used for all house care and their employment status (-.18) was the strongest of the several variables examined. Employment status also was related to wives' time use for each of the separate activities—regular house care (-.16), special house care (-.12), and yard and car care (-.11). Employment status was slightly interrelated with the effects of number of children and family type on wives' time use for regular house care (a decline in the correlation value from -.16 to -.13 when either of the two variables was held constant).

Employment of wives also was more closely related to husbands' use of time on regular house care (.12) than the other variables, although the relationship was not strong. This relationship was the opposite of the one with wives' time, and was independent of the effects of family composition. Husbands used slightly more time on regular house care when their wives were employed, without regard to number or ages of children.

Teenagers' time spent on regular house care was also slightly related to employment of wives. Although comparatively low (.11) this relationship was independent of the effects of family composition. Teenagers spent slightly more time on regular house care when their mothers were employed.

Education of Wives and Husbands (Table 6.2). Wives' time spent on regular house care was related to their education (.15), as was their time spent on all house care (.10). Both relationships indicated a little higher time use when wives' educational level was lower. Wives' time for regular house care also was weakly related to husbands' education (.08).

    Husbands' Hours of Employment (Tables 6.2 and 6.3). The relationships between husbands' hours of employment and wives' time use were low; the correlation values were .06 and .07, respectively, for wives' time spent for all house care and regular house care.

    The correlation coefficients between husbands' time use and their hours of employment were a little higher than those for wives' time and in the opposite direction (-.10 for all house care, -.08 for regular house care, and -.09 for yard and car care). Husbands spent slightly less time on these activities when they had longer workweeks.

Time Used for Care of the House

Total Time of All Workers

Number of Children and Employment of Wives (Table 6.4). The marked effect of number of children on total time used by all workers for regular house care is shown in Table 6.4. Whether or not wives were employed, total time generally increased as the number of children increased. Between families with no children and those with five or six children the amount of increase was the same in employed- and nonemployed-wife households—a little over an hour a day.

    The weakness of the correlation between number of children and total time spent on yard and car care can be seen in the small variations in time according to family size, especially when wives were not employed. The slight increase in total time spent on yard and car care was more apparent when wives were not employed than when they were. Although employment of wives was not significantly correlated with total time spent on this activity, at least 6 minutes less time per day was used in all family sizes in employed-wife households. Differences between employed- and nonemployed-wife households were greater in the larger families. The average time spent by all workers in special house care in both non-employed- and employed-wife households was the same, .7 hour a day.

    Total time used on all house care increased fairly regularly with increases in number of children when wives were not employed. When they were, total time did not increase regularly by family size but more time was spent in larger than in smaller families. Except in families with three children, less total time of all workers was spent on all house care in all family sizes when wives were employed.

    Age of Youngest Child and Employment of Wives (Table 6.5). There was a decrease of about half an hour a day in total time spent on regular house care between families with older and those with younger children when wives were not employed but no consistent difference when they were. The effect of employment of wives in reducing time spent by all workers can be seen in the lower time used on regular house care at most ages of youngest child in employed-wife households, and particularly in the difference of about 18 minutes a day in households with the oldest children.

    More total time of all workers was spent on yard and car care in families with older children than in those with younger children, whether or not wives were employed.

    Table 6.5 shows inconsistent variations in time spent on special house care by age of youngest child. The relatively large amount of time spent in families with a child 1 year old, 1.0 hour a day when the wives were employed, is typical of the high reported times of less frequent activities in which certain families performed considerable work on the record days.

    Age of the youngest child had a consistent effect on total time spent on all house care only when wives were not employed, but this relationship was fairly strong; about an hour a day more was used in families with older children than in those with children under 2. When wives were employed, considerably less time was spent on all house care in families when children were of school age, and more time was spent when children were under age 2. This relationship reflects the variations in time spent on the two less regular activities.

    Family Type and Employment of Wives (Table 6.6). The separate effects of number of children and age of the youngest child are apparent in the higher use of time for regular house care in larger families and in those with older children than in smaller families and those with younger children. Whether or not wives were employed, the least time tended to be spent on regular house care in families with no children (with no association with age of wives) and in small families with preschool-age children. Employment of wives had little effect on regular house care time in families with preschool-age children, in which about the same amount of time was used in both nonemployed- and employed-wife households. The principal effect of wives' employment was in families with no children and small families with older children, in which less time usually was spent when wives were employed.

In general, the relationship of family type with time use for all house care activities was similar to the relationship between this variable and time use for regular house care, the major component of the category. The somewhat erratic distribution of all house care time in relation to family type was mostly the result of sharp variations in time spent on the two less regular activities. The effect of employment of wives on time use for all house care was relatively strong when examined with family type. In most family types less time was used when the wives were employed than when they were not, and the decreases were substantial in some family types. In families without children, total time used for all house care activities increased consistently with increasing age of wife only in nonemployed-wife households, by an average of over half an hour a day between households with wives in the youngest and oldest age groups. No such relationship was apparent when the wives were employed.

In families with no children, all work time for special house care tended to increase with age of wives, and some of these family types spent more time than families with children, especially when the wives were not employed. The smaller amount of time spent on special house care when wives were employed was apparent in most family types. The major exceptions to this general trend were the family types with employed wives in which some of the more time-consuming subtasks in special house care apparently had been done on record days.

Data in Table 6.6 show that, in general, whether or not wives were employed, more time was spent on yard and car care in the family types with older than with younger children. Less time was spent on yard and car care in employed-wife households in almost all family types, but these differences were apparently more the result of variations in time spent on special house care projects between nonemployed- and employed-wife households than a consistent difference because of employment status.

House Type (Table 6.8). Because house type was related to time spent on some aspects of house care but was also interrelated with family size, the extent of the relationship was explored further. To eliminate the possible effects of the varying age levels of the houses in the sample, age of house was held constant for this analysis. About one-quarter of the homes had been built in the 1960's, a third between 1940 and 1959, 19% between 1920 and 1939, and 20% before 1920. (Four percent of wives did not know the age of their dwelling.) As can be seen from Table 6.8, age of house had no effect on time use; the most time was spent in one-family houses whether they were new or old. Also, time use for this activity usually increased between apartments and one-family houses at nearly all levels of house age.

Since house type and number of children exercised separate effects on time used for regular house care, these two variables are shown together in Table 6.8. Time increased regularly with number of children in the two principal housing types (apartments and one-family houses). Only the small number of mobile homes showed an inconsistent pattern in this respect. In apartments, twice as much time was spent in the largest families (1.4 hours a day, on average) as in the smallest (.7 hour a day), and in one-family houses three times as much time (2.8 hours a day) was used in the largest as in the smallest families (.9 hour).

The effect of house type was less clear-cut. More time was not consistently spent in one-family houses than in other types of dwellings at all family sizes, and only in the largest families was the time spent appreciably higher. In most family sizes the time used on regular house care tended to be about the same in apartments as in two-family houses.

Persons-per-Room Ratio (Table 6.8). Since each house type represents an amount of space to be cared for, the effects of space available and family size together may be seen by using a persons-per-room ratio (Table 6.8). Contrary to the usual method of computing such a ratio, bathrooms were included in the count of rooms used because of the amount of work they create. More time was spent on regular house care as houses became more crowded.

Time Spent by Individual Workers

Number of Children and Employment of Wives (Table 6.4). The increase in wives' time use for regular house care in relation to number of children was mostly between families with no children or one child and the larger families; wives spent about the same amount of time in all family sizes of two or more children. The effect of employment in reducing wives' time input was somewhat stronger than the effect of number of children in increasing it; employed wives spent less time than nonemployed wives on regular house care in all family sizes. When the wives were employed, there was no consistent relationship with family size in time spent on this activity. Average time of employed wives for regular house care was .9 hour a day, compared with 1.1 hours a day for those not employed.

Wives' time on all house care activities was not consistently related to number of children. When they were not employed, the net change in their time between small and large families was very slight; when they were employed, the principal difference was between families with no children (.9 hour a day) and those with children (averages of over an hour a day).

Employment of wives had a stronger effect than did number of children on wives' use of time on all house care work; in all family sizes less time was spent on overall house care by employed wives than by nonemployed wives. This decline averaged about half an hour a day in some sizes of families and at least .2 hour in all others. It was evident that in some family sizes the decreased time of employed wives was not made up by increased time from other family or nonfamily workers.

Nonemployed wives, in general, spent about .3 hour a day on special house care in all family sizes. Employed wives spent a little less time than nonemployed ones in most family sizes (about .2 hour a day). When there were no children in the households, nonemployed wives used .5 hour and employed wives .3 hour a day for special house care.

Although wives' time use on yard and car care was related to family size, the correlation was too weak and their time contribution too low to affect their average daily time use.

Husbands' time use for regular house care did not relate to number of children (6 minutes or less at each family size when wives were employed and less than 3 minutes per day at each family size when they were not). Husbands' time use for regular house care was slightly related to wives' employment, but the increase in husbands' time use in employed- over nonemployed-wife households was only an average of a few minutes a day.

Husbands' time use on all house care, special house care, and yard and car care was not related to family composition or wives' employment. Among families with more than one child, husbands did, however, tend to consistently spend a little more time on all house care activities when the wives were employed than when they were not. Husbands averaged .3 hour a day on special house care in all households, and .2 or .3 hour a day

respectively on yard and car care, depending on wives' employment.

Teenagers' time use for regular house care tended to increase as the number of children increased, whether or not their mothers were employed. In nearly all family sizes except the smallest they spent more time on regular house care when the wives were employed. Teenagers' lower time use in small families could have been affected by a smaller number of teenagers. Probably as a result of these variations, the average time of teenagers was only a little higher when the wives were employed (.4 hour a day) than when they were not (.3 hour a day). In most family sizes when the wives were employed, teenagers' contribution of time for regular house care was second only to their mothers'.

The relationship between teenagers' time spent on all house care activities and number of children was not consistent by changes in family size. Rather, in both nonemployed- and employed-wife households it was the result of their greater use of time in larger families.

Children 6 to 11 averaged a little more time on regular house care when their mothers were employed but this was not consistent in all family sizes. In the largest families, children 6 to 11 spent the most time when the wives were not employed. In these families, their time use (1.0 hour a day) was greater than that of teenagers and, in other family sizes, time use of younger children approximated teenagers' time. When the wives were employed, the time of this age group was usually lower than that of teenagers, and only when the wives were not employed was it related fairly consistently to number of children.

When the wives were not employed, the time use of children 6 to 11 on all house care activities combined increased as the number of children increased. Although the time of children 6 to 11 was not related to number of children when the mothers were employed, they did spend about as much average time on all house care as when their mothers were not employed (.4 hour a day).

The 6- to 11-year age group spent very little time on special house care, an average of less than 3 minutes a day, but they spent a little more time on yard and car care. Much of the work in special house care requires more attention and skill than could be expected from these children without fairly close supervision. On both less frequent activities, children 6 to 11 spent about the same amount of time in large as in small families and tended to spend a little more time when the mothers were not employed than when they were.

It seemed apparent that the increased work load for house care in families with more children and older children was shared by school-age children, whether or not the wives were employed.

The time use of adult female and male workers other than wives and husbands for all house care was .1 hour a day, on the average. Time for adult female workers other than wives was generally used for regular house care and that of adult male workers other than husbands was for special house care.

Age of Youngest Child and Employment of Wives (Table 6.5). The only time spent by wives on house care activities that was statistically related to the age of the youngest child was their time use for yard and car care. Although this relationship was weak, there was a consistent increase in time inputs of nonemployed wives as children in the family were older. Employed wives spent less time than nonemployed wives on this type of work at all ages of youngest child.

Family Type and Employment of Wives (Tables 6.6 and 6.7). In general, both nonemployed and employed wives spent less than average time on regular house care in households with no children. Nonemployed wives spent less than average time in one-child households only when the youngest child was of preschool age; in other family types, they usually spent a little more than average time. The time use of employed wives varied inconsistently among family types.

Employment of wives could be expected to have a somewhat stronger effect on wives' time use for regular house care than for some other kinds of housework, since some of the work in regular house care can be delegated to other family members. The effect of employment on wives' time use for regular house care and all house care combined was stronger than the effect of family composition. In small families with teenage children, employed wives spent much less time than those nonemployed. In general, this lower time use was not completely made up by that of any other worker; therefore, it probably reflected less work because of lower family complexity. Employed wives also spent less time, by varying amounts, than nonemployed wives on regular house care and all house care in most other family types, particularly in families with no children and those with teenagers. In some of these family types, the time use of some other household worker for all house care and regular house care increased.

Wives, whether employed or not, fairly consistently spent more time on yard and car care in families with older children. Employed wives spent a little less time than nonemployed ones in nearly all family types and the least amount of time in more complex families.

In most family types, wives and husbands spent about the same average time on special house care. In the family types in which an average of over an hour a day was spent by all workers on special house care, the time was usually that of both wives and husbands except in a few cases in which a high proportion of the time was husbands' alone. This similarity results mostly from the nature of the subtasks in special house care, in which the time-consuming operations in interior home maintenance have traditionally been done by husbands. Some of the special house cleaning work (which usually is the wives' province) may take less time, but there are more such jobs and many of them typically are done more frequently.

Characteristics and Content of Work in Care of the House

The Dwellings

The characteristics of the house occupied are important in defining the amount of space to be cleaned and the work environment in which house care is done. The distribution of house types in the sample by selected family characteristics is shown in Table 2.14 and discussed in Chapter 2.

Dwelling characteristics examined because of their possible effect on the amount of work in house care included: number of levels, number of rooms, number of bathrooms, number of rooms in use, persons-per-room ratio, heating and cooling equipment, and special features that might either increase or decrease work.

Dwelling Space (Tables 6.9, 6.10, and 6.11). Half of the dwellings in the sample had two stories, 40% were one story, and 3% had three stories. (In this study apartments were classified as one-story dwellings when they were all on one level.) Only 7% of the sample lived in split-level homes. Most of the homes in the study were fairly large; 48% of the families lived in houses with six or seven rooms not counting bathrooms, and almost one-quarter were in houses with more than six rooms (Table 6.9). Apartments and mobile homes had about the same number of rooms (two to five) and two-family houses typically had six or seven rooms. The largest houses, as would be expected, were one-family dwellings; only one-fifth of these dwellings had fewer than six rooms.

The number of rooms in the house was closely

related to the number of children. As family size advanced, the proportion living in dwellings with fewer than six rooms declined fairly regularly, while the proportion living in dwellings with eight or more rooms increased progressively.

In families with no children, households with younger wives (under age 40) tended to be living in smaller dwellings, while those with older wives usually lived in dwellings with at least six rooms. The proportion of families without children living in dwellings of eight or more rooms increased from 2% of those with the youngest wives to 24% of those with wives 40 to 54. Increases in house size were not consistently related to socioeconomic level; however, families at lower levels tended to occupy dwellings with fewer rooms than families at the two highest levels. More families with nonemployed wives lived in dwellings with eight or more rooms than those with employed wives, although both groups typically had six or seven rooms.

About three-fifths of the houses had only one bathroom, about one-fifth had an additional half bath, and another fifth had two or more bathrooms. The proportion of families with one bathroom declined as family size advanced, from 70% of those with one child to 44% of those with five or more children, while the proportion with two or more bathrooms increased, from 12% to 36%.

Most houses in the sample, as measured by the persons-per-room index of crowding, had ample space: 93% of all dwellings had persons-per-room ratios of one or fewer persons per room (the national standard), and about two-thirds had persons-per-room ratios of .75 or less (Table 6.10). With respect to degree of crowding, there was very little difference between dwellings in the city and those in the suburbs (95% of urban houses and 92% of suburban ones had persons-per-room ratios of one person or less).

The number of rooms in daily use is another factor that has some bearing on the amount of work in regular house care. Most of the households in the sample (84%) had used all the rooms in the house during the previous 7 days, and another 10% had used all except one room (Table 6.11).

The proportion of families that used all the rooms in the house increased fairly consistently with number of children; also, the families not using all rooms tended to be those with none or only one child at home. In families without children the older wives (age 40 or over) more than the younger wives tended to have rooms not in use.

Heating and Cooling Equipment of Dwellings (Table 6.12). Automatic heating systems were standard equipment in the houses; only 22 families (less than 2%) did not have automatic heating. The heating systems most commonly used were warm air furnaces (84%), though a small portion (13%) used steam heat (Table 6.12).

Because of the effects of heating systems on need for cleaning, the participants subjectively evaluated the dirt-producing effects of their heating systems. Some dirt was caused by most of the heating systems, although a third of the wives stated that their heating systems caused very little (26%) or no dirt (4%). About two-fifths reported "some dirt," and almost a third said that it caused "much dirt."

Air conditioners contribute to the residential environment and help to create more comfortable working and living conditions. They have the effect of reducing dust coming into the house and may, therefore, cut down on some types of cleaning. In the sample, only 14% had one air-conditioning unit and only 6% had two or more units or a central air-conditioning system.

A fireplace is another feature usually considered as enhancing to the residential environment. This feature, like air conditioners, was not common in the sample; less than a third of families (29%) lived in houses with indoor fireplaces. The use of fireplaces by sample families was low: when used at all, they tended to have been used at most only 1 or 2 days during the previous week, and only 2% of all families had used a fireplace on the record days.

Selected Work-Increasing and Work-Reducing Factors

Work Increasers (Table 6.13). Six factors found in previous research to increase the amount of work in routine house cleaning and inquired about in the survey were: inadequate storage space, room arrangement, extra dirt from outside, neighborhood construction, weather conditions, and entertaining. Responses from all families showed that extra cleaning resulted from weather conditions such as rain, snow, or mud (59%); extra dirt from outside (57%); entertaining (47%); inadequate storage space (35%); room arrangement (17%); and neighborhood construction (9%). The principal differences by employment were the lower proportions of employed wives who reported extra work caused by neighborhood construction (6% versus 10%) or entertaining (41% versus 49%).

Some of the extra time caused by these six factors was related to the presence of children or to the size of the family. If there were children, especially when there were two or more, wives more often mentioned inadequate storage and room arrangement, extra dirt from outside the house, and weather conditions. Socioeconomic level was related to extra time spent on cleaning caused by extra dirt from outside; the proportion mentioning this item increased as socioeconomic level declined (from 50% of the highest level to 62% of the lowest). The most frequent reports of room arrangement causing extra cleaning were made by families at the two lowest levels.

Two of the special situations that might cause extra cleaning work were features of the house. Inadequate storage was less bothersome in one-family houses than in apartments or two-family houses, and room arrangement was less trouble in both one-family houses and apartments than in two-family dwellings. On the other hand, extra dirt brought in from outside was more bothersome in both one- and two-family houses than in apartments; this relationship is probably a result of the higher amount of indoor-outdoor activity by families in such dwellings. The factor of dirt from outside was the most troublesome of the six factors studied for families in one-family dwellings (60%). Weather conditions caused extra work for a large portion of families and was the chief cause of extra cleaning time reported for the previous week in two-family houses (64%) and apartments (50%). Possibly this relates to confinement to more restricted space in bad weather. Weather conditions were reported more often as resulting in extra cleaning for those living in newer than in older homes.

Inadequate storage and inefficient room arrangement were more often reported as troublesome by families living in houses built after 1960 and least often reported as troublesome by families living in the oldest houses.

Work Reducers (Table 6.14). Wives were asked whether or not they had taken certain steps to reduce cleaning time during the previous 7 days by keeping outside dirt from being tracked through the house—by using mats at the entrances, a special entrance or mud room, frequent cleaning of entrance areas, or having shoes or clothing changed near the entrance.

Use of mats at the entrance was the action most frequently taken by over four-fifths of the wives. Almost two-thirds, however, cleaned entrance areas frequently; three-fifths had shoes, work, or play clothes changed near the entrance;

and half had special entrances or mud rooms.

Special entrances and mud rooms were related to the number of children, and their use increased from 40% of one-child families to 68% of families with five or more children. Entrance areas were cleaned more frequently when there were two or more children in the family and most frequently (by 74%) when there were five or more children. The practice of changing shoes or outdoor clothing near the entrance increased with number of children to more than 70% of families doing so if there were four or more children.

In families without children, the use of any of these features was somewhat related to age of homemaker. Older wives more than younger ones had mats at the entrance, used special entrances, or cleaned entryways frequently. On the other hand, having shoes or outdoor clothing changed near the entrance declined as age of wives increased, from 64% of families with a wife under 25, to 29% of those in which the wives were 55 or older.

Availability and Use of Cleaning Equipment and Services (Table 6.15)

Practically all of the families in the sample had vacuum cleaners (96%) (Table 6.15). About the only variations from this were in families without children, in which a somewhat smaller proportion of the youngest wives (88%) than wives of other age groups had a vacuum cleaner. Over half of the sample (54%) also owned either a carpet sweeper or an electric broom (equipment used for light pickup cleaning). Ownership of this equipment was somewhat higher among families with children than among families with no children. Among families at different socioeconomic levels, the lowest ownership of carpet sweepers or electric brooms (45%) was at the lowest level.

Use of Cleaning Equipment on Record Days and the Previous 7 Days (Table 6.15). Vacuum cleaners had been used by less than half the households on the record days (45%) and were used less in employed-wife households (39%) than in those where the wives were not employed (47%). Nearly all (91%) of the households had used a vacuum cleaner on at least 1 day during the previous 7. The most common frequency was on 2 or 3 days (two-fifths); about one-fifth of families had used a vacuum cleaner on 5 or more days. The average number of days on which a vacuum cleaner had been used was 3.0. Vacuum cleaners had been used on fewer days in households in which the wives were employed than in those where they were not, averages of 2.7 and 3.1 days, respectively.

The frequency of using a vacuum cleaner was related fairly closely to the number of children. Families with no children used a vacuum cleaner on an average of 2.2 days during the previous 7, while families with five to nine children had used one on an average of 4 days.

Carpet sweepers or electric brooms were used on an average of about 1.5 days during the previous 7. Only 7% of the families had used a rug shampooer or floor scrubber at least once in the previous 7 days, and only 8% had used a floor polisher.

Use of Paid Help and Commercial Services for Cleaning (Table 6.16). A substantial number of families (78%) reported not using paid help for regular house care; and only on 26 days (1% of the record days) had paid help been used. On the record days, a slightly higher proportion of employed-wife households had used paid help with cleaning (3%) than those with nonemployed wives (1%).

Only 5% of all families reported having used paid help with cleaning during the previous 7 days. More employed-wife (9%) than nonemployed-wife (4%) households had used these services.

A slightly higher proportion of the households of employed wives (26%) versus those of the nonemployed (21%) reported that they sometimes used paid help with regular house cleaning. The average time spent on this work by paid help on the record days in those households that had used such help was 5 hours when the wives were not employed and 4.8 hours when they were. Employed-wife households used paid help on somewhat more days during the previous 7 than nonemployed-wife households (an average of 1.8, compared with an average of 1.3 days).

The use of commercial cleaning services by sample families for special house care was too low to have had much effect on overall time. Only 2% of the families had used such services or rented cleaning equipment during the previous 7 days, and, for the most part, this use had been on 1 day only.

Regular House Care

Regular house care consists of two kinds of work, cleaning the house and keeping the house in order. Each of these types has different characteristics. Amounts of daily time spent on regular house care may vary among typical households from less than an hour to several hours. Most studies, and the Purdue project in particular (Manning, 1968, p. 22), have found a number of factors related to time spent and work accomplished in regular house care, with no one factor predominant. In fact, no general activity area of time-consuming household work has been more difficult to measure in relation to time use than regular house care, a result of the extensive variability in amounts of work undertaken and amounts of time spent in any one period.

Number of Rooms (Including Bathrooms) Given Care (Tables 6.17 and 6.18). Practically all of the households had done some regular house care work on the record days (less than 1% reported not having performed such work in any rooms); over half had cared for from five to seven rooms, including bathrooms (Table 6.17).

The typical number of rooms (including bathrooms) cared for on the record days in nonemployed-wife households was from five to seven, and about one-fifth had given care to eight or more rooms. In employed-wife households, the typical number of rooms given care was also five to seven, but a higher proportion of this group (35%) than of nonemployed-wife households (21%) had given care to fewer than five rooms on the record days.

Less than one-fifth of the sample had cared for fewer than five rooms during the previous 7 days; almost half had cared for six or seven rooms (Table 6.18). The principal difference by employment status of wives was the lower proportion of employed-wife households in which care had been given to eight or more rooms (33% versus 40% of nonemployed-wife households).

The proportion of households giving care to eight or more rooms during the previous week increased with each additional child from 22% of families with no children to 66% of families with five to nine; fewer than five rooms were given care mostly by families with no children or only one or two. In families without children, the number of rooms given care in the previous 7 days increased with the age of wives. Households in which wives were under 25 usually cared for from two to five rooms in contrast to those with wives over age 40, three-quarters of which had cared for at least six rooms. The proportion of families caring for six or seven rooms in the previous 7 days increased, and the proportion caring for more than 7 rooms declined with socioeconomic level. Families living in two-family houses had typically cared for six or seven rooms in the previous week; those in one-family houses tended to have cared for eight or more.

It was clear that the number of rooms given care was largely a matter of intensity of use brought about by variations in family size and composition. This relationship is in line with the earlier research of Walker (1955), Hook (1963), and Wiegand (1954), all of which showed some relationship between family composition and number of rooms given care.

Frequency of General Cleaning (Table 6.18). In order to distinguish regular cleaning from daily pickup operations, the term "general cleaning" was used. This term included the regular routine cleaning tasks performed at some regular interval such as once or twice a week or month.

For the most part, families in the sample tended to do routine house cleaning more frequently than weekly; the average number of days on which general cleaning work was performed was 4.1. This average was a little lower when wives were employed (3.7 days, or half a day less than in nonemployed-wife households).

The frequency of cleaning was not related to the number of children nor, in families without children, to age of wives. However, among families with no children the youngest group of wives tended to do general cleaning work frequently (on an average of 3.6 days, compared with averages of 3 days or less among families with older wives). Among different socioeconomic levels, general cleaning work was performed on fewer days by families at the highest level. Apartments, two-family, and one-family houses were given general cleaning on about the same average number of days in the previous 7 (4.1). Mobile homes received general cleaning more frequently than other types of houses (an average of 5.1 days).

Special House Care

The only household work activity performed less frequently than special house care was special food preparation. The average daily time used on special house care, however, was high enough to classify it as one of the more time-consuming activities (an average of .7 hour a day whether or not the wives were employed) (Table 6.4). The range of time spent varied from an average of less than 3 minutes to over an hour a day. These variations were not related to family composition but rather reflected the fact that certain families had scheduled different kinds of special house care work on the record days. The average time per day spent by the families that reported some major work in special house care was 1.4 hours a day, or

about twice as much time as the average for the entire sample.

Three categories of special house care were analyzed: special house cleaning, house maintenance, and making household furnishings. Most of the house maintenance work was done by the families themselves, although somewhat more did use hired help for this activity than for other household work. Of the total sample, 16% reported using hired help with house maintenance work at some time during the previous 12 months.

Responsibility for House Maintenance (Table 6.19). Of the families in the sample, four-fifths were responsible for maintenance of house and equipment. Responsibility for maintenance increased among the types of families likely to be living in units other than apartments. This responsibility was, for example, related to the number of children; it increased from 61% of families with no children to 94% of families with five or more. In families without children, much higher proportions of households with wives over age 40 than those with younger wives had house maintenance responsibility.

Frequency of Special House Care (Table 6.18). In the total sample, 759 families (59%) reported spending some time on one or more kinds of special house care work on the record days. Of the three groups, special house cleaning was performed on the record days more often than house maintenance, while making household furnishings was a minor activity for most of the families. The order of importance was the same whether or not the wives were employed, but employed-wife households had performed all of these activities less frequently than nonemployed-wife households, particularly house maintenance and special house care.

During the previous week, special house cleaning had likewise been performed a little more frequently than house maintenance, and both of these activities were much more frequent than making household furnishings. About two-thirds of the families had done some type of special house cleaning during the previous 7 days; about half had done house maintenance work, and 13% had made household furnishings. The average number of days in the previous week on which each of these groups of activities was performed were, respectively, 1.2, 1.0, and .3.

The frequency of doing special house cleaning and house maintenance was somewhat related to the number of children, in that the average number of days increased slightly between families with no children or one child and families with five or more. The lower frequency of interior house maintenance in the smallest families may also reflect differences in types of houses lived in.

In no-children households, house maintenance and making household furnishings were done more often as wives were older. Making household furnishings was most frequent at the highest socioeconomic level (an average of .4 day in the previous 7). Each group of activities was performed less frequently when the wives were employed.

Care of Yard and Car Combined

The work in yard and car care has many of the same characteristics as the work in special house care, particularly with respect to variability in amounts of time used at any one work period and frequency of the work. Unlike special house care, yard and car care rated low in both average time used and frequency (Table 3.8). The average daily time spent on this activity was .6 hour a day in nonemployed-wife households and .4 hour a day in employed-wife households. In both cases, the time spent represented 5% of all household work time (the same as the average time use on the more regularly performed activity of washing by machine but less than the average time used on special house care). In the total sample 80% reported spending some time on record days on work related to yard or car care, or both.

In order to have specific information on the content of work in yard care, data were collected separately on five categories of outside house work: care of drives and/or walks, care of lawns, care of shrubs and trees, care of flower beds or gardens, and care of vegetable gardens.

Responsibility for Care of Grounds (Table 6.19). Four-fifths or more of respondents were responsible for some type of yard care. Care of drives, walks, and lawns, the most frequently named responsibilities, was the responsibility of almost nine-tenths of the sample. Care of vegetable gardens was the least frequently named responsibility (one-third of the families). When the wives were employed, the proportions reporting each kind of responsibility were a little less than when the wives were not employed; the highest difference was for care of vegetable gardens (29% compared with 35%).

Responsibility for care of the grounds around the house was related to the number of children and increased consistently as number of children increased. The highest proportion of families

responsible for care of vegetable gardens were the largest families (48%) and the lowest proportion were those without children or with only one child (25% and 27%, respectively).

In families without children, many more were responsible for care of driveways and grounds when the wives were age 40 or older than were families with younger wives.

Size of House Lots (Table 6.20). One gross measure of the amount of maintenance work in yard care is the size of the house lot. Of the total number of families responsible for some kind of outside work, the highest proportions, 34% and 23%, respectively, had small (from 6,000 to 10,000 sq. ft.) or medium-size (10,000 to 20,000 sq. ft.) lots.

The proportion of families living in houses on small or medium-size lots tended to increase with the number of children in the family, but the number of children was not related to having very small or large lots. Number of children did have an effect on whether or not families had house lots for which they had care responsibility; the proportion having such responsibility increased with advancing number of children to 100% for families with five or more. In families without children, a substantially higher proportion of households with wives over age 40 than of those with younger wives were responsible for care of house lots.

Availability and Use of Equipment and Services for Care of Yard (Table 6.21). No attempt was made to investigate the use of the numerous items of equipment used in outdoor household work, except for power lawnmowers, which have become fairly standard equipment in homes, and snowblowers or snowplows. Since the use of such equipment is seasonal, it was asked whether or not each of these items was used over the previous 12 months.

As might be expected, the use of power lawnmowers was much more general than the use of power snow removal equipment (Table 6.21). Over seven-tenths of the entire sample had used a power lawnmower in the previous year, while only one-fifth had used a snowblower or snowplow. There was no difference between nonemployed- and employed-wife households in the proportion using a power lawnmower, but more employed-wife households (24%) had used snow-removal equipment than had nonemployed-wife households (19%).

As with special house care work, most of the subtasks in yard care were done by the family members. The activity for which the highest proportion (18%) had sometimes hired help was snow removal. Only 12% had paid help for lawn mowing and only 10% for yard and garden care. Employed-wife households used hired help for snow removal somewhat less (14%) than non-employed-wife households (19%); the proportions hiring help for the other two activities were similar in both types of households. Hired help for one or more kinds of yard care was used most by families with no children and least by families with four or more. In families without children, hired help was used most by households in which the wives were age 40 or older. Families in the three highest socio-economic levels used hired help on each kind of work more often than those in the two lower ones.

Frequency of Yard and Car Care Activities (Tables 6.18 and 6.22). Families had put garbage and refuse out for collection on 49% of the record days (Table 6.22). Cars and walks or driveways were each cared for by about 14% of the families; care of grounds received a little more attention (by 18% of the sample). The only differences between nonemployed- and employed-wife households for these activities were the smaller proportions that had cared for walks and grounds when wives were employed.

Walks, driveways, and cars were each given care on at least 1 day out of the previous 7 by a much higher proportion of families (almost three-fifths) than cared for lawns and gardens (a little less than half) (Table 6.18).

Families took care of walks and driveways an average of 1.2 days in the previous 7; this was a little less frequent when wives were employed, .9 day. Frequency of such care was related to age of wives in families without children, and the difference between families with younger and older wives was substantial (an increase from .2 day when wives were under 25 to 1.7 days when they were 55 and older). Care of walks and driveways was also related to socioeconomic level, with families at the lowest level doing such work more frequently than others (on an average of 1.4 days).

Although a smaller proportion of families had done some care of the grounds in the previous 7 days than had cared for walks or driveways, they did this work on about the same average number of days, 1.1, with a similar decline (to .9 day) when wives were employed. There was some relationship between frequency of this work and number of children, in that the work was done more frequently in larger than in smaller families. In families without children, the frequency was related to age of wives, with a substantial difference between families with the youngest and

oldest wives. Care of grounds was not closely related to socioeconomic level.

Use and Care of Family Cars
(Tables 6.23 and 6.24)

Like most other American families, households in the sample used the automobile as the primary means of transportation. Only 1% of the sample had not used at least one automobile, and over one-third used more than one regularly (Table 6.24). In employed-wife households, 45% used more than one automobile regularly. Among families with children, the proportion using more than one car increased from 32% of one-child families to 42% of those with five or more children. Families without children with wives in the oldest age groups and those in the lower socio-economic levels were somewhat less likely than other families to use more than one automobile regularly.

Over 80% of wives in the sample were drivers. Those who did not drive were mostly wives in the oldest age group (33%) or at the lowest socio-economic level (38%). Families typically had two drivers, but the proportion with three or more drivers was over 10% in employed-wife households and 5% in nonemployed-wife ones.

Four categories of car care were set up for the analysis: washing car at home, taking car to car wash, waxing car, and servicing car at home. A high proportion of families performed some kind of work related to car care; the most common was taking a car to a car wash (80%) or washing a car at home (74%) (Table 6.23). About seven-tenths (69%) of the families did the more time-consuming job of sometimes waxing their own car and almost half of them did some car servicing themselves (46%).

Car washing, either at home or at a car wash, was most likely to be performed at some kind of regular interval, either weekly, semimonthly, or monthly, though for over a third of the families it was an occasional activity. The other two types of care were occasional rather than regular ones, though waxing the car was performed annually by one-quarter of the families.

The proportion of families washing the car at home tended to increase and the proportion using a commercial car wash tended to decline as the number of children increased. Waxing the car at home declined a little between one-child families and those with five or more. In families without children, those with wives under age 40 waxed and serviced cars at home more than did families in which wives were over age 40. Servicing the car at home also was done by more families at the two lowest socioeconomic levels than by those at higher levels.

Transportation Used on the Record Days and in the Previous 7 Days (Tables 6.24 and 6.25). Although the amount of use of an automobile would not necessarily be related to the amount of care given it by family members, the extent of such use provides some background information on the importance of car care to families.

The importance of the private automobile in family transportation patterns in the sample can be seen from its extensive use and the general lack of use of other available methods of transportation. Of all families, 96% had used the family car on the record days, compared with about 25% that had used a bus, 6% that had used a carpool, and 1% that had used a taxi (Table 6.24). Though the use of the bus increased when wives were employed, children were about the only family members who used this type of transportation (22% for all families; 34% of families with school-age children).

The principal uses of the automobile on the record days were by parents and children or husbands and wives together or by husbands alone. When wives were employed, use of the automobile by husbands alone declined and use by husband and wife together increased, while other types of use remained unchanged. Some of this use was for transportation to the place of employment, since the automobile provided most of such transportation for both husbands (89%) and wives (20%). Automobiles also were used by 3% of the families to transport helpers from outside the household, usually by the husband or wife alone. Use of the family car was not reported as transportation by children in the sample unless at least one parent was with them; families in the sample had no children over 18 living at home.

Only 1% of the families had not used a family automobile during the previous 7 days (Table 6.25). Use of the family cars during this period was not related to number of children or age of wives, and varied only slightly by socioeconomic level.

Buses were used by someone in almost half the total group in the previous 7 days and by someone in over half of the employed-wife households. The use of a bus was directly related to number of children and increased from 19% of families with no children and 30% of those with one child to 69% of those with five or more children. The increased use of buses was mostly by children; the proportion of children using a bus increased from 23% in one-child families to 60% of families with four or more children. Buses were used somewhat more frequently by families with no children when wives were over age 40 than by those with younger wives and by children in more families at the three lowest socioeconomic levels than by those in families at the higher levels.

Carpools were used more frequently over the previous 7 days by larger families than by smaller ones, and in the larger families they were used mostly by children or husbands. Use of carpools increased between the highest and lowest socioeconomic levels; at the higher levels they were used more by children and at the lower levels more by husbands.

Travel Time (Table 6.26)

Travel time was considered part of the primary time used for a work activity, but it was recorded separately from the time used to perform the work. Averages of travel time and of primary time for each household work activity were computed separately, then combined for the particular activities.

An average of about 2 hours was spent on daily travel for household or other work by all workers in the household. The largest proportion of this time, 1.3 hours, was for travel to and from employment or other obligatory activities. Husbands spent an average of .8 hour a day on travel, most of which (.6 hour) was for daily travel to and from work. Wives spent about half as much time (.4 hour) as husbands for daily travel; most of wives' travel time was in connection with household work (.3 hour).

The average daily time spent on travel in connection with household work was .6 hour. Among the household work activities, the highest amount of travel time (an average of .4 hour a day by all workers) was used in connection with marketing.

No travel time was reported in connection with food preparation activities, and travel time was only a negligible part of total time or wives' or husbands' time spent on work related to clothing care or house care. Although chauffeuring family members is part of family care, when time spent on travel for this purpose was averaged for the entire sample, it was .2 hour per day by all workers and .1 hour each by wives and husbands.

Wives and husbands tended to spend about the same amount of time on travel for household work (.3 and .2 hour, respectively). The only household work area in which wives spent more time for travel than husbands was for marketing (.2 hour compared with .1 hour for husbands).

Undesirability of Combining Yard Care with Car Care in Analysis of Output

There was some relationship between certain family characteristics and the kinds of work done in both yard care and car care, but there were some differences in the characteristics of families that more often performed the two kinds of work. For example, the families more likely to do the more time-consuming car care work (waxing and servicing) themselves were those with younger wives, smaller families, and lower socioeconomic status. The families who had the largest house lots and were responsible for some or all kinds of care of grounds, on the other hand, were those with more children, older wives, and higher socioeconomic status. Therefore, it seems inappropriate to continue this combined classification in future measurement of household production. Although it had correctly been assumed that these two activities would be more likely than others to be done by husbands, the disadvantage of association of work frequency with different variables negates the choice of combining them.

TABLE 6.1—Rank and partial rank correlation coefficients for house care time of all workers and major variables
(1,260 husband–wife households, Syracuse, N.Y., 1967-68)

Total time of all workers in:	Kendall Tau[a]	Partial rank correlations[b] with major variables held constant					
		Number of children	Age of youngest child	Family type	Empl. of wives	House type	Location of residence
ALL HOUSE CARE ACTIVITIES							
Family composition variables							
Number of children	.20		.20		.19	.17	
Age of youngest child	-.15	-.15			-.18	-.11	
Age of oldest child	-.17						
Family type	.16				.14	.14	
Employment							
Wives	-.11	-.08	-.15	-.08			
Socioeconomic level							
Wives' education	.04**						
Husbands' education	.08						
Housing							
House type	.18	.15	.15	.16			.17
Location of residence	.05*						
REGULAR HOUSE CARE							
Family composition variables							
Number of children	.26		.26		.25	.24	
Age of youngest child	-.10	-.11			-.13	-.08	
Age of oldest child	-.16						
Family type	.22				.21	.20	
Employment							
Wives	-.08	-.04	-.11	-.04			
Husbands' hours	.09						
Socioeconomic level							
Wives' education	.06						
Husbands' education	.13						
Housing							
House type	.12	.07	.10	.08			.12

SPECIAL HOUSE CARE

Family composition variables

Number of children	.05*				
Age of oldest child	-.04+				
Family type	.05**				
Employment					
Wives	-.09	-.08		-.10	-.08
Housing					
House type	.09	.08	.09	.09	.08
Location of residence	.04+				

YARD AND CAR CARE

Family composition variables

Number of children	.08	.08	.08	.06	
Age of youngest child	-.12	-.12	-.13	-.09	
Age of oldest child	-.09				
Family type	.06		.05	.04	
Employment					
Wives	-.05*				
Socioeconomic level					
Husbands' education	.03+				
	.05*				
Housing					
House type	.13	.12		.11	
Location of residence	.08		.13	.04	.11

[a] All Tau values reported were significant at the .001 level unless otherwise indicated as: * = .005, ** = .01 or .02, and + = .03 to .05. For discussion of effects of ranking of variables on positive and negative values, see pp. 30-31. Correlation coefficients were based on 1,260 households except for age of youngest child, for which only families with children were used (1,092).

[b] Partial rank correlation values are reported only for major variables at the .001 level of significance.

TABLE 6.2—Rank and partial rank correlation coefficients for house care time of wives and major variables
(1,260 husband–wife households, Syracuse, N.Y., 1967-68)

Total time of wives in:	Kendall Tau[a]	Partial rank correlations[b] with major variables held constant			
		Number of children	Age of youngest child	Family type	Empl. of wives
ALL HOUSE CARE ACTIVITIES					
Family composition variables					
Number of children	.11		.11		.08
Family type	.10				.07
Employment					
Wives	-.18	-.17	-.18	-.17	
Husbands' hours	.06				
Education					
Wives	.10				
Husbands	-.04				
REGULAR HOUSE CARE					
Family composition variables					
Number of children	.16		.16		.14
Family type	.15				.13
Employment					
Wives	-.16	-.13	-.16	-.13	
Husbands' hours	.07				
Education					
Wives	.15				
Husbands	.08				

SPECIAL HOUSE CARE

Employment						
Wives	-.12	-.12	-.12	-.12		
Education						
Husbands	-.04†				-.07	.05

YARD AND CAR CARE

Family composition variables						
Number of children	.07		.07			
Age of youngest child	-.09	-.09				
Family type	.05**					
Employment						
Wives	-.11	-.10	-.09	-.10		
Husbands' hours	.04**					

[a] All Tau values reported were significant at the .001 level unless otherwise indicated as: * = .005, ** = .01 or .02, and † = .03 to .05. For discussion of effects of ranking of variables on positive and negative values, see pp. 30-31. Correlation coefficients were based on 1,260 households except for age of youngest child, for which only families with children were used (1,092)

[b] Partial rank correlation values are reported only for major variables at the .001 level of significance.

TABLE 6.3—Rank and partial rank correlation coefficients for house care time of husbands (*1,260 husband–wife households, Syracuse, N.Y., 1967-68*)

Time in:	Kendall Tau[a]	Husbands' time[c] Partial rank correlations[b] with major variables held constant			
		Number of children	Age of youngest child	Family type	Empl. of wives
ALL HOUSE CARE					
Family composition variables					
Number of children					
Age of youngest child					
Family type					
Employment					
Husbands' hours	-.10				
REGULAR HOUSE CARE					
Family composition variables					
Number of children	-.06		-.06		-.04
Age of youngest child	.04+				
Family type	-.05*				-.03
Employment					
Wives	.12	.11	.11	.11	
Husbands' hours	-.08				
Education					
Wives	-.04+				
Husbands	-.04+				
SPECIAL HOUSE CARE					
Family composition variables					
Number of children	.06*		.06		.05
Family type	.05*				.05
Employment					
Wives	-.04+				
Husbands' hours	-.04+				
YARD AND CAR CARE					
Family composition variables					
Number of children	-.04+				
Age of youngest child					
Family type	-.04+				
Employment					
Wives					
Husbands' hours	-.09				
Education					
Husbands	.04**				

[a]All Tau values reported were significant at the .001 level unless otherwise indicated as * = .005, ** = .01 or .02, and + = .03 to .05. For discussion of effects of ranking of variables on positive and negative values, see pp. 30-31.

[b]Partial rank correlation values are reported only for major variables at the .001 level of significance.

[c]Correlation coefficients were based on 1,260 households except for age of youngest child, for which only families with children were used (1,092).

[d]Tau values computed on basis of 378 families with teenagers.

and teenagers and major variables

| Kendall Tau[a] | Teenagers' time[d] | | | |
| | Partial rank correlations[b] with major variables held constant | | | |
	Number of children	Age of youngest child	Family type	Empl. of wives
.12		.12		.12
-.08≠				
-.07≠				
.15		.15		.17
-.07≠				
.10*				.12
.11	.14	.13	.13	
.09**				
.07≠				
-.06≠				
-.08**				
-.09*				

TABLE 6.4—House care time of all workers and individual workers, by number of children
(1,296 husband-wife households, Syracuse, N.Y., 1967-68)

Activity	Number of children	Total number of families NE[a]	E	All workers (Total)[b] NE	E	Wives NE	E	Husbands NE	E	Other workers Females NE	E	Males NE	E
								Average hours per day[c]					
All house care	0	97	71	2.2	1.4	1.5	.9	.6	.4	.1			
	1	149	61	2.3	2.0	1.5	1.3	.6	.5		.1	.1	
	2	295	83	2.5	2.4	1.7	1.1	.6	.8			.1	.1
	3	233	61	2.9	3.2	1.7	1.4	.6	.7	.1	.1	.1	
	4	139	30	2.8	2.7	1.7	1.3	.6	.7		.2		
	5-6	47	9	3.9	3.0	1.7	1.1	.7	.8			.1	
	7-9	19	2	4.2		1.5		.6					
	Average	979	317	2.7	2.3	1.6	1.2	.6	.6		.1	.1	
Regular house care	0			1.0	.7	.9	.6		.1				
	1			1.1	1.1	1.0	.9		.1				
	2			1.3	1.2	1.2	.9		.1				
	3			1.5	1.8	1.2	1.1						
	4			1.6	1.6	1.3	.9				.1		
	5-6			2.2	1.8	1.2	1.0						
	7-9			2.9		1.2							
	Average			1.4	1.2	1.1	.9		.1				
Special house care	0			.8	.4	.5	.3	.3	.1				
	1			.7	.5	.3	.3	.3	.2			.1	
	2			.7	.7	.3	.1	.3	.4				.1
	3			.8	.8	.3	.2	.3	.4				
	4			.7	1.0	.2	.3	.3	.6				
	5-6			.9	.8	.3	.1	.4	.7			.1	
	7-9			.7		.2		.3					
	Average			.7	.7	.3	.2	.3	.3				
Yard and car care	0			.4	.3	.1	.1	.3	.2				
	1			.5	.4	.1	.1	.3	.2				
	2			.6	.4	.2	.1	.3	.3				
	3			.6	.5	.2	.1	.3	.3				
	4			.6	.2	.2	.1	.3	.1				
	5-6			.7	.4	.2		.3	.1				
	7-9			.5				.2					
	Average			.6	.4	.1	.1	.3	.2				

[a]NE and E indicate households with nonemployed or employed wives.

[b]Sum of average time for individual workers may not equal total time of all workers because of rounding and because averages of children's time include only households with children of specified ages.

[c]Time is reported only if there were three or more families and if average time was 3 minutes or more.

and employment of wives

Number of households with children 12-17 years NE E		Time of children 12-17 NE E		Number of households with children 6-11 years NE E		Time of children 6-11 NE E	
		Av. hrs. per day[C]				Av. hrs. per day[C]	
22	20	.6	.3	23	19	.2	.1
82	44	.4	.5	128	40	.3	.3
91	35	.6	1.0	156	38	.5	.6
43	19	.7	.7	91	18	.5	.3
31	6	1.0	1.0	46	8	.6	.5
18	2	.9		19	2	1.3	
287	126	.6	.6	463	125	.4	.4
		.2	.1			.2	.1
		.2	.3			.1	.2
		.2	.7			.2	.4
		.3	.5			.3	.3
		.7	.9			.5	.2
		.6				1.0	
		.3	.4			.2	.3
			.1			.1	
		.1	.1				.1
		.1	.2			.1	.1
		.3	.1				
		.1					
		.1				.1	
		.1	.1				
		.4	.1				
		.2	.1			.1	.1
		.2	.1			.2	.1
		.2				.1	.1
		.2	.1			.1	.3
		.1	.2			.2	.1
		.2	.1			.2	.1

TABLE 6.5—House care time of all workers and individual workers, by age of the youngest
(1,128 husband-wife households, Syracuse, N.Y., 1967-68)

Activity	Age of youngest child (years)	Number of families NE[a]	E	All workers (Total)[b] NE	E	Wives NE	E	Husbands NE	E	Other workers Females NE	E	Males NE	E
								Average hours per day[c]					
All house care	12-17	80	61	3.3	2.4	1.9	.8	.6	.6	.1	.1		
	6-11	210	86	3.3	2.7	1.7	1.4	.7	.5			.1	
	2-5	248	63	2.8	2.5	1.6	1.4	.6	.7		.1	.1	.1
	1	163	20	2.4	2.7	1.6	1.3	.6	1.1				
	Under 1	181	16	2.1	2.4	1.4	1.1	.4	1.0				
	Average	882	246	2.8	2.6	1.6	1.2	.6	.7		.1	.1	
Regular house care	12-17			1.6	1.3	1.3	.6			.1	.1		
	6-11			1.7	1.6	1.2	1.1						
	2-5			1.4	1.3	1.2	1.1		.1				
	1			1.3	1.2	1.2	.9		.1				
	Under 1			1.2	1.4	1.1	1.0		.1				
	Average			1.4	1.4	1.2	.9						
Special house care	12-17			.7	.6	.3	.2	.3	.3			.1	
	6-11			.9	.7	.3	.2	.4	.3			.1	.1
	2-5			.8	.8	.3	.2	.3	.4			.1	.1
	1			.6	1.0	.3	.3	.3	.7				
	Under 1			.5	.7	.3		.2	.7				
	Average			.7	.7	.3	.2	.3	.4			.1	
Yard and car care	12-17			1.0	.5	.3	.1	.4	.3				
	6-11			.7	.4	.2	.1	.3	.2				
	2-5			.5	.4	.2	.1	.3	.2				
	1			.5	.4	.1		.3	.3				
	Under 1			.3	.3	.1		.2	.2				
	Average			.6	.4	.1	.1	.3	.2				

[a]NE and E indicate households with nonemployed or employed wives.

[b]Sum of average time for individual workers may not equal total time of all workers because of rounding and because averages of children's time include only households with children of specified ages.

[c]Time is reported only if there were three or more families and if average time was 3 minutes or more.

child and employment of wives

Number of households with children 12-17 years		Time of children 12-17		Number of households with children 6-11 years		Time of children 6-11	
NE	E	NE	E	NE	E	NE	E
		Av. hrs. per day[c]				Av. hrs. per day[c]	
80	61	.7	.8				
87	41	.7	.5	210	86	.5	.5
85	17	.5	.5	133	24	.4	.2
20	5	.5	.3	77	9	.3	.4
15	2	1.0		43	6	.6	.4
287	126	.6	.6	463	125	.4	.4
		.3	.5				
		.4	.3			.3	.3
		.2	.2			.2	.1
		.2	.2			.1	.4
		.5	1.6			.3	.3
		.3	.4			.2	.3
		.1	.1				
		?	]			.1	.1
		.1	.2				
		.1					
		.3				.1	
		.1	.1				
		.3	.1				
		.1				.2	.1
		.2				.1	
		.2	.1			.1	
		.2	.2			.2	.1
		.2	.1			.1	.1

TABLE 6.6—House care time of all workers, wives, husbands
(1,296 husband–wife households, Syracuse, N.Y.

	Number		All house care		Reg. house care		Special house care		Yard and car care	
Family type	NE[a]	E	NE	E	NE	E	NE	E	NE	E
	Average hours per day[c]									
No-child households by age of wives										
under 25	16	26	1.8	1.1	1.0	.6	.5	.2	.4	.3
25-39	19	23	2.2	1.7	1.0	.9	.7	.5	.6	.3
40-54	30	12	2.2	1.4	1.0	.5	.9	.8	.3	.2
55 and over	32	10	2.4	1.2	1.0	.8	1.1	.4	.3	.1
Number of children by age of youngest child										
1 child										
12-17 years	22	20	4.1	2.2	1.6	1.0	1.3	.6	1.1	.6
6-11	23	19	2.4	2.3	1.3	1.5	.8	.6	.3	.3
2-5	26	16	2.6	1.7	1.0	1.0	.8	.5	.6	.2
1	37	5	2.0	1.2	1.0	.8	.5	.2	.5	.3
under 1	41	1	1.5		.9		.5		.1	
2 children										
12-17 years	27	15	3.6	2.1	1.7	1.2	.8	.3	1.1	.6
6-11	60	24	3.1	2.4	1.4	1.2	.7	.8	.9	.5
2-5	93	28	2.4	2.3	1.3	1.2	.8	.8	.4	.3
1	50	9	2.6	3.7	1.3	1.3	.7	1.8	.6	.6
under 1	65	7	1.7	1.6	1.0	1.2	.4	.1	.3	.2
3 children										
12-17 years	26	16	2.7	2.5	1.5	1.5	.4	.7	.8	.4
6-11	58	26	3.6	3.5	1.6	2.2	1.1	.8	.8	.5
2-5	70	13	3.0	3.7	1.6	1.6	.8	1.3	.7	.8
1	48	2	2.2		1.3		.5		.5	
under 1	31	4	2.7	1.5	1.3	1.2	.8	.1	.6	.1
4 children										
12-17 years	5	9	1.8	3.0	1.2	1.4	.2	1.3	.4	.3
6-11	51	15	3.3	2.5	1.8	1.6	.8	.7	.7	.2
2-5	32	1	2.5		1.4		.7		.4	
1	19	3	3.1	1.9	1.5	1.3	.9	.6	.7	
under 1	32	2	2.4		1.4		.5		.5	
5-6 children										
12-17 years	0	1								
6-11	16	2	4.8		2.9		1.1		.8	
2-5	17	3	3.5	1.9	1.8	1.3	.8	.2	.9	.4
1	6	1	2.4		1.3		.8		.3	
under 1	8	2	3.7		2.5		.9		.3	
7-9 children										
6-11 years	2	0								
2-5	10	2	3.5		2.6		.3		.5	
1	3	0	4.9		3.1		1.2		.6	
under 1	4	0	4.4		2.9		1.2		.3	

[a]NE and E indicate households with nonemployed or employed wives.

[b]Sum of average time for individual workers may not equal total time of all workers because of rounding and because averages of children's time include only households with children of specified ages.

[c]Time is reported only if there were three or more families and if average time was over 3 minutes.

and other workers, by family type and employment of wives
1967-68)

	Wives' time								Husbands' time								Other workers' time			
	All house care		Reg.house care		Special house care		Yard and car care		All house care		Reg. house care		Special house care		Yard and car care		All house care			
																	Females		Males	
	NE	E	NE	E	NE	E	NE	E	NE	E	NE	E	NE	E	NE	E	NE	E	NE	E
							Average hours per day^c													
	1.3	.7	.9	.5	.4	.1		.1	.4	.4			.1		.1	.4	.2				
	1.8	1.1	1.0	.8	.6	.3	.3		.4	.6		.1	.2	.2	.3	.3					
	1.5	1.1	1.0	.4	.4	.6	.2	.1	.7	.3			.5	.2	.1	.1					
	1.4	1.0	.8	.7	.6	.2			.8	.1	.1		.4	.1	.3	.1	.2			.1	
	2.2	1.0	1.3	.6	.5	.2	.3	.1	1.1	.7		.1	.7	.3	.4	.4	.1	.2	.1		
	1.6	1.8	1.2	1.3	.4	.5	.1	.1	.6	.3			.4	.1	.2	.2		.1			
	1.4	1.2	1.0	.9	.2	.2	.1	.1	.9	.5		.1	.4	.3	.5	.1			.3		
	1.3	1.0	1.0	.8	.2	.2	.1	.1	.7	.2			.2		.4	.2					
	1.2		.9		.3				.2		.1		.1		.1						
	2.1	.8	1.4	.7	.4	.1	.3	.1	.7	.4			.1	.1	.6	.2	.2				
	1.6	1.1	1.1	.8	.3	.2	.2	.1	.7	.7		.1	.3	.3	.4	.3	.1		.1	.2	
	1.7	1.2	1.2	1.0	.4	.1	.1	.1	.6	.8			.3	.5	.2	.2			.1	.1	
	1.8	1.2	1.3	.8	.4	.4	.1		.7	2.0		.1	.3	1.4	.4	.5		.1	.1		
	1.3	1.2	1.0	1.2	.2		.1		.4	.4			.2	.1	.2	.2					
	1.5	.6	1.2	.4	.2	.1	.1		.3	.8			.1	.5	.2	.3		.1			
	1.8	1.5	1.2	1.3	.4	.2	.2	.1	.8	.7			.4	.4	.3	.2	.1		.1		
	1.7	2.2	1.3	1.5	.3	.5	.2	.2	.6	1.1			.3	.5	.3	.5	.1	.2	.1		
	1.5		1.2		.3		.1		.5				.3		.2						
	1.8	.7	1.2	.8	.4		.2		.5	.2		.1	.3	.1	.2				.1		
	1.1	1.1	.9	.5		.5	.2	.1	.1	.6				.5	.1	.2		.1	.1		
	1.9	1.4	1.3	1.1	.3	.2	.3	.1	.6	.5		.1	.4	.4	.2			.2			
	1.7		1.3		.3		.1		.6				.4		.2						
	1.8	1.2	1.3	1.1	.4	.1	.1		.9	.5			.4	.5	.5						
	1.4		1.2		.1		.1		.5				.2		.3						
	1.8		1.3		.3		.2		1.0		.1		.7		.2				.1		
	1.6	.7	1.1	.7	.3		.2		.7	.5			.3	.2	.4	.3					
	1.1		.9		.1				.3				.1		.2		.3		.4		
	2.0		1.7		.2		.1		.7				.5		.2						
	1.3		1.2		.1				.5		.1		.2		.2						
	1.7		1.5		.3				.1						.1						
	1.8		1.2		.6				.8				.6		.1						

TABLE 6.7—House care time of children 12 to 17 and 6 to 11 years, by family type and
(413 husband-wife households with teenagers and 588 with children 6-11

| | Number | | All house care | | Reg. house care | | Special house care | | Yard and car care | |
Family type	NE[a]	E	NE	E	NE	E	NE	E	NE	E
					Average hours per day[b]					
Number of children by age of youngest child										
1 child										
12-17 years	22	20	.6	.3	.2	.1		.1	.4	.1
6-11										
2 children										
12-17 years	27	15	.6	.9	.2	.5	.1	.1	.3	.3
6-11	26	16	.3	.2	.1	.1	.1	.1	.1	
2-5	26	11	.3	.3	.2	.2	.1	.1	.1	
1	2	2								
under 1	1	0								
3 children										
12-17 years	26	16	.8	1.1	.3	.9	.1	.1	.4	.1
6-11	27	15	.6	.9	.3	.6	.2	.2	.1	.1
2-5	29	2	.5		.2		.2		.2	
1	6	1	.4		.1				.2	
under 1	3	1	.4		.3				.1	
4 children										
12-17 years	5	9	.6	1.2	.3	.9	.1	.3	.2	
6-11	20	8	.6	.2	.3	.2	.3			
2-5	9	1	.4		.2		.1		.1	
1	6	1	.6		.1		.1		.4	
under 1	3	0	2.8		1.1		1.1		.7	
5-6 children										
12-17 years	0	1								
6-11	12	2	1.6		1.2				.4	
2-5	11	1	.8		.3		.2		.2	
1	3	1	.3		.2		.1		.1	
under 1	5	1	.7		.4		.3			
7-9 children										
6-11	2	0								
2-5	10	2	.8		.6		.5		.1	
1	3	0	1.2		.6				.1	
under 1	3	0	.5		.5					

[a]NE and E indicate households with nonemployed or employed wives.

[b]Time is reported only if there were three or more families and if average time was 3 minutes or more.

employment of wives
years, Syracuse, N.Y., 1967-68)

Number		All house care		Reg. house care		Special house care		Yard and car care	
NE	E	NE	E	NE	E	NE	E	NE	E
				Average hours per day[b]					
23	19	.2	.1	.1	.1	.1			
60	24	.4	.4	.2	.2		.1	.2	.1
32	10	.1	.1		.1			.1	
23	5	.1	.5	.1	.5				
13	1	.1		.1					
58	26	.7	.8	.2	.6	.1	.1	.3	.1
53	9	.4	.1	.2	.1	.1		.1	.1
31	1	.2		.1				.1	
14	2	.4		.1				.3	
51	15	.6	.4	.4	.3			.2	.1
21	0	.2		.1				.1	
14	2	.3		.2		.1			
5	1	1.1		.5		.2		.5	
16	2	.7		.7				.1	
17	3	.6	.4	.4	.4			.2	.1
6	1	.2		.1		.1			
7	2	.8		.6		.1		.1	
2	0								
10	2	.9		.8				.1	
3	0	1.8		1.0		.4		.4	
4	0	1.5		1.4				.1	

TABLE 6.8—Regular house care time of all workers by type and age of house, number of children, and persons-per-room ratio
(1,296 husband–wife households, Syracuse, N.Y., 1967-68)

	Number	All types	Apartment	Mobile homes[a]	2-family	1-family
				Type of house		
				Average hours per day[b]		
N =	1,296	1,293[c]	165	7	146	975
Year house built						
1960 or later	302		.9	1.2	1.2	1.5
1940–1959	434		.9		1.1	1.4
1920–1939	242		.9		1.4	1.4
1900–1919	136		1.2		1.3	1.6
Before 1900	125		1.1		1.3	1.4
Don't know	57		.9		1.1	1.3
Number of children						
0	168		.7		1.0	.9
1	210		1.0		1.0	1.2
2	378		1.1		1.1	1.3
3	294		1.3		1.7	1.5
4	169		1.4		1.5	1.8
5 or more	77				1.4	2.8
Persons-per-room ratio (including bathrooms)						
.50 or less	564	1.1				
.51 – .75	517	1.5				
.76 – 1.00	189	1.7				
1.01 – 1.50	25	1.9				
1.51 or more	1					

[a]Time is reported only for age of house because of number of cases.

[b]Time is reported only if there were three or more families and if average time was 3 minutes or more.

[c]Three houses classed as "other" are not included.

TABLE 6.9—Size of dwelling, by selected variables
(1,296 husband-wife households, Syracuse, N.Y., 1967-68)

Households	Number	Number of rooms (without bathrooms)			Number of bathrooms		
		2–5	6–7	8 or more	1	1 1/2	2 or more
				Percent			
Total group	1,296	29	48	23	61	19	20
Nonemployed wives	979	28	48	24	59	20	21
Employed wives	317	32	51	17	66	19	15
Number of children							
0	168	53	33	14	66	18	16
1	210	40	45	15	70	17	12
2	378	32	51	17	65	18	17
3	294	17	55	28	54	23	24
4	169	19	50	31	53	21	27
5 or more	77	8	47	45	44	21	36
Age of wives in families without children							
Under 25	42	81	17	2	88	5	7
25–39	42	65	21	14	64	24	12
40–54	42	31	50	19	60	24	17
55 and over	42	36	43	21	52	21	26
Socioeconomic level							
Class 1 (highest)	163	18	39	43	38	29	34
Class 2	163	31	43	26	48	22	30
Class 3	402	26	48	26	55	22	24
Class 4	483	33	53	14	73	15	11
Class 5	85	42	50	8	85	9	6
Type of housing[a]							
Apartment	165	80	20	—			
Mobile home	7	86	14	—			
2-family	146	36	58	7			
1-family	975	19	52	29			

[a]Three houses classed as "other" are not included.

TABLE 6.10—Persons-per-room ratio, by location of residence
(1,296 husband-wife households, Syracuse, N.Y., 1967-68)

Persons-per-room (not including bathrooms)	Total group	City	Suburbs
	Percent		
.50 or less	26	27	26
.51 - .75	39	41	37
.76 - 1.00	28	27	29
1.01 - 1.50	6	5	7
1.51 or more	1	<1	1
Total	100	100	100

TABLE 6.11—Number of rooms not used in previous 7 days, by selected variables
(1,296 husband-wife households, Syracuse, N.Y., 1967-68)

Households	Number	Number of rooms not used			
		0	1	2	3 or more
		Percent			
Total group	1,296	84	10	4	2
Nonemployed wives	979	84	11	4	2
Employed wives	317	84	11	4	1
Number of children					
0	168	60	23	13	4
1	210	80	15	3	1
2	378	89	8	2	
3	294	88	8	2	1
4	169	90	7	1	2
5 or more	77	96		3	1
Age of wives in families without children					
Under 25	42	74	21	2	2
25-39	42	67	14	14	5
40-54	42	48	24	24	5
55 and over	42	50	33	12	4
Socioeconomic level					
Class 1 (highest)	163	80	12	4	3
Class 2	163	88	7	3	1
Class 3	402	85	10	3	1
Class 4	483	83	12	4	1
Class 5	85	89	7	2	1

TABLE 6.12—Heating and cooling equipment of dwellings
(1,296 husband-wife households, Syracuse, N.Y., 1967-68)

Equipment	Total group
	Percent
Heating equipment	
Automatic	98
Warm-air furnace	84
Steam heat	13
Built-in electric	1
Space heater	1
Other	1
Air conditioning	
None	80
1 unit	14
2 or more units	3
Central	3
Fireplace	
Owned	29
Used on record days	2

TABLE 6.13—Causes of extra cleaning work reported for previous 7 days, by selected variables

(1,296 husband–wife households, Syracuse, N.Y., 1967-68)

Households	Number	Special situations reported					
		Inade-quate storage	Room arrange-ment	Extra dirt from outside	Construc-tion in neighbor-hood	Weather condi-tions	Enter-taining
		Percent reporting					
Total group	1,296	35	17	57	9	59	47
Nonemployed wives	979	35	17	58	10	59	49
Employed wives	317	36	18	54	6	60	41
Number of children							
0	168	27	10	45	7	49	48
1	210	31	15	51	5	54	51
2	378	36	18	58	11	58	44
3	294	39	18	62	9	66	48
4	169	37	24	66	7	62	47
5 or more	77	35	18	60	12	68	44
Socioeconomic level							
Class 1 (highest)	163	31	17	50	7	61	50
Class 2	163	42	14	57	11	53	56
Class 3	402	31	13	58	9	59	47
Class 4	483	37	20	58	8	59	45
Class 5	85	32	27	62	8	68	35
House type							
Apartment	165	45	18	45	5	50	46
2-family	146	42	24	55	5	64	45
1-family	975	31	16	60	10	36	48
Age of dwelling							
1960 or later	302	47	22	59	3	69	42
1940–1959	434	35	19	54	4	60	46
1920–1939	242	36	18	57	3	62	52
1900–1919	136	36	17	56	12	56	46
Before 1900	125	29	16	57	14	57	46
Don't know	57						

TABLE 6.14—Cleaning time reduction techniques reported for previous 7 days, by selected variables

(1,296 husband-wife households, Syracuse, N.Y., 1967-68)

Households	Number	Techniques used			
		Mats at entrance	Special entrance or mud room	Frequent cleaning of entrance area	Changing shoes or clothing near entrance
		Percent using			
Total group	1,296	82	50	65	61
Nonemployed wives	979	83	51	66	60
Employed wives	317	79	47	60	64
Number of children					
0	168	80	40	51	51
1	210	81	40	60	58
2	378	84	53	69	61
3	294	81	53	67	64
4	169	83	53	64	73
5 or more	77	84	68	74	71
Age of wives in families without children					
Under 25	42	76	24	33	64
25-39	42	71	40	55	55
40-54	42	86	50	62	55
55 and over	42	86	48	55	29
Socioeconomic level					
Class 1 (highest)	163	88	50	57	56
Class 2	163	81	47	52	58
Class 3	402	83	54	66	62
Class 4	483	80	48	68	62
Class 5	85	80	52	78	62

TABLE 6.15—Availability and use of equipment for care of house, by selected variables
(1,296 husband–wife households, Syracuse, N.Y., 1967-68)

Households	Number	Equipment available		Equipment used in previous 7 days	
		Vacuum cleaner	Carpet sweeper or electric broom	Vacuum cleaner	Carpet sweeper or electric broom
		Percent		Average days of use	
Total group	1,296	96	54	3.0	1.4
Nonemployed wives	979	96	54	3.1	1.5
Employed wives	317	95	54	2.7	1.2
Number of children					
0	168	94	49	2.2	.9
1	210	95	60	2.5	1.5
2	378	96	53	3.0	1.4
3	294	97	53	3.3	1.6
4	169	96	53	3.4	1.5
5 or more	77	96	56	4.0	1.8
Age of wives in families without children					
Under 25	42	88	48	1.9	.6
25–39	42	93	43	2.5	.6
40–54	42	98	55	2.5	1.1
55 and over	42	95	50	1.9	1.1
Socioeconomic level					
Class 1 (highest)	163	97	55	2.8	1.4
Class 2	163	96	52	3.0	1.3
Class 3	402	97	57	3.0	1.4
Class 4	483	94	53	3.0	1.5
Class 5	85	92	45	3.2	1.2

TABLE 6.16—Use of paid help for regular house care, by employment of wives
(1,296 husband–wife households, Syracuse, N.Y., 1967-68)

	All households	Nonemployed-wife households	Employed-wife households
	1,296	979	317
		Percent	
Percent reporting they sometimes used paid help	22	21	26
Percent reporting use of paid help with activity in previous 7 days	5	4	9
Percent reporting use of paid help on record days	1	1	3
		Average days	
Average number of days in previous 7 on which paid help was used[a]	1.5	1.3	1.8
		Average hours	
Average hours spent on regular house care by paid help on record days[b]	5.0	5.1	4.8

[a]64 households (36 with nonemployed and 28 with employed wives)
[b]13 households (6 with nonemployed and 7 with employed wives)

TABLE 6.17—Number of rooms cared for on the record days, by employment of wives
(1,296 husband–wife households, Syracuse, N.Y., 1967-68)

	All households	Nonemployed-wife households	Employed-wife households
Number	1,296	979	317
Number of rooms, including bathrooms, cared for		Percent	
0	1	1	2
1	1	1	3
2	4	3	5
3	8	6	10
4	12	10	15
5	19	20	18
6	21	24	16
7	17	16	16
8	9	9	9
9 or more	8	11	6

TABLE 6.18—Type of activities performed in care of house, yard,
(1,296 husband-wife households, Syracuse, N.Y.,

Households	Number	Regular house care Number of rooms cared for in previous 7 days		
		Number of rooms		
		2-5	6-7	8 or more
		Percent		
Total group	1,296	16	46	38
Nonemployed wives	979	15	45	40
Employed wives	317	19	48	33
Number of children				
0	168	40	38	22
1	210	25	49	26
2	378	14	52	34
3	294	6	49	45
4	169	7	40	53
5 or more	77	3	31	66
Age of wives in families without children				
Under 25	42	71	24	5
25-39	42	43	36	21
40-54	42	24	45	31
55 and over	42	24	45	31
Socioeconomic level				
Class 1 (highest)	163	15	29	56
Class 2	163	20	37	43
Class 3	402	11	45	44
Class 4	483	17	54	29
Class 5	85	22	61	17
House type[a]				
Apartment	165	58	36	6
Mobile home	7	43	57	--
2-family	146	19	71	10
1-family	975	8	44	48

[a]Three houses classed as "other" are not included.

and car during previous 7 days; by selected variables
1967-68)

General cleaning	Special house cleaning	House maintenance	Making household furnishings	Care of lawns/ gardens	Care of walks/ driveways	Care of car
			Average days			
4.1	1.2	1.0	.3	1.1	1.2	.8
4.2	1.3	1.1	.3	1.2	1.2	.8
3.7	1.0	.9	.2	.9	.9	.9
3.0	1.2	.9	.3	.8	1.0	.8
4.0	1.2	.9	.2	.8	1.0	.8
4.4	1.2	1.0	.2	1.1	1.2	.9
4.2	1.2	1.1	.2	1.3	1.2	.8
4.5	1.3	1.1	.3	1.4	1.0	.8
4.4	1.4	1.3	.2	1.3	1.7	.8
3.6	1.2	.4	.1	.3	.2	1.0
2.8	1.1	1.0	.3	.7	.7	.7
3.0	1.4	1.1	.4	.9	1.3	.8
2.6	1.1	1.2	.5	1.2	1.7	.7
3.7	1.2	1.2	.4	.9	1.0	.7
4.3	1.3	1.0	.3	1.0	1.0	.9
4.0	1.3	1.1	.3	1.1	1.2	.9
4.3	1.1	1.0	.2	1.2	1.2	.8
4.1	1.2	1.2	.2	1.1	1.4	1.0
4.1						
5.1						
4.2						
4.1						

TABLE 6.19—Responsibility for yard care, by selected variables
(1,296 husband-wife households, Syracuse, N.Y., 1967-68)

Households	All house-holds	Kinds of care					
		Drives/ walks	Lawns	Shrubs/ trees	Flowers	Vegetable gardens	House mainte-nance
		Percent					
Total group	1,296	87	87	84	80	33	81
Nonemployed wives	979	88	87	84	80	35	81
Employed wives	317	86	85	82	79	29	79
Number of children							
0	168	68	66	64	63	25	61
1	210	78	78	75	68	27	70
2	378	90	88	85	82	31	83
3	294	95	94	92	85	41	87
4	169	96	96	93	92	37	90
5 or more	77	100	99	96	92	48	94
Age of wives in families without children							
Under 25	42	33	31	31	33	10	24
25-39	42	60	57	50	48	26	48
40-54	42	93	93	93	90	33	93
55 and over	42	86	83	81	81	31	81
Socioeconomic level							
Class 1 (highest)	163	85	85	85	80	34	81
Class 2	163	78	76	74	73	28	72
Class 3	402	91	91	88	83	36	85
Class 4	483	88	87	83	80	35	81
Class 5	85	89	89	85	76	27	75

TABLE 6.20—Size of house lots, by selected variables
(1,296 husband–wife households, Syracuse, N.Y., 1967-68)

Households		Lot size[a]				
		Very small Less than 6,000 square feet	Small 6,000 to 9,999 square feet	Medium 10,000 to 19,000 square feet	Large 20,000 square feet or more	Not responsible for care of grounds
				Percent		
Total group	1,296	17	34	23	12	14
Nonemployed wives	979	16	36	23	12	13
Employed wives	317	22	30	21	14	14
Number of children						
0	168	10	27	15	14	34
1	210	20	32	17	8	23
2	378	19	34	25	11	11
3	294	18	37	24	16	5
4	169	14	40	28	13	5
5 or more	77	22	39	27	12	0
Age of wives in families without children						
Under 25	42	5	19	5	2	69
25–39	42	5	17	12	21	45
40–54	42	12	40	24	17	7
55 and over	42	19	31	19	17	14
Socioeconomic Level						
Class 1 (highest)	163	14	29	32	10	15
Class 2	163	10	35	23	8	24
Class 3	402	16	36	25	13	10
Class 4	483	20	35	18	14	13
Class 5	85	31	34	14	11	10

[a]Example of lot sizes:
   very small — less than 60' x 100'
   Small — 60' x 100' to 99' x 100'
   Medium — 100' x 100' to 199' x 100'
   Large — 100' x 200' or more — approx. 1/2 acre.

TABLE 6.21—Use of equipment and hired help with yard care in previous 12 months, by selected variables
(1,296 husband–wife households, Syracuse, N.Y., 1967-68)

Households	Number	Equipment used		Kinds of care for which help was hired		
		Power lawnmower	Snowplow or snowblower	Lawn mowing	Snow removal	Yard and garden care
		Percent using				
Total group	1,296	72	20	12	18	10
Nonemployed wives	979	73	19	12	19	10
Employed wives	317	72	24	10	14	10
Number of children						
0	168	55	26	14	23	15
1	210	63	18	11	17	10
2	378	75	18	13	15	10
3	294	78	20	12	20	10
4	169	83	22	10	18	5
5 or more	77	73	21	4	14	6
Age of wives in families without children						
Under 25	42	31	5	10	7	2
25-39	42	52	12	7	14	14
40-54	42	76	45	26	36	26
55 and over	42	62	43	14	33	17
Socioeconomic level						
Class 1 (highest)	163	69	15	17	24	17
Class 2	163	62	16	20	20	17
Class 3	402	77	25	14	25	12
Class 4	483	74	20	6	10	5
Class 5	85	67	21	2	13	4

TABLE 6.22—Kinds of special house care, yard, and car care on record days, by employment of wives (*1,296 husband–wife households, Syracuse, N.Y., 1967-68*)

Kinds of care	All households	Nonemployed–wife households	Employed–wife households
Number	1,296	979	317
		Percent	
House maintenance	22	23	19
Special house cleaning	25	26	21
Household furnishings made	4	4	3
Care of walks/driveways	15	16	12
Care of lawns/gardens	18	20	12
Care of car	14	14	14
Care of garbage and trash	49	50	48

TABLE 6.23—Kinds of car care, by selected variables
(1,296 husband–wife households, Syracuse, N.Y., 1967-68)

Households	Number	Wash car at home	Take car to car wash	Wax car	Service car
			Type of care		
			Percent doing		
Total group	1,296	74	80	69	46
Nonemployed wives	979	75	80	68	45
Employed wives	317	71	79	72	47
Frequency of care					
Weekly		16	14	<1	3
Semimonthly		16	17	1	3
Monthly		8	13	3	5
Occasionally		34	36	41	35
Annually		1	<1	24	1
Number of children					
0	168	60	86	61	39
1	210	71	83	74	45
2	378	76	79	72	52
3	294	78	77	68	42
4	169	77	78	66	53
5 or more	77	82	77	64	35
Age of wives in families without children					
Under 25	42	48	88	64	57
25–39	42	64	81	74	45
40–54	42	67	90	55	24
55 and over	42	60	83	50	29
Socioeconomic level					
Class 1 (highest)	163	73	79	64	40
Class 2	163	76	78	68	48
Class 3	402	76	84	67	37
Class 4	483	73	76	74	52
Class 5	85	71	85	58	60

TABLE 6.24—Transportation used on record days, by employment of wives
(1,296 husband–wife households, Syracuse, N.Y., 1967-68)

Households	All households	Nonemployed-wife households	Employed-wife households
Total group	1,296	979	317
		Percent	
Number of cars used regularly			
0	1	1	1
1	61	64	54
2	36	34	43
3 or more	1	1	2
Percent of wives who drive	84	83	88
Number of drivers in family			
0	1	1	<1
1	15	16	14
2	78	78	76
3	6	5	10
4	<1	<1	1
Transportation used on record days			
Family car			
No one	4	4	3
Husband	26	29	16
Wife	4	4	6
Husband and wife	26	23	35
Parents and child	35	35	35
Husband and child	3	3	3
Wife and child	2	2	3
Bus			
No one	73	75	68
Husband	1	1	2
Wife	2	1	4
Parents and child	1	1	3
Child	22	22	23
Carpool			
No one	94	94	92
Husband	2	2	2
Wife	2	1	4
Child	2	2	2
Taxi	1	<1	1

TABLE 6.25—Transportation by car and bus used in the previous 7 days, by selected variables
(*1,296 husband–wife households, Syracuse, N.Y., 1967-68*)

Households	Number	Family car used by				Bus used by			
		Someone	Wife	Husband	Children	Someone	Wife	Husband	Children
		Percent using							
Total group	1,296	99	93	97	70	47	11	4	39
Nonemployed wives	979	98	93	98	72	45	9	4	38
Employed wives	317	99	96	97	64	55	17	6	42
Number of children									
0	168	99	93	98		19	14	7	
1	210	100	96	100	77	30	14	3	23
2	378	97	94	96	80	50	10	4	41
3	294	99	94	98	81	59	10	3	53
4	169	98	97	97	88	66	10	6	60
5 or more	77	99	92	98	80	69	12	3	61
Socioeconomic level									
Class 1 (highest)	163	99	94	98	65	39	10	5	31
Class 2	163	99	95	100	64	47	12	10	33
Class 3	402	100	96	98	73	46	8	2	41
Class 4	483	97	93	97	71	51	14	4	42
Class 5	85	96	88	94	74	56	14	10	47

TABLE 6.26—Average daily time used by all workers, wives, and husbands for travel, household work, and all work, by type of activity
(*1,296 husband–wife households, Syracuse, N.Y., 1967-68*)

Work activities	All workers' time		Wives' time		Husbands' time	
	Travel	All	Travel	All	Travel	All
	Average hours per day					
Food preparation	--	2.6	--	2.1	--	.2
Family care	.2	2.3	.1	1.6	.1	.4
House care	<.1	2.6	<.1	1.5	<.1	.6
Clothing care	<.1	1.3	<.1	1.2	<.1	<.1
Marketing/Management	.4	1.6	.2	1.0	.1	.4
All household work	.6	10.5	.3	7.3	.2	1.6
Other work	1.3	15.6	.1	1.7	.6	7.6
All work (household and other work combined)	1.9	26.1	.4	9.0	.8	9.2

Chapter VII

Care of Clothing

This area of household work was made up of three activities, washing by machine, ironing, and special care of clothing. Washing by machine was a frequently performed activity (on 66% and 56% of the record days in nonemployed- and employed-wife households, respectively) while ironing and special clothing care were carried on less frequently (Table 3.8). None of the activities was rated as time consuming in comparison with time spent in other areas of household work. Although the distribution of total time spent on a combination of all clothing care work was fairly uniform among the three activities, somewhat more time was spent on washing by machine (39%) than on ironing (31%) or special clothing care (30%).

The time reported for washing by machine included time spent primarily on the preparation and cleanup operations since the various washing operations are most often automatic. If the machines used were nonautomatic, time used for rinsing and wringing clothes was included. The preparation activities included collecting and sorting soiled articles for washing, pretreating them, and loading the washer. The after-washing activities included unloading the washer, loading and unloading the dryer or hanging up articles to dry and taking them down, and folding and storing unironed articles.

The time when the washers and dryers were in operation was not included in the time reported. When the machine is operating, the full attention of the worker is not required and the worker can spend the inactive work time on other activities.

The time spent on ironing included the time when direct attention was given to preparing clothing and household textiles for ironing, ironing or pressing the articles, getting out and putting away equipment, and folding and returning articles to storage.

Special care and construction of clothing and household linens included any work on clothing and household textiles not specifically a part of household washing or ironing. Washing by hand was classified as special care of clothing and linens since this is a special requirement of items made of

certain materials. The other types of work included in this category were dry cleaning, seasonal storage of clothing, mending, spot removal, shoe care, and construction, repair, or adjustment of clothing and household textiles.

The reasons for including such diverse kinds of work in one category were (1) to separate these various kinds of clothing care from such relatively clear-cut activities as household washing and ironing, and (2) because not enough time is spent on any of the subtasks in typical households for a relationship between amount of work and time spent to be determined. Making such household furnishings as slipcovers and draperies was included under special house care.

Rank Correlations of Time Used for Clothing Care[1,2]

Rank Correlations of Total Time of All Workers and Major Variables

Number of Children (Table 7.1). This variable had a closer relationship than other major variables with total time spent by all workers on washing by machine (.24) and had one of the two closest associations with total time spent on all clothing care (.15) and on ironing (.09). Each of these values declined slightly when either employment of wives or house type was held constant. The increase with number of children in total time used for all clothing care, washing by machine, or ironing was a little less when wives were employed. The weak relationship between number of children and

---

[1]All Tau values reported in tabular form or referred to in the text were significant at the .001 level unless otherwise stated. Although correlation coefficients were determined for all major variables, only significant relationships are reported in tables and only the correlations strong enough to change the amount of time used daily are discussed to any extent.

[2]For an explanation of meaning of positive and negative correlation values as related to the different variables, see pages 30-31.

ironing time probably resulted from the infrequent performance of this activity.

Ages of Youngest and Oldest Child (Table 7.1). These two variables had weak relationships with all workers' time spent on washing by machine (.11 and .07) and with total time spent on special clothing care (-.08 and -.07). The relationships between age of child variables and total time used on these two activities were in opposite directions, but both could logically be expected; more time was used on household washing when children in the family were younger, and more time was spent on special kinds of clothing care when children were older. Though weak, the correlation values of these two variables with total time spent on special clothing care were the closest of any of the major variables.

The effects of age of the youngest child were slightly interrelated with those of employment of wives in relation to time spent on machine washing; the value for the age variable declined to .08 when the employment variable was held constant. In contrast, the correlation between age of youngest child and total time spent on special clothing care was slightly higher (-.10) when employment of wives was held constant. Though small, these changes indicated a decrease in time spent on washing by machine when wives were employed at all ages of youngest child and indicated an increase in time for special clothing care as children became older, whether or not wives were employed.

In previous research, the family composition variables most closely related to time spent on household washing were the number of persons in the household and age of the youngest child. In Warren's research (1938, p. 424), time increased as the number of persons increased and when the youngest child was under 4 years. Warren combined these two variables as a measure of work load in household washing. Walker (1955, p. 60) found some relationship, though not a clear-cut one, between number of persons in the household and time use for this activity. In her research, age of youngest child was found to affect time use for household washing principally when the youngest child was a baby.

Family Type (Table 7.1). This variable had about the same relationship with total time spent on clothing care work as number of children. Correlation values of family type with total time spent on washing by machine (.23), all clothing care (.13), and ironing (.08) were almost as high as those for number of children. The similarity between these two variables could be expected

from the relative strength of the correlations with number of children, and the relative weakness of the correlations of age of youngest child with total time spent on most kinds of clothing care.

With respect to time spent by all workers on washing by machine, ironing, and all clothing care, the interrelationships between family type and other variables were similar to those between number of children and the same variables.

Employment of Wives (Table 7.1). Employment of wives was correlated negatively with total time spent on all clothing care (-.15), washing by machine (-.14), and ironing (-.09). The relationships between employment of wives and time used for all clothing care and ironing were as close as those for number of children.

When either number of children or family type was held constant, the correlation values for employment of wives and time used for washing declined from -.14 to -.11 and -.10, and those for time used for all clothing care from -.15 to -.13 each. When the wives were employed, a small part of the decline in time spent on all clothing care and washing by machine was the result of smaller or less complex families. Employment of wives was interrelated with age of youngest child only in relation to time spent on washing by machine; the small decline in its value (from -.14 to -.12) when the latter variable was held constant indicated that a small part of the decreased time use with employment was the effect of age of youngest child.

House Type (Table 7.1). House type had weak correlation coefficients with total time spent on all clothing care (.09), washing by machine (.10), and ironing (.07). Some of the effect of house type on time spent on all clothing care, washing, and ironing was the effect of number of children or family type, as shown by the small decline in correlation values when either of these variables was held constant.

Socioeconomic Level (Table 7.1). This variable had a weak correlation with total time used on washing by machine (.06).

Education of Wives (Table 7.1). Total time spent on washing by machine was weakly related to educational level of wives (.07) as was total time spent on special clothing care (-.06). Slightly more time, in terms of minutes per day, was used on washing by machine when wives had lower levels of education and slightly more time was used on special clothing care when they had higher levels of education.

Number of Loads Washed and Pieces Ironed. Although loads of clothes had been used as a measure of the work load in washing by machine in earlier research (Walker, 1957, and Purcell, 1965), it was given only limited consideration as a unit for quantifying work in the present study. Both time spent and loads washed are measures of the work load, and, therefore, they correlate highly. As expected, a close relationship was found between number of loads of clothes washed on the record days and amount of time used (correlation value of .66).

Number of pieces ironed was the basis for the original work unit developed for household ironing by Warren (1938) and for the later work unit developed by Walker (1955). The rank correlation value between time spent on ironing and number of pieces ironed was .80. This very high correlation between the two measures indicated that number of pieces was a significant indicator of the work load in ironing. Like the measure of loads of clothes for washing, number of pieces ironed was not given serious consideration for work load measurement due to the complexity of data collection required for its use.

Rank Correlations of Time Used by Individual Workers and Major Variables

Individual Workers' Share in Clothing Care. Wives' time accounted for over nine-tenths of all workers' time spent on all clothing care activities combined and on each separate activity. The correlations between wives' time use for this work and the major variables were the same as, or very similar to, correlations of the major variables with total time of all workers. With respect to all clothing care activities combined, 94% of total time use was spent by the average nonemployed wife and 86% by an employed one. The proportion of total time spent by both husbands and teenagers on washing by machine increased somewhat when the wives were employed, from 2% to 4% and from 1% to 2%, respectively (Table 3.10). Teenagers' proportionate time in doing ironing and special clothing care also increased when their mothers were employed to 7% and 16% of total time, respectively.

Number of Children (Tables 7.2 and 7.3). Wives' time spent on washing by machine, all clothing care, and ironing correlated with the number of children in the family (correlation coefficients of .23, .13, and .08).

The partial rank correlations showed some interrelationship between number of children and employment of wives in effects of each on wives' time use for all clothing care and washing by machine; number of children had a little less effect in increasing wives' time when wives were employed than when they were not.

Husbands' use of time on all clothing care and special clothing care had a very weak relationship (-.06) with number of children.

Age of Youngest Child (Tables 7.2 and 7.3). Like number of children, age of youngest child had a closer correlation with wives' time use for washing by machine (.11) than with their time use for other types of clothing care. For washing by machine the change in correlation value for age of youngest, when employment was held constant, indicated that wives' time increased slightly as youngest children in the family were older, whether or not the wives were employed.

The only significant correlation between husbands' clothing care time and age of youngest child was with husbands' time spent on washing by machine (.07); for teenagers the only significant correlation was with their time for ironing (-.11).

Family Type (Table 7.2). This variable was as closely related to wives' time spent on any kind of clothing care and on all clothing care as was number of children. As family type became more complex, wives spent more time on all clothing care, washing, and ironing. Interrelationships with employment of wives also were the same as those for number of children; when wives were employed, increase in family complexity had slightly less effect in extending the wives' time spent on washing, ironing, or all clothing care.

Employment of Wives (Tables 7.2 and 7.3). This variable had the best relationship of any of the major variables with wives' time use for all clothing care (-.18), ironing (-.11), and special clothing care (-.07). For washing by machine, however, wives' time use was more closely associated with number of children and family type than with their employment (-.16). When either of these family composition variables was held constant, employment of wives was a relatively weaker variable than number of children or family type in relation to time for washing by machine, as shown by the decline in the correlation coefficients (from -.16 to -.12, in each case). A similar interrelationship was evident between employment and the two family composition variables as related to wives' time use for all clothing care. In contrast, employment reduced wives' time spent on ironing and special clothing care regardless of family size or complexity. Unlike number of children and family type the correlation value of employment and time use for washing increased from -.16 to -.19 when age of the youngest child was held constant.

The relationship between employment of wives and teenagers' use of time on washing by machine (.12) indicated that they spent slightly more time on household washing when their mothers were employed. These correlations were independent of the effects of any family composition variables.

Education of Wives and Husbands (Tables 7.2 and 7.3). Wives' education had a weak association with their time spent on washing by machine (.07) and special clothing care (-.07). Wives with higher levels of education spent slightly less time on washing by machine and slightly more time on special clothing care. Though low, the relationship between wives' time use for special clothing care and their education was stronger than relationships between wives' time use and any of the family composition variables.

Husbands' time spent on all clothing care activities combined was related to wives' education (-.07) but not to their own. Both education variables were slightly related to husbands' time use on special clothing care (-.07 and -.06 for education of wives and husbands, respectively).

Time Used for Clothing Care

Total Time of All Workers

Number of Children and Employment of Wives (Table 7.4). Total time use by all workers for all clothing care combined increased as the number of children increased, except in the largest employed-wife families. When wives were employed, less time was spent on all clothing care than when they were not in nearly all family sizes.

In households of both nonemployed and employed wives, all workers' time spent on washing by machine also increased consistently as family size advanced. On the average, .6 hour a day more time was spent on household washing in nonemployed-wife households with seven to nine children than in those with no children. When wives were employed, about .4 hour a day more time was spent in families with five or six children than in those with no children. All workers' time spent on washing by machine was relatively less affected by wives' employment than by number of children; differences were small between non-employed- and employed-wife households (on the average, about 6 minutes less a day in the latter).

Total time used on both ironing and special clothing care varied only slightly and inconsistently by family size. On the other hand, employment of wives had a stronger effect in decreasing time spent on ironing than number of children had in increasing it. Less time was spent on ironing in nearly all family sizes when the wives were employed; these differences were fairly large in families without children and in those with five or more. Whether or not wives were employed, the difference in ironing time between larger and smaller families was fairly small. Total time use for special clothing care averaged about half an hour a day, irrespective of family size when wives were not employed, while the time use was more variable by family size when wives were employed.

Age of Youngest Child and Employment of Wives (Table 7.5). The decline in time used for household washing as age of youngest child increased was small. When wives were employed, a little less time was used on this activity at all ages of youngest except when the youngest was under 1 year.

Age of youngest child had more effect on all workers' time spent on special clothing care than on other kinds of clothing care. In both nonemployed- and employed-wife households total time spent on this activity increased somewhat as the youngest child was older. When wives were employed, less time was spent on special clothing care than when they were not at any age of youngest child, except in teenage groups. The weak effect of employment of wives on all workers' time used for special clothing care is shown by the lack of change in the average time, which was .4 hour a day in both nonemployed- and employed-wife households.

Family Type and Employment of Wives (Table 7.6). Family type was more closely related to total time use for washing by machine, the regularly performed activity, than to time use for other kinds of clothing care. Basically, this relationship was due to number of children. In most family types, less total time was spent on clothing care in employed- than in nonemployed-wife households; there was no consistent relationship to family type in the few cases in which considerably more time, on the average, was spent when wives were employed than when they were not.

Season of the Year. There was a slight tendency for household washing and ironing to be done more frequently in the spring and summer months (May to August) than in other seasons. More pieces were ironed in the summer months and the overall average time spent on ironing then was .5 hour as compared with .3 hour for January to April and .4 hour for September to December.

When the effect of season on use of time for washing and for ironing was examined in relation to the family composition variables, it was found to be so closely interrelated with the latter as to have no measurable effect on time use.

Time of Individual Workers

Except for the combination of all clothing care activities, the time of workers other than wives is not shown in the tables or discussed since in only a few cases did any other worker spend as much time as an average of .1 hour a day.

Number of Children and Employment of Wives (Table 7.4). Since the time of wives accounted for nearly all total time spent, their time use on clothing care followed the same trends as all workers' time. Wives, whether employed or not, spent more time on all clothing care in larger than in smaller families, and in all family sizes they consistently spent less time on this work when they were employed. For both nonemployed and employed wives, the increased time between smaller and larger families averaged about half an hour a day. The decrease in wives' time with employment tended to be less in larger families than in smaller ones, except those with five or six children. This substantial decline was mostly the result of the lesser time spent by employed wives on ironing (from .6 to .2 hour a day) and special clothing care (from .4 to .1 hour a day).

Number of children had a more consistent effect on wives' time spent on washing by machine than on their time spent on all clothing care, but their employment had less effect. Wives' time use for washing by machine increased fairly steadily as the number of children increased. This effect was apparent whether wives were employed or not, though employed wives spent a little less time than nonemployed wives at most family sizes. In households of both employed and nonemployed wives, the relatively strong effect of number of children is apparent from an increase of almost half an hour a day between families with no children and those with five or six. The effect of employment was considerably less; on the average, employed wives spent only about 6 minutes a day less on machine washing than nonemployed wives.

For wives' time spent on ironing, the relationship with their employment was slightly stronger than the one with number of children. Wives' average time use for ironing was slightly less when they were employed (.3 hour a day

average, compared with .4 hour), and employed wives spent consistently less time than nonemployed wives at all family sizes.

Age of Youngest Child and Employment of Wives (Table 7.5). Wives' time spent on washing by machine increased by only a small amount between families with teenagers and those with a baby as youngest, in keeping with the weak relationship for age of youngest child.

Teenagers' time use on ironing had some relationship with age of youngest child but it was too weak to affect their average daily time. Similarly, the slight relationship between husbands' time use on washing by machine and age of youngest child did not change their average daily time of less than 3 minutes.

Family Type and Employment of Wives (Table 7.6). The closest relationship between family type and wives' time use for clothing care was that with washing by machine. Wives' time used for this activity increased, though not regularly, as family type became more complex. This relationship was more apparent for the time of nonemployed than employed wives. Employed wives spent a little less time on this activity than nonemployed ones in most family types; their time use had no perceptible relationship with family type.

The relationship between family type and wives' time spent on ironing was weak with no consistent time change by family type (Table 7.6). In most family types, employed wives spent a little less time on ironing than nonemployed ones, especially in households with children of school age or some of the more complex family types in which teenagers contributed some time.

The time used by nonemployed wives for all clothing care increased with family size when the youngest child was under 1; with a few exceptions nonemployed wives spent more time in the larger than in the smaller families. Employed wives' time showed no consistent relationship to family type; in most, and especially in households without children, they spent less time on all clothing care than nonemployed wives.

Characteristics and Content of Work in Care of Clothing

Washing by Machine

The use of automatic equipment has reduced the physical labor of household washing, but time still has to be spent on collecting articles for washing and returning them to storage as well as the pre- and post-washing operations of loading and unloading. Time use also varies according to the kind and location of equipment used (automatic versus nonautomatic, at home or away from home) and the frequency of washing. Further, changes in standards that increase or decrease time use may also accompany improvements in equipment. Ease of performance may be another source of time variations. If household washing is more easily accomplished than ironing, decisions of selection of clothing and textiles may be made to shift some of the work in ironing to washing and thus increase time use on the latter activity.

The type of equipment used, frequency of washing, and loads washed have been important variables in past research on household washing. Frequently, one or more of these variables have been related to time use. For example, most previous studies have reported a much higher time use for household washing when nonautomatic equipment is used. In the present study, particular attention was given to examining interrelationships among kind of equipment used, frequency of washing, and number of loads washed in terms of relationships with the family composition variables.

Equipment and Laundry Services Used on Record Days and the Previous 7 Days (Tables 7.7, 7.8, and 7.9). An automatic washer was used on the record days by almost three-fifths of the households in the sample. Only 3% used a nonautomatic washer and 1% a combination washer-dryer. Automatic dryers were used by about two-fifths of the households, a much lower proportion than had used automatic washers (Table 7.7). Employed-wife households used automatic washers less on the record days (50%) than those with nonemployed wives (59%).

Neither commercial laundry service nor diaper service was used extensively by households in the sample. In nonemployed- and employed-wife households 3% and 2% had used a commercial laundry on the record days; 4% of nonemployed-wife households and 1% of employed-wife households had used diaper service. Of families with children under 2 years of age, 11% had used diaper service when wives were not employed as compared with only 6% when they were (Table 7.7).

Though no paid help was used for washing by machine alone, such help was used by 5 out of the 1,296 families for washing and ironing and by 1 family for washing, ironing, and washing by hand. All of this paid help was used at home, and 5 of the

6 paid workers were in employed-wife households.

In line with common practice in the United States, most of the household washing was done at home; only 8% reported that the washing machines used on the record days were at coin laundries (6%) or elsewhere (2%), such as at a relative's house or in apartment house laundries. In general, the families that had used washing machines away from home were those without children; in these households in which the wives were under age 25, less than half had used washers at home (Table 7.8). Use of a washer at home increased substantially when there was one child in the household, and only 2% to 5% of households with two or more children had used a machine away from home. Only a slightly higher proportion of families with employed wives (9%) than of those with nonemployed wives (6%) had used a coin laundry on the record days.

During the previous 7 days, when an automatic washer was used at home, household washing was distributed fairly evenly by number of days of the week in all households, regardless of wives' employment. Nine-tenths of all families had used an automatic washer on at least 1 day out of the previous 7. Between nonemployed- and employed-wife households some difference was evident in the frequency of using an automatic washer at home; 72% of households in which the wives were not employed compared with 59% of those with employed wives had used an automatic washer on 3 or more days (Table 7.9). Employed-wife households had used an automatic washer at home an average of 3.3 days during the previous week compared with an average of 3.9 days for nonemployed-wife households. In the previous 7 days, a nonautomatic washer had been used by only 8% of households of nonemployed wives and 4% of those with employed wives.

Coin-operated laundry facilities were used by only 7% of the nonemployed-wife households and 13% of the employed-wife households, and most of this was on only 1 day a week. Use of a commercial laundry was also typically on 1 day a week.

Nonautomatic washers at home, though used by only a small proportion of families, were used relatively frequently (on from 1 to 5 days) in nonemployed-wife households and less often (on from 1 to 3 days) by employed-wife households.

Frequency of Washing by Machine During the Previous 7 Days (Tables 7.10, 7.11, and 7.12). In addition to the actual quantity of work, several subjective factors such as standards and household routines may be related to the frequency of household washing. Frequency of washing also may vary in response to decisions in other areas of homemaking, such as quantities of clothing required by growing children. The mother may decide to buy fewer clothes and wash more frequently or vice versa.

In the sample households, washing by machine was usually not done every day, but was much more frequent than once a week. Only 1% of all families had not washed some article during the previous 7 days; articles were washed on an average of 4.2 of these days. This average increased progressively by number of children from 3.7 days in one-child families to 6.6 days in those with seven to nine children.

When use of automatic washers alone was considered, the frequency of use increased by number of children, from an average of about 3 days per week in families with one child to about 5 days per week in families with five or more children. The relationship between number of children and frequency of using an automatic washer tended to hold whether or not wives were employed; however, the average number of days an automatic washer was used was lower in employed- than in nonemployed-wife households (3.8 versus 4.4 days).

The frequency of washing by automatic washer during the previous 7 days tended to increase with declines in age of the youngest child; whether or not wives were employed, the highest frequency (4.5 to 5.0 days) was in families with a youngest child under age 2. There were only minor variations in frequency of using an automatic machine by employment of wives when age of the youngest child was held constant.

When the frequency of household washing by automatic washer during the previous 7 days was related to family type, most frequent use of an automatic washer was typically in families with children under 2 years old and in families with four or more children (Table 7.11). When wives were not employed, the decrease in average number of days on which household washing was done by an automatic washer as the youngest child became older was quite apparent, as was the increased frequency between smaller and larger families. When wives were employed, the variations by age of youngest child and number of children were somewhat more inconsistent, though in general they followed the same pattern as when wives were not employed.

In families without children, there was no relationship between age of wives and average number of days on which an automatic washer was

used, except that such use was least frequent when wives were under age 25, whether employed or not.

Size of family, more than kind of equipment used, was associated with the frequency of washing (Table 7.12); for families of the same size, a similar percentage washed on the record days, whether they used a nonautomatic or automatic washer.

Loads of Clothes Washed on Record Days and the Previous 7 Days (Tables 7.13, 7.14, and 7.15). In Walker's previous research (1955), the focusing of time use for household washing on machine use made it possible to quantify the work load for this activity in terms of number of loads washed at one time. In the present study, particular attention was given to analysis of loads of clothes washed as related to the family composition variables to demonstrate the interchangeability of loads of clothes washed and family composition as quantifying variables for measurement of the work in washing clothes and household textiles.

The typical quantity of washing consisted of from one to three loads washed on 1 day; only about one-tenth of the sample households had washed four or more, and less than 1% had washed 9 loads or more. The average number of loads of washing on the record days was 1.5, including washing at home and at laundromats (Table 7.13). This average was somewhat lower than the average number of loads found in previous studies and may reflect a trend toward more frequent washing with less done at one time.

There was a well-defined relationship between the number of loads of household washing on the record days and number of children in the family; the average number of loads washed increased as the number of children increased, whether or not the homemaker was employed. Families with seven to nine children washed an average of three loads on the record days, while those with one child washed an average of one load.

The number of loads washed on the record days varied somewhat according to age of youngest child, with a total difference of less than half a load between households in which the youngest was 12 to 17 and those in which the youngest was a baby.

In families with children, differences between nonemployed- and employed-wife households were usually small and inconsistent. The differences seemed to occur mainly because there were fewer employed-wife households in the larger and more complex families in which more loads tended to be washed. Overall, the average number of loads washed on the record days in employed-wife households (1.3) was only a little less than that in nonemployed-wife households. As pointed out earlier (Table 7.5), since employed-wife households spent an average of 12 minutes less a day on washing by machine than others, it appears that the small differences in time between employed- and nonemployed-wife households were in the direction of less time spent to produce a similar quantity of work.

The stronger effect of number of children than of youngest child on number of loads washed was apparent when complexity of family type was considered (Table 7.14). Larger families had higher average numbers of loads washed on the record days than smaller families at all ages of youngest child. This pattern was the same whether or not wives were employed, but when they were employed the average number of loads was more varied and less related to family type. The differences in average number of loads by employment of wives and family type were minor and mostly in smaller families; the larger households with employed wives tended to wash almost as many loads on the record days as those with nonemployed wives.

In families without children, although there was no relationship between age of wives and average number of loads washed on the record days, employed-wife households washed a higher average number of loads than nonemployed ones at all ages of wives except the youngest group.

During the previous 7 days, households in the sample were fairly evenly divided between those that had washed 9 or fewer loads (52%) and those that had washed 10 or more. Washing of 10 to 12 loads was most common (24% of households). The average number of loads washed per week was 9.9 and the average number of loads washed per week for each family member was 2.3. Although 6% and 7% of employed- and nonemployed-wife households, respectively, had washed 19 or more loads, more loads were washed weekly in households in which wives were not employed (Table 7.15). The typical weekly washing for those households was from 7 to 12 loads, while in employed-wife households it was from 4 to 9 loads. A higher proportion of nonemployed-wife households had washed 10 or more loads (51% compared with 38%), and fewer had washed from 1 to 6 (25% compared with 43% of employed-wife households).

The average number of loads washed during the previous 7 days increased substantially as the number of children in the family increased, from an average of 4.3 loads in families with no children and 7.1 loads in families with one child to an average of 20.7 loads in families with seven to nine children (Table 7.13). As in past research, the average number of loads per person per household declined slightly in larger households, from a high of 2.5 loads per person in families with two children to 2.1 loads per person in families with seven to nine children.

Although the average number of loads washed on the record days was not closely related to age of youngest child, the average number of loads washed weekly was. This weekly average declined consistently as age of youngest child increased, from 7.8 loads when the youngest was a baby to 6.6 loads when the youngest was 12 to 17 (Table 7.13).

Number of Loads Washed and Time Spent

The definite relationships between the family composition variables and the frequency of household washing (by automatic washer or other facilities) and the number of loads washed at one time indicated that family composition was closely related to the work load in household washing. This is indicative of the equivalent value of the number of loads washed and time spent as measures of the work load in household washing.

Ironing

In the present study, ironing as a household work activity was neither time consuming nor frequently performed. Largely, the low frequency and relatively low amount of time used for ironing have come about through eliminating the amount of work required rather than by a major change in equipment used. The development of no-iron materials and permanent-press clothing are examples. The steam iron eliminates much, and in some cases all, of the need to dampen articles before ironing them.

The analysis of characteristics of ironing was devoted principally to the kinds of ironing (clothing or household textiles), frequency of ironing, and number of pieces ironed on the record days. The particular focus was on relationships between family composition variables and these characteristics of ironing.

Use of Paid Help with Ironing. Nearly all of the ironing was done at home and by wives or teenagers; only 14 of the 1,296 wives in the sample had paid help for ironing. In addition to the six who had paid help for household washing and ironing discussed under washing by machine, six wives sent ironing out and two others had used paid help with ironing at home. These latter two families had wives who were employed, and the average time spent by paid help on ironing was about 2 hours. In contrast, all except one of the six families that had sent ironing out had non-employed wives.

Frequency of Ironing on Record Days and the Previous 7 Days (Tables 7.9, 7.10, and 7.15). Because ironing clothing was much more frequent than ironing textiles, the two types have been considered separately in some of the analyses in order to provide a better picture of the work load.

The greater importance of clothing than household textiles in ironing work is evident in Table 7.15. Clothing was ironed on about 40% of the record days whether or not wives were employed, while textiles were ironed on 18% of the days in nonemployed-wife families and on only 12% in those with employed wives.

During the previous 7 days, clothing was ironed on an average of 2.5 days. Household textiles were ironed much less frequently, an average of 1.1 days (Table 7.9). The frequency of ironing clothing was the same whether or not wives were employed and the frequency of ironing household textiles was only a little lower in employed-wife households (an average of 1.0 day) than in nonemployed-wife households (an average of 1.2 days).

The average number of days in the previous 7 on which either kind of ironing was done tended to increase with the number of children (Table 7.10) as did the average number of days on which clothing was ironed. Households with five or more children ironed clothing on an average of twice as many days (3.3) as families without children (1.5). Household textiles were ironed on an average of about 1 day in families of all sizes.

Number of Pieces Ironed on Record Days and the Previous 7 Days (Tables 7.13 and 7.15). Ironing, like household washing, is an activity in which the unit of processing the work was a focus of analysis of the time spent. The number of pieces ironed provides a means of quantifying the work load because each piece has to be prepared for ironing as a separate unit, handled separately, and folded and stored after ironing. Other measures of output have been number of baskets of clothes ironed and types of articles ironed. In Walker's previous research in 1955, number of pieces ironed was the quantifying variable related to time use as the measure of the work load in ironing. In the present study, relationships

between number of pieces ironed and selected family composition variables were determined and compared with the relationships between the same variables and time spent on ironing.

Each article ironed, regardless of its size, was counted as one piece; for example, a shirt or a handkerchief each counted as one piece. The variations in work and time caused by differences in types of articles ironed could be expected to average out over typical ironing periods in a large sample.

An average of 6.5 pieces per family were ironed on the record days, an average of 5.5 pieces of clothing and 1.0 piece of household textiles (Table 7.13). For those who ironed, the typical number of pieces of either clothing or textiles ironed on the record days was 1 to 9 (Table 7.15). There seems to have been a marked decrease in the amount of ironing over the years; Walker (1955) reported an average of 22 pieces ironed on the record days.

Employment of wives was the only variable that showed a consistent relationship with number of pieces ironed on the record days. More articles were ironed in households where wives were not employed, an average of 7.0, compared with an average of 4.8 pieces when wives were employed (Table 7.13). Thus, though the same proportions of nonemployed- and employed-wife households had ironed clothing on the record days, the amount of work output in the latter households was considerably less, an average of 4.1 pieces, or almost 2 pieces a day less than in nonemployed-wife households. Fewer employed-wife households (12%) than nonemployed-wife ones (18%) had ironed textiles on the record days, but the difference in average number of pieces was not large (1.1 pieces in nonemployed-wife households and .7 piece when wives were employed).

The average number of all pieces ironed on the record days was slightly related to number of children, in that number of pieces generally increased with the number of children. Families with no children or only one child ironed the smallest average number of pieces.

The seasonal variations in number of pieces ironed on the record days were small; the smallest average number was ironed in the winter (5.2) and the largest average number in the summer (7.7).

Number of Pieces and Time Spent. The relationships found between family composition variables and number of pieces were similar to those found between the same variables and time spent on ironing. Fewer pieces were ironed and less time spent when wives were employed than when they were not, and there was a general tendency for more pieces to be ironed and more time spent as family size increased. This comparison is indicative of the equivalency of the number of pieces variable and time spent as measures of the work accomplished in household ironing.

Special Clothing Care

Special clothing care represents a collection of subtasks that are integrated chiefly by their purpose; i.e., the provision and renewal of clothing and household textiles for the family's use. Special care of clothing and other items is a sporadic activity that may be carried on intensively in some households and not at all or very little in others. Some of the subtasks, such as washing by hand, may be performed frequently, while others, such as shoe care and dry cleaning, are likely to be needed less often. Sewing work, especially if often done by machine, is one of the more variable subtasks and may be postponed until a fairly long period, relatively free of interruptions, is available. Sewing was one of the categories that could be classified more as a goods producing activity than as a service producing activity. For further research it would, therefore, seem desirable to keep it separate.

Considerable detail was collected on two of the subtasks on which the most time was likely to be spent; i.e., sewing and washing by hand. The purpose was to determine, if possible, what family characteristics or other variables might be most closely related to the amount of work.

Use of Commercial Facilities and Paid Help (Table 7.7). About 6% of the families had used commercial dry cleaner services on the record days but less than 1% had used coin-operated dry cleaning facilities. The variable use of commercial dry cleaning services has also been evident in past research.

On 3 of the 2,592 record days, the paid helper at home also did washing by hand. These paid helpers were in households in which wives were not employed and in an upper socioeconomic class.

Sewing and Washing by Hand on Record Days and the Previous 7 Days (Tables 7.7, 7.9, 7.10, 7.13, and 7.15). Of respondents in the sample, 30% had used sewing equipment on the record days. Employed-wife households had used such equipment somewhat less frequently (26%) than those in which wives were not employed (31%) (Table 7.7).

As might be expected, washing articles of clothing by hand was much more frequent than washing household textiles, though neither activity was widespread. Only 1% of families had washed household textiles by hand on the record days (Table 7.15). Of the total group, 32% of the employed-wife households and 25% of the nonemployed-wife households had washed clothing by hand. Hand-washing was usually of a small quantity of articles, an average of 1.2 pieces per day for both employed- and nonemployed-wife households (Table 7.13).

During the previous 7 days, 88% of the nonemployed- and 84% of the employed-wife households had sewed or mended (Table 7.9). About three-fifths of both types of households had done this work on 1 or 2 days and about one-fifth on 3 or 4. The frequency of sewing or mending was about the same when the wives were employed (an average of 1.9 days) as when they were not (an average of 2.0 days).

The frequency of sewing or mending for the present sample was somewhat related to the number of children (Table 7.10). Among families with children, the average number of days on which this work was done increased from 1.7 in families with one child to 2.4 in families with five or more. It was also related to age of wives in families without children, in which the frequency increased by more than half a day between the youngest and oldest age groups. The frequency of sewing or mending in the previous 7 days was not related to socioeconomic level.

About four-fifths of families had done some washing by hand during the previous 7 days, in both employed- and nonemployed-wife households (Table 7.9). Employed-wife households also washed articles by hand on more days (10% had washed by hand on all 7 days versus 4% of nonemployed-wife households). This higher frequency with wives' employment was evident in the relatively high average number of days on which this work was performed (2.6 days versus 1.9 when the wives were not employed).

The frequency of washing by hand varied inconsistently by number of children (Table 7.10). Families without children tended to do this kind of work more frequently than other families and the frequency of washing by hand tended to increase with advancing age of wives. The frequency of washing by hand was slightly less at the lowest socioeconomic level.

It was apparent that, although most families did some work in sewing and washing by hand, the two types of activities were not related to the same characteristics. The amount of sewing tended to increase as the number of children increased and employment of wives tended to reduce the frequency of this activity. Washing by hand was not related to the number of children and its frequency increased when the wives were employed. For any precise determination of output and input in these types of work, each would have to be considered as separate activities. It is probable, also, that the opposing relationships between amount of work in these two major subtasks and some of the major variables were partly responsible for a general lack of correlation between most of the variables and time spent on special care of clothing.

TABLE 7.1—Rank and partial rank correlation
(1,260 husband–wife households,

Total time of <u>all workers</u> in:	Kendall Tau[a]
ALL CLOTHING CARE ACTIVITIES	
Family composition variables	
Number of children	.15
Family type	.13
Employment	
Wives	-.15
Husbands' hours	.04⊬
Housing	
House type	.09
Location of residence	.03⊬
WASHING BY MACHINE	
Family composition variables	
Number of children	.24
Age of youngest child	.11
Age of oldest child	.07
Family type	.23
Employment	
Wives	-.14
Socioeconomic level	.06
Wives' education	.07
Husbands' education	.05*
Housing	
House type	.10
Location of residence	.04**
IRONING	
Family composition variables	
Number of children	.09
Family type	.08
Employment	
Wives	-.09
Housing	
House type	.07
Location of residence	.05*
SPECIAL CLOTHING CARE	
Family composition variables	
Age of youngest child	-.08
Age of oldest child	-.07
Employment	
Wives	-.05*
Socioeconomic level	-.04⊬
Wives' education	-.06
Husbands' education	-.04⊬
Housing	
House type	.04⊬

[a]All Tau values reported were significant at the .001 level unless otherwise indicated as: * = .005, ** = .01 or .02, and ⊬ = .03 to .05. For discussion of effects of ranking of variables on positive and negative values, see pp. 30-31. Correlation coefficients were based on 1,260 households except for age of youngest child, for which only families with children were used (1,092).

[b]Partial rank correlation values reported only for major variables at the .001 level of significance.

coefficients for clothing care time of all workers and major variables
Syracuse, N.Y., 1967-68)

Partial rank correlations[b] with major variables held constant					
Number of children	Age of youngest child	Family type	Empl. of wives	House type	Location of residence
	.15		.13	.13	
			.11	.12	
-.13	-.15	-.13			
.07	.10	.07			.09
	.24		.22	.22	
.11			.08	.13	
			.21	.22	
-.11	-.12	-.10			
.06	.13	.07			.10
	.09		.08	.08	
			.07	.07	
-.08	-.10	-.08			
.05	.06	.05			.05
-.08			-.10	-.08	

TABLE 7.2—Rank and partial rank correlation coefficients for clothing care time of wives and major variables
(1,260 husband–wife households, Syracuse, N.Y., 1967-68)

Total time of wives in:	Kendall Tau[a]	Partial rank correlations[b] with major variables held constant			
		Number of children	Age of youngest child	Family type	Empl. of wives
ALL CLOTHING CARE ACTIVITIES					
Family composition variables					
Number of children	.13		.13		.11
Age of youngest child	.04†				.10
Family type	.13				
Employment					
Wives	-.18	-.16	-.19	-.16	
Husbands' hours	.03†				
Education					
Wives	.04†				
WASHING BY MACHINE					
Family composition variables					
Number of children	.23		.24		.21
Age of youngest child	.11	.11			.15
Family type	.23				.21
Employment					
Wives	-.16	-.12	-.19	-.12	
Education					
Wives	.07				
Husbands	.04†				

IRONING

Family composition variables				
Number of children	.08		.08	.07
Family type	.08			.06
Employment				
Wives	-.11	-.10	-.11	-.10

SPECIAL CLOTHING CARE

Family composition variables				
Number of children	-.04†			
Age of youngest child	-.04**			
Family type	-.04**			
Employment				
Wives	-.07	-.08	-.07	-.08
Education				
Wives	-.07			
Husbands	-.05*			

[a]All Tau values reported were significant at the .001 level unless otherwise indicated as: * = .001, ** = .01 or .02, and † = .03 to .05. For discussion of effects of ranking of variables on positive and negative values, see pp. 30-31. Correlation coefficients were based on 1,260 households except for age of youngest child, for which only families with children were used (1,092).

[b]Partial rank correlation values are reported only for major variables at the .001 level of significance.

TABLE 7.3—Rank and partial rank correlation coefficients for clothing care time of
(*1,260 husband–wife households, Syracuse, N.Y., 1967-68*)

| Time in: | Kendall Tau[a] | Husbands time[c] Partial rank correlations[b] with major variables held constant | | |
		Number of children	Age of youngest child	Empl. of wives
ALL CLOTHING CARE				
Family composition variables				
Number of children	-.06		-.06	-.05
Age of youngest child				
Family type	-.05*			-.04
Employment				
Wives	.04⁄			
Husbands' hours	-.04⁄			
Education				
Wives	-.07			
WASHING BY MACHINE				
Family composition variables				
Age of youngest child	.07	.07		.06
Employment				
Wives	.03⁄			
Husbands' hours	-.04⁄			
Education				
Wives	-.04⁄			
Husbands	.03⁄			
IRONING				
Family composition variables				
Age of youngest child				
Employment				
Husbands' hours				
SPECIAL CLOTHING CARE				
Family composition variables				
Number of children	-.06		-.06	-.06
Age of youngest child				
Family type	-.06			-.06
Employment				
Wives				
Education				
Wives	-.07			
Husbands	-.06			

[a]All Tau values reported were significant at the .001 level unless otherwise indicated as * = .05, ** = .01 or .02, and ⁄ = .03 to .05. For discussion of effects of ranking of variables on positive and negative values see pp. 30-31.

[b]Partial rank correlation values are reported only for major variables at the .001 level of significance.

[c]Correlation coefficients were based on 1,260 households except for age of youngest child, for which only families with children were used (1,092).

[d]Tau values were computed on basis of 378 families with teenagers.

husbands and teenagers and major variables

| | Teenagers' time[d] | | | |
| | Partial rank correlations[b] with major variables held constant | | | |
Kendall Tau[a]	Number of children	Age of youngest child	Family type	Empl. of wives
−.09*	−.09			−.11
.12	.13	.13	.13	
.06≠				
.09*				
−.11	−.11			−.12
−.08**				
−.07≠				
.06≠				

TABLE 7.4—Clothing care time of all workers and individual workers, by number of
(1,296 husband-wife households, Syracuse, N.Y., 1967-68)

Activity	Number of children	Total number of families NE[a]	E	Time of All workers (Total)[b] NE	E	Wives NE	E
				Average hours per day[c]			
All clothing care	0	97	71	1.1	.6	1.1	.6
	1	149	61	1.2	.9	1.1	.8
	2	295	83	1.4	1.1	1.4	.9
	3	233	61	1.4	1.3	1.3	1.1
	4	139	30	1.5	1.6	1.4	1.2
	5-6	47	9	1.8	1.0	1.6	1.0
	7-9	19	2	1.8		1.6	
	Average	979	317	1.4	1.1	1.3	.9
Washing by machine	0			.3	.3	.3	.2
	1			.4	.3	.4	.3
	2			.6	.4	.5	.3
	3			.6	.5	.5	.5
	4			.7	.6	.7	.6
	5-6			.7	.7	.7	.6
	7-9			.9		.9	
	Average			.5	.4	.5	.4
Ironing	0			.4	.2	.4	.2
	1			.4	.3	.4	.3
	2			.4	.4	.4	.3
	3			.5	.4	.4	.3
	4			.4	.3	.4	.3
	5-6			.6	.3	.6	.2
	7-9			.5		.3	
	Average			.4	.3	.4	.3
Special clothing care	0			.5	.2	.5	.2
	1			.4	.3	.3	.3
	2			.4	.4	.4	.2
	3			.4	.4	.3	.3
	4			.4	.6	.3	.4
	5-6			.5	.1	.4	.1
	7-9			.4		.3	
	Average			.4	.4	.3	.3

[a]NE and E indicate households with nonemployed or employed wives.

[b]Sum of average time for individual workers may not equal total time of all workers because of rounding and because averages of children's time include only households with children of specified ages.

[c]Time is reported only if there were three or more families and if average time was 3 minutes or more.

children and employment of wives

Number of households with children 12-17 years		Time of children 12-17		Number of households with children 6-11 years		Time of children 6-11	
NE	E	NE	E	NE	E	NE	E
		Av. hrs. per day[c]				Av. hrs. per day[c]	
22	20	.1	.1	23	19		
82	44	.1	.2	128	40		
91	35	.2	.3	156	38		
43	19	.3	.5	91	18		
31	6	.2	.1	46	8		
18	2	.2		19	2	.1	
287	126	.2	.2	463	125		
		.1	.1				
		.1	.1				
		.1					
		.1					
			.1				
		.1	.1				
		.2	.4				
		.1					
		.1	.1				

TABLE 7.5—Clothing care time of all workers and individual workers, by
(1,128 husband-wife households, Syracuse, N.Y., 1967-68)

Activity	Age of youngest child (years)	Number of families NE [a]	E
All clothing care	12-17	80	61
	6-11	210	86
	2-5	248	63
	1	163	20
	Under 1	181	16
	Average	882	246
Washing by machine	12-17		
	6-11		
	2-5		
	1		
	Under 1		
	Average		
Ironing	12-17		
	6-11		
	2-5		
	1		
	Under 1		
	Average		
Special clothing care	12-17		
	6-11		
	2-5		
	1		
	Under 1		
	Average		

[a]NE and E indicate households with nonemployed or employed wives.

[b]Sum of average time for individual workers may not equal total time of all workers because of rounding and because averages of children's time include only households with children of specified ages.

[c]Time is reported only if there were three or more families and if average time was 3 minutes or more.

age of youngest child and employment of wives

Time of All workers (Total)[b]		Wives		Number of households with children 12-17 years		Time of children 12-17	
NE	E	NE	E	NE	E	NE	E
Average hours per day[c]						Av. hrs. per day[c]	
1.4	1.5	1.1	1.2	80	61	.1	.3
1.5	1.2	1.4	1.0	87	41	.2	.2
1.4	.9	1.4	.8	85	17	.1	.1
1.3	1.2	1.2	1.1	20	5	.3	
1.3	.9	1.3	.9	15	2	.1	
1.4	1.2	1.3	1.0	287	126	.2	.2
.5	.4	.5	.4				
.5	.4	.5	.4				
.6	.4	.5	.4				
.6	.5	.6	.5				
.6	.6	.6	.6				
.6	.4	.6	.4				
.4	.4	.3					.1
.5	.4	.5	.3			.1	
.5	.3	.5	.3				
.4	.5	.4	.5			.1	
.4	.2	.4	.2				
.4	.3	.4	.3			.1	.1
.4	.4	.5	.7			.1	.2
.4	.3	.5	.4			.2	.2
.4	.2	.4	.2			.1	
.3	.2	.3	.2			.2	
.3	.1	.3	.1				
.4	.4	.3	.3			.1	.1

TABLE 7.6—Clothing care time of all workers, wives, and teenagers,
(1,296 husband-wife households, Syracuse, N.Y.,1967-68)

Family Type	Number NE[a]	E	All workers' time (total time)[b]							
			All clothing care NE	E	Washing by machine NE	E	Ironing NE	E	Spec. clothing care NE	E
No-child households by age of wives			Average hours per day[c]							
under 25 years	16	26	.7	.6	.2	.2	.2	.2	.3	.2
25-39	19	23	1.2	.8	.3	.4	.4	.2	.5	.2
40-54	30	12	1.4	.4	.4	.2	.4	.1	.7	.1
55 and over	32	10	1.1	.7	.3	.1	.4	.1	.4	.5
Number of children by age of youngest child										
1 child										
12-17 years	22	20	1.2	1.0	.3	.3	.4	.3	.5	.4
6-11	23	19	1.5	.9	.4	.2	.5	.3	.6	.4
2-5	26	16	1.0	.7	.3	.3	.4	.2	.4	.2
1	37	5	.9	1.4	.4	.6	.3	.8	.2	.1
under 1	41	1	1.2		.5		.4		.3	
2 children										
12-17 years	27	15	1.4	1.8	.5	.4	.4	.5	.4	.9
6-11	60	24	1.6	1.0	.5	.3	.5	.3	.5	.4
2-5	93	28	1.5	.9	.6	.4	.5	.3	.4	.2
1	50	9	1.4	1.0	.6	.4	.4	.4	.4	.2
under 1	65	7	1.2	.9	.5	.6	.4	.2	.3	.1
3 children										
12-17 years	26	16	1.4	1.1	.6	.3	.4	.4	.5	.4
6-11	58	26	1.3	1.7	.5	.6	.5	.6	.4	.6
2-5	70	13	1.4	.9	.5	.5	.5	.2	.4	.1
1	48	2	1.4		.6		.5		.4	
under 1	31	4	1.4	.5	.7	.4	.5	.1	.3	
4 children										
12-17 years	5	9	1.7	2.7	.9	.9	.4	.5	.4	1.3
6-11	51	15	1.5	1.1	.6	.4	.5	.2	.4	.4
2-5	32	1	1.7		.7		.5		.5	
1	19	3	1.3	1.0	.8	.6	.3	.3	.2	.1
under 1	32	2	1.5		.8		.5		.2	
5-6 children										
12-17 years	0	1								
6-11	16	2	2.0		.6		.8		.5	
2-5	17	3	1.8	.7	.7	.3	.6	.4	.4	
1	6	1	1.2		.6		.3		.4	
under 1	8	2	1.8		.7		.5		.6	
7-9 children										
6-11 years	2	0								
2-5	10	2	1.6		.8		.3		.5	
1	3	0	2.4		1.3		.7		.4	
under 1	4	0	1.8		.7		.8		.4	

[a]NE and E indicate households with nonemployed or employed wives.

[b]Sum of average time for individual workers may not equal total time of all workers because of rounding and because averages of children's time include only house holds with children of specified ages.

[c]Time is reported only if there were three or more families and if average time was 3 minutes or more.

by family type and employment of wives

All clothing care		Wives' time Washing by machine		Ironing		Spec. clothing care		House-holds with teen-agers		All clothing care		Teenagers' time Washing by machine		Ironing		Spec. clothing care	
NE	E	NE	E	NE	E	NE	E	NE	E	NE	E	NE	E	NE	E	NE	E
Average hours per day[c]										Average hours per day[c]							
.7	.6	.2	.2	.2	.2	.3	.2										
1.2	.7	.2	.3	.4	.2	.5	.2										
1.4	.4	.4	.2	.4	.1	.6	.1										
1.0	.7	.3	.1	.4	.1	.4	.5										
1.1	.9	.3	.3	.4	.2	.4	.4	22	20	.1	.1					.1	
1.5	.8	.4	.2	.5	.3	.6	.3										
1.0	.6	.3	.2	.4	.1	.3	.2										
.9	1.4	.4	.6	.3	.8	.2	.1										
1.1		.4		.4		.3											
1.3	1.2	.5	.3	.4	.4	.4	.5	27	15	.1	.3			.1			.2
1.5	.8	.5	.3	.5	.3	.5	.2	26	16	.1	.2			.1			.2
1.4	.9	.6	.4	.5	.3	.4	.2	26	11		.1	.1					
1.4	1.0	.6	.4	.4	.4	.4	.2	2	2								
1.2	.9	.5	.6	.4	.2	.3	.1										
1.2	.7	.5	.3	.3	.2	.4	.2	26	16	.2	.4			.1	.1	.1	.2
1.2	1.6	.5	.6	.4	.5	.3	.5	27	15	.1	.2			.1			
1.3	.9	.5	.5	.5	.2	.3	.1	29	2	.2						.2	
1.3		.6		.4		.3		6	1	.8				.2		.6	
1.4		.7	.4	.5	.1	.3		3	1								
1.4	2.1	.9	.9	.4	.4	.2	.8	5	9	.3	.6			.1		.2	.5
1.3	.8	.6	.4	.4	.1	.3	.2	20	8	.5	.4			.1		.4	.4
1.6		.7		.5		.4		9	1	.1							
1.3		.8	.6	.3	.3	.2	.1	6	1								
1.4		.8		.5		.2		3	0	.1		.1					
								0	1								
1.7		.6		.8		.3		12	2	.3						.3	
1.7		.7	.3	.6	.3	.4		11	1	.1							
.9		.4		.2		.2		3	1								
1.8		.7		.5		.6		5	1								
								2	0								
1.5		.8		.3		.4		10	2	.1							
1.9		1.3		.5		.1		3	0	.3				.2		.1	
1.6		.7		.5		.4		3	0	.2				.2			

TABLE 7.7—Percentage of households using selected equipment and services for washing and special clothing care on record days, by employment of wives
(1,296 husband–wife households, Syracuse, N.Y., 1967-68)

	All house- holds	Nonemployed- wife households	Employed- wife households
N =	1,296	979	317
		Percent	
Washing by machine			
No equipment used on record days	40	38	46
Automatic washer	57	59	50
Combination washer-dryer	1	1	1
Dryer	42	44	37
Nonautomatic washer	3	3	2
Commercial laundry	3	3	2
Diaper service	3	4[a]	1[b]
Paid help for washing	1	1	2
Special clothing care			
Sewing equipment	30	31	26
Commercial drycleaning	6	7	6
Coin-operated drycleaning	<1	<1	<1

[a]Of the 343 nonemployed-wife households with children under 2, 11% used diaper service.
[b]Of the 35 employed-wife households with children under 2, 6% used diaper service.

TABLE 7.8—Percentage of all households using laundry equipment on the record days at various locations, by selected variables
(1,296 husband–wife households, Syracuse, N.Y., 1967-68)

Households	Number of families	At home	Coin laundry	Elsewhere
			Percent	
Number of children				
0	168	71	20	9
1	210	89	7	4
2	378	95	5	
3	294	97	2	
4	169	95	4	1
5-9	77	97	3	
Age of wives in families without children				
Under 25	42	45	42	13
25 39	42	68	21	11
40-54	42	90	7	2
55 and over	42	81	10	10
Socioeconomic level				
Class 1 (highest)	163	92	5	3
Class 2	163	89	10	2
Class 3	402	92	5	3
Class 4	483	92	7	2
Class 5	85	92	8	
Nonemployed wives	979	92	6	2
Employed wives	317	88	9	3

TABLE 7.9—Frequency, during previous 7 days, of use of selected equipment or sewing, and washing by hand, by employment of wives
(*1,296 husband–wife households, Syracuse, N.Y., 1967-68*)

Number of days Per week	Automatic washer at home		Coin laundry		Nonautomatic washer at home		Commercial laundry	
	NEa	E	NE	E	NE	E	NE	E
N =	979	317						
			Percent of households					
0	10	11	92	87	92	95	88	87
1	6	14	5	10	2	1	9	11
2	12	16	2	3	2	2	2	1
3	15	17			2	1	1	
4	13	11			1			
5	14	7			1			
6	15	11						
7	15	13						
Average number of days	3.9	3.3						

aNE and E indicate households with nonemployed or employed wives.

commercial services for washing by machine and frequency of ironing,

Ironing				Special clothing care			
Clothing		Household textiles		Sewing or mending		Washing by hand	
NE	E	NE	E	NE	E	NE	E
Percent of households							
5	9	34	37	12	16	20	17
22	27	36	41	30	32	27	22
30	21	18	14	29	26	25	22
22	17	7	6	14	15	13	9
10	11	3	1	7	5	6	8
6	7	1	1	4	4	4	8
2	3			2	1	1	5
2	6			2	1	4	10
2.5	2.5	1.2	1.0	2.0	1.9	1.9	2.6

TABLE 7.10—Frequency of clothing care activities during previous 7 days, by
(1,296 husband-wife households, Syracuse, N.Y., 1967-68)

Variable	Number of households NE[a]	E	Washing with automatic washer NE	E
			Average number of days	
Number of children				
0	97	71	1.7	1.5
1	149	61	3.3	3.2
2	295	83	4.1	3.6
3	233	61	4.2	4.5
4	139	30	4.8	4.3
5 or more	66	11	5.1	4.9
All households	979	317	4.4	3.8
Age of youngest child				
12-17 years	80	61	3.3	3.5
6-11	210	86	3.9	3.6
2-5	248	63	4.1	4.0
1	163	20	4.5	5.0
Under 1	181	16	4.6	4.7
Age of wives in families without children				
Under 25				
25-39				
40-54				
55 and over				
Socioeconomic level				
Class 1 (highest)				
Class 2				
Class 3				
Class 4				
Class 5				

[a]NE and E indicate households with nonemployed or employed wives.

selected variables

Number of households	Ironing			Special clothing care	
	All ironing	Clothing ironed	Household textiles ironed	Sewing or mending	Washing by hand
			Average number of days		
168	1.5	1.5	.9	1.8	2.5
210	2.2	2.2	1.0	1.7	2.1
278	2.5	2.3	1.2	2.0	2.1
294	2.9	2.9	1.1	2.1	2.0
169	2.8	2.8	1.1	2.1	1.4
77	3.3	3.3	1.2	2.4	2.0
42				1.6	2.3
42				1.6	2.3
42				1.9	2.8
42				2.2	2.7
163				2.2	2.0
163				2.1	2.2
402				1.9	2.1
483				1.9	2.1
85				2.1	1.8

TABLE 7.11—Frequency of washing by automatic washer during previous 7 days, by family type and employment of wives
(*1,296 husband-wife households, Syracuse, N.Y., 1967-68*)

Family type	Nonemployed-wife households	Employed-wife households
	N = 979	N = 317
	Average number of days	
No-child households by age of wives		
under 25 years	1.1	1.3
25-39	2.0	1.5
40-54	1.9	2.0
55 and over	1.5	1.5
Number of children by age of youngest child		
1 child		
12-17 years	2.9	2.7
6-11	3.1	3.3
2-5	3.2	2.9
1	3.2	5.0
under 1	3.7	
2 children		
12-17 years	3.0	3.1
6-11	3.5	2.9
2-5	4.2	4.1
1	4.5	4.4
under 1	4.6	4.3
3 children		
12-17 years	3.8	4.6
6-11	3.9	4.3
2-5	3.9	4.5
1	4.8	
under 1	4.6	<.1
4 children		
12-17 years	4.2	3.6
6-11	4.1	4.0
2-5	4.7	
1	5.4	<.1
under 1	5.1	
5-6 children		
12-17 years		
6-11	4.8	
2-5	4.0	<.1
1	4.5	
under 1	6.8	
7-9 children		
6-11 years		
2-5	5.0	
1	<.1	
under 1	<.1	

TABLE 7.12—Percentage of all households using selected washing equipment or commercial services, by number of children

(1,296 husband-wife households, Syracuse, N.Y., 1967-68)

Number of children	Percent of families in sample	Automatic washer at home	Nonautomatic washer at home	Coin laundry	Commercial laundry
		Percent of record days equipment was used			
0	13	5	9	27	25
1	16	14	10	24	17
2	29	31	28	25	23
3	23	26	27	10	17
4-6	17	22	24	14	13
7-9	2	2	2	--	5
Total families	1,296				
Total days equipment or service used in previous 7 days		4,887	236	175	192

TABLE 7.13—Average loads washed, average pieces of clothing and household textiles ironed, and pieces hand washed, by selected variables
(1,296 husband-wife households, Syracuse, N.Y., 1967-68)

Variables	Total households	Loads washed On record days	Loads washed In 7 days	Pieces ironed on record days All	Clothing	Textiles	Pieces washed by hand on the record days
All families	1,296	1.5	9.9	6.5	5.5	1.0	1.2
Nonemployed wives	979	1.5		7.0	5.9	1.1	1.2
Employed wives	317	1.3		4.8	4.1	.7	1.2
Number of children							
0	168	.7	4.3	3.6			
1	210	1.0	7.1	5.1			
2	378	1.5	9.8	6.7			
3	294	1.8	11.4	7.4			
4	169	2.1	14.1	7.0			
5-6	56	2.2		9.3			
7-9	21	3.0	20.7	6.6			
Age of youngest child							
12-17 years	141	1.4	6.6	6.1			
6-11	296	1.6	6.7	7.4			
2-5	311	1.5	7.0	6.9			
1	183	1.7	7.2	6.5			
less than 1	197	1.8	7.8	7.1			
Socioeconomic level							
Class 1 (highest)	163			5.2			
Class 2	163			5.7			
Class 3	402			6.6			
Class 4	483			7.1			
Class 5	85			6.5			
Season of the year							
January-April	431			5.2			
May-August	429			7.7			
September-December	436			6.5			

TABLE 7.14—Average number of loads washed on record days, by family type and employment of wives
(1,296 husband-wife households, Syracuse, N.Y., 1967-68)

Family type	Nonemployed-wife households	Employed-wife households
	N = 979	N = 317
	Average loads washed	
No-child households by age of wives		
under 25 years	.6	.4
25–39	.7	.9
40–54	.6	1.3
55 and over	.5	.6
Number of children by age of youngest child		
1 child		
12–17 years	1.0	1.1
6–11	1.0	.8
2–5	.7	.8
1	.9	1.3
under 1	1.4	
2 children		
12–17 years	1.5	1.2
6–11	1.5	1.2
2–5	1.5	1.2
1	1.6	1.7
under 1	1.4	1.4
3 children		
12–17 years	1.5	1.3
6–11	1.7	2.0
2–5	1.6	1.9
1	1.8	
under 1	2.3	1.5
4 children		
12–17 years	2.4	2.3
6–11	2.0	1.8
2–5	2.0	
1	2.4	1.8
under 1	2.2	
5–6 children		
12–17 years		
6–11	1.9	
2–5	1.9	1.7
1	2.8	
under 1	2.6	
7–9 children		
6–11 years		
2–5	2.7	
1	3.8	
under 1	2.0	

TABLE 7.15—Distribution of numbers of loads washed, pieces ironed and washed by hand, by employment of wives

(1,296 husband-wife households, Syracuse, N.Y., 1967-68)

| | | | Ironed | | | | Washed by hand | | | |
| | | | Clothing | | Textiles | | Clothing | | Textiles | |
	Washed NE[a]	E	NE	E	NE	E	NE	E	NE	E
					Percent					
Number of loads washed in previous 7 days										
0	1	2								
1-3	6	11								
4-6	19	32								
7-9	23	20								
10-12	26	20								
13-15	11	10								
16-18	7	2								
19+	7	6								
Number of pieces ironed on record days										
0			59	61	82	88				
1-9			17	23	14	10				
10-19			12	9	3	2				
20-29			6	5	1					
30+			5	2						
Number of pieces washed by hand on record days										
0							75	68	99	99
1-2							12	18	1	1
3-6							8	10		
7+							5	4		

[a]NE and E indicate households with nonemployed or employed wives.

Chapter VIII

Marketing and Management

Rank Correlations with Time Used for Marketing[1,2]

Marketing was a frequently performed activity (68% of the record days in both nonemployed- and employed-wife households) and one which required a proportionally large expenditure of time (Table 3.8). The time spent on marketing made up as high a proportion of total household work time as did regular house care (12% in nonemployed- and 14% in employed-wife households). Of the total time spent on marketing, .4 hour represented travel time (Table 6.26).

Marketing included all shopping, whether or not purchases were made, by any member of the household or by other workers for the household. This shopping was for food, clothing, household supplies and equipment, or other types of purchases for the use of the whole family or its individual members. Time recorded included time for shopping in person, by telephone, by mail, or in home sales; time for putting purchases away; and transportation time involved in shopping.

Rank Correlations of Total Marketing Time of All Workers and Major Variables

Number of Children (Table 8.1). Number of children was slightly related to the time spent by all workers on marketing and shopping (.09). Though weak, the relationship was relatively independent of the effects of other variables.

Ages of Youngest and Oldest Child (Table 8.1). These two variables had the strongest relationships of any of the major variables with total time spent on marketing and shopping (-.16

and -.18). The correlation value for age of oldest child was a little closer than the correlation value for age of youngest child; this difference indicated a relatively greater strength for age of oldest child than for age of youngest child for all workers' time spent on marketing.

Of the three major family composition variables, age of youngest child had the highest correlation (-.16) with marketing time, and there was very little change in the correlation when other variables were held constant. The stronger correlation of age of youngest child than of number of children with time spent on marketing and shopping probably comes from the increased complexity of the buying process as children become older, as Manning (1968, p. 38) has pointed out.

Rank Correlations of Time of Individual Workers and Major Variables

Individual Workers' Share in Marketing. The participation of employed and nonemployed wives in marketing was considerably less frequent than the total participation of all workers (Table 3.11). Though wives were the most frequent workers, they did marketing on about half the record days, in contrast to a total of seven-tenths of record days on which the activity was performed. Both husbands and teenagers marketed on about a third of the record days; children 6 to 11 were involved on 14% of the record days. Except for an increase in teenagers' frequency of participation, the distribution of the work in this activity was the same in both employed- and nonemployed-wife households. Wives' proportion of total time in marketing declined only a small amount when they were employed, from 58% to 53% (Table 3.10). The difference was offset by an increased proportion of time from teenagers (from 9% to 15%). Husbands' time was a quarter of all workers' time for marketing in households with either employed or nonemployed wives.

Age of Youngest Child (Table 8.2). This variable had the closest relationship of any of the variables with wives' time spent on marketing

---

[1]All Tau values reported in tabular form or referred to in the text were significant at the .001 level unless otherwise stated. Although correlation coefficients were determined for all major variables, only significant relationships are reported in tables and only the correlations strong enough to change the amount of time used daily are discussed to any extent.

[2]For an explanation of meaning of positive and negative correlation values as related to the different variables, see pages 30-31.

(-.10). Although the relationship was not strong, wives spent a little more time on marketing when children in the family were older.

Teenagers' time use for marketing work was somewhat related to age of youngest child (-.11), and this relationship was independent of the effects of other variables.

Education of Husbands (Table 8.2). There was only slight association (-.06) of wives' time for marketing and husbands' education.

Husbands' Hours of Employment (Table 8.2). The only variable related to husbands' time use on marketing was their hours of employment (-.12); husbands spent a little less time on marketing when they worked longer hours.

Time Spent on Marketing

Total Time of All Workers

Number of Children and Employment of Wives (Table 8.3). Although total time use for marketing was not closely correlated with number of children, more time usually was spent in larger than in smaller families, whether or not wives were employed. The differences in marketing time by employment of wives were not related to size of family.

Age of Youngest Child and Employment of Wives (Table 8.4). The relationship between age of youngest child and total time use for marketing was apparent in nonemployed-wife households. When wives were not employed, total marketing time increased consistently by age groups of youngest children (from an average of .9 hour a day when the youngest was a baby to an average of 2.0 hours a day when the youngest was a teenager). The greatest difference (about half an hour a day) was between groups with the youngest child 2 to 5 and those with the youngest child between 6 and 11. When wives were employed, total time spent on marketing was highest in families with teenagers as youngest (1.8 hours a day, on the average) but varied inconsistently among other age groups.

Family Type and Employment of Wives (Tables 8.5 and 8.6). Although family type did not show a significant correlation with time use of all workers for marketing, the average times for each family type are presented in tabular form. This table shows the somewhat stronger relationship between age of the youngest child and total time than that for total time and number of children.

Time Spent by Individual Workers

Number of Children and Employment of Wives (Table 8.3). Neither nonemployed nor employed wives' time use for marketing showed a relationship to number of children. In both nonemployed- and employed-wife households the average time use for marketing was the same (.7 hour for wives, .3 for husbands, .4 for teenagers, and .2 for children 6 to 11).

Age of Youngest Child and Employment of Wives (Table 8.4). Nonemployed wives' time for marketing was related to age of youngest child, tending to increase as age of the youngest child increased. Employed wives spent a little less time on marketing than nonemployed wives, except when there were children under 1 year, but their time use did not vary consistently by age groups of children. The time of nonemployed wives increased by an average of half an hour a day between the time spent when their youngest child was a baby and when the youngest was a teenager.

Whether or not their mothers were employed, teenagers' time use on marketing usually increased between families in which the youngest was a baby and those in which teenagers themselves were the youngest children. The time spent by children 6 to 11 and by other workers on marketing showed no relationship with age of the youngest child.

Rank Correlations with Time Used for Management

Probably the most significant and least quantifiable part of household production related to the managerial function. Reporting of management activities was limited in both frequency and in total time for households of both employed and nonemployed wives. Under-reporting may account for some of the low average time of management as a separate activity. Management is an ongoing activity and some of it can be carried on while doing other activities; thus, time used for it is not easily identified and may often have been reported as part of other activities. On the other hand, some managerial activities, such as preparing income tax returns or planning for family parties, may require a large amount of easily identified time. It is extremely difficult to obtain an accurate measurement of time used in management as a separate activity.

Management does comprise some operations that are distinctive and that provide a core around which some basic features of the activity may be identified. In this study, time for management as a separate activity was identified primarily as that time recognized and recorded for decision-making and planning—such as thinking about and discussing alternatives to long- and short-range plans, measuring space for planning renovations, figuring out how much money would be available to carry out plans; organizing, checking plans as they are carried out, supervising work of others, keeping records, and evaluating the results of completed plans. In addition, certain kinds of planning for specific household work activities such as planning menus and making out shopping lists were classified as management activities.

Rank Correlations of Total Time Used by All Workers and Major Variables

Number of Children, Age of Children, and Family Type (Table 8.1). None of the family composition variables correlated significantly with total time use for management.

Employment of Wives (Table 8.1). Time use of all workers for management was only weakly related to employment of wives (-.06).

Socioeconomic Level (Table 8.1). The highest correlation between socioeconomic level and time use for any household work activity was in management (-.09). The change in time use, however, between higher and lower socioeconomic levels was found to be very small; time used at the two highest socioeconomic levels was .5 hour, in contrast with .3 hour at the two lowest levels.

Education of Wives and Husbands (Table 8.1). The relationships between these two variables and total time use for management were in the same direction as that for socioeconomic level. The correlation values of -.13 and -.10, respectively, for wives' and husbands' education with all workers' time used for management were higher than for other variables; this indicated that more time was used on this activity in households in which either wives or husbands had a higher level of education.

Rank Correlations of Time Used by Individual Workers and Major Variables

Individual Workers' Share in Management. Wives were the principal workers in management whether or not they were employed (Table 3.10). Husbands were the only other workers who participated to any extent in management; their

time accounted for over a third of all workers' time. Teenagers' management time was 2% of total management time when mothers were not employed and 3% when they were.

Employment of Wives (Table 8.2). The time used by wives for management was slightly associated with their employment (-.08).

Education of Wives and Husbands (Table 8.2). Wives' time use for managerial activities was related to the education of both wives and husbands (-.14 and -.10); these relationships were higher than those of family composition or wives' employment. Wives who had a higher level of education or whose husbands had a higher level of education spent a little more time on management than those with lower education. Husbands' time use for management was weakly related to wives' education (-.06). Teenagers' time use on management was also somewhat related to their mothers' education (-.11); this indicated a slightly increased use of time by teenagers as mothers' education increased.

Husbands' Hours of Employment (Table 8.2). The only significant correlation between this variable and time use of any worker in management was with teenagers' time (-.11). Teenagers' time was, however, a relatively minor part of all workers' time in management, and their decreased time when their fathers worked longer hours did not affect the distribution of total time.

Time Spent on Management

Total Time of All Workers and Individual Workers' Time (Tables 8.3 to 8.6)

Number of Children, Age of Youngest Child, Family Type, and Employment of Wives. Although none of the family composition variables related significantly to time use in management, average times of all workers and individual workers are presented in tabular form. The relationship of employment of wives with all workers' time was weak; however, its effects can be seen in the lower time use in employed-wife households compared to nonemployed-wife households. The average time spent on management by all workers was .4 hour when wives were not employed and .3 hour when they were (Table 8.3). The lower time use of employed wives in smaller families and in some families with older children was not enough to change wives' average daily time of .2 hour (Tables 8.3 and 8.4).

Characteristics and Content of Marketing Activities

The time demands for shopping obviously differ according to the types of products for which shopping is done. Food marketing, which typically also includes purchases of various types of household supplies, is performed more frequently than the other kinds of marketing and also more regularly, usually on a certain day of the week. Purchases of clothing may also be fairly regular but usually are less frequent, and may take a considerable amount of time of several family members. Some purchases, such as medical supplies, are typically irregular in nature, may or may not be made quickly, and frequently are part of a general shopping expedition. Major items of household equipment, on the other hand, are purchased infrequently but may require considerable time for family consultations or several shopping trips before a decision is reached and purchase accomplished.

Various considerations from outside the household also enter into shopping decisions and time used. Since transportation is a key factor in shopping, decisions on amount to be done at one time may depend on various problems involved in reaching the shopping center, such as distance and times of traffic congestion. Also, since shopping usually means travel from the home, it may be dovetailed with the schedules of family members, such as stopping to shop on the way home from work or in conjunction with chauffeuring children to school or to other activities. Another factor in time spent on marketing is that frequently, but not regularly, more than one family member takes part in the activity.

The variations in marketing time brought about by the range of decisions that affect any one component of the time have made it difficult to identify any one variable related to the activity as an indicator of output.

In the present study data were collected for three factors expected to be associated with the content of work in marketing. These were: planning methods used for shopping, kinds of shopping on the 2 record days, and the person who did the shopping. Because marketing for food (including household supplies) was the most frequent and likely to be the most widespread type, additional data were collected on frequency of shopping for food and the number of trips made in the previous 7 days for food and household supplies.

Planning Methods Used for Shopping
(Table 8.7)

No shopping had been done on the record days in over a third of either the nonemployed- or employed-wife households; three-fifths of wives reported having shopped. The most popular method of planning was to have in mind the supplies and goods needed, that is, "in-the-head" planning. About two-thirds of the shoppers had used this method in contrast with about one-fourth who had used a written list; 9% reported a combination of the two methods.

Practically no differences were evident between nonemployed- and employed-wife households in their planning for shopping or in type of planning method used. Planning for shopping was not closely related to family size; more families with children (55% to 65%) planned for shopping than families without children (48%). Use of a written list was somewhat related to family size; about a third of the families with either no children or with one child and about a fourth of other family sizes used this method. In families without children, planning had been done by more of the younger wives (under age 40) than by those who were older; use of a written list declined from 64% of wives under 25 to 19% of those 55 and older. Neither planning nor method of planning was related to socioeconomic level.

Frequency of Major Shopping for Food
(Table 8.8)

The regularity of major food marketing activities can be seen from Table 8.8, which shows that 97% of wives, employed or not, reported a regular frequency for major food shopping. The usual frequency was weekly (79%) for both nonemployed and employed wives. Of the remainder, about as many said they shopped more frequently (8%) as less often (10%). The only employment difference was that the employed wives tended to shop a little more frequently.

The frequency of shopping was not significantly related to the presence or number of children. The largest families (five or more children) were a little more likely to shop biweekly (12%) than families with fewer children. The frequency of shopping for food was not directly related to age of wives, but households in which wives were 55 or older were more inclined to have no set pattern (14%) than those in which wives were younger (7%).

Marketing on the Record Days and Previous 7 Days (Table 8.9)

Of the 1,296 families in the sample, 57% reported shopping for food and household supplies on the record days, 11% for household equipment and furnishings, 16% for clothing, and 23% for other items.

Wives were the principal shoppers for each kind of purchasing. Husbands were the second most frequent shoppers for food and household supplies (14%), followed by a combination of family members (8%). Two or more family members had shopped together for household equipment and furniture in 3% of the households, though 2% of husbands and 6% of wives had made such purchases by themselves. Only a few husbands and children had purchased clothing alone (1% each), and in only 2% of the households did children shop for miscellaneous items such as medical supplies or gifts. Shopping for the household by anyone other than a family member was minimal.

The kinds of shopping done and the principal shoppers were about the same in both non-employed- and employed-wife households. Although the amount of shopping for food and household supplies was not closely related to the number of children, more of the larger families (at least three-fifths) than of smaller ones (over half) had shopped. The type of person who did the shopping was not related to number of children.

The highest percentage of families without children that shopped for food and supplies on the record days were those with wives age 55 or over. Shopping by wives alone predominated in each age group and for each type of shopping; however, shopping for food and supplies by husbands in childless households increased with age of wives.

Shopping for household furniture and equipment on the record days was not related to any of the selected variables.

The amount of shopping for clothing on the record days was related to the presence of children and somewhat related to number; clothing shopping increased from 6% of households with no children to 12% of those with one child and about one-fifth of those with two or more children.

Number of Trips in Previous 7 Days to Shop for Food and Household Supplies (Table 8.10)

Although major food shopping was reported as once per week, additional trips were made by various family members to purchase food and household supplies. About seven-tenths of the wives and over half of the husbands had made from one to three trips for this purpose during the previous 7 days. When eight or more trips had been made during the previous week, they had mostly been made by the wife. Employed wives had made a few more food-shopping trips in the previous 7 days than nonemployed wives (23% versus 19% had made four or more food-shopping trips).

The number of trips for food shopping by wives or husbands increased between families with no children and those with children; however, about one-fifth of the wives and one-tenth of the husbands had made four or more shopping trips in all families with children. Making four or more trips by children increased as family size advanced, from less than 1% of families with one child to one-fifth of those with five or more.

In families with no children at home, wives under age 40 tended to have made from one to three food-shopping trips during the previous 7 days. Wives over age 40 were more inclined than younger ones to have made no food-shopping trips, or conversely to have made four or more. In these families with no children, husbands' frequency of food shopping increased when wives were 55 or older (to 55% making three trips and 12% making four or more), but their number of trips was not closely associated with age of wives.

Trips by wives for food shopping were not associated with socioeconomic level, nor were husbands', although the proportion of husbands who had made four or more food-shopping trips was highest at the lowest level (18%). The number of trips for food shopping by children tended to increase with declining socioeconomic level, from 14% of the highest level who had made one or more such trips to 38% of the lowest.

Characteristics and Content of Management

The aspects of management explored in the present study were: techniques used by wives to organize their use of time; wives' evaluation of themselves as managers; and the performance of management and record keeping on the record days and during the preceding week. Only seven families reported no time for managerial activities on the record days; the average time spent was .4 hour a day for all families.

Techniques for Organizing Use of Time
(Table 8.11)

As Steidl and Bratton have pointed out (1968, p. 212), methods of organizing to accomplish household work are partly determined by the kind of work involved. There is, therefore, no one ideal method that will apply to all households or all wives, nor even to the same household at all times. The interest in the present study was in the extent to which certain common methods of organizing work on a particular day were used.

Wives in the sample reported using more than one technique to organize their time. They most frequently (84% of the sample) said that they did some mental scheduling of activities; 75% said they did some planning for their time use; 71% depended on daily routine to organize their activities; and over half used a regular weekly routine. Only a small portion (16%) used written schedules, and half of the wives reported that they assigned tasks to other family members. About the only difference between nonemployed and employed wives in the techniques used was the higher proportion of employed than nonemployed wives who assigned work to others.

Only one planning method seemed to be associated with the number of children in the family; assignment of tasks to family members increased fairly regularly as the number of children increased (from 15% of those with no children and 31% of those with one child to 90% of those with five or more children). The highest use of planning was in one-child households (80%) and the lowest when there were five or more children (68%), but this method was not directly associated with number of children. Daily routine was related to the presence of children in the household: three-fifths of those with no children used this method, in contrast with three-fourths of families with children. Use of a written schedule was somewhat related to family size; more of those with no children or one child used this method than did those with two or more children.

The only type of organizing method consistently related to age of wives in childless families was weekly routine, the use of which increased slightly by age (from 50% of wives under 25 to 55% of wives 55 and older). Of the groups, wives aged 40 to 54 in households with no children had the smallest percentages who reported planning (55%), written schedules (14%), mental scheduling (71%), or assignment of tasks to other family members (2%), while wives under 25 had the highest proportional use of any of the methods

except daily or weekly routines.

The organizing techniques of the two lowest socioeconomic classes differed from those of the two highest; use of a written schedule declined with socioeconomic level from 27% of the highest class to 8% of the lowest. Planning was reported somewhat more frequently at the three highest socioeconomic levels (about four-fifths) than at the two lowest (about seven-tenths). The highest levels used weekly routine as a planning guide less (about half) than the three lowest levels (about three-fifths); they also were somewhat less likely to assign tasks to other family members than the three lowest classes. Daily routines were used about equally at all socioeconomic levels.

Wives as Good Managers (Table 8.11)

In response to the direct question, "Do you consider yourself a good manager?" over four-fifths of the wives, whether employed or not, said "yes." A small proportion did not answer definitely "yes" or "no" to this question; some qualified their answers, and some were uncertain. In response to the question of why they evaluated their management as they did, almost half of the 1,155 wives who responded to the question related their evaluation to their organization and control of planning; more than a quarter gave a subjective overall evaluation, such as that their families are well cared for, they get things done, or they make good use of resources; for about 10% the evaluation related to their types of plans and planning; and for another 10% it related to their personal qualities such as flexibility, thriftiness, efficiency, or enjoyment of life.

Wives' view of themselves as good managers declined slightly as number of children increased (from 86% of those with one child to 79% of those with five or more children). In families without children, the youngest wives (under 25) were more inclined than older ones to consider themselves good managers (90%, compared with about 80% of each other age group). Socioeconomic status did not seem to relate to wives' evaluation of themselves as managers. Wives' view of themselves as good managers made no difference in the total time spent on management and record keeping; an average of .4 hour a day was used in either case.

Participants in Management Activities on the Record Days and During the Previous 7 Days (Table 8.12)

Because of differences in frequencies, management activities and record keeping were kept separate for this part of the analysis.

Of the total sample, 62% reported that someone in the household had performed some management activity on the record days. Such activities were reported for husbands and wives together (31% of the total sample) or for only wives (29%). In only 2% of the households were husbands reported as the only ones who had performed management work. Only six children were reported to have done some management activity on the record days. Fewer employed-wife households (58%) than nonemployed-wife households (64%) had reported management activities on the record days.

Record keeping was reported by a much smaller proportion of families (32%) than was management. A similar proportion of employed- and nonemployed-wife households had done some record-keeping activities on the record days (34% and 31%). Record keeping had been done by wives only (18%) or to a lesser extent by husbands only (9%), and in a small proportion of households (5%) by husbands and wives together.

The extent of managerial activities in the scheme of household work can be seen much more clearly from performance over a week. Almost all (98%) of the 1,296 families reported some management and record keeping during the previous 7 days, whether or not wives were employed. Management activities were most likely to be done by both husbands and wives (63%), although in about one-third of the households wives were the only ones for whom such work was reported. In only 3% of the families were management activities reported for husbands exclusively for the previous 7 days.

Record keeping was also done by husbands and wives together, but to a lesser extent than management (37%); about the same proportions of wives (31%) and husbands (29%) did such work exclusive of the other during the previous 7 days. Although more employed (36%) than nonemployed wives (30%) had done the record keeping, slightly fewer husbands of employed wives (26%) than of those whose wives were not employed (30%) had done this work.

The performance of management during the previous 7 days was not related to number of children. Usually this activity had been done by husbands and wives together (three-fifths to two-thirds) without regard to the number of children. In families without children, performance of management activities during the previous 7 days was somewhat associated with age of wives; a smaller proportion of households with wives in the two older groups reported this activity. A sizable difference was evident between the childless households with younger and those with older wives in the proportion of households in which management was done jointly by husbands and wives; 74% to 79% of the wives and husbands had managed jointly in the two younger groups, in contrast with 50% and 62% in the two older ones. Performance of management activities by wives only was reported somewhat less frequently when wives were under 40 than when they were older.

Performance of joint management activities by husbands and wives was highest (75%) at the highest socioeconomic level and declined to 56% at the lowest level. Report of performance of managerial activities by wives only also was related to socioeconomic level, but increased as status lowered (from 22% of the highest level to 39% of the lowest). Management performance by only husbands seemed not to be related to socio-economic level.

Number of children was not related to record-keeping activities during the previous 7 days, or to whether records were kept individually or jointly by husbands and wives. Among families without children, record keeping was a joint activity for wives and husbands a little more often when wives were under age 40 than when they were older. Record keeping by only husbands during the previous 7 days was highest when wives were under 25 (29%) and when they were 55 or older (26%).

Socioeconomic level had no apparent effect on the proportion of families doing record keeping in the previous 7 days. Joint performance of this activity by wives and husbands was not related to socioeconomic level. The proportions of wives in the two lowest socioeconomic levels who did this work alone were about double those of the two highest (two-fifths versus one-fifth). On the other hand, husbands who did record keeping alone declined in percentage with socioeconomic level (from 36% at the two highest levels to 19% at the lowest level).

TABLE 8.1—Rank and partial rank correlation coefficients for
(1,260 husband-wife households, Syracuse, N.Y.,

Total time of <u>all workers</u> in:	Kendall Tau[a]
MARKETING	
Family composition variables	
Number of children	.09
Age of youngest child	−.16
Age of oldest child	−.18
Family type	.05*
Employment	
Husbands' hours	−.04≠
Education	
Husbands	−.05*
Housing	
House type	.05**
MANAGEMENT AND RECORD KEEPING	
Family composition variables	
Number of children	.05**
Age of oldest child	−.04≠
Family type	.04≠
Employment	
Wives	−.06
Socioeconomic level	−.09
Wives' education	−.13
Husbands' education	−.10
Housing	
House type	.05*
Location of residence	.03≠

[a]All Tau values reported were significant at the .001 level unless otherwise indicated
positive and negative values, see pp. 30-31. Correlation coefficients were based on

[b]Partial rank correlation values are reported only for major variables at the .001 level

marketing and management time of all workers and major variables
1967-68)

Number of children	Partial rank correlations[b] with major variables held constant			
	Age of youngest child	Family type	Empl. of wives	House type
	.09		.09	.08
-.16			-.16	-.15
-.06	-.07	-.06		

as: * = .005, ** = .01 or .02, and ✝ = .03 to .05. For discussion of effects of ranking of variables on
1,260 households except for age of youngest child, for which only families with children were used (1,092).

of significance.

TABLE 8.2—Rank and partial rank correlation coefficients for marketing and management (*1,260 husband–wife households, Syracuse, N.Y., 1967-68*)

Time in:	Kendall Tau[a]	Partial rank correlations[b] with major variables held constant			
		Number of children	Age of youngest	Family type	Empl. of wives
MARKETING					
Family composition variables					
Number of children	.04†				
Age of youngest child	−.10	−.10			−.10
Employment					
Husbands' hours					
Education					
Wives	−.04†				
Husbands	−.06				
MANAGEMENT AND RECORD KEEPING					
Family composition variables					
Number of children	.05*				
Age of youngest child					
Family type	.04†				
Employment					
Wives	−.08	−.07	−.08	−.07	
Husbands' hours					
Education					
Wives	−.14				
Husbands	−.10				

[a]All Tau values reported were significant at the .001 level unless otherwise indicated as: * = .005, ** = .01 or .02, and † = .03 to .05. For discussion of effects of ranking of variables on positive and negative values, see pp. 30-31.

[b]Partial rank correlation values reported only for major variables at the .001 level of significance.

[c]Correlation coefficients were based on 1,260 households except for age of youngest child, for which only families with children were used (1,092).

[d]Tau values were computed on basis of 378 families with teenagers.

time of wives, husbands, and teenagers and major variables

Husbands' time[c]	Teenagers' time[d]			
		Partial rank correlations[b] with major variables held constant		
Kendall Tau[a]	Kendall Tau[a]	Number of children	Age of youngest	Empl. of wives
	.10* -.11	-.11		-.12
-.12				
-.03≠				
.03≠	-.07≠			
-.04**	-.11			
-.06 -.05**	-.11			

TABLE 8.3—Marketing and management time of all workers and individual workers, by
(1,296 husband-wife households, Syracuse, N.Y., 1967-68)

Activity	Number of children	Total number of families NE[a]	E	All workers (Total)[b] NE	E	Wives NE	E	Husbands NE	E
				Average hours per day[c]					
Marketing	0	97	71	1.0	.9	.7	.6	.3	.3
	1	149	61	1.1	1.0	.7	.5	.3	.3
	2	295	83	1.1	1.4	.7	.7	.3	.3
	3	233	61	1.5	1.4	.8	.7	.3	.3
	4	139	30	1.4	1.6	.7	.7	.3	.2
	5-6	47	9	1.5	1.4	.8	.8	.2	.4
	7-9	19	2	1.7		.8		.4	
	Average	979	317	1.3	1.2	.7	.7	.3	.3
Management and record keeping	0			.4	.3	.2	.2	.2	.1
	1			.4	.3	.2	.2	.1	.1
	2			.4	.3	.2	.2	.2	.1
	3			.4	.3	.3	.2	.1	.1
	4			.4	.2	.2	.2	.1	
	5-6			.5	.2	.3	.1	.1	.1
	7-9			.5		.3		.1	
	Average			.4	.3	.2	.2	.1	.1

[a]NE and E indicate households with nonemployed or employed wives.

[b]Sum of average time for individual workers may not equal total time of all workers because of rounding and because averages of children's time include only households with children of specified ages.

[c]Time is reported only if there were three or more families and if average time was 3 minutes or more.

number of children and employment of wives

Number of households with children 12-17 years		Time of children 12-17		Number of households with children 6-11 years		Time of children 6-11	
NE	E	NE	E	NE	E	NE	E
		Av. hrs. per day[c]				Av. hrs. per day[c]	
22	20	.2	.3	23	19	.1	.2
82	44	.3	.4	128	40	.1	
91	35	.5	.4	156	38	.2	.3
43	19	.5	.9	91	18	.4	.2
31	6	.4	.1	46	8	.2	.1
18	2	.5		19	2	.1	
287	126	.4	.4	463	125	.2	.2
							.1
			.1				

TABLE 8.4—Marketing and management time of all workers and individual workers, by (*1,128 husband-wife households, Syracuse, N.Y., 1967-68*)

Activity	Age of youngest child (years)	Number of families NE[a]	E	All workers (Total)[b] NE	E	Wives NE	E	Husbands NE	E
				Average hours per day[c]					
Marketing	12–17	80	61	2.0	1.8	1.0	.8	.5	.4
	6–11	210	86	1.7	1.3	.9	.6	.3	.2
	2–5	248	63	1.2	.9	.8	.6	.3	.3
	1	163	20	1.0	1.1	.6	.6	.3	.3
	Under 1	181	16	.9	1.4	.5	.8	.3	.5
	Average	882	246	1.3	1.3	.7	.7	.3	.3
Management and record keeping	12–17			.5	.3	.3	.2	.1	.1
	6–11			.4	.3	.3	.2	.1	.1
	2–5			.4	.3	.2	.2	.1	.1
	1			.4	.3	.2	.2	.2	.1
	Under 1			.4	.2	.2	.2	.1	
	Average			.4	.3	.2	.2	.1	.1

[a]NE and E indicate households with nonemployed or employed wives.

[b]Sum of average time for individual workers may not equal total time of all workers because of rounding and because averages of children's time include only households with children of specified ages.

[c]Time is reported only if there were three or more families and if average time was 3 minutes or more.

age of youngest child and employment of wives

Number of households with children 12-17 years		Time of children 12-17		Number of households with children 6-11 years		Time of children 6-11	
NE	E	NE	E	NE	E	NE	E
		Av. hrs. per day[c]				Av. hrs. per day[c]	
80	61	.5	.6				
87	41	.4	.4	210	86	.3	.2
85	17	.3	.2	133	24	.1	.1
20	5	.3	.2	77	9	.1	.2
15	2	.3		43	6	.2	.2
287	126	.4	.4	463	125	.2	.2
		.1					
		.1	.1				

TABLE 8.5—Marketing and management time of all workers, wives, and husbands, by family type and employment of wives
(1,296 husband–wife households, Syracuse, N.Y., 1967-68)

Family type	Number NE[a]	Number E	All workers' time[b] Marketing NE	Marketing E	Management and record keeping NE	E	Wives' time[b] Marketing NE	Marketing E	Management and record keeping NE	E	Husbands' time[b] Marketing NE	Marketing E	Management and record keeping NE	E
							Average hours per day[c]							
No-child households by age of wives														
under 25 years	16	26	1.3	.9	.3	.5	.9	.6	.2	.3	.3	.3	.1	.3
25-39	19	23	.9	.7	.5	.2	.6	.4	.3	.2	.3	.2	.2	.1
40-54	30	12	1.1	1.2	.4	.1	.7	1.1	.2	.1	.4	.2	.2	
55 and over	32	10	.9	.9	.3	.3	.6	.5	.2	.1	.3	.3	.2	.2
Number of children by age of youngest child														
1 child														
12-17 years	22	20	1.5	1.5	.4	.4	.8	.7	.2	.2	.5	.4	.1	.1
6-11	23	19	1.2	1.1	.3	.2	.8	.6	.2	.2	.3	.2	.1	
2-5	26	16	1.2	.5	.2	.2	.9	.2	.2	.1	.3	.3	.2	.1
1	37	5	1.1	.4	.4	.4	.8	.4	.2	.3	.3		.2	.1
under 1	41	1	.7		.5		.5		.3		.2		.2	
2 children														
12-17 years	27	15	2.1	2.1	.4	.4	1.0	.8	.3	.2	.6	.6	.1	.2
6-11	60	24	1.2	1.4	.5	.3	.7	.8	.2	.1	.2	.2	.2	.2
2-5	93	28	1.2	1.1	.5	.3	.8	.8	.2	.2	.3	.3	.2	.1
1	50	9	.8	1.2	.3	.5	.6	.6	.2	.3	.3	.6	.1	.2
under 1	65	7	.8	.9	.3	.2	.5	.6	.2	.2	.3	.2	.1	
3 children														
12-17 years	26	16	2.5	1.5	.5	.2	1.2	.8	.3	.1	.4	.4	.1	.1
6-11	58	26	1.8	1.3	.5	.5	.9	.5	.3	.2	.4	.2	.1	.2
2-5	70	13	1.3	1.2	.3	.3	.8	.8	.2	.2	.3	.3	.1	.1
1	48	2	1.1		.5		.6		.3		.3		.2	
under 1	31	4	.8	1.4	.3	.1	.5	.8	.2		.2	.5	.1	

	NE	E	NE	E	NE	E	NE	E	NE	E	NE	E	NE
4 children													
12–17 years	5	9	1.7	2.5	.8	.4	1.2	.9	.5	.3	.4	.1	.3
6–11	51	15	2.0	1.2	.4	.2	.9	.6	.3	.2	.3	.2	.1
2–5	32	1	1.1		.4		.6		.3		.2		.1
1	19	3	.8	1.3	.4		.5	.9	.1		.3	.3	.2
under 1	32	2	1.2		.3		.7		.2		.3		.2
5–6 children													
12–17 years	0	1											
6–11	16	2	2.4		.5		.9		.4		.3		.1
2–5	17	3	1.1	.7	.4		.7	.4	.3		.2		.1
1	6	1	1.0		.5		1.0		.4				.2
under 1	8	22	.9		.6		.5		.3				.3
7–9 children													
6–11 years	2	0											
2–5	10	2	1.3		.5		.7		.2		.3		.2
1	3	0	1.8		.6		.5		.5		.3		.1
under 1	4	0	1.7		.6		.8		.5				.1

[a] NE and E indicate households with nonemployed or employed wives.

[b] Sum of average time for individual workers may not equal total time of all workers because of rounding and because averages of children's time include only households with children of specified ages.

[c] Time is reported only if there were three or more families and if average time was 3 minutes or more.

TABLE 8.6—Marketing and management time of children 12-17 and 6-11, by family type and employment of wives

(413 husband–wife households with teenagers and 588 with children 6-11 years, Syracuse, N.Y., 1967-68)

Family type	Time of children 12-17 years						Time of children 6-11 years					
	Number NE[a]	E	Marketing NE	E	Mgmt & record keeping NE	E	Number NE	E	Marketing NE	E	Mgmt & record keeping NE	E
	Average hours per day[b]						Average hours per day[b]					
Number of children by age of youngest												
1 child												
12-17 years	22	20	.2	.3								
6-11							23	19	.1	.2		
2 children												
12-17 years	27	15	.5	.6								
6-11	26	16	.1	.4			60	24	.1			
2-5	26	11	.1	.2			32	10	.1			
1	2	2					23	5			.1	
Under 1	1	0					13	1				
3 children												
12-17 years	26	16	.9	.3	.1							
6-11	27	15	.4	.5			58	26	.3	.3		
2-5	29	2	.3				53	9	.2	.2		.1
1	6	1	.7			.1	31	1	.1			
Under 1	3	1					14	2	.1			
4 children												
12-17 years	5	9	.2	1.5		.1						
6-11	20	8	.5	.4			51	15	.6	.2		
2-5	9	1	.8				21	0	.1			
1	6	1					14	2	.1			.1
Under 1	3	0	.9				5	1	1.0			
5-6 children												
12-17 years	0	1										
6-11	12	2	.7				16	2	.6			
2-5	11	1	.3				17	3			.1	
1	3	1	.1				6	1				
Under 1	5	1	.3			.1	7	2	.1			
7-9 children												
6-11 years	2	0					2	0				
2-5	10	2	.3				10	2				
1	3	0	.5				3	0	.6			
Under 1	3	0					4	0				

[a]NE and E indicate households with nonemployed or employed wives.

[b]Time is reported only if there were three or more families and if average time was 3 minutes or more.

TABLE 8.7—Planning for marketing on record days, by selected variables
(1,296 husband–wife households, Syracuse, N.Y., 1967-68)

Households	Number	Percent who planned for shopping on record days	Number of shoppers	Planning method for those who shopped		
				"In-the-head"	Written list	Combina-tion
				Percent		
Total group	1,296	59	842	64	27	9
Number of children						
0	168	48	91	56	36	8
1	210	55	132	57	32	11
2	378	59	247	64	28	8
3	294	65	203	67	25	8
4	169	64	118	74	18	8
5 or more	77	56	51	67	25	8
Age of wives in families without children						
Under 25	42	48	22	32	64	5
25–39	42	56	26	54	35	11
40–54	42	43	22	64	27	9
55 and over	42	45	21	76	19	5
Nonemployed wives	979	59	632	63	28	9
Employed wives	317	59	210	67	25	8
Socioeconomic level						
Class 1 (highest)	163	58	106	65	26	8
Class 2	163	58	104	56	33	11
Class 3	402	62	275	61	29	9
Class 4	483	57	303	70	23	7
Class 5	85	59	54	65	26	9

TABLE 8.8—Frequency of marketing for food and household supplies, by selected variables
(1,296 husband–wife households, Syracuse, N.Y., 1967-68)

Households	Number	No set pattern	Daily	Biweekly	Weekly	Semimonthly	Monthly
				Row percent			
Total group	1,296	3	1	7	79	9	1
Number of children							
0	168	7	2	6	76	8	1
1	210	3	1	8	80	7	1
2	378	2	1	7	78	12	
3	294	1		8	82	8	
4	169	2	2	6	80	8	1
5 or more	77			12	80	8	
Age of wives in households without children							
Under 25	42	2		7	79	10	2
25–39	42	7	2	7	74	10	
40–54	42	5		7	81	7	
55 and over	42	14	5	5	69	7	
Nonemployed wives	979	2	1	7	80	10	1
Employed wives	317	3	2	9	78	7	1

TABLE 8.9—Marketing on record days, by selected variables
(1,296 husband–wife households, Syracuse, N.Y., 1967-68)

Households	Number	Type of shopping			
		Food supplies	Household equipment	Clothing	Miscellaneous
		Percent			
Total group	1,296	57	11	16	23
Number of children					
0	168	51	14	6	15
1	210	56	11	12	20
2	378	56	11	21	24
3	294	63	9	19	27
4	169	65	12	20	25
5 or more	77	64	10	18	20
Age of wives in households without children					
Under 25	42	50	17	--	24
25–39	42	48	12	7	12
40–54	42	45	17	14	14
55 and over	42	60	12	5	10
Nonemployed wives	979	57	11	16	23
Employed wives	317	57	10	15	21
Principal shoppers					
Wives		32	6	11	11
Husbands		14	2	1	6
Children		3	<1	1	2
Other workers		<1	--	<1	<1
Combinations		8	3	3	4
No shopping done		43	89	84	77

TABLE 8.10—Number of trips made in previous 7 days for food marketing, by
(1,296 husband–wife households, Syracuse, N.Y., 1967-68)

Households	Number	Wives		
		0	1-3	4+
		Percent		
Total group	1,296	13	67	20
Number of children				
0	168	17	68	15
1	210	12	70	18
2	378	16	63	21
3	294	10	68	22
4	169	12	67	21
5 or more	77	6	72	22
Age of wives in households without children				
Under 25	42	14	79	7
25-39	42	5	81	14
40-54	42	19	60	21
55 and over	42	31	52	17
Socioeconomic level				
Class 1 (highest)	163	10	73	17
Class 2	163	14	64	22
Class 3	402	12	68	20
Class 4	483	14	66	20
Class 5	85	13	66	21
Nonemployed wives	979	14	67	19
Employed wives	317	10	67	23

selected variables

	Number of trips by							
Husbands			Children			Combinations		
0	1-3	4+	0	1-3	4+	0	1-3	4+
			Percent					
36	53	11	79	16	5	65	32	3
49	45	6	--	--	--			
31	57	12	91	8	<1			
35	55	10	82	14	4			
34	55	11	67	26	7			
37	50	13	69	24	7			
34	56	10	48	31	21			
55	40	5						
55	43	2						
55	40	5						
33	55	12						
41	53	6	86	12	2			
36	53	11	88	10	2			
32	58	10	79	16	5			
37	52	11	75	18	7			
40	42	18	62	28	10			
36	54	10	80	15	5	65	31	4
37	50	13	74	21	6	65	32	3

TABLE 8.11—Wives' evaluation of their management and use of techniques
(1,296 husband–wife households, Syracuse, N.Y., 1967-68)

Households	Number	Evaluation of management "good"
Total group	1,296	83
Number of children		
0	168	83
1	210	86
2	378	85
3	294	81
4	169	80
5 or more	77	79
Age of wives in families without children		
Under 25	42	90
25–39	42	79
40–54	42	81
55 and over	42	83
Socioeconomic level		
Class 1 (highest)	163	82
Class 2	163	84
Class 3	402	82
Class 4	483	83
Class 5	85	87
Nonemployed wives	979	83
Employed wives	317	83

[a]Since more than one technique was frequently reported, percentages do not add to 100.

for organizing time, by selected variables

Techniques of organization of time					
"In-the-head" scheduling	Planning	Daily routine	Regular weekly routine	Assigning tasks	Written schedule
Percent[a]					
84	75	71	58	50	16
81	74	62	52	15	20
83	80	77	52	31	21
87	75	72	64	48	14
83	76	69	59	67	16
80	74	72	54	66	14
86	68	80	60	90	16
88	86	60	50	24	24
81	79	64	52	12	19
71	55	62	52	2	14
83	79	62	55	21	21
85	85	70	53	48	27
81	76	69	51	45	25
84	79	72	62	54	17
84	70	72	58	49	11
82	68	69	58	52	8
83	76	71	57	48	16
85	74	73	62	56	17

TABLE 8.12—Participants in management and record keeping on record days and during
(1,296 husband–wife households, Syracuse, N.Y., 1967-68)

Households	Number	Someone	Wives and Husbands	Wives only	Husbands only
			Percent		
Record days					
Total group	1,296	62	31	29	2
Nonemployed wives	979	64	31	30	2
Employed wives	317	58	29	26	3
Previous 7 days					
Total group	1,296	98	63	32	3
Nonemployed wives	979	98	63	32	3
Employed wives	317	96	61	33	2
Number of children					
0	168	95	66	26	3
1	210	98	60	36	2
2	378	98	66	30	2
3	294	99	60	35	4
4	169	96	59	33	4
5–9	77	99	68	30	
Age of wives in households without children					
Under 25 years	42	100	79	19	2
25–39	42	98	74	24	
40–54	42	90	50	36	5
55 and over	42	93	62	26	5
Socioeconomic level					
Class 1 (highest)	163	98	75	22	2
Class 2	163	99	69	25	4
Class 3	402	98	63	34	2
Class 4	483	96	58	36	3
Class 5	85	97	56	39	4

previous 7 days, by selected variables

| | Record Keeping | | |
Someone	Wives and Husbands	Wives only	Husbands only
	Percent		
32	5	18	9
31	5	18	8
34	5	18	11
97	37	31	29
96	37	30	30
98	36	36	26
97	42	30	24
96	38	28	31
96	34	29	32
98	33	37	28
97	44	30	23
95	34	34	26
100	43	29	29
98	48	29	21
95	40	33	21
95	38	31	26
96	39	22	36
97	41	20	36
97	39	30	28
96	32	38	26
96	38	40	19

Chapter IX

Summary and Recommendations for Future Research

The purpose of this study was to find a means of measuring the work load in household production that could be relatively simple to use and for which data could be easily collected. The project was a continuation of research on time used for household work begun at Cornell as early as 1926 as a part of a study sponsored by the Bureau of Home Economics of the United States Department of Agriculture.

The measure of household work, like other measures, has to be expressed in terms of a quantity of production output from a given amount of some resource input—in this case, *time*. Although either amount of work accomplished or time used to accomplish it can be used to express the work load, the time input in relation to work output is a more usable measure. Previous research had been directed toward measuring the amount of work in each household work activity by identifying one or more quantifying variables, then relating such variables to the time used to accomplish each quantity of work. The major problems with this approach had been the large amount of data that had to be collected and analyzed and the very real difficulty of finding a variable that would quantify all of the work involved in each area of household production.

In the present study, the emphasis was placed on time spent on household work as the major dependent variable. On the basis of previous research, the hypothesis to be tested was that the amount of work in the household varied principally in relation to some characteristic of family composition such as number of children, age of youngest child, or a combination of family size and ages of children. If the hypothesis were true, the amount of household work accomplished would vary principally in relation to changes in family composition. The relationship between family composition and amount of time used for household work would be a relationship between amount of work accomplished and the time used to accomplish it. Thus, by knowing the composition of the household, it would be possible to

predict how much time would have to be spent to produce the goods and services a family needed to function as a unit. That is, on the average, a certain amount of time would be used to produce goods and services for a family of a given composition.

The principal components of family composition for this study were number of children and ages of youngest and oldest children, variables known to be related to household work. The random sample of 1,296 husband-wife families was drawn from names of families stratified by 32 different combinations of family composition. These types of family composition varied from families with no children, stratified by age of the wife, to those with seven to nine children, stratified by number of children and age of the youngest and oldest child.

The total time spent by all workers on household work was the central focus of the study. Time-use records for all family members over age 6 were collected for 2 days from each wife in the sample in the form of estimates made and recorded in 5- and 10-minute intervals. Since some household work varies in quantity by season and day of the week, an equal number of records for each of the 7 days of the week and approximately equal numbers for each season were collected. To eliminate differences in household production caused by residential location, approximately half of the records were collected from families living in the city and half from families living in the suburbs. Within these controls, other characteristics of the households were assumed to vary randomly.

The time reported as spent on each type of household work and on all household work was in terms of daily time and represented the amount of time spent on a household work activity if all activities were performed daily. The number of records collected and the length of the period of collection made it possible to minimize the normal variability of daily household work and also to collect records of time use for all kinds of household work, some of which are performed less frequently than daily.

The types of household workers were: wives, husbands, children 12 to 17, children 6 to 11, and other female and male workers who were not regular members of the household. The time use of each of the individual types of workers was analyzed separately, since different factors were related to the amount of time various workers spent on household work. Wives made the largest time contributions; the total time spent on most activities usually consisted of a large component of wives' time plus smaller and varying time contributions from other family and nonfamily workers.

Household work was defined as the production of goods and services within the household for family use and consumption in six areas: (1) food preparation, (2) house care, (3) family care, (4) clothing care, (5) marketing, and (6) management. Although the activities that made up the categories were essentially related to producing the same service, each activity placed somewhat different demands on time and was distinct from other activities in content, types of operations, methods of processing, subtasks, equipment, and workplace. Each of 13 household work activities, therefore, was analyzed separately for relationships with the variables.

Extensive nonparametric statistical analyses of rank correlation coefficients were made of relationships between control and random variables and time used by all workers and different types of workers for each of the 13 household work activities, alone and in combination. The results of these analyses showed that four variables were more closely correlated to time use than others. These were: number of children, age of youngest child, employment of wives, and family type (a composite variable made up of number of children and age of the youngest child). Other variables that were related less closely with time use on one or more types of household work activities were: age of the oldest child, house type, location of residence, socioeconomic status, education of wives, education of husbands, and hours of employment of husbands.

To examine the empirical effects of these variables on time use, time spent by each type of worker on each household work activity was summed and averaged over the 1,296 families for each activity and for all household work combined. In order to compute average daily time use by all workers, the time of children 6 to 11 and 12 to 17 was also averaged in the same manner.

However, since families did not have an equal chance to report time used by children of specified ages, averages of time inputs of children based on all families in the sample did not provide a meaningful measure of time contributions of children. For this reason, the rank correlations and time reported for children 12 to 17 were based on the time spent by these children in families that had teenagers, and averages of time use reported for children 6 to 11 years were based on the families that had children in this age group.

Both results of statistical analyses and empirical evidence supporting the statistical analyses are reported in the monograph to provide pertinent information for further research efforts.

Effects of Characteristics of Household Work on Time-Use Measurement

In addition to the effects of the variables themselves on time use, the measurements of correlation were influenced by several characteristics of each household work activity. In general, effective correlations were found for major variables when activities were regularly performed, were relatively time consuming, and had a clearly defined work content. When they were infrequently performed or when their composition was not well defined, only weak or nonsignificant correlations resulted.

Activities that were performed regularly (defined as having been performed on over half the record days) and that had high time demands (an average of around an hour or more a day) were regular meal preparation, regular house care, physical and nonphysical care of family members, and after-meal cleanup. Time spent on each of these activities was related to one or another of the principal variables with the relationships well defined by correlation values of .25 or higher and by clear-cut changes in amount of time used with changes in the variable.

Variability of activities within a household work category and also in factors not studied in this project could be expected to affect the relationships between time use and major variables. For example, although marketing was a regularly performed activity and used a comparatively large amount of time, the highest correlation coefficient with time spent on this activity was -.16 with age of the youngest child. This activity varied considerably in relation to such factors as kind of shopping, location of markets, amount and kind of shopping done at one time, and number of shoppers.

As in other studies of household work time, no effective relationships were found between any of the variables and time spent on less regularly performed household work on which relatively little average time was spent. In the present study, these less regular and less time-consuming activities were: special house care, ironing, special clothing care, yard and car care, management, and special food preparation. All of the correlations with time use on each of these types of household work were less than $\pm.15$.

When the individual activities were grouped into overall classifications such as all food preparation and all house care, relationships with time use were usually weaker than those with the separate activities. To a large extent, the strength of relationships between time use for the grouped activities and the variables depended on whether or not the activities of which they were composed were regular and time consuming and had consistent relationships with one variable. For example, all food preparation had a slightly higher correlation coefficient with number of children than did either regular meal preparation or after-meal cleanup. (The time spent on special food preparation was too small a proportion of total food preparation time to have any effect on the grouped activities.) It was clear that the relationships of number of children and time use for the two major food preparation activities were sufficiently strong to increase the time spent on all food preparation work as family size was larger.

All family care consisted of two time-consuming and regular activities, but the component activities related more closely to different variables—age of youngest child for physical care and number of children for nonphysical care. As a result of the strength of the relationship of age of youngest child with physical care, its relationship with all family care was also strong. All house care, on the other hand, was made up of only one regular activity and two less regular ones, and the best relationships with each were with different variables. In this group of activities, the one regular activity was a time-consuming one, and the relationship between number of children and regular house care was strong enough to maintain an effective relationship with all house care (.20). The grouped activities, however, provided a way to measure the time inputs for some of the less frequent activities, which, in themselves, had only weak associations with time use.

Relationships Between Significant Variables and Total Time of All Workers for Household Work[1,2]

Number of Children

Rank Correlations (Summary Table 1). This variable had the strongest statistical relationship (Kendall Tau Value .37) of any of the variables tested with total time spent by all workers on all household work combined. It was likewise the variable most closely related to total time spent on four regularly performed activities: regular meal preparation (.31), after-meal cleanup (.28), regular house care (.26), and washing by machine (.24). Number of children was about as closely related as any other variable to total time spent on nonphysical care of family members (.27). Together, the total time of all workers spent on these five activities accounted for more than half the total average daily time reported for all household work in the total sample.

Number of children was also the variable either most closely related or as closely related as any variable to total time spent on three of the major groups of activities: all food preparation (.33), all house care (.20), and all clothing care (.15). Together these three grouped activities accounted for about 60% of time reported for all household work.

Number of children was also significantly related to time use for all family care (.29) and physical care of family members (.25), although the age of the youngest child had a much closer relationship to all family care (.56) and to physical care (.70). Time for marketing also was more closely related to age of the youngest child than to number of children (-.16 versus .09). Similarly, time spent on yard and car care was related to number of children (.08) but was more closely related to age of youngest child (-.12).

When tested by partial correlation, the effects of number of children were interrelated with those of employment of wives for time spent on all

---

[1] All Tau values reported in tabular form or referred to in the text were significant at the .001 level unless otherwise stated. Although correlation coefficients were determined for all major variables, only significant relationships are reported in tables and only the correlations strong enough to change the amount of time used daily are discussed to any extent.

[2] For an explanation of meaning of positive and negative correlation values as related to the different variables, see pages 30-31.

household work and on the frequent and time-consuming activities of regular meal preparation, after-meal cleanup, and washing by machine. In each case, number of children had the stronger effect. Similarly, the effects of number of children on time spent by all workers on regular house care were stronger than the effects of house type, which also were interrelated with it.

Number of children and employment of wives were equal in their effect on total time spent for all clothing care. The only household work activity in which number of children did not have a statistically significant relationship with all workers' time was special clothing care.

The relationships of number of children with total time use on most of the less regular activities were weak, although number of children was as closely related to all workers' time use on ironing (.09) as any other major variable. For three of the specific task areas (special food preparation, special house care, and management), the correlation coefficients between time use and number of children were not statistically significant at the .001 level. In total, these four activities plus special clothing care accounted for about 15% of all household work time reported.

Average Total Time Spent (Summary Table 2). The rank correlation coefficients showed the effectiveness of number of children as a predictor of total time use by all workers on household work and its relative strength in relation to other variables. Summary Table 2 shows the distribution of total time use on household work by number of children, without reference to employment of wives. For all household work, daily average time increased consistently with each increment in the number of children. Time spent increased about 3 hours per day for families with one child over those with no children, followed by an increase of around 1 hour per additional child from that point on.

For each of the grouped activities itemized in Summary Table 2, time use generally increased with increase in family size, although the extent of the increase varied among the activities. Time spent for food-related activities and all house care increased from an average of 2 hours per day in families with no children or only one child to almost 3 hours per day in those with two to four children, and to 4 or 5 hours per day in larger families. Family care time was more variable by number of children than was food preparation or house care time but increased from an average of 2.2 hours per day in families with one child to an average of 4.2 hours a day in those with seven to

nine children.[3] The range of time for all clothing care between family sizes was less than for other kinds of household work, but total time use increased gradually with family size from an average of about an hour a day in families with one child to almost 2 hours a day in families with five or more children.

The individual activities that had the closest correlation between time use and number of children also showed a gradual increase in average daily time use with an increase in number of children. Although the increases in time by each change in family size were generally small, the overall increases between one-child families and the largest families were about 1½ hours per day for regular meal preparation, after-meal cleanup, and regular house care, and about 2 hours per day for nonphysical care of family members. Time spent on washing by machine varied less from small to large families; nevertheless, there was a consistent increase in time used with increase in family size. Ironing and physical care of family members increased inconsistently in time use with increments in family size, partly because of the interrelationship between number of children and employment of wives. Although marketing time was only weakly related to number of children, it was evident that the least time was used in the smallest families. There was no meaningful increase in marketing time by increments of family size when there were three or more children in the household.

Age of Youngest Child

Rank Correlations (Summary Table 1). Age of youngest child had the closest correlation of any of the variables with all workers' time use for two regularly performed and time-consuming activities, physical care of family members (.70) and marketing (-.16); and also with total time spent on one group of activities, all family care (.56). These relationships were not affected when number of children, employment of wives, or house type were held constant.

The regular activities of physical care and marketing accounted for about one-fifth of

---

[3]While correlation coefficients were based on 1,260 families, the average times reported for 1,296 households show that the relationships held when the 21 families with seven to nine children and the 15 families with four or more teenagers were included.

average daily time used on all household work. The relationships between age of youngest child and time spent on physical care and all family care were the strongest of any tested in the project. Whether or not wives were employed, much more time was spent on physical care when children were preschoolers or babies than when they were of school age. The relationship between age of the youngest child and total time use by all workers for marketing was in the opposite direction from those with family care; that is, more time was used as the children in the family were older.

Age of youngest child had a generally weak relationship with all workers' time use on most household work other than family care and marketing. Its relationship with time use on non-physical care was only somewhat less close (.23) than that for number of children (.27). Among the less regularly performed activities, the weak relationships found between age of youngest child and all workers' time use were the closest of any of the variables tested for special clothing care (-.08, or -.10 when employment of wives was held constant). Age of youngest child also was as closely related to yard and car care time (-.12) as house type; the relationship, however, weakened to -.09 when house type was held constant.

Average Total Time Spent (Summary Table 3). This summary table shows the total time use of all workers (without reference to employment of wives) for the household work activities that were most closely related to age of youngest child. The effectiveness of age of youngest child as an indicator of total time likely to be used for physical care and all family care is shown by the substantial decreases in average time with decreases in age of youngest child. Total time used by all workers increased regularly and substantially in physical care, from an average of .1 hour a day spent in households with only teenage children to 3 hours a day in households with a baby as the youngest child. Similarly, total time use for all family care was over 4 hours a day more in families with a baby than in families with only teenage children.

The relationship between age of the youngest child and total time use on marketing indicated that more time was used as age of the youngest child advanced. This increase was progressive in all workers' total time spent on marketing; the averages ranged from about 1 hour a day in families with the youngest child a baby to 2 hours a day in those with the youngest a teenager.

Although the relationship was not close, age of youngest child had a perceptible effect on total time spent on special clothing care and yard and car care. The special clothing care time of all workers tended to increase with increments in age of youngest child with a low overall average change in time of only .1 hour. Yard and car care time of all workers also increased with age of youngest child, about half an hour for families with a teenager over those with a baby as the youngest child.

Employment of Wives

Rank Correlations (Summary Table 1). Employment of wives was negatively and significantly related (at the .001 level) to total time used by all workers on all household work and on each of the separate household work activities, with the exception of marketing, yard and car care, special clothing care, and special food preparation. The highest correlation was -.24 (for physical care of family members) and the lowest -.06 (for management). The relationships between wives' employment and time use of all workers varied in strength and, like those of the other two major variables, were more closely correlated with time use for the regularly performed and time-consuming activities than for less regular ones.

The effects of employment of wives on the total time used by all workers for most kinds of household work tended to be interrelated with the effects of number of children. When number of children was held constant, employment of wives had a reduced effect on total time used for all household work, all food preparation, all house care, regular meal preparation, after-meal cleanup, regular house care, and washing by machine. The interrelationships with number of children, however, usually indicated only the relatively greater strength of family size than of employment on household work time. When the effects of number of children were removed, employment of wives had sufficiently close relationships to time use to bring about a reduction of all workers' time spent on most kinds of household work. Among the less regular activities, employment of wives was as closely related to ironing time as number of children and to special house care as house type.

When age of the youngest child was held constant, the correlation coefficients for employment of wives and time use frequently increased, as did the values for age of youngest child when employment of wives was held constant. This independence was probably the result of the relatively strong effects both variables had on wives' use of time and the relatively close relationship between age of the youngest child and employment of wives. The major exception to this general trend was for family care time. When age of the youngest child was held constant employment of wives had only a minimal effect on total time used for physical care, nonphysical care, or all family care.

Average Total Time Spent (Summary Tables 4 and 5). For all household work, employed-wife households spent almost 2½ hours a day less total time, on the average, than nonemployed-wife households. The group of activities in which time was reduced the most in employed-wife households was family care, with a reduction of an hour a day. Other reductions were lower, and were distributed over all groups of activities (an average of about half an hour a day less on both all food preparation and all house care and about a quarter hour less on all clothing care). The effects of employment of wives and its interrelationships with family composition were apparent in total time spent by all workers on all household work, on the major groups of activities, and on most of the regular and time-consuming household work except marketing. For this latter activity, total time spent varied inconsistently with employment of wives, as would be expected from the lack of correlation.

The large reduction in total time spent on all family care was principally the result of increased numbers of wives being employed as children were older combined with decreased time spent on physical care of family members with increased age of the youngest child. Employed-wife households spent less time on physical care at any family size (on the average, .7 hour a day less) (Summary Table 4). This effect was slightly interrelated with that of number of children (the time spent in employed- and nonemployed-wife households was similar in the largest families), and was strongly interrelated with effects of age of the youngest child. When a child over age 2 was the youngest child, only a little less time was spent on physical care in employed- than in nonemployed-wife families (Summary Table 5). In employed-wife households with a baby, the decrease probably reflected some child care away from home.

The effects of employment of wives on total time used for nonphysical care were nearly all the effects of changes in age of the youngest child. Both types of households spent about the same time for this work except when children were under age 2. The higher amount of nonphysical care time in employed-wife households probably resulted from the time of employed babysitters.

There also were some interrelationships with family size.

The interrelationships of employment of wives with number of children were evident in the time reductions on regular activities. The lower time of employed-wife households on nonphysical care was mostly in families with three and four children. In other family sizes, about the same or more time was spent when the wives were employed than when they were not. Employed-wife households spent a little less time than those with nonemployed wives on regular meal preparation and after-meal cleanup in nearly all family sizes. Employment of wives was only weakly related to time use of all workers for regular house care, especially when number of children was held constant; only employed-wife families with no children or those with five or six children spent much less time on this work than nonemployed-wife families.

Among the less regular activities, though the changes in time were small, employed-wife families spent less time on ironing than non-employed-wife families in nearly all family sizes.

Family Type

Family type was made up of two variables, number of children and age of youngest child. Because these two variables did not have equal effects on household work time, the relationships of family type with time use tended to be skewed toward those of the stronger variable. Except for a few activities, number of children had stronger effects than age of the youngest child; the effects of family type, therefore, closely paralleled those of number of children.

Rank Correlations. Family type had a slightly closer relationship than any other major variable with time spent on one household work activity, nonphysical care of family members (.28). The slightly closer correlation between time use for this activity and family type than with either of the two component variables (number of children at .27 and age of youngest at .23) indicates that more time was spent on nonphysical care of family members when children were younger as well as when families were larger; that is, when family type was more complex.

Given the definition of the most complex families as those with a large number of children and a low age of youngest child, an effective relationship with family type required a positive relationship with time use for each of the two component variables. The correlation coefficients for time use for each of the 13 household activities studied were all positive with number of children while with age of youngest they were sometimes positive and sometimes negative. When the relationships of number of children and age of youngest child with time use on an activity were both positive, then the relationship of family type with time use was relatively strong also. Examples of this situation were all household work, family care activities, and washing by machine. When the relationships of age of youngest child with total time use were negative—that is, when time use increased as children in the family were older— the correlations for family type were weaker. When the relationship for age of youngest child was negative and relatively strong and the relationship with number of children was weak (as in relation to time use on marketing), there was no measurable relationship with family type.

The generally weaker relationships of family type with time use compared to relationships of one or the other of its components makes this variable of considerably less practical importance than number of children, even though its correlation values were frequently as good as those of number of children and time use. Combining the two component variables tended to weaken rather than to strengthen evident relationships. Probably this was the effect of the independent relationships of number of children and their ages with household work time and their different effects on different kinds of household work. The complexity of the family type variable and the problems associated with its use are additional factors in our recommendation that its use should not be pursued as a time predictor in the form used for this project. It is possible that number of children could be effectively combined with age of youngest child for some activities and with age of oldest child for others.

The use to be made of the data would determine the importance of continued effort to combine these two important variables. If the time use data were to be aggregated to show the extent of household production in the country, number of children and age of youngest as separate variables rather than combined would seem appropriate. However, if the time estimates were to be used by an individual family, as in estimating the monetary value of its time use in household production, development of an improved method of combining the variables would seem appropriate.

Average Total Time Spent. The use of family type presented some analysis problems with

respect to numbers of cases. In some categories very few cases from the sample were available for use. This was especially true for the large families and those with young children in which wives were employed; these also were less usual types in the general population. However, the detailed tables that report time use by family type show clearly the sharp fluctuations in household work time brought about by family composition and the relationships of number of children and age of the youngest child with time use.

Age of Wives in Families Without Children

No correlation coefficients were determined for age of wife in childless households apart from those for the overall variable of family type. Effective relationships between age of wives and total daily average time were very few. Employment of wives had more effect on use of time when there were no children in the household than did age of wives. In all except two of the regularly performed activities, and in all of the less regular ones, less time was used in households of employed wives with no children at home than of nonemployed wives; the two exceptions were nonphysical care and washing by machine. At any age of wives in no-children families, employed-wife households spent less time on all household work (on the average, about 2 hours a day less), and they spent much less time, at any age of wives, on all food preparation, all house care, and all clothing care. Only when the wives were 40 or older did employed-wife households spend as much time on marketing as those with a nonemployed wife.

Age of Oldest Child

For four individual tasks—meal preparation, after-meal cleanup, marketing, and regular house care—the age of the oldest child correlated slightly more closely with total time of all workers than did age of the youngest. For these activities, however, the negative value with age of the youngest child shows the same basic result, that more time was used as the children were older rather than younger. Age of the youngest child is recommended as a variable for further research, because it is the more closely related variable with time use for other activities and also because the correlation values for the two age variables were of comparable strength.

House Type

House type was more closely related to time use for house care work than to other kinds of household work, in which its effects tended to be mostly those of number of children. The correlation coefficients for house type and number of children in relation to all workers' time use on all house care were similar (.18 versus .20), but in relation to time use for regular house care the correlation coefficient for house type (.12) was weaker than for number of children (.26). House type was a slightly stronger variable than number of children in relation to total time spent on yard and car care (.13 versus .08). House type was as closely related to time spent on special house care (.09) as employment of homemaker (-.09). The apparent relationship between house type and total time spent on all household work was largely the effect of number of children.

It is probable that total time spent for yard and car care and some kinds of special house care varies between the extremes of housing types (apartments and one-family houses). However, evidence throughout this study pointed to a high interrelationship between house type and family composition, which is borne out by common observation. Families with children tend to live in one-family houses on individual lots, and their houses tend to be larger when they have more children. The lack of effect of house type on regular house care and on all household work when number of children was held constant leads to the conclusion that this variable is a redundant one in relation to studies of household work time. That is, like family type, it would not supply sufficient additional information about time use on household work to make its use profitable.

Location of Residence

The highest correlation value between time use and residential location was .08, and the only relationships between this variable and all workers' time that were not the effects of house type, as shown by the partial rank correlations, were those with time spent on all family care and on physical care. These two correlations indicated that, regardless of the type of house the family lived in, a slightly higher amount of time was spent on family care in suburban areas than in the city; these slight relationships were not meaningful, however, in view of the large amount of time spent on this kind of work at some stages of the family cycle.

It was concluded from the results of this study that, although some minor fluctuations in time use on some kinds of household work might be found, a city or suburban location of residence had no measurable effect on household work time.

Socioeconomic Level of Households and Education of Wives and Husbands

With only a few exceptions, these three variables tended to be related to total time spent on the same activities and the relationships tended to show weak but similar correlation values.

None of the three variables (socioeconomic level, education of wives, and education of husbands) was related to total time spent on all household work. Among the grouped activities, the only relationship with a correlation value significant at the .001 level was that between wives' education and total time spent on all house care (.08). This relationship was too low to change the average daily time spent on this work.

Total time spent on regular house care and after-meal cleanup was more closely related to wives' education than to husbands' education or socioeconomic level with respective correlation values of .13 and .10. With these weak relationships no consistent increase was found in the high average daily time spent on these tasks.

The correlation coefficients between all workers' time spent on management were -.13 with wives' education, -.10 with husbands' education, and -.09 with socioeconomic level. These three variables were related more closely than any other variable to time use reported for management.

It seems clear from the results of this study that socioeconomic level of the family had little effect on time used for any major household work. Also, for the activities with which socioeconomic level showed a relationship, wives' education was the variable with a closer correlation. On the assumption that wives' education is not highly interrelated with family composition or wives' employment, this variable seems to have some possible explanatory power in relation to time spent on some activities, notably managerial ones.

Because of a general assumption that education of parents is related to care of children, the two education variables were examined further for relationships between total time and time of wives and husbands as spent only in families with children and in families with specified ages of the youngest child. For all families with children the rank correlations between time of all workers used for physical care and the educational level of wives and husbands were closer than those for all 1,260 families; but they still remained weak. Although weak, the values for wives' education and all family care time (-.10) and nonphysical care (-.09) were statistically significant at the .001 level. The highest correlation coefficient between wives' education and all workers' time for family care was when the youngest child was 6 to 11 (-.17). When wives had a higher educational level, more total time was spent on nonphysical care when the youngest child was of elementary school age.

Relationships between husbands' education and all workers' time used for physical care were on the same order of weakness as those with education of wives. Neither husbands' nor wives' education was related to all workers' time use on physical care; the highest correlation coefficients for all workers' time used for all family care and husbands' education were -.12 and -.13 when the youngest child was 6 to 11 or 2 to 5.

The relationships between education of husbands and time spent for nonphysical care at different ages of youngest child were similar to those between all workers' time use and wives' education. Higher educational levels of husbands tended to increase nonphysical care time of all workers in families with children only when the youngest child was 6 to 11 (-.14).

Husbands' Hours of Employment

The variable, husbands' hours of employment, was significantly related to total time use of all workers for only one activity, regular house care (.09). The relationship was too weak to have any consistent effect on total time used for this work.

Husbands' hours of employment was, however, a useful variable because of its relationships with husbands' household work time. In spite of generally low correlation coefficients with time use of other workers in most activities, for future research it could provide a means of measuring time changes in those less regularly performed activities in which husbands are usually the principal workers. Also, as more wives enter the labor force, hours of employment of husbands may become a more significant variable.

Relationships Between the Selected Variables and Time Used by Wives for Household Work

With only three exceptions, wives spent over half (and usually substantially more than half) of all workers' time used on all household work and on the work activities individually or grouped. Husbands were the principal workers in yard and car care. Employed wives remained the principal single providers of nonphysical care of family members, but their proportionate share dropped from 55% when not employed to 38% when employed. Husbands and nonemployed wives spent about equal portions of the time on special house care; when wives were employed, their share declined and husbands' share increased.

Rank Correlations for Wives' Time

The two variables that had the most effect on wives' household work time were their employment and age of the youngest child. One or the other of these two variables was the most closely related to wives' time spent on all household work, all the groups of activities, and nearly all of the regular and time-consuming kinds of household work.

Employment of Wives (Summary Table 6). Some relationship between wives' employment and their time use for all household work activities was evident from the rank correlations for each type of household work activity except marketing. Wives' employment had the closest relationship with wives' time spent on all household work (-.36), on three groups of activities (all food preparation, -.29; all house care, -.18; and all clothing care, -.18), and on two of the more time-consuming activities (regular meal preparation, -.26, and after-meal cleanup, -.27). Some correlation values were higher between wives' employment and their time use when age of the youngest child was held constant (the greatest increases were from -.36 to -.46 for all household work, from -.26 to -.50 for all family care, from -.26 to -.60 for physical care, and from -.12 to -.31 for all food preparation).

Employment of wives was the variable most closely related to wives' use of time for all the less regular household work activities except management and special food preparation. For the latter activity, the correlation values were all equally low and not significant.

Number of Children (Summary Table 6). Number of children related less closely (.27) to wives' time on all household work than either their employment (-.36) or age of the youngest child (.30). Further, when employment was held constant, number of children and wives' time use dropped in correlation from .27 to .23. Number of children had about the same relationship as employment with wives' time use for all family care, for physical care of family members, and for regular house care. Number of children correlated better than any other variable with wives' time use on nonphysical care of family members and on washing by machine.

Age of Youngest Child (Summary Table 6). The age of the youngest was more closely related than number of children or employment of wives to wives' time use on one group of activities, all family care (.60); as well as on two specific tasks, physical care of family members (.70) and marketing (-.10). The correlation values for age of youngest child with wives' time use for nearly all kinds of household work remained the same or increased when wives' employment was held constant. Similarly, the correlations between wives' employment and wives' time usually increased or were unchanged when age of youngest child was held constant. When employment was held constant, the values for age of youngest child and wives' time spent increased from .60 to .70 for all family care, from .70 to .81 for physical care, and from .30 to .42 for all household work.

Age of the youngest child was not significantly related to wives' time use on some kinds of very time-consuming household work, such as all house care, regular house care, regular meal preparation, and all clothing care.

Education of Wives. Wives' time use on a few kinds of household work was related to their education at least as well as it was to other variables. In fact, the best relationship with their time spent on management was with their education (-.14). In view of the generally low time reported for this activity, it is probable that wives' time increased by small amounts with increments in their educational level. In relation to wives' time spent on special clothing care, the correlation value for their education was -.07, the same as that for their employment; also, their time use on regular house care correlated almost as well with their education (.15) as with the two best related variables, number of children (.16) and wives' employment (-.16). In the case of regular house care the correlation value indicated some decrease in wives' time use with increase in education.

Wives' education was not significantly related to their time spent on family care work except for weak correlations with their time use for all family care and nonphysical care (-.07 each) when only families with children were considered.

Education of Husbands. Correlations between wives' time use and husbands' education were usually lower than those with their own education and relatively ineffective for predicting

time use. The correlation between husbands' education and wives' time use on management, however, was higher (-.10) than that with wives' employment (-.08), though lower than the correlation with wives' education (-.14).

Hours of Employment of Husbands. Wives' time use had a few weak relationships with husbands' hours of employment, all of which were positive. None of them was high enough to consistently affect wives' average daily use of time. The highest correlation (.08) was that with wives' time spent on all household work; their time tended to increase by a few minutes a day with increments in husbands' hours of employment.

Average Daily Time Used by Wives

Employment of Wives (Summary Tables 7 and 8). The effectiveness of the variable of wives' employment in decreasing their household work time is very apparent. For all of the regular household work activities except marketing, employed wives spent less time than those nonemployed in all or nearly all family size and age of youngest child categories. Average daily time spent by employed wives on all household work was from 2 to 2½ hours less than that of the nonemployed at each number of children, and from 1½ to 2¼ hours less at each age of youngest child.

When employed, wives' time use for all food preparation, all house care, and all clothing care was less than that of nonemployed wives at each family size and at nearly all age groups of youngest child. Employed wives' time spent on all family care likewise was substantially less than that of nonemployed wives in families with children. These differences tended to be especially high; employed wives spent at least an hour a day less on all family care in all family sizes except the largest.

The effect of employment on wives' time was more variable in relation to the less regular activities; this effect was consistent enough to reduce the average time spent by employed wives for special house care and ironing.

Number of Children and Employment of Wives (Summary Table 7). In general, number of children did not have a regular and consistent effect on wives' time use for many household work activities. For two activities number of children had the closest correlation with wives' time: their time spent on washing by machine increased fairly regularly as number of children advanced, while for nonphysical care the increase was mainly between families with no children and any number above one child. The inconsistent variations by number of children in wives' time use for family care probably resulted from varying ages of youngest child in different sizes of family.

Although wives' household work time on the individual and grouped activities tended to vary inconsistently by family size, it nevertheless did relate to number of children. The general effectiveness of the relationships is especially apparent in wives' use of time for all household work which, whether or not wives were employed, increased fairly consistently with increments in the number of children. The increase in wives' time was substantial between one-child families and those with five or more—over an hour a day when wives were employed and at least 1½ hours a day when nonemployed.

Age of Youngest Child and Employment of Wives (Summary Table 8). Age of youngest child was strongly related to wives' use of time for all family and physical care; the time spent on these activities by the nonemployed and also by the employed wives increased regularly and substantially. Wives, employed or not, also spent more time on all household work when age of the youngest child was lower. Both nonemployed and employed wives spent more time on special clothing care in families with older than in those with younger children. The increase in wives' time spent on either marketing or yard and car care with increments in age of youngest child was evident only for nonemployed wives.

Age of Wives and Employment in Families Without Children. The time spent by wives with no children at home varied inconsistently by their age but, as age level advanced, it tended to increase slightly for all food preparation, regular meal preparation, and after-meal cleanup. When they were employed, wives' time use for management declined as they became older, and the older wives who were employed tended to spend less time on ironing than did the younger ones who were employed.

In families without children, employment had a much more consistent and stronger effect than age of wives; employed wives spent an average of 2 hours less a day on all household work than did those who were not employed, and they consistently spent less at each age of wives. Employed wives also spent less time on all the regular household work activities except family care and washing.

Relationships Between Selected Variables and Time Used by Husbands for Household Work

Husbands spent an average of 1.6 hours a day on all household work and their time use tended to be concentrated in relatively few activities. As a group, husbands spent some time daily on nearly all kinds of household work. However, their amount of time varied widely between kinds of work, from an average of less than 3 minutes a day for all clothing care to an average of 36 minutes per day for all house care work.

In both nonemployed- and employed-wife households, the most time of husbands was spent on weekends. Their time on Sundays averaged 2 hours in each type of household; on Saturdays it averaged almost 3 hours in the nonemployed-wife households. It was below the average (around 1.2 or 1.3 hours) on all other days in both types of households except for Fridays when it was 1.7 hours in households with employed wives.

Rank Correlations for Husbands' Time

Hours of Employment of Husbands. The variable that most frequently had the closest relationship with the household work time of husbands was their hours of employment. All of the relationships were negative; that is, husbands generally spent less time on household work as their hours of employment increased.

Hours of husbands' employment was the only variable related to husbands' time spent on all household work (-.15). Husbands' hours of employment also was more closely related than, or as closely related as, other major variables to their time spent on all food preparation (-.12), all house care (-.10), after-meal cleanup (-.10), marketing (-.12), yard and car care (-.09), and special food preparation (-.06).

Family Composition. Among the family composition variables, age of the youngest child had the closest relationships with husbands' time use for all family care (.23), physical care (.35), nonphysical care (.12), and washing by machine (.07). Age of youngest child, however, had little effect on husbands' time use on other household work activities. Number of children had some relationship with husbands' time use for more kinds of household work than age of the youngest child.

Husbands' time use for marketing, yard and car care, and all house care was not related to

family composition variables or employment of
wives. For husbands' time contributions for these
kinds of work to be analyzed, it would be necessary
to examine them in relation to husbands' hours of
employment.

The relationships of number of children and
age of the youngest child with husbands' time for
family care were effective. Husbands' time spent
on nonphysical care and all family care generally
increased when number of children was larger and
age of youngest child was lower.

Employment and Education of Wives. Wives'
employment had the closest relationship with
husbands' time use on two activities, regular house
care (.12) and regular meal preparation (.13).

Education of wives was more closely related
than other variables to husbands' time spent on
management (-.06). In families with children,
when the youngest child was between 6 and 11, the
correlation coefficients for wives' education and
husbands' time use on all family care and
nonphysical care were -.14 and -.18, respectively.

Education of Husbands. Husbands' time use
had only a few weak relationships with their
education level. The highest correlation value was
-.11 for husbands' time use for all family care and
for nonphysical care. When age of the youngest
child was held constant in families with children,
the correlation coefficient for husbands' time use
for all family care increased to -.16 for families
with the youngest child under 1 year old; the
values for nonphysical care increased to -.14 when
the youngest child was 6 to 11 years old and to -.15
when the youngest was under 1 year. Husbands'
time was used primarily in nonphysical rather than
physical care of children.

Average Daily Time Used by Husbands

Time contributed by husbands to household work
was closely related to their time for employment;
that is, work on their primary productive activity.
Their average time ranged from 2.1 hours per day
when they were employed less than 40 hours per
week to 1.2 hours a day when they were employed
50 hours or more per week.

The groups of household work activities for
which husbands spent most of their time were all
house care (.6 hour a day) and all family care (.4
hour a day, but less when wives were employed, .3
hour a day). For house care, husbands spent most
of their time on special house care and yard and
car care and very little on regular house care (.1
hour a day). They contributed from one-fifth to
one-fourth of total time spent on nonphysical care

of family members and on marketing.

Several of the correlations of variables with
husbands' time use were ineffective in showing
differences in average time because husbands
spent only a negligible amount of time on a
particular kind of work, especially on clothing
care. Other relationships showed only small
changes in husbands' average daily time. For
example, husbands' average time spent on all food
preparation increased from 6 minutes per day
when wives were not employed to 12 minutes per
day when they were. Husbands spent only 6
minutes a day or less, on the average, on such
regular and generally time-consuming household
work activities as regular meal preparation,
regular house care, physical care, and after-meal
cleanup. Although husbands' average daily time
use on these activities increased a little when wives
were employed, the general effect was very low.
Husbands' time contribution for physical care
increased with lower age of the youngest child, but
the overall increase was only about 18 minutes a
day when wives were employed.

Husbands' time use for household work in
families with no children at home varied by age of
wives but had very few consistent relationships
with wives' age. When wives were not employed,
husbands spent more time on all household work
as age of wives increased. However, when wives
were employed, husbands' time varied by age of
wives, and they spent less time on all household
work when wives were older than when they were
younger. When the wives were not employed,
husbands' time use on all house care in
no-children families also tended to increase with
age of wives.

Employment of wives in no-children families
had more effect on husbands' time than age of
wives. For the two activities on which husbands
spent the most time in no-children households,
special house care and yard and car care, they
tended to spend less time, on the average, when
wives were employed, though not at all ages of
wives. Husbands' time use on marketing was the
same whether or not wives were employed and
varied inconsistently by wives' age.

Relationships Between Selected Variables and Time Used by Children and Nonfamily Workers for Household Work

In the 413 families with teenagers, children in this
age group did some work in one or more household

activities on about 88% of the record days. Over half of the families reported teenagers' work in 1 to 3 activities, and another quarter reported work in 4 to 6 of the 13 household work activities studied. The accumulated average time of teenagers was 2.0 hours per day in nonemployed-wife households and 2.2 hours in those of employed wives. This amount of time was a meaningful proportion of the total in households with teenagers. Saturday was the day on which more time was used by teenagers than any other, on the average about 3½ hours.

Rank Correlations for Teenagers' Time

Number of Children and Age of Youngest Child. Number of children was the variable most closely related to teenagers' time use for all household work and for the kinds of household work on which they spent the most time, except marketing, with correlation values as follows: all household work (.21), all food preparation (.21), all house care (.12), regular meal preparation (.17), after-meal cleanup (.15), regular house care (.15).

Age of the youngest child was the next most important variable in relation to teenagers' household work time. In six household work activities, teenagers' time had some relationship with age of the youngest child. This variable had the closest relationship of any with teenagers' time spent on all family care (.21), physical care (.22), nonphysical care (.19), marketing (-.11), and ironing (-.11).

Employment of Wives and Husbands' Hours of Employment. Employment of wives was more closely related than other variables to teenagers' time use on only one household work activity, washing by machine (.12). This relationship was relatively unimportant since teenagers' average time use on such work was less than 3 minutes a day.

Their fathers' hours of employment was related to teenagers' time use on two activities, after-meal cleanup (-.10) and management (-.11). Husbands' hours of employment had the same correlation value (-.11) in relation to teenagers' time use on management as did education of wives. The relationship between teenagers' time and their fathers' hours of employment, though weak, offers further evidence of the possible importance of fathers' hours of employment as a variable for future study in relation to certain kinds of household work.

Education of Wives and Husbands. Education of wives was the only variable besides fathers' hours of employment related to teenagers' time use on management (-.11). Though teenagers spent only a small portion of the total time reported for management, the relationship between their time and education of mothers is a further indication of possible relationships for this variable with time use on some less regular household work activities.

Education of fathers was not related to teenagers' time spent on household work.

Average Daily Time Used by Teenagers

The relationships between number of children and teenagers' time use for their major activities were effective ones in measuring time contributions for all teenagers in families with teenagers. Whether the mothers were employed or not, teenagers spent more time as the number of children increased or as families were larger on all household work, all food preparation, all house care, and on the time-consuming activities of regular meal preparation, regular house care, and after-meal cleanup. In households with nonemployed wives, teenagers' time for all household work varied from 1 hour in families with one or two children to 3 hours in those with five or more children. In employed-wife households, the time of teenagers varied from 1 hour in one-child households to 1½ hours in those with two children, 3 hours in those with three, and about 4 hours in those with five or six.

For those activities in which age of the youngest child was the most highly related variable, most of the relationships were not strong; most of these were activities on which teenagers as a group did not spend much time. Whether or not the mothers were employed, teenagers' time use for all family care increased with decreasing age of the youngest child and their time spent on marketing increased with increments in age of the youngest child.

Relationships between age of the youngest child and teenagers' time use for most food work tended to be weak. However, their time spent on regular meal preparation diminished slightly with declining age of youngest child whether or not mothers were employed.

Employment of wives had some effect on teenagers' household work time. Teenagers spent a little more time when the mothers were employed at most or all family sizes on all food preparation work and on regular house care. Their time use for all household work was not significantly related to employment of mothers but in most family sizes they tended to spend slightly more time when the mothers were employed. In most other kinds of household work, teenagers did not consistently spend more time in employed-wife than in nonemployed-wife households.

Time Used for Household Work by Children 6 to 11 Years

In families with children in the 6- to 11-year age group, the children had done some work in one or more activities on 69% of the record days. The areas in which they most frequently participated were regular house care, regular meal preparation, and after-meal cleanup. The time use of children 6 to 11 for all household work was about the same when their mothers were employed (1.0 hour) and when they were not (1.1 hours). No correlation values were determined because their time use in each activity was relatively limited.

Some relationship was evident between size of family and the accumulated time use of children of these ages for all household work. For families with nonemployed mothers the time ranged from about half an hour in those households with one child to a total of 2½ hours in the largest families. For families with employed mothers, the time was not directly related to number of children; it ranged from about half an hour in small families to 1½ hours in three-child households, and then dropped to 1 hour in larger families.

Time Used for Household Work by Female and Male Nonfamily Workers

In employed-wife households only 5% of all household work time reported was that of female workers other than family members; it was 3% of all time in nonemployed-wife households. Time for nonfamily male workers made up only 1% of the total time, whether or not wives were employed.

For all household work, the time of other workers, male or female, did not vary by number of children, whether wives were employed or not; however, nonfamily workers tended to spend more time in households in which there were younger children, especially in employed-wife households. About three-fifths of all time of female workers other than family members was used for nonphysical care of children; their time represented 14% and 24% of the total time used for this activity in nonemployed- and employed-wife households, respectively. Although their second most common activity was regular house care, their time accounted for only 3% of total time for this activity. Time of nonfamily male workers went

mainly into special house care, yard care, and nonphysical care of children.

Recommendations for Future Analysis of Time Use for Household Production

Variables

If only one variable could be used to predict time costs of household production the best one would be *number of children* in the household. This variable was related to total time use of all workers more closely or as closely as any other variable for all household work and for the five regular activities that accounted for more than half of all time use reported for household work. It was most closely related to time use in the three groups of activities that accounted for about 60% of all time reported. It was significantly related to time use for 12 of the 13 household activities studied. However, it was not as closely related to two regular, time-consuming activities as was age of the youngest child; these were physical care of family members and marketing.

Number of children was also significantly related to time use of the wives and also to time use of teenagers for all household work and some individual activities.

Either age of the youngest child or number of children was most closely or as closely related to time use as any other variable in eleven household activities that made up about 90% of total average daily time. When the activities of family care and marketing that correlated best with age of the youngest child were added to the three groups of activities for which time use related most closely to number of children, practically all household work time could be accounted for.

The authors recommend the use of *number of children* as a predictor of time use for:

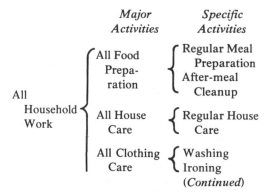

	Major Activities	*Specific Activities*
All Household Work	All Food Preparation	Regular Meal Preparation / After-meal Cleanup
	All House Care	Regular House Care
	All Clothing Care	Washing / Ironing

(*Continued*)

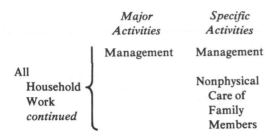

	Major Activities	Specific Activities
All Household Work *continued*	Management	Management
		Nonphysical Care of Family Members

The authors recommend the use of *age of the youngest child* as a prediction of time use for:

	Major Activities	Specific Activities
	All Family Care	Physical Care of Family Members
	Marketing	Marketing
		Yard and Car Care

Although *employment of wives* was not in itself the best predictor of all workers' time use on any major household work activity, it nevertheless was an important factor in the amount of time used on household work. Employment was strongly correlated with wives' household work time. The authors recommend that data for employed- and nonemployed-wife households be analyzed separately for the measurement of household production.

Husbands' hours of paid employment was the only variable found to relate effectively with husbands' work time in the household. The authors recommend that hours of husbands' employment be used as a major variable because of its possible value in explaining variations in the household work time of husbands.

Household Work Categories

For this study, 13 types of individual household work activities and 6 major household work areas were defined on the basis of previous research.

The decision to use grouped or individual activity categories for future research in time measurement must depend on purposes of the time analysis. For example, if the purpose were to put a monetary value on household production, individual activities should be used since not all activities could have the same monetary value. If the researcher were interested in work roles of various family members, refined categories would also seem essential. On the other hand, if the researcher were interested in household work in total for the various family members, three categories—family care, marketing, and other household work—might be desirable.

In general, as indicated earlier, few difficulties were found in the analysis of the specific work activities that were time consuming and frequently performed. However, among the less frequently performed work activities, various problems were encountered because of combining some subtasks into one activity category; for example, the combination of sewing and washing by hand into special clothing care and the combination of yard care and car care into one category.

One recommendation made on the basis of findings in the present study is that special food preparation be combined with regular meal preparation for future study. The amount of time spent on special food preparation was too small to appreciably affect the large amount of time spent on regular meal preparation. Another possibility may be to combine special house care with regular house care. However, combining these activities would result in loss of information as to the principal worker in each area; as work is now distributed in families, females are the principal workers in regular house care while males do much special house care.

Sample and Data Collection

Before time use can be effectively utilized as a measure of production, it will be necessary to collect time-use data from a large sample of households from many geographical locations in the country and to collect these data from all kinds of households, some of which were not included in this survey (e.g., one-parent households and one-, two-, or more-adult households). Data also need to be collected from cities and communities of different sizes. Data reported in this monograph related to one urban-suburban area, Syracuse, N.Y. As a part of the time-use research project conducted at Cornell, data were collected from a small supplementary sample of rural families in 1971, but these data were analyzed separately and not reported here.

Surveys need to be done in such a manner that time of wives, husbands, boys, and girls can either be combined for household analysis or be kept separate for analysis of time of individual types of workers in households; to average the household work time contributed by males and females produces meaningless data. Data should be collected to include days of the week and seasonal variations. Surveys need to be done frequently enough to determine changes brought on by changes in technology, economic conditions, and culture.

National time accounts, collected by households on an ongoing basis, will be essential if measurement of household production becomes a serious national goal. Research is also needed to determine appropriate methods for incorporating household production in national indicators and in economic analysis.

Before a national time survey can be undertaken, coordinated surveys should be conducted in various regions of the country, including replication in Syracuse, N.Y., to determine regional and city size variability. Ideally, such surveys would be conducted in 1977-78 to determine possible changes in time use over a 10-year period. Replication in Syracuse would be critical to determine whether variability in other locations is due to changes over time or variability caused by climatic conditions or demographic characteristics of the areas studied. If such studies are undertaken, we highly recommend coordination of sampling method, instruments, methods for data collection, data coding, and methods of analysis. We also recommend tests of alternate methods of data collection; for example, comparison should be made of data on time use collected from wives only with data collected from all family members over 12 years of age.

Before household production data can be compared among researchers in one country or internationally, a definition of the term needs to be agreed upon.[4] A significant question is: What are the limits for activities and types of workers to be included?

---

[4]In the summer of 1975 a working party on time-use measurement of household work and its economic value was convened under the auspices of the Department of Home Economics of the Agricultural University of the Netherlands. This party of nine Dutch, German, and American home economists tentatively defined household work and household production as follows: "Household work comprises the activities performed for and by the household member(s) that result in household production, the goods and services that enable a household to function." This definition differs from the one used in this monograph only in the exclusion of time use of nonfamily workers.

Major Accomplishments of Cornell Study

The study reported in this monograph is viewed as one more significant step toward the goal of measurement of household work, although it would be unfortunate to assume more extensive accomplishments than the project was set up to do.

In the judgment of the researchers involved, three significant variables (number of children, age of the youngest child, and employment of wives) have been identified for future research. Other variables, often assumed to relate to time use, have been shown to be of only minor importance in a total picture of time use for household work.

It was the hypothesis of the research that family composition relates more closely to time use for household work than any other variable. Statistical analysis of the data affirm this hypothesis and the extensive tabular descriptions of time use according to number of children and age of youngest child empirically show the effects of these variables on time use of all workers and individual types of workers. These descriptive data also show the relevance of the statistical differences; they permit interpretation of the meaningfulness of the statistically significant differences in terms of the extent of such differences for specific work activities and total household production.

Of the three variables identified as most closely related to time use for household work, number of children is the one most conveniently used and most appropriate for measurement of all household work activities except care of family members and marketing; for these work activities age of the youngest child is a more adequate measure. The third variable, employment of wives, is negatively associated with time use by all workers and by wives for each household work activity; it could, therefore, be used as a third control variable for further research. This variable was a random rather than a control variable for the project reported here and its relative importance emerged in the process of data analysis.

Another accomplishment of the study was the development of a means of recording the data on time use that is easy to use, provides for accurate reporting, and is economical to administer. For measurement of time use for household work the time-use chart and method for reporting time use of family members in this study proved very satisfactory for respondents' ease of reporting and for ease of preparing data for analysis. The form was subjectively evaluated very positively by the researchers and could be used without significant changes for further research on household production.

The one major drawback is that the household work time as reported by this instrument cannot be analyzed along with nonwork time. For some purposes it would be not only desirable but essential to include all time use in one record. The advantages of a time diary over the system used for this study are that (1) all types of time may be reported, and (2) that reporting is done in the words of the respondent. The advantage of the time chart developed for this study over the diary method is that coding of the activities is done by the respondent, decreasing significantly the costs of coding vast quantities of varied data while avoiding potential errors in interpreting the purpose of the activities reported. The survey interview instrument used for the study served the purpose of the present research but would require considerable revision by deleting information found not to be critical for further analysis.

The time-use study project has resulted in the development of an extensive data bank of household work information and familial descriptive data combined with time-use data. The current project used nonparametric statistical measures for analysis, but much of the data are amenable to a variety of multivariate analytical techniques. Some of the data have been selected for testing hypotheses by researchers at Columbia University and at the University of Wisconsin and continue to be used by researchers within the New York State College of Human Ecology at Cornell University (see Appendix C, 1974 and 1975).

In addition to use of the data for research the time-use data have many uses for families. Possibly the outcome of the research that has had the greatest immediate social impact has resulted from reporting of data on the distribution and monetary value of the work of household production within the family unit at a point in time when there is great interest in work roles of men and women. The data also have implications for family decision making for which time cost facts are relevant, such as an estimation of the time costs of combining household work at various stages of the family cycle with employment work or the time costs of operating households of various sizes. Time-cost facts resulting from this survey also have potential usefulness (1) to professionals such as family counselors, extension workers, and social workers as they attempt to assist families in time-use choices and (2) to educators as they assist young people in realistic planning for future work roles in terms of time demands.

The publications that were used for disseminating results of analyses at interim phases of the research project (1969 to 1975) are reported in Appendix C. This dissemination of research results was viewed as a significant part of the research project.

The most important result of the study has been the confirmation of a direct relationship between family composition and time spent on household work, thus allowing the use of amount of time spent on the work to become a measure of household production. The family characteristic is the indicator of the work accomplished in each activity in the time spent; for example, age of youngest child expresses the work accomplished in family care in different types of households for a given period of time. Thus, both time spent and work accomplished are expressed as a unit. The advantages of time as a measure of household production are that it varies principally with the amount of work, measures the work accomplished in each work activity, is additive, is expressible in different units (such as an hour, day, week), and can be developed from data that are relatively easy to collect. Additionally, it may be expressed in units to which wage rates, which are usually computed in units of time, may be applied. Continued research is needed to devise the most appropriate means of attaching monetary value to this time use.

SUMMARY TABLE 1—Rank correlation coefficients[a] for number of children, age of youngest child, and employment of wives and all workers' time use for (1) all household work, (2) groups of work activities, and (3) specific work activities

(1,260 husband-wife households, Syracuse, N.Y., 1967-68)

Activity	Number of children	Age of youngest (N = 1,092)	Employment of wives
All household work	[.37]	.13	-.23
All food preparation	[.33]	-.08	-.19
All family care	.29	[.56]	-.19
All house care	[.20]	-.15	-.11
All clothing care	[.15]		[-.15]
Specific task areas			
Regular meal preparation	[.31]	-.06*	-.19
After meal cleanup	[.28]	-.07	-.18
Special food preparation	[.06*]	-.05*	
Physical care of family members	.25	[.70]	-.24
Nonphysical care of family members	[.27]	.23	-.10
Regular house care	[.26]	-.10	-.08
Special house care	.05*		[-.09]
Yard and car care	.08	[-.12]	-.05*
Washing by machine	[.24]	.11	-.14
Ironing	[.09]		[-.09]
Special clothing care		[-.08]	-.05*
Marketing	.09	[-.16]	
Management	.05**		[-.06]

[a]All correlation coefficients reported are significant at the .001 level unless otherwise indicated as: * = .005, ** = .01 or .02. Tau correlations for other variables are reported in respective chapters on each activity.
[ ] The highest of the three variables in correlation with time use of all workers on the activity.

SUMMARY TABLE 2—Total time[a] used by all workers for (1) all household work, (2) groups of work activities, and (3) specific work activities, by number of children

(1,296 husband–wife households, Syracuse, N.Y., 1967-68)

Number of children	Number of families	All household work	All food activities	All family care	All house care	All clothing care
			Average hours per day[b]			
0	168	6.3	2.0	.2	1.8	.9
1	210	9.1	2.2	2.2	2.2	1.1
2	378	10.7	2.6	2.7	2.5	1.4
3	294	11.4	2.9	2.4	3.0	1.4
4	169	12.1	2.9	3.0	2.8	1.5
5-6	56	14.1	3.8	3.1	3.7	1.7
7-9	21	16.9	4.7	4.2	4.1	1.8
Average	1,296	10.5	2.6	2.3	2.6	1.3

Number of children	Number of families	Regular meal preparation	After-meal cleanup	Physical care	Nonphysical care	Regular house care	Yard and car care	Washing by machine	Ironing	Marketing
0	168	1.1	.7		.2	.9	.3	.3	.3	1.0
1	210	1.3	.9	1.0	1.1	1.1	.4	.4	.4	1.1
2	378	1.5	.9	1.3	1.3	1.3	.5	.5	.4	1.2
3	294	1.7	1.1	1.1	1.3	1.5	.6	.5	.5	1.5
4	169	1.9	1.1	1.4	1.6	1.6	.5	.7	.4	1.5
5-6	56	2.2	1.6	1.3	1.8	2.2	.5	.7	.6	1.5
7-9	21	2.7	2.2	1.4	2.8	2.7		.9	.4	1.6
Average	1,296	1.5	1.0	1.1	1.2	1.4	.5	.5	.4	1.3

[a]Time is reported for activities with correlation values significant at the .001 level.

[b]Time is reported only if there were three or more families and if average time was 3 minutes or more.

SUMMARY TABLE 3—Total time[a] used by all workers for all family care and for five specific work activities, by age of youngest child
(1,128 husband–wife households, Syracuse, N.Y., 1967-68)

Age of youngest child	Number of families	All family care	Physical care	Nonphysical care	Marketing	Yard and car care	Special clothing care
			Average hours per day[b]				
12-17	141	.7	.1	.5	1.9	.8	.4
6-11	296	1.4	.3	1.1	1.6	.7	.4
2-5	311	2.5	1.0	1.5	1.1	.5	.4
1	183	3.4	1.8	1.6	1.0	.5	.3
Under 1	197	5.2	3.2	1.9	.9	.3	.3
Average	1,128	2.6	1.2	1.4	1.3	.5	.4

[a]Time is reported for activities with correlation values significant at the .001 level.

[b]Time is reported only if there were three or more families and if average time was 3 minutes or more.

SUMMARY TABLE 4—Total time[a] used by all workers for (1) all household work, (2) groups children and employment of wives

(1,296 husband–wife households, Syracuse, N.Y., 1967-68)

Number of children	Number NE[c]	E	All household work NE	E	All food activities NE	E	All house care NE	E
				Average hours per day[b]				
0	97	71	7.2	5.0	2.3	1.5	2.2	1.4
1	149	61	9.7	7.7	2.3	2.0	2.3	2.0
2	295	83	11.0	9.8	2.6	2.4	2.5	2.4
3	233	61	11.6	10.8	2.9	2.8	2.9	3.2
4	139	30	12.3	10.9	2.9	3.0	2.8	2.7
5-6	47	9	14.5	13.0	4.1	3.3	3.9	3.0
7-9	19	2	17.4		4.7		4.2	
Average	979	317	11.1	8.7	2.8	2.3	2.7	2.3

Number of children	Number NE	E	Regular meal preparation NE	E	After-meal cleanup NE	E	Regular house care NE	E
0	97	71	1.2	.9	.8	.5	1.0	.7
1	149	61	1.3	1.2	.9	.7	1.1	1.1
2	295	83	1.5	1.4	.9	.9	1.3	1.2
3	233	61	1.7	1.5	1.0	1.1	1.5	1.8
4	139	30	1.8	1.9	1.2	1.0	1.6	1.6
5-6	47	9	2.2	1.9	1.6	1.2	2.2	1.8
7-9	19	2	2.7		2.2		2.9	
Average	979	317	1.6	1.3	1.0	.8	1.4	1.2

[a]Time is reported for activities with correlation values significant at the .001 level.

[b]Time is reported only if there were three or more families and if average time was 3 minutes or more.

[c]NE and E indicate households with nonemployed or employed wives.

of work activities, and (3) specific work activities, by number of

All family care NE	E	All clothing care NE	E
		Average hours per day[b]	
.2	.3	1.1	.6
2.4	1.5	1.2	.9
2.8	2.2	1.4	1.1
2.5	1.8	1.4	1.3
3.3	1.6	1.5	1.6
2.9	4.0	1.8	1.0
4.5		1.8	
2.5	1.5	1.4	1.1

Physical care NE	E	Nonphysical care NE	E	Washing by machine NE	E	Ironing NE	E	Marketing NE	E
		.1	.2	.3	.3	.4	.2	1.0	.9
1.3	.4	1.1	1.1	.4	.3	.4	.3	1.1	1.0
1.5	.7	1.3	1.4	.6	.4	.4	.4	1.1	1.4
1.2	.7	1.4	1.1	.6	.5	.5	.4	1.5	1.4
1.6	.5	1.7	1.1	.7	.6	.4	.3	1.4	1.6
1.3	1.1	1.6	2.9	.7	.7	.6	.3	1.5	1.4
1.5		3.0		.9		.5		1.7	
1.2	.5	1.3	1.1	.5	.4	.4	.3	1.3	1.2

SUMMARY TABLE 5—Total time[a] used by all workers for all family care and for five specific work activities, by age of youngest child and employment of wives

(1,128 husband-wife households, Syracuse, N.Y., 1967-68)

Age of youngest child	Number of families NE[c]	E	All family care NE	E
			Average hours per day[b]	
12–17	80	61	.7	.6
6–11	210	86	1.5	1.3
2–5	248	63	2.5	2.5
1	163	20	3.4	3.8
Under 1	181	16	5.1	5.8
Average	882	246	2.8	1.9

Age of youngest child	Number NE[c]	Number E	Physical care NE	E	Nonphysical care NE	E	Marketing NE	E	Yard and car care NE	E	Special clothing care NE	E
12–17	80	61	.1	.1	.5	.5	2.0	1.8	1.0	.5	.4	.4
6–11	210	86	.4	.2	1.1	1.1	1.7	1.3	.7	.4	.4	.3
2–5	248	63	1.0	.8	1.5	1.7	1.2	.9	.5	.4	.4	.2
1	163	20	1.8	1.9	1.5	1.9	1.0	1.1	.5	.4	.3	.2
Under 1	181	16	3.2	2.7	1.8	3.1	.9	1.4	.3	.3	.3	.1
Average	882	246	1.4	.6	1.4	1.3	1.3	1.3	.6	.4	.4	.4

[a]Time is reported for activities with correlation values significant at the .001 level.

[b]Time is reported only if there were three or more families and if average time was 3 minutes or more.

[c]NE and E indicate households with nonemployed or employed wives.

SUMMARY TABLE 6—Rank correlation coefficients[a] for number of children, age of youngest child, and employment of wives and wives' time used for (1) all household work, (2) groups of work activities, and (3) specific work activities

(1,260 husband–wife households, Syracuse, N.Y., 1967-68)

Activity	Number of children	Age of youngest (N = 1,092)	Employment of wives
All household work	.27	.30	[-.36]
All food preparation	.21	.07	[-.29]
All family care	.28	[.60]	-.26
All house care	.11		[-.18]
All clothing care	.13	.04+	[-.18]
Specific task areas			
Regular meal preparation	.22	.04**	[-.26]
After-meal cleanup	.14	.11	[-.27]
Special food preparation	.04+	-.04**	-.04+
Physical care of family members	.25	[.70]	-.26
Nonphysical care of family members	[.25]	.18	-.16
Regular house care	[.16]		[-.16]
Special house care			[-.12]
Yard and car care	.07	-.09	[-.11]
Washing by machine	[.23]	.11	-.16
Ironing	.08		[-.11]
Special clothing care	-.04+	-.04**	[-.07]
Marketing	.04+	[-.10]	
Management	.05*		[-.08]

[a]All correlation coefficients reported are significant at the .001 level unless otherwise indicated as: * = .005, ** = .01 or .02, and + = .03 to .05. Tau correlations for other variables are reported in respective chapters on each activity.

[‾ ‾ ‾] The highest of the three variables in correlation with time use of wives in each activity.

SUMMARY TABLE 7—Time[a] used by wives for (1) all household work, (2) groups of work of children and employment of wives

(1,296 husband-wife households, Syracuse, N.Y., 1967-68)

Number of children	Number NE[c]	E	All household work NE	E	All food activities NE	E	All house care NE	E
					Average hours per day[b]			
0	97	71	5.7	3.7	2.0	1.3	1.5	.9
1	149	61	7.4	5.1	2.1	1.6	1.5	1.3
2	295	83	8.4	5.9	2.3	1.8	1.7	1.1
3	233	61	8.1	6.0	2.3	1.8	1.7	1.4
4	139	30	8.7	6.2	2.3	1.9	1.7	1.3
5-6	47	9	9.0	6.3	2.7	1.9	1.7	1.1
7-9	19	2	9.4		2.6		1.5	
Average	979	317	8.0	5.3	2.3	1.7	1.6	1.2

			Regular meal preparation NE	E	After-meal cleanup NE	E	Regular house care NE	E	Special house care NE	E
0	97	71	1.1	.8	.7	.4	.9	.6	.5	.3
1	149	61	1.2	.9	.8	.5	1.0	.9	.3	.3
2	295	83	1.4	1.1	.8	.6	1.2	.9	.3	.1
3	233	61	1.4	1.0	.8	.6	1.2	1.1	.3	.2
4	139	30	1.6	1.2	.9	.6	1.3	.9	.2	.3
5-6	47	9	1.7	1.3	.8	.6	1.2	1.0	.3	.1
7-9	19	2	1.8		.9		1.2		.2	
Average	979	317	1.4	1.0	.8	.6	1.1	.9	.3	.2

[a]Time is reported for activities with correlation values significant at the .001 level.

[b]Time is reported only if there were three or more families and if average time was 3 minutes or more.

[c]NE and E indicate households with nonemployed or employed wives.

activities, and (3) specific work activities, by number

All family care		All clothing care	
NE	E	NE	E
Average hours per day[b]			
.1	.1	1.1	.6
1.8	.7	1.1	.8
2.1	1.1	1.4	.9
1.8	.9	1.3	1.1
2.3	1.0	1.4	1.2
1.8	1.4	1.6	1.0
2.7		1.6	
1.8	.8	1.3	.9

Yard and car care		Physical care		Nonphysical care		Washing by machine		Ironing		Marketing	
NE	E	NE	E	NE	E	NE	E	NE	E	NE	E
.1	.1			.1	.1	.3	.2	.4	.2	.7	.6
.1	.1	1.2	.3	.6	.4	.4	.3	.4	.3	.7	.5
.2	.1	1.4	.6	.7	.5	.5	.3	.4	.3	.7	.7
.2	.1	1.0	.5	.8	.4	.5	.5	.4	.3	.8	.7
.2	.1	1.4	.4	.9	.6	.7	.6	.4	.3	.7	.7
.2		1.1	.8	.8	.6	.7	.6	.6	.2	.8	.8
		1.2		1.5		.9		.5		.8	
.1	.1	1.1	.4	.7	.4	.5	.4	.4	.3	.7	.7

SUMMARY TABLE 8—Time[a] used by wives for (1) all household work, (2) groups of work activities, and (3) specific work activities, by age of youngest child and employment of wives (1,128 husband–wife households, Syracuse, N.Y., 1967-68)

Average hours per day[b]

Age of youngest child	Number[c] NE	E	All household work NE	E	All food activities NE	E	All house care NE	E	All family care NE	E	All clothing care NE	E
12-17	80	61	7.0	4.8	2.2	1.5	1.9	.8	.4	.3	1.1	1.2
6-11	210	86	7.6	5.8	2.4	1.8	1.7	1.4	1.0	.7	1.4	1.0
2-5	248	63	8.2	6.0	2.5	1.9	1.6	1.4	1.7	1.2	1.4	.8
1	163	20	8.6	7.0	2.4	1.8	1.6	1.3	2.5	1.9	1.2	1.1
Under 1	181	16	9.6	7.5	2.3	1.8	1.4	1.1	3.8	2.7	1.3	.9
Average	882	246	8.3	5.8	2.4	1.8	1.6	1.2	2.0	1.0	1.3	1.0

Age of youngest child	Number NE	E	Yard and car care NE	E	Physical care NE	E	Nonphysical care NE	E	Special clothing care NE	E	Marketing NE	E
12-17	80	61	.3	.1	.1	.1	.3	.3	.5	.7	1.0	.8
6-11	210	86	.2	.1	.3	.2	.7	.5	.5	.4	.9	.6
2-5	248	63	.2	.1	.9	.6	.9	.5	.4	.2	.8	.6
1	163	20	.1		1.6	1.2	.8	.7	.3	.2	.6	.6
Under 1	181	16	.1		2.9	2.2	.9	.5	.3	.1	.5	.8
Average	882	246	.1	.1	1.2	.5	.8	.5	.3	.3	.7	.7

[a]Time is reported for activities with correlation values significant at the .001 level.
[b]Time is reported only if there were three or more families and if average time was 3 minutes or more.
[c]NE and E indicate households with nonemployed or employed wives.

References in Text

Anderson, N. *Work and Leisure.* New York: Free Press of Glencoe, 1961.

Boalt, C. *1000 Husmödrar om Hemarbetet (Household Work of 1000 Homemakers).* Stockholm, Sweden: Konsument Institutet Meddelar, Statens Institut för Konsumentfrågor, 1961.

Chapin, F. S., Jr. *Human Activity Patterns in the City: Things People Do in Time and in Space.* New York: John Wiley, 1974.

daFonseca, D. M. Analysis of dishwashing time in selected Indiana families. Unpublished master's thesis, Purdue University, 1964.

Fabricant, S. Comment. In V. R. Fuchs (Ed.), *Production and Productivity in the Service Industries.* Studies in Income and Wealth, No. 34, New York: National Bureau of Economic Research, 1969.

Foote, N. N. Methods for study of meaning in use of time. In R. W. Kleemeier (Ed.), *Aging and Leisure.* New York: Oxford Press, 1961.

Fraisse, P. Time: Psychological aspects. In D. L. Sills (Ed.), *International Encyclopedia of the Social Sciences,* Vol. 16. New York: Macmillan and Free Press, 1968.

Friedan, B. *The Feminine Mystique.* New York: Dell, 1963.

Fuchs, V. R. (Ed.) *Production and Productivity in the Service Industries.* Studies in Income and Wealth, No. 34. New York: National Bureau of Economic Research, 1969.

Gage, M. G. *The Work Load and Its Value for 50 Homemakers, Tompkins County, New York.* (Doctoral dissertation, Cornell University) Ann Arbor, Mich.: University Microfilms, 1960, No. 61-1440.

Gauger, W. H. Household work: can we add it to GNP? *Journal of Home Economics,* 1973, *65* (October), 12-15.

Girard, A. Le budget-temps de la femme mariee dans les agglomerations urbaines (Time-budgets for urban married women). *Population,* 1958, *13* (4), 591-618.

Gitobu, J. K. Use of time for household activities by employed and nonemployed rural homemakers. Unpublished master's thesis, Cornell University, 1972.

Goody, J. Time: Social organization. In D. L. Sills (Ed.), *International Encyclopedia of the Social Sciences,* Vol. 16. New York: Macmillan and Free Press, 1968.

Gross, I., and Crandall, E. W. *Management for Modern Families.* New York: Appleton-Century-Crofts, 1954.

Hoffman, L. W. The decision to work. In F. I. Nye and L. W. Hoffman (Eds.), *The Employed Mother in America.* Chicago: Rand McNally, 1963.

Hollingshead, A. B. Two factor index of social position. Box 1965, Yale Station, New Haven, Conn.: Author, 1957. (Mimeographed)

Hook, N. C. Use of time in regular care of the house in selected Indiana families. Unpublished master's thesis, Purdue University, 1963.

Hoppen, K. K. Teenage contribution to the work of the home in 28 families, Baldwin, New York. Unpublished master's thesis, Cornell University, 1966.

Jarmon, C. G. Relationship between homemakers' attitudes toward specific household tasks and family composition, other situational variables and time allocation. Unpublished master's thesis, Cornell University, 1972.

King, W. I., and Epstein, L. *The National Income and Its Purchasing Power.* Publication No. 15. New York: National Bureau of Economic Research, 1930.

Levy, S. *The meanings of work.* Chicago, Ill.: Center for the Study of Liberal Education for Adults, 1963.

Lynch, M. C. Participation in household work by children 6-17 years of age. Unpublished master's thesis, Cornell University, 1975.

Manning, S. L. *Time Use in Household Tasks by Indiana Families.* Purdue University Agricultural Experiment Station Research Bulletin No. 837, 1968.

Nie, N., Bent, D. H., and Hull, C. H. *Statistical Package for the Social Sciences.* New York: McGraw-Hill, 1970.

Parker, S. *The Future of Work and Leisure.* London: McGibbon and Lee, 1971.

Purcell, C. E. Development of an Indiana home-making work unit for washing clothes. Unpublished master's thesis, Purdue University, 1965.

Reid, M. *Economics of Household Production.* New York: John Wiley, 1934.

Ruggles, N., and Ruggles, R. *The Design of Economic Accounts.* General Series No. 89. New York: National Bureau of Economic Research, 1970.

Saurio, E. *Maalaisemännän ajankäytto* (Use of time of rural Finnish homemakers). Helsinki-Porvoo: Werner Söderström, 1947.

Siegel, S. *Nonparametric Statistics for the Behavioral Sciences.* New York: McGraw-Hill, 1956.

Smith, R. Testing a measure of household work for use in studying work load and labor efficiency. Unpublished master's thesis, Cornell University, 1940.

Steidl, R. E., and Bratton, E. C. *Work in the Home.* New York: John Wiley, 1968.

Suneson, D. I. Use of time for family food shopping activities. Unpublished master's thesis, Cornell University, 1961.

Szalai, A. (Ed.) *The Use of Time: Daily Activities of Urban and Suburban Populations in Twelve Countries.* The Hague, Paris: Mouton, 1972.

U.S. Bureau of the Census. *Statistical Abstract of the United States: 1969.* (90th ed.) Washington, D.C.: U.S. Government Printing Office, 1969.

U.S. Bureau of the Census. *Census of Population: 1970 Detailed Characteristics,* Final Report PC(1)-D34, New York. Washington, D.C.: U.S. Government Printing Office, 1972.

Walker, K. E. *Homemaking Work Units for New York State Households.* (Doctoral dissertation, Cornell University) Ann Arbor, Mich.: University Microfilms, 1955, No. 15,437.

Walker, K. E. *Homemaking Work Units for New York State Households.* Cornell University Agricultural Experiment Station Memoir No. 353, 1957.

Walker, K. E. *Homemakers' Use of Time for Care of Children in Sweden 1957.* Konsument Institutet Meddelar Nr. 11. Stockholm, Sweden: Statens Institut för Konsumentfrägör, 1964.

Walker, K. E. Homemaking still takes time. *Journal of Home Economics,* 1969. *61,* 621-624.

Walker, K. E. How much help for working mothers? The children's role. *Human Ecology Forum,* 1970, *1,* 13-15.

Walker, K. E., and Gauger, W. H. *The Dollar Value of Household Work.* Information Bulletin No. 60, New York State College of Human Ecology, Cornell University, 1973.

Walker, K. E., and Nordenstedt, B-S. Helpers' time in household activities. Unpublished data. State Research Project No. 75, Department of Household Economics and Management, New York State College of Home Economics, Cornell University, Ithaca, N.Y., 1966.

Warren, J. Use of time in its relation to home management. Unpublished doctoral dissertation, Cornell University, 1938.

Warren, J. *Use of Time in Its Relation to Home Management.* Cornell University Agricultural Experiment Station Bulletin No. 734, 1940.

Wiegand, E. Comparative use of time of farm and city full-time homemakers and homemakers in the labor force in relation to home management. Unpublished doctoral dissertation, Cornell University, 1953.

Wiegand, E. *Use of Time by Full-time and Part-time Homemakers in Relation to Home Management.* Cornell University Agricultural Experiment Station Memoir No. 330, 1954.

Wilson, M. *Use of Time by Oregon Farm Homemakers.* Oregon Agricultural Experiment Station Bulletin No. 256, 1929.

Wright, C. W. *Economic History of the United States.* (2nd ed.) New York: McGraw-Hill, 1949.

Appendix A

Methodology

The conceptual rationale and objectives for this research are reported in Chapter 1, The Measurement of Household Production. Details of procedure are reported in this section.

The primary objective of this project was the further development of a method of measuring the production of services and goods in family households. Earlier studies had demonstrated that time variations in household work were caused principally by variations in the amount of work to be done. It was assumed that the amount of time used for household work activities could provide a reliable measure of the amount of work being carried on in typical households.

Selection of Variables

The conceptual design defined amount of time used on household production as the dependent variable; this variable was the primary determinant of the data to be collected, the method used to collect the data, and the size of the sample.

For time use to be an effective measure of household work, it was necessary to determine what factor or factors affected this work time the most. A number of previous studies on the amount of time used for household work had primarily emphasized the importance of number of children in the family and the age of the youngest child. Everyday experience supported such findings, but there remained many unanswered questions, such as: How much difference does one more child make in the total work load of a family with a designated number of children at designated ages? What are the differences in the work load in families with children of varying combinations of ages? How does the time use vary for families at different stages of the family cycle? What is the impact of employment of wives on the amount of household work and who does it? Answering these questions required a study of a relatively large number of families with many patterns of family composition being adequately represented.

The research centered on family composition as the principal explanatory variable of the amount of work done to produce goods and services in family households. It was hypothesized that this work in contemporary households varies in relation to the number and ages of children in families with children and in families without children that age of wives would act as a predicting variable. The family composition variables determined the type of sample selected. Family composition has the practical advantage as a predicting variable of being readily ascertained from known information. Data on family composition are a standard part of sample surveys conducted by the U.S. Bureau of the Census.

It was not expected that family composition would be the best predictor for all categories of household activities. The hypothesis to be tested was that it would be the best predictor of time use for some activities and at least adequate for others. In previous research it had been found that several secondary variables were close to family composition in effectiveness of predicting time use. A study to determine average time input values should indicate those activities for which the secondary variables were important and the activities (if any) for which family composition was not the primary predictor. Previous research had shown that the work output in some household activities could be defined by some specific characteristic of the activity, e.g., loads of clothes washed. The effectiveness of these work output variables needed to be tested by use of a more representative sample and in relation to the effect of family composition.

With a major change in life style to urban-suburban from the former city-farm type of living, location of residence became a second control variable critical in selecting the site for the study. To determine the effects on time use caused by urban and suburban residence, it was necessary that each type of family composition be equally represented in these residential areas.

Two additional variables that could affect time use were controlled by interview scheduling—season of the year and day of the week. Most families must adjust their households to standard schedules set by schools, family vacations, and occupations at different times of the year. Each season has characteristics and special activities that affect the total work load or the work required by a special activity. Other considerations related to average household work time are the varying amounts of time used on some activities on different days and on weekends as compared with weekdays. Household work activity patterns may vary in frequency from several times a day to daily, semiweekly, weekly, biweekly, monthly, or only occasionally. These varying frequencies were more adequately represented by using season of year and day of week as controls.

To examine effects of other factors that relate to amount of household work and its time use, data were collected for selected variables related to the socioeconomic characteristics of the household and the physical aspects of the work environment. These were random rather than control variables. The characteristics considered as attributes of the social environment in which the household work was conducted were: socioeconomic status, characteristics of the wives and husbands (age, education, employment status, and occupation), and characteristics of the household as a unit, such as amount of time family members spent at home and away from home on the record days, special family situations, and household practices. The physical characteristics selected as most likely to describe the typical household work environment were: features of the housing (number of stories, number of rooms, age of the house, number of rooms in use, availability of adequate work and storage space, and other special-use spaces); availability and use of household equipment.

The quantity of demographic and other data needed to give these random variables adequate explanatory power strongly influenced decisions made with respect to each aspect of the study design. Any of these variables could be expected to combine with family composition to explain time use, some variability on work output, or to modify effects of family composition.[1]

Employment of wives was expected to be a significant variable. However, employment of wives was used as a random rather than a control variable for practical reasons. With the number and age of children as a control measure it would be almost impossible to have a large sample and to control on employment in addition to number and ages of children, because married women are more likely to work at some stages of the family cycle than others. With employment as a random variable it was assumed that employed women would be included in the sample in proportion to their representation in the labor force in the population area.

Random selection was desirable in order that the other family characteristics would occur in the sample in the same proportion found in the general population. A completely random sample, however, would provide an inadequate data base for some types of families and more than needed for others (for example, households with no children). The plan, therefore, was to first stratify a population by family composition and then select randomly within it. The random selection of families within each stratum of family composition assumed that the socioeconomic and physical characteristics to be studied would appear in the sample in about the same proportion as they occurred in the population of the city selected for the survey.

Site for the Study

Since the urban-suburban population has become predominant in the latter half of the twentieth century in the United States, it was considered essential that households in the sample be chosen from a predominantly urban area, preferably with demographic characteristics of the population as close as possible to their proportion in the population of New York State.

Because the nature of the study was such that close supervision of the field work was essential and because collection of the data was expected to extend over a long period, it was centered in only one area.

Population analyses[2] were made of three major cities with Standard Metropolitan Statistical Areas (SMSA) of 250,000 or more population within a radius of 150 miles of Ithaca, N.Y. (Buffalo, Rochester, and Syracuse) as they compared with each other, with New York State, and with the United States. Criteria used for comparisons were family income, median school years completed by age and sex, employment of men and women by type of occupation and industry, and participation in the labor force of women with husbands present by presence and age of children in household.

The city and suburbs of Syracuse were selected because the population characteristics of this area were more like those of New York State as a whole than were those of the other cities considered. Relevant demographic characteristics

---

[1]See Chapter 2 for distribution of various random variables within the sample and among family types.

[2]These analyses were done by Professor Ethel Vatter, Department of Consumer Economics and Public Policy.

of the Syracuse SMSA for 1970 are shown in Appendix Table 1.

Pilot Study

Before the plan was developed fully, an important question with respect to control variables had to be answered: Were there enough differences in household work and time use between households on different socioeconomic levels to require that socioeconomic status be used with family composition as a control variable? A second question related to the number of categories of family composition to be included, since it was clearly advisable to test the number of categories of family composition before making definite plans for the major study. In addition, instruments of data collection being developed during the sample selection phase needed to be tested.

A pilot study was designed to provide answers to these questions and to test data-collection procedures and instruments. Sixty families were selected from pools of names stratified according to three socioeconomic levels and 20 categories of family composition based upon number and ages of children. The families were selected from three segments of the broad strata of middle class— lower-middle, middle, and upper-middle. Very poor and very rich families were excluded. Differences in household work and time use could be expected between the extremes of economic classes, but what was not known was whether significant differences existed between groups within the middle class.

From the pilot study it was found that there were no consistent differences in time use for household work between families in the three socioeconomic groups. Socioeconomic status as a control variable, therefore, was eliminated.

The pilot study showed the expected differences among families of different compositions in time used for household work, but it also indicated that 20 categories of family composition would not be sufficient for the analysis. The number of categories selected was increased to 31, the additional categories being defined from the findings of the pilot study. One age category, as used by the U.S. Bureau of the Census, was adjusted when findings indicated that there was no substantial difference in time use between families with a 2-year-old child and those in which there was a child between the ages of 3 and 5; these two preschool-age categories were combined for the major study to 2 to 5 years, making five rather than six categories of children's ages.

Family Composition of Sample Families

The family composition variable determined the type of sample selected. It was the purpose of this project to study a sample of families broadly representative, demographically, of the majority of families in the general population. Husband-wife families with or without children at home and with no other adults living in the households make up the majority of families. The sample selected, therefore, included only complete, nuclear families with or without children at home.

Not included were such households as single-parent families, one-person households, and households in which adults other than husband and wife lived. Patterns of living in these households may be different than in households of parents and children, but it was not possible to include in one research project all the possible variations of family composition.

The preliminary plan was to have a stratified sample of at least 1,000 families, with an equal number of husband-wife families with one, two, three, or more children under age 18 in each category. Some of these categories should have all children in the same age groups and others should have children from more than one age category. Age categories were selected on the basis of the results of time-use analysis from Walker's previous research, the age classifications of children used in the 1960 Census of Population, and the results of the pilot study. Five age categories were selected (12 to 17, 6 to 11, 2 to 5, 1 year, and under 1 year).

One problem of using a sample stratified by number and ages of children is the instability of the population for sample drawing and interviewing. The combination of age of children and number of children made the population selected subject to almost constant shifting. Families moved from one classification of family size to another with the birth of a baby or with an older child reaching age 18. As each child had a birthday, families could move into new classifications of ages of children. To reduce the age classification problem, the age of a child was considered for the study as not changed from the age at the first sample selection when the interview was held within 4 months of his birthday.

Four types of childless households were selected to be compatible with data from the U.S. Census. These types, by age of wives, were: under age 25 years, between 25 and 39, between 40 and 54, or 55 years and older.

A sample size of at least 30 households per category seemed essential to provide an adequate data base for analysis, and the number selected should be divisible by seven to permit equal representation of days of the week within each category. The number selected for each family type was 42. Control of day of the week was maintained by scheduling of interviews and record days.

To control for season of the year, the data collection phase had to extend over a year's time. Each type of family needed to be equally represented in each season. Three season categories appropriate to the climatic conditions of Syracuse, N.Y. were set as: winter-early spring (January through April), late spring-summer (May through August), and fall-early winter (September through December). These categories were selected to include the effects of school vacations and also because families tend to have a different pattern of activities during the fall and holiday season from those they follow from January through early spring. Controls on season of the year were maintained by the distribution of scheduled interviews.

Establishing the Population for Drawing Sample

In order to establish the population from which to draw the sample of families with children, it was necessary to have complete and up-to-date records of the number of children and the birthdate of each child in all, or nearly all, households in both the city and suburban areas of Syracuse. For the sample of families without children, an equally complete list of childless families in the city and suburbs was needed.

Data that include family composition are collected by several agencies: the U.S. Bureau of the Census, school systems, publishers of city directories, city and civic agencies, and consumer research groups. A thorough investigation of these and other sources by the research associate, Irma Telling,[3] showed that no one set of data was available that met the requirements of being up-to-date and complete for both city and suburban families or for families with and without children in the study area.

New York State education laws require that a school census of all families with minors between birth and 18 years of age be taken annually in all school districts, except cities with populations of 125,000 or more. Since the population of the city

of Syracuse was over 216,000 in 1960, school census records were not available. The school census for each suburban area around the city, however, was geographically complete and provided current information on the number of children and age of each child under 18 years of age in the school district as well as names and addresses of parents. School census records, therefore, provided a good basis for the list of suburban families with children.

An intensive search was undertaken for some type of records in the city that would provide some of the essential data on the composition of families. School data were considered, and in a conference with the director of research for the Syracuse city schools, it was learned that a school research project related to the city school population for both public and private schools was in progress. For this research a list of 45,000 children of school age attending both public and private schools in Syracuse had been compiled with the name, birthdate, and home address of each child, but children were not listed by families and there was no record of children under school age. The exploration of other possible sources of census data for the city, however, showed that the list was the only alternative that was even remotely feasible.

The Polk Company, publishers of city directories, was enumerating households in the Syracuse area in 1966 to prepare a household census for sales and marketing organizations. Their listing provided the age range of children and number of children but neither exact ages nor birthdates. The Polk Company listing did solve one part of the sample problem, since they had a list of childless families in the Syracuse area that included both urban and suburban families. A 10% sample of a purchased computer printout of about 22,000 names of no-children families was used for random selection of households without children. Information on the age of wives was not available from this listing, and it was necessary to combine randomization of husband-wife, no-children households with information obtained by interview to determine the proper age categorization.

Before a final decision could be made to use the list of school-age city children from the education research project, a source of information on children under school age in Syracuse had to be found. Although birth records are confidential, it was possible to examine the lists of births as published periodically in the newspapers during the previous 6 years. The lists could be

---

[3]Mrs. Irma Telling served as research associate throughout the project.

obtained from microfilm copies of local papers on file in the Syracuse public library, and current lists in the newspapers could be collected as they were published. Such listings made it possible to collect information on names and addresses of children born in Onondaga County in the preceding 6 years as well as the surname and first name of the father. Not all parents give permission for announcement of their child's birth, thus families of these children were excluded from the sampling population.

Once the problem of obtaining a listing of preschool-age children was resolved, permission to use the list of school-age children was requested from the school administrative officials. This permission was granted after explanation was given as to the nature and purpose of the proposed study, the way the data were to be used, and the potential usefulness of the data to the schools themselves. The data-processing card available for each student enrolled in the public and private schools of Syracuse was reproduced. On the assumption that children with the same surname and address were members of the same family, the data collected for preschool children and the data for school-age children in the city were combined into family groups. The method used was a merge-sort program, which matched the last name of the family, the first name of the father, and the address. The resulting list was verified by checking in the 1966 city directory the address, number of children in the household, and whether the family was a husband-wife family. The names of approximately 7,000 eligible families with children within the city limits were thus available for the random selection of the city sample.

The population lists for the suburban families were compiled from the school census records. Nine of the 16 school districts in Onondaga County had their census information recorded on data-processing cards.[4] After a comparative analysis showed that these districts were representative in many ways of the entire county and accounted for 83% of the total county population according to the 1960 census, it was decided to use the school census records of only these 9 districts in compiling the lists of suburban families by number and age of children. Authorization to use the school census data was obtained from the school board in each of the districts. All of the school census records were sorted into family groups. The names of approximately 20,000 suburban families with children were available for the random drawing of the suburban sample. This listing from consolidated school districts included rural house-

holds proportionally to the extent that they were found in the district.

Each family on the city and suburban listing was coded by the number and ages of children. Childless families were coded only by absence of children. To provide the stratification needed, the coded family cards were sorted into different family types separately by city and suburban residence. A sample of the desired number of 42 names was drawn randomly by means of data-processing equipment from pools of names for each of the family groups according to place of residence. A backup sample for each cell was also randomly drawn at the same time. Incomplete or other ineligible families could not be eliminated before the sample was drawn, since the information on the listings showed number and age of children and the presence or absence of children but not whether the children lived in complete families or in households in which adults other than the parents also lived.

Family composition information had to be verified and age of the wives had to be obtained as part of the initial interview; only families eligible according to their current family composition were interviewed. Sometimes by the time of an interview a new baby had been born or a child had left home for college, and this changed the family composition classification. If any specification was not met, the name was deleted and the interviewer checked the qualifications of the next family on the list. If, after a minimum of three "call backs" at different hours of the day, it was impossible to contact the person selected, or if the selected person refused to schedule an interview, the next name on the list was used until each cell was filled.

The plan followed for control of the urban-suburban variable was that 21 families for each cell were chosen randomly from urban families listed according to family composition characteristics, and 21 families were chosen randomly from the suburban list.[5] Although the aim was to have an equal division between the urban and suburban residential locations in each of the cells, this was not always possible, largely due to the pattern of families with school-age children moving to

---

[4]The school districts included were: East Syracuse-Minoa, Jordan-Elbridge, Liverpool, Marcellus, North Syracuse, Skaneateles, Tully, West Genesee, and Westhill.

[5]A separate study of 60 rural families was conducted in Cortland County in 1971. The results of this study are not included in the analysis of data reported in this monograph but are reported in a master's thesis by Julia Gitobu (1972).

suburbs. Where particular family types were lacking in a certain cell in either the city or suburban list, additional names were drawn from the corresponding list of the other residential location (Appendix Table 2). It was considered more important to have an equal number of families in the cells than to have an even division according to place of residence. Although only a few of the original cells were exactly divided between urban-suburban residence, the distribution for the entire sample was 48% urban and 52% suburban.

The Sample Selected

The final sample consisted of 27 types of families with children stratified by number of children and age of youngest and oldest child and 4 types of childless families stratified by age of wives (Appendix Table 2). With two exceptions, each cell contained 42 families. Only 15 families were found with four to six children between the ages of 12 and 17, and an additional cell was added during the last 6 months of interviewing for families of seven to nine children under 18 years of age. This group had not been included in the original design, but when six-child families were contacted, it was found that in some cases another child had been born. However, only one-half as many records were collected for this category as for the others.

To obtain the 1,296 records used for analysis, 1,948 households in Syracuse and environs were contacted in the 12-month period from April 1967 to April 1968. Of these, 68% of the wives were interviewed (Appendix Table 3). Eight percent did not fit the cell, primarily because of only one or more than two adults in the household and 4% had either moved or could not be contacted in three attempts. Twenty percent refused because of lack of interest, time pressures, or language problems. Problems of obtaining cooperation on the study were greater in households without children (35% refusal) than in those with children (14% refusal). Of the 1,324 completed records, 28 were not used due to over-sampling on a specified day in a specific cell.

Records of Time Use

Time of All Workers

The goal of the research, to determine the factor or factors that most closely related to time use on household work, required that total time spent by all workers should be the basis of the study. Although wives were known to be the principal workers, it was also known that husbands and children contribute varying amounts of time to household production. Some families also have time contributed by paid help or by unpaid or reciprocal assistance from relatives and friends. The time spent on household work by each family member and other type of worker, therefore, needed to be recorded.

It was assumed that children under 6 years of age were likely to be learning rather than contributing to household production, so a report of their time use was omitted, but time use was reported for each older child by sex and age, and for the wives, husbands, and other adult female and male workers.

An accounting for all time use in 24 hours was desirable because it has been found to be an aid to recall. It also was assumed that this complete reporting would reduce incorrect recall associated with liking or disliking an activity and/or other psychological factors. A disliked activity seems to consume a great deal of time, while time spent on an enjoyed task seems to pass quickly (Fraisse, 1968). Since recent activities are more accurately recalled than less recent ones, respondents were asked to recall time use for the immediate past. It is also easier to recall activities on which large blocks of time have been spent than those which have taken only a few minutes. The latter, consequently, may be overlooked unless the discipline of accounting for the 24-hour day is imposed.

Definition of Household Work Time

The major concern in collecting the time-use data was with primary household work time, that is, the time when the activity engaged the worker's full or main attention. To have clear-cut records of primary time, two other kinds of time had to be recorded separately—secondary time and travel time.

Secondary time is that spent on an activity in combination with another (primary) activity that receives the worker's principal attention. Since large segments of time may be used for some household work activities and small segments for others, these small segments are sometimes dovetailed into the larger segments without interrupting them. Household activities are sometimes combined when one does not require the full attention of the worker as, for example, listening to a child's report of school while preparing dinner. They may also be carried on simultaneously when one task has a period of inactive work time, as in waiting for certain types of food to be cooked before resuming food preparation activities. Work on one household operation may be interwoven with work on another related task in such a way that both can be carried on at the same time. In all such situations, one activity is the principal activity receiving the worker's attention. Other activities are combined with it for convenience or for more effective use of time. This kind of time had to be kept separate from primary time in order to avoid problems of longer-than-24-hour days in the analysis.

In all households, and especially in urban households, the time spent on transportation accounts for a large portion of the time used for several household activities; in the present study such time, unlike secondary time, was considered an integral part of time use for the activity. Thus, time spent in travel to stores for shopping was included with marketing time, time of travel to laundromats was recorded as part of clothes-washing time, and other travel time was similarly reported. If a trip covered multiple purposes, the time of travel was allocated among activities. Time used for chauffeuring or transporting others was allocated in accordance with the purpose of the trip, such as physical care of family members, nonphysical care of family members, or other activities.

Number of Time Records for Each Household

A plan was developed to interview each wife on 2 days. Records of time use for 2 days were used to increase the amount of data and to allow more meaningful comparisons without enlarging the size of the sample. It was assumed that a 2-day report would reduce the chances of sample dropout so often experienced when respondents are asked to keep records for relatively long periods. In the present study, that risk was higher because the time-use record desired was a complete record of all use of time by each member of the household aged 6 years or older for the full 24 hours. It was assumed that the full day's record was essential to prevent exaggeration or error of recall in recording use of time; such complex records, however, could place a heavy burden on cooperating families if they were asked to keep records for an extended period. Given the large sample size in the present study, continuous

records for a long period of time from each family seemed unnecessary for reliable statistical analysis.

The validity of the information was increased over a record for 1 day, because infrequently performed household work activities are more likely to be reported in 2 days than on only 1 day for each family. It was recognized that the advantages of a sample of families more intensively studied would be lost. Time-chart records from different families on each day and in each season are not, of course, the same as time records from the same family over a consecutive period. The families selected for a smaller sample might or might not have typical characteristics of the population, and the sample might have to be too small to measure statistically the effects of the major control variables and the random variables on time variations.

The validity of the time-use data depended on how accurately wives and interviewers classified the use of time of all household members in the categories on the time-record chart. Safeguards were set up by strategic use of questions in the interviews to decrease the possibility of incomplete or unusable records.

Intervals of Time Reporting

No attempt was made to obtain precise records of time use, partly because of the variation in ability to estimate time use accurately, partly because of the practical difficulty of getting wives to record beginning and ending clock time for many activities, and partly because it was assumed that absolute precision in time records would not enhance the measurement of production sufficiently to make up for the added problems of data collection.

The time interval chosen for reporting related to the degree of precision required in the time record as well as to the amount of work that could be expected of respondents. Records of large blocks of household work time collected over a long period provide considerable data but are somewhat less precise than those in which smaller intervals of time are used. At the same time, too small an interval is unrealistic and places an undue burden on the recorder, unless such precision is an absolute essential for the research. For the purposes of the present study, 5-minute intervals were considered too small and intervals of 15 or 30 minutes too large. Many household work operations take less than 10 minutes and some continue for longer periods than 30 minutes. The

10-minute interval was, therefore, selected with the possibility of dividing this block in half for operations related to any activity for which the 5-minute interval was appropriate for reporting (e.g., 5, 15, or 25 minutes).

Categories of Household Work

It was not considered necessary to know what particular household work operation was performed in the time reported. The classification system used in the present study was developed by Walker and her graduate students by adapting coding systems used in earlier studies. The major categories set up for the Warren (1938) and Wiegand (1953) studies were adapted to current household practices; the revised classification was tested by Hoppen (1966) and again in the pilot survey prior to the present study.

Thirteen precategorized classifications were set up to measure time use for household production of services and goods. These household work categories were: food preparation, after-meal cleanup, and special food preparation; regular house care, special house care and maintenance, and care of yard and car; washing, ironing, and special care of clothing; physical and nonphysical care of family members; marketing and management. To provide categories for a record of the full 24-hour period, two additional blocks were used to record time spent on nonhousehold work activities: (1) "other work" (work other than household work) including school, paid, and volunteer work, and (2) "other activities," including all personal, family, and social activities.

The use of precategorized household work activities meant that the activities were coded as time use was recorded. The use of preclassified activities reduced the time and expense of later coding detailed records and may have increased accuracy since attention was directed toward the recording of time use by the participants rather than to the details of tasks.

The Time-Record Chart

A primary objective in the design of the chart for collecting time-use data was to have it easy to use, since wives were much more likely to cooperate if time use could be recorded without excessive effort. Household work activities were listed along the vertical axis of the chart and time units of 10 minutes each were listed across the horizontal axis (Chapter 2, Figure 2.1). A method of folding the chart was devised so that the vertical listing was in view whenever time was recorded in the horizontal unit.

To record the activities of any family members and their time spent for the various types of household work on the time chart, a method was developed to identify each participant by means of letters and numbers in different colors (Appendix B). The letter and number identified the household worker or workers and the colors indicated sex. The participants' symbol was circled if the time was secondary rather than primary in use; to identify the portion of time used for travel an additional symbol was used.

The focus of the study was on the time all family members contributed for household production, but it was desirable to have, if possible, only two time records from each family, one for each day of record. An important question considered was whether the wives could provide the information for the entire family or whether each family member should keep his own record. It was assumed that wives have extensive knowledge of the commitments and household work activities of family members. The use of only one time chart for an entire family would save considerable time and expense in both the data collection and analysis phases, and it could provide greater control over the accuracy of the records since only one family member would need to be instructed.

A small-scale study was conducted in a suburban area of Baldwinsville, N.Y., by a graduate student (Hoppen, 1966) to test the hypothesis that data on time use of all family members could be recorded adequately by the wives. In that study, wives reported time use by all family members while teenage children reported their own time use. Some differences were found between the two sets of records, but for the most part the records of household work kept by the wives were very similar to the reports of the teenagers. On the basis of this study, the decision was made to have all the time reported by the wives on a single form for each day.

Data Collection

Interviews with each wife in the selected families and the time-record charts were the means used to collect the data (Appendix B and Chapter 2, Figure 2.1). A principal advantage of the personal interview was its potential for obtaining the designated number of complete and usable records for each type of family composition. Some personal contact with the sample families was required in order to ensure that only eligible families would be selected and to classify families into the appropriate family types. If the name randomly drawn did not fit the cell to which it was assigned, it was placed on a reserve list to be used if needed for the new cell to which it correctly belonged. The purpose of the study could be explained in an interview, at length if necessary, and any other background information about the study could be provided to encourage the wives' cooperation. Questions as to the meaning of terms could be answered to increase chances of accuracy of responses. Since personal contact usually reduces the number of unusable records, the cost of obtaining the required number of complete records was expected to be lower by this means than by others.

Preparing for the Interviews

Extensive preinterview preparations were made to avoid, as much as possible, the high refusal rate that sometimes accompanies attempts to collect data on use of time. The wife in a family selected for the sample received a letter requesting her cooperation, and the family was considered only tentatively selected until the interviewer called on the family for an affirmation and to arrange for the day and time of the first interview. Wives were paid a small sum for their cooperation.

The purpose of the study received much publicity in the local papers and brief descriptions of it were made over local radio and television networks. The Syracuse Better Business Bureau and local police officers also were informed that interviewers would be calling on families in the area. The interviewers were provided with insignia identifying them as connected with the Cornell time-use-study project.

Most of the interviewers were alumnae of the New York State College of Home Economics. Training sessions were conducted by the principal investigator and the research associate in charge of data collection. The purposes of the study were explained and emphasis was placed on the means of eliciting recall of the previous day's activities without influencing responses. Techniques for maintaining all the controls established for the sample were carefully explained. For example, if the composition of a family had changed between the time of selecting the sample and the time of the interview, the interview was not held.

As part of her training, each interviewer conducted a trial interview with a wife not included in the sample. In conference with the field supervisor questions of procedure were clarified and the results of the first trial interview were checked before further assignments were made.

Interview Schedule

In developing the interview schedule for the present study, questions from instruments developed over a period of years for the study of time use for household work provided a starting point. Questions were revised and updated. The length of the schedule was a matter of concern, since the time for the interview had to be kept within reasonable limits. Phrasing the questions presented some problems, since there should be no connotation that certain features, characteristics, methods, equipment, or standards of performance were more desirable than others.

A major portion of the schedule was made up of questions to elicit supplementary data related to the major categories of household activities. A review of recent and past literature on household work, household production, and work roles of men and women was undertaken in order to assure the inclusion of pertinent questions to provide a picture of the environment in which the household work was being carried on. Most of these questions were asked for each day of record and some, mostly pertaining to equipment used or activities performed less frequently than daily, covered the preceding 7 days or the past 12 months. For food preparation activities, detailed information was obtained on design features of the kitchen and household equipment available.

Many questions were precoded. For these questions International Business Machines scanner forms were designed for ease of administration during the interviews and in tabulations for the analysis (Appendix B). Hand coding was required for other questions that were of the open-end type.

The Interviews

The first interview with a respondent consisted of (1) an explanation of the study, (2) the collection of demographic and other data on the family, (3) collection of background data on the household activities performed and equipment used on the preceding day, (4) reading the definitions of activities to the wife while she also read them, (5) reading aloud instructions for recording the use of time of family members on the time chart while the wife also read them, (6) recording the use of time on the preceding day for all family members 6 years of age or older, (7) leaving the completed chart and a second chart with the wife for her to record activities on the following day, and (8) making an appointment for the second interview.

Use of the time-record chart was demonstrated and wives were instructed on how to keep the next day's record. Particular attention was paid to distinguishing between and recording primary and secondary time. The interviewers asked questions, assumed to be neutral, to provide clues for recall of the sequence of events on the previous day and to show how wives could use such clues in making their records. Included were such questions as: What time did you get up? What time did the children leave for school? What did you do in this period? When did you eat your first meal? What did you do before that?

The interviewers also explained the organization of household work around the concepts of get ready, perform, and clean up so that wives could readily distinguish the categories under which to record the time-use records. Wives had little difficulty in recognizing how their household work fitted into the activity categories. When in doubt about how to record time used for some unusual operations, interviewers and wives both were instructed to call the field office. A record was kept in the office of all such decisions for future use to avoid inconsistent recording.

The interviewers used information about the previous day's activities to instruct the wives on the method of recording time use. The interviewer recorded household activities for the first record day, which was the day preceding the first interview, and demonstrated the method of keeping the time record for each family member, classifying the numerous household operations into the categories on the time chart, and distinguishing between primary and secondary activities. The wife was provided with a copy of the time chart so that she could follow the interviewer's method of recording the household operations, and the interviewer and the wife reviewed the instructions together. This method reduced chances of error in the time records, since wives filled out only one time chart and completed it relatively soon after receiving detailed instructions and a demonstration.

The completed time record for the previous day was left with the wife so that other family members could review her recording of their activities for accuracy and completeness. A second time-record chart was also left, together with the list of activities included in the household work categories and the instruction sheet. This record chart also was to be checked by other family members.

The second interview, usually held 2 days after the first interview, consisted of (1) collecting the time-record charts from the wife, (2) carefully going over the wife's record of activities on the preceding day, (3) checking the second time-record chart for completeness, (4) collecting background data on the household activities performed and equipment used on the preceding day, and (5) collecting general supplementary information on activities or equipment for the preceding 7 days or other period. Any corrections necessary were made with the help and consent of the wife.

The first interview took about an hour and the second interview lasted about three-quarters of an hour. Interviews were scheduled so that an equal number of first-day and second-day records were available for each day of the week, including Sundays.

Field Office

A field office was established in Syracuse to provide the close supervision needed. The office opened in April 1967 when field operations began and was maintained until the field work was completed in April 1968.

The field office operated under the immediate supervision of the research associate responsible for the collection of data for the study and under the general direction of the principal investigator. The office was responsible for:

Developing publicity for good public relations;

Hiring, training, and supervising the interviewers;

Scheduling the interviewers' work;

Verifying interviews and time record charts;

Maintaining master control records of interviews with each family type;

Editing and coding.

All of the time charts and schedules were edited for omissions and inconsistencies. For example, the time chart was checked to see that all the pieces of time recorded added up to 24 hours for each family member, and questions that had been included in the interview schedule to permit cross-checking between the time chart and the schedule were checked. The computer was used for some of this cross-checking; for example, when washing by machine was reported on the time chart, the corresponding schedule was scanned to verify that data on the number of loads of washing and type of machine used had also been recorded. Further validating was done by the research associate telephoning a random sample of respondents and asking a few key questions from the schedule. Interviewers were paid only for complete and validated interviews.

The field office was an important factor in saving time and reducing costs in the data collection phase, but its primary function was in maintaining high standards of accuracy in the data collection. Because the completed forms were checked promptly, the errors, discrepancies, or omissions were found in time to correct them. It was possible to replace unsatisfactory interviews, such as those made on a day of the week already sampled in that season.

Data Bank Development

Coding Data

Time Chart Data. By use of preclassified work activities most decisions needed for time-use coding were made when the data were collected. However, these data had to be tallied by a coding system according to kind of time (primary, secondary, and travel) for each family member for each work activity. These data were tallied by use of a printing calculator, and the tapes were used for checking and for key punching directly.

Interview Schedule Data. The use of the scanner forms as part of the interview schedule permitted mechanical punching directly onto cards by optical scanner equipment. Some demographic data and certain work output questions required hand coding. The most complex coding procedures were those for coding types of meals served. Each menu item was coded at the time of the interview as to preparation state (e.g., fresh, frozen, canned) and as to number of cooking and noncooking operations involved in its preparation. Home economists were employed as special coders to check the consistency of the coding and to tally each type of operation for each menu item, for each meal, and for the day's food preparation.

Data Files

All data were punched on data processing cards. The decks punched consisted of: 19 each for coding primary, secondary, and travel time for each worker; 5 for demographic data; 15 for precoded data from the scanner sheets, and about 10 preliminary working decks. By the end of the project a total of 111 decks had been prepared. In addition, data were recorded on one magnetic tape organized by family identification and also on a second magnetic tape organized by task areas. Data from 40 of the decks were also stored on a disk for use on an IBM 360-65 computer system.

All files have been used in the analysis. Often card decks were used to read in the data for computer analysis; the tapes were used for selected analyses and for permanent storage; and the disk was used for the most complex operations.

Methods of Analysis

The analysis of data was made in two stages. The first stage consisted of descriptive analyses, identification of factors for further study, and choice of statistical tools for the major analysis. In the second stage, each household work activity was analyzed to determine the strength of the relationships between time use and selected variables as potential predictors of time use. The interrelationships of the variables found to be significantly related to time use in each household work activity were also explored.

Descriptive Analysis

The descriptive analytic stage consisted of measures of central tendency, two-way plots, product moment correlations, and univariate analysis.

Measures of central tendency and dispersion were used to describe the amount of primary time used for the major household task areas and for 13 specific task areas by (a) all workers combined, (b) wives, (c) husbands, (d) children 12 to 17 years, (e) children 6 to 11, and (f) workers other than family members. Primary time, by definition, included travel time; the amount of travel time used was determined for the major task areas and for each task area separately, then added to the primary time. (See Chapter 6, Table 6.26.) Descriptive analysis was also done for the secondary time used in each activity; however, extensive analyses were confined to primary time.

Segments of time spent, recorded in 10-minute blocks, on each activity for each household worker were added together to give the total time spent by all workers combined and by each type of worker on a household work activity for each of the 2 record days. To reflect the approximation of the time intervals, daily time was averaged to the nearest tenth of an hour. Time-use means and marginals were computed for the task areas by subclassifications of many variables including the following: (a) number of children; (b) ages of the youngest and oldest children, (c) age of the youngest child alone, (d) family type, defined by number of children and age of the youngest child combined, (e) employment of wives and husbands, (f) socioeconomic level, (g) education of wives and husbands, (h) urban-suburban residence, and (i) type of housing.

Cross tabulations of time-use averages by different types of workers in each general task area were developed for variables assumed to be interrelated. Emphasis was placed on the inter-relationship of employment of the wives to many other variables. Some cross tabulations of averages were also developed for socioeconomic variables, but these analyses were not extensive because results of a preliminary analysis of the socio-economic variable did not prove fruitful. The analyses of physical environment factors in relation to time use were carried out for selected circumstances and activities (e.g., automatic washers related to time for washing).

To examine types of variability and nature of relationships, extensive efforts went into plotting (a) time use of individual families within each cell and (b) averages of time use by both control and dependent variables. Two-way analysis of variance was used to describe the significance of apparent variations in time input by wives and by all workers according to the family composition variables of number of children and age of youngest child, and according to employment of wives.

Product moment correlations were also used early in the project, essentially in a screening process to evaluate the strength of the relationship of a wide range of variables with the total time use of all workers and wives on each household work activity. In order to use this technique certain assumptions had to be made: that the data distributions were reasonably normal and that the variables could all be quantitatively scaled. These exploratory tests provided an additional basis for selecting variables for further analysis. Since it was only one of the screening techniques used, the noncompliance with essential assumptions was not considered critical.

As a further test of the age groups of youngest child in a family, actual age of youngest child was used in some of the first correlations. This arrangement did not prove to be correlated substantially more closely with time than the original categories of grouped ages of the sample; it complicated the program without compensating benefits. For the remainder of the analyses, only the grouped-age categories were used.

The categories for employment status of wives that had been set up in the descriptive analysis were later reanalyzed and tested in various combinations. No change was made, however, in the original classification of 0 to 14 hours of paid work representing the nonemployed and 15 or more hours identifying the employed wives.

At this stage of the project it became apparent that time records for the 2 record days could be combined. There had been some concern that asking questions on the first record day might have influenced the records and the answers for the second day. Analysis of time recorded on each record day separately, however, showed that there were no substantial differences in the product moment correlations of the variables analyzed and time spent on an activity for the 2 days. Use of the combined time was much preferred, since certain household tasks are done less frequently than daily. If it had been necessary to analyze the 2 days separately, there would have been many more households for which no work in some activities was reported.

Choice of Statistical Measures

A nonparametric measure of correlation was chosen as the chief statistical measure for analysis after consultation with Associate Professor Scott Urquhart in Statistics and Biometry at Cornell University, and after two doctoral candidates (Larry Male and James Harner) in that department had done extensive analysis of two-variable plots, types of linear relationships, and measures of central tendency for all work activities included in the study.

A general problem with several of the statistical techniques considered was that the data did not meet their requirements of normal or near normal distribution and quantitative scaling. For example, although regression was seriously considered, the statisticians strongly advised against it.[6] Covariant analysis was tried on a few

---

[6]Regression was used for analysis of these data by two other researchers: Arleen Leibowitz, working with Jacob Mincer on a doctoral thesis at Columbia University; and Professor Peter Lindert, University of Wisconsin. These researchers contracted with Cornell University for use of the data from the Syracuse survey.

combinations of number and ages of children, but this technique led to highly complex analyses because of the size of the sample and number of variables.

Another important decision was based on an attempt to estimate weekly time for two of the household activities. The analysis of estimated weekly time compared with analysis of reported time use for the 2 days showed only slight differences in relationships between time use and several of the variables. Use of reported time, however, greatly reduced the complexity of the analysis. Use of estimated weekly time did improve the relationships for nondaily activities, but with a highly complex method of estimating weekly time, there seemed little justification for using weekly estimated time on some activities and daily time on others. Slightly higher precision in the relationships with time spent on a few activities was rejected, therefore, in favor of the practicality of using recorded time for 2 days throughout the analysis.

To determine the degree of statistical relationships between time use by all workers and by individual types of workers for 2 days in each area of household work and the major variables of the study, the nonparametric measure of rank correlation, Kendall Tau (Siegel, 1956) was chosen.

Examination of the graphs plotted from the descriptive analysis showed clearly that the variables were sometimes skewed and had nonnormal distributions. Several reasons for the various distribution patterns among the household tasks were easily identified. Much variability is normal in kinds of household production carried on at different stages of the family cycle; also, at the respective stages, there is variability in the frequency with which some activities are done. For example, food preparation and dishwashing are daily activities in most homes; washing and ironing vary considerably in the frequency of performance; and family care may be a regular, infrequent, or nonexistent activity depending upon the composition of the family.

Many of the variables were not quantitative and could only be imperfectly defined on an ordinal scale. Some variables were quantitative enough and some distributions normal enough to meet the requirements of parametric statistical techniques, but it was considered better to use one technique consistently throughout the analysis. Kendall Tau was chosen as a better measure of association than other rank-correlation measures for a sample of large size and with many ties, i.e.,

more than one observation with the same value.

The Kendall rank-correlation coefficient is designed to measure the degree of correlation between the ordinal rankings of two variables and determine the probability of the occurrence of a correlation as large as the one observed in the sample. The range of possible values is from -1.0 to +1.0; a correlation of zero shows that the two ranked variables are not related in the sample population. According to Siegel (1956), with a sample size larger than eight, the sampling distribution of Tau becomes similar to a normal distribution and the significance of the values may be determined.

Median rather than mean times are preferred for use in the rank-correlation analysis, but to determine medians throughout the analysis would have been a very complex and time-consuming task since no computer program was available when needed for a sample of this size. Median time as well as mean time was determined for some of the computations. Since the two values were fairly close for most of the activities, the decision was made to use the mean.

Two sets of nonparametric Kendall Tau values were calculated. On the basis of relationships indicated by the first set, the major variables to be used for the analysis were selected. These variables were: number of children, age of youngest child, age of oldest child, family type, employment of wives, socioeconomic status, house type, residence location, husbands' hours of employment, education of wives, and education of husbands. Not all of these variables had close relationships with the total time of all workers or of the individual workers. However, each of them was related relatively closely to either all workers' or some individual worker's time use on one or more household work activities and, therefore, was retained for the major analysis.

Other variables such as season or type of equipment also were tested in the first set of rank-correlation analysis but were not used for continued analysis; the few relatively weak relationships found for such variables have been reported under a particular activity.

The Kendall Tau values from the second set of analyses are the ones reported in this monograph. These values were obtained from analysis of time records for 2 days from 1,260 families. This number rather than 1,296 was used to maintain equality in the number of cases according to number and ages of children as sampled. Data from two of the cells were eliminated because fewer than 42 families were interviewed.[7] For this final set of correlation values reported in this document, time use for 2 days of records for each family were analyzed.

Another part of both the first and second set of rank-correlation coefficients had to do with the analysis of the work quantifying variables (e.g., number of pieces ironed, etc.) developed as measures of household work in previous research. In the second rank-correlation analysis, coefficients were calculated that showed the relationships between each of these variables and the amount of time spent on the particular activity on the 2 record days (for meal types, only 1 day's record was used because of the extensive amount of data for about 11,000 meals on 2 days). These values have been reported for the appropriate activities. The quantifying variables correlated highly with time throughout the analysis, a further indication that quantity of work and time spent were measures of household production.

Correlation values were determined for the major variables and the total time spent by all workers and by wives, husbands, and children 12 to 17 on all household work, major task areas, and specific tasks. Values were computed for all of the major variables in relation to all workers' time; for the three types of individual workers, values were computed for all major variables except socioeconomic status, house type, and location of residence. These latter variables had generally not tested as being highly correlated with all workers' time use. In calculating these correlations, time spent was ranked in minutes per day in order that all relationships of at least an .05 level of significance would be identified. In the tables of correlation coefficients, all of the significant values have been reported, but only coefficients significant at the .001 level have been discussed in the text. Most correlation coefficients of less significance than .001 reflected time variability as low as 5 minutes a day in a specific activity, and this was judged too small a difference to be generally meaningful.

At the early stage of measurement by Kendall Tau, "canned programs" were not available for handling large quantities of data; therefore, a statistical programer was employed to write the programs. For the final analyses a canned program included in the *Statistical Package for the Social Sciences* (Nie, Bent, and Hull, 1970) proved to be far more economical and adequate.

Since some of the variables related to time use are likely to be interrelated, it was essential to determine the effect of a given variable on work time when a third variable was held constant. Partial rank correlations were computed for variables significantly related to time use that were assumed to be interrelated (various family composition variables, employment of wives, house type, and location of residence). In computing the partial rank-correlation coefficients, the following formula suggested by Kendall (Siegel, 1956, p. 226) was used:

$$T_{xy.z} = \frac{T_{xy} - T_{zy} T_{xz}}{\sqrt{(1 - T_{zy}^2)(1 - T_{zx}^2)}}$$

The constants used in these computations are shown in Chapter 3, Table 3.1. Since some variables were highly correlated with others, it was apparent that sometimes one could substitute for the other; other variables that were independent of each other had to be considered independent in each work activity.

Ranking of Variables. Ranking the variables for the correlation analysis was a major problem in some instances. Certain variables were qualitative and built into the study design (the original cells, season, location of residence), while others were either qualitatively or quantitatively random (socioeconomic status, education, employment of wives, and others). Some variables did not have meaning on an ordinal scale, and considerable experimentation was necessary before they could be ordered.

The basis for the rankings varied. Season, for example, was not ranked by natural seasonal order but by progression in the order of its relationship to time as shown by the descriptive analysis: (1) January to April, (2) September to December, and (3) May to August. Several different rankings were tried for house types before ordering by: apartment, mobile home, two-family, and one-family dwellings. Equipment, whenever relevant, was usually ranked from most to least automatic.

The quantifying variables caused less trouble since most of them were ordered naturally by quantity of work. In ranking such variables as number of pieces and number of loads, fairly natural breaks were defined by histograms. The distributions of some of the quantifying variables were skewed toward larger values in each of the categories; in such cases, mean, median, and interquartile ranges were computed. Much effort was put into the development of ranking classifications for meal types to test the relationship

---

[7]Those eliminated were 15 records for families with four to six children all in the 12- to 17-year-age range and 21 records for families of seven to nine children.

between time use in meal preparation and the complexity of meals prepared. Meals were first classified by type and then by the food preparation complexity for the day ranked by number of complex and simple meals.

One classification problem was the use of other combinations of numbers and ages of children than had been used for the original cells. Ages of the youngest and oldest child made the cell variable difficult to arrange in the kind of progressive order required for rank correlations, and the descriptive analysis had shown that the results would be difficult to interpret. Some preliminary analyses of the three components of the cell variable had indicated that age of the oldest child made less difference in the time spent than age of the youngest child, and the latter alone expressed the relationship about as well as ages of both youngest and oldest as used in sample selection.

Although the sample had been stratified by the cell variable, family type became a random variable when reordered by number of children and age of the youngest child. Some categories had unequal numbers and some had very few or no cases. The advantages of an equal number of cases in the original variable cell were given up in favor of a simpler arrangement that could be ranked in a theoretical progression so that time relationships could be more readily interpreted. The variable described as family type in tabular presentation throughout this monograph combines number of children and age of youngest child, ordered from the simplest to most complex family structure, i.e., from young families with no children to large families with the youngest child a baby. Both as a component of family type and as a separate variable, age groups of youngest child were ranked from oldest (12 to 17) to youngest (under 1 year).

The categories for levels of education and occupation of husbands were ordered for the interview questions to fit the Hollingshead (1957) scale; the lower coding numbers indicated higher social position. (See Chapter 2, Table 2.5.) Likewise, for the education of the wives and husbands, low numbers indicated a higher level of education. As indicated on tables showing correlation of either socioeconomic or education levels with time use, negative values signify an increased use of time with increase in level of socioeconomic status or education, and a positive correlation indicates an increase in time use as either level declines.

Data Storage

Decks of data processing cards used for the study were stored by the Department of Consumer Economics, New York State College of Human Ecology, Cornell University. Data tapes were filed in the department's storage facilities in the tape library of the Office of Computing Services at Cornell; the disk used in processing of data was discarded. Plans have been made to store the original data, along with earlier New York State time-use data, in the University Archives.

APPENDIX TABLE 1—Selected demographic characteristics in 1970 of Syracuse, N.Y., Standard Metropolitan Statistical Area (SMSA) compared with the State of New York

Characteristics	Syracuse, N.Y. SMSA	New York State
Median income	$10,531	$10,719
Median years of school completed	12.2	12.0
	Percent	
Employment of wives		
All husband-wife families	40	38
Own children under 6	25	21
Own children 6 to 17 (only)	50	45
Husband-wife households	(N = 132,469)	(N = 3,846,468)
No children	41	45
1 child	18	18
2 children	18	18
3 children	12	10
4 or more	12	9

Source: U.S. Bureau of the Census. *Census of Population: 1970 Detailed Characteristics,* Final Report PC(1)-D34 New York. Washington, D.C.: U.S. Government Printing Office, 1972.

APPENDIX TABLE 2—Cell structure for stratified random sampling pool
(1,296 husband–wife households, Syracuse, N.Y.,

Cell number	Cell structure – by number and age of children
1	no children; age of wife under 25 years
2	no children; age of wife 25–39 years
3	no children; age of wife 40–54 years
4	no children; age of wife 55 years and over
5	1 child; under 1 year
6	1 child; 1 year
7	1 child; 2–5 years
8	1 child; 6–11 years
9	1 child; 12–17 years
10	2 children; both under 2 years
11	2 children; both 2–5 years
12	2 children; both 6–11 years
13	2 children; both 12–17 years
14	2 children; one under 2, one 2–5 years
15	2 children; one under 2, one 6–11 years
16	2 children; one under 6, one 12–17 years
17	2 children; one 2–5 years, one 6–11 years
18	2 children; one 6–11 years, one 12–17 years
19	3 children; all under 6 years
20	3 children; all 6–11 years
21	3 children; all 12–17 years
22	3 children; youngest under 2, oldest 6–11 years
23	3 children; youngest under 6 years, oldest 12–17 years
24	3 children; youngest 2–5 years, oldest 6–11 years
25	3 children; youngest 6–11 years, oldest 12–17 years
26	4–6 children; all under 6 years
27	4–6 children; all 6–11 years
28	4–6 children; all 12–17 years
29	4–6 children; youngest under 6, oldest 6–11 years
30	4–6 children; youngest under 6, oldest 12–17 years
31	4–6 children; youngest 6–11 years, oldest 12–17 years
32	7–9 children; youngest under 6 years, oldest 12–17 years

and sample interviewed
1967-68)

City Maximum number of families	Number in sample	Suburbs Maximum number of families	Number in sample	Population of families from which sample was drawn	Sample size
19,871	89	2,761	79	22,632	168
536	24	170	18	706	42
236	26	679	16	915	42
413	19	1,251	23	1,664	42
376	26	1,291	16	1,667	42
704	28	2,099	14	2,803	42
25	20	23	22	48	42
249	22	786	20	1,035	42
365	21	1,068	21	1,433	42
391	23	1,061	19	1,452	42
243	16	454	26	697	42
39	9	89	33	128	42
48	16	170	26	218	42
256	24	1,225	18	1,481	42
461	20	1,260	22	1,721	42
166	18	352	24	518	42
109	23	390	19	499	42
76	21	218	21	294	42
94	20	311	22	405	42
161	23	512	19	673	42
304	19	1,485	23	1,789	42
505	18	1,381	24	1,886	42
28	10	47	32	75	42
42	11	66	31	108	42
12	4	24	11	36	15
525	24	1,544	18	2,069	42
575	14	1,525	28	2,100	42
413	23	984	19	1,397	42
7,352		20,465		27,817	
---		---		---	(21)
TOTAL 27,223	611	23,226	664	50,449	1,275
					(1,296)

APPENDIX TABLE 3—Random sample drawing—percentage of noncontacts, refusals, and completed interviews
(1,296 husband-wife households, Syracuse, N.Y., 1967-68)

	Total sample		Childless couples		Couples with children	
	No. of families	Percent of families	No. of families	Percent of families	No. of families	Percent of families
Contacts	1,948		485		1,463	
Completed	1,324	68	171	35	1,153	79
Did not fit sample	164	8	93	19	71	5
Noncontacts	80	4	51	11	29	2
Nonresponse	380	20	170	35	210	14

Instruments and Instructions
Used for Data Collection

Instructions for Keeping Time Record [1]

We need to have a record of how each member of your family used his time for two days. To show you how to keep the record, we'll record yesterday's use of time while I am here. For the second record we would like you to record your family's use of time for a second day.

On the left side of the time record, household work and other activities are listed; across the top of the record, the twenty-four hours of the day are listed. We are asking that you keep a time record for the entire family, and that you ask your husband and each child to look over the charts to check your recording of their use of time. For ease in recalling and recording the time, we have broken each hour into six ten-minute periods.

A combination of colors and letters or numbers is used to record each family member's time. The activity that a family member has done is identified by symbols placed in the appropriate time and activity blocks. All female members of the family are represented by red; the homemaker is represented by a red W and each girl is represented by her age in red. The male members are reported in blue; the husband's symbol is a blue H, and each boy is represented by his age in blue. If both the husband and wife have done the same activity, a black P for parents would be used. A black F would be used if the entire family participated; and a black C would be used for all the children participating. Other male helpers would be designated by a blue O and other female helpers by a red O.

If from 8:00 to 8:10 a.m. you prepared the breakfast, you write a red W in the first block after 8 a.m. in the meal preparation row. If you continued this for another ten minutes, you put another red W in the following block at 8:10. For longer, continuous activities, an arrow and line can be drawn from the time of starting an activity to the time the activity was completed, using the individual's letter at each end. (W ⟵⟶ W) Time recorded is active time use: that is, time involved in getting ready for the job, working at the job and cleaning up after the job, but it does not include the time required for a machine to function without your full attention. If two tasks are done within the 10-minute period, but not simultaneously, draw a line to divide the time block into approximate 5-minute periods and write in the worker's symbol.

If you or any other worker did two or more things at the same time, record the time in the same manner as above, but circle the letter for the secondary activity. For example, if you were preparing dinner and listening to a child's spelling lesson, place a W under Meal Preparation and a (W) under Other Care of Family Members; if you were ironing but at the same time thinking about redecorating the living room, put the (W) under Management; if while you were ironing you were also watching TV, place a (W) under Other Activities. Use the (W) to indicate the time of responsibility for care of children when your primary attention is going to something else. For example, if you were not free to leave the house

---

[1]For time-record chart (see Figure 2.1, Chapter 2).

-2-

because the children were playing in the back yard, or if you had to be home because the children were home from school, use the (W) under Other Care of Children and a W under the activity to which your main attention was given.   If a child accompanied you to the supermarket because you were responsible for his care during that time, place a W in Marketing and a (W) in Other Care of Family Members.

Include transportation time with the activity for which the trip was made, but use a T after the family symbol to indicate time spent in travel (WT).   If more than one thing was done on a trip, include the time enroute to the activity of the first stop and assign the time for return trip to the last activity.   For example, if you went to the dry cleaners and then did your marketing, include time to dry cleaners under Special Care of Clothing and include the time traveling home under Marketing. If you went to the laundromat, the grocery store, and back to the laundromat, include all travel time under Washing by Machine.

Key:

Workers' symbols for recording primary time:

Wife *W*	Husband *H*	Parents P	Other male helpers *o*
		Children C	
Girl *12*	Boy *10*	Family F	Other female helpers *☉*

Symbols for recording secondary time:
   Use symbols as above with circle.   For example: (*w*)

Symbols for recording transportation time:
   Use symbol for primary time plus T.   For example: *WT*

Time blocks

10 minutes   5 minutes

NEW YORK STATE COLLEGE OF HOME ECONOMICS
A Statutory College of the State University
At Cornell University, Ithaca, New York 14850

Department of Household Economics and Management

Use-of-time Research Project
Definition of Household Activities

HOUSEHOLD ACTIVITIES

1. Regular Meal Preparation

Preparation of food for all regular meals served on record days.
    Breakfast, noon and evening meals
    Snacks, packed lunches
    Special foods (baby formula, cocktails, etc.)
Cleanup incidental to meal preparation
Setting the table
Serving the food

2. Special Food Preparation

Preparation of food for future use.
    Food baked or prepared for another day
    Canning and freezing
Preparation of food for guests and special occasions
    Holiday meals
    Party refreshments
    Food gifts and donations of food served at functions outside the home
Cleanup incidental to this preparation

3. After-Meal Cleanup

After-meal care of table, dishes, leftovers, kitchen equipment and refuse.
(also include unloading dishwasher or dish drainer for storage.)

                         ****

4. Regular House Care

Daily, semi-weekly, weekly, and biweekly care and cleaning of house and
appliances.
    Cleaning tasks, such as
        mopping
        dusting
        vacuuming
    Making beds
    Putting rooms in order
    Tending the house heating system
    Caring for house plants or flowers

5. <u>Special House Care and Maintenance</u>

Occasional or seasonal care and cleaning of house, such as:
    Washing windows
    Cleaning closets
    Waxing floors
    Defrosting and cleaning freezer
    Special cleaning of oven

Repair and upkeep of home, appliances and furnishings, such as:
    Painting and papering
    Repairing furniture
    Repairing equipment
    Reupholstering
    Redecorating

****

6. <u>Care of Yard and Car</u>

Daily and seasonal care and maintenance of yard, garden areas, walks, garage, car, and equipment used for these activities. (Also include care of garbage and trash.)

****

7. <u>Washing by Machine</u>

Washing clothes and household textiles at home or at laundromat.
    Collecting and sorting soiled things for washing
    Pretreating
    Loading and unloading washer or dryer (do not include time taken by machine)
    Hanging things on line and taking them down
    Cleanup incidental to washing
    Folding and storing unironed clothes

8. <u>Ironing</u>

Ironing and pressing of clothes. Also include:
    Preparing clothes and household linens for ironing
    Getting out and putting away equipment used
    Folding and storing ironed articles

9. <u>Special Care and Construction of Clothing and Household Linens</u>

All activities related to clothing production and upkeep not included in 7. and 8. For example, include:
    Hand washing
    Mending
    Spot removal
    Shoe care
    Dry cleaning
    Seasonal storage
    Construction of clothing and household furnishings

****

10. Physical Care of Family Members

All activities related to physical care, such as:
     Bathing, feeding and dressing of family members
     Giving bedside care
     First aid
     Taking family members to dentist or physician, beauty or barber shop

11. Other Care of Family Members

All activities related to social and educational development of family
members, such as:
     Helping with lessons
     Reading to children
     Taking children to social and educational functions
     Taking care of family pets

****

12. Marketing (or Shopping)

All activities related to shopping, whether or not purchases are made.
Include:
     Time for shopping in person, by telephone, mail, or home sales or delivery
     Time for putting purchases away

13. Management and Record Keeping

All management activities of the household.
     Making decisions and planning, such as:
          Thinking about and discussing alternatives
          Planning menus
          Making out market lists
          Looking around for ideas
          Measuring space for something
          Figuring out how much money is available
     Checking plans as you carry them out
     Supervising work of others
     Thinking back to see if plans worked

All record keeping activities, such as:
     Paying bills
     Making bank deposits
     Making and working on records of receipts and expenditures

****

OTHER WORK

14. School, Paid and Volunteer Work
Time for each family member going to and from work or school as well as
time at work or school.

****

OTHER ACTIVITIES

15. All Other Personal, Family and Social Activities
All activities not included in 1-14 above. For example:
     Personal activities as eating and sleeping
     Social activities as letter writing, visiting, recreation and play
     (individual, family or community)

Record No. _____ - _____

NEW YORK STATE COLLEGE OF HOME ECONOMICS
A Statutory College of the State University
At Cornell University, Ithaca, New York 14850

Department of Household Economics and Management

Household Activity Survey

Name _____ Address _____

Telephone No. _____   _____

How many persons over 18 are living in your home? _____ If only one adult
or more than 2 adults, discontinue interview. If 2 adults, ask "What is the
name of the head of the household?" _____. If
this is the same as above, ask: "What is the relationship of the second adult
to head of household?" If husband/wife, circle the H & W below, otherwise
discontinue interview.

Please check this card to tell me the letter of age group to which your
husband and you belong. (enter below)

How many children under 18 are living in your home? _____

If 7 or more, discontinue interview. If less than 7, ask "Starting with the
youngest child, please tell me whether it is a boy or girl and the age and
birth date of each. "(Interviewer list below)

No.	Family member	Age	Birthdate
	H		X
	W		X
1			
2			
3			
4			
5			
6			

The House and Its Care (1)   Record No. _____

```
000   100   200   300   400      500   600   700   800   900        00    10    20    30    40        50    60    70    80    90
====  ====  ====  ====  ====     ====  ====  ====  ====  ====       ====  ====  ====  ====  ====      ====  ====  ====  ====  ====
 0     1     2     3     4        5     6     7     8     9   Record  000   100   200   300   400        500   600   700   800   900
====  ====  ====  ====  ====     ====  ====  ====  ====  ====   No.  ====  ====  ====  ====  ====      ====  ====  ====  ====  ====
 00    10    20    30    40       50    60    70    80    90         0     1     2     3     4        5     6     7     8     9
====  ====  ====  ====  ====     ====  ====  ====  ====  ====       ====  ====  ====  ====  ====      ====  ====  ====  ====  ====
```

1. Is your home:

AN APARTMENT	A SINGLE HOUSE	2–FAMILY HOUSE	MOBILE HOME	OTHER
=====	=====	=====	=====	=====

2. How many stories does your home have?

1	2	3	SPLIT LEVEL	OTHER
=====	=====	=====	=====	=====

3. Do you have an attic used for anything but storage?

NO	YES
=====	=====

4. Do you have a basement used for anything but storage?

NO	YES
=====	=====

5. How many rooms are in your home?

(count kitchen; do not count halls or bath)

1	2	3	4	5	6	7	8	9+
=====	=====	=====	=====	=====	=====	=====	=====	=====

6. How many bathrooms are in your home?

0	1	1½	2	2½	3	3½	MORE
=====	=====	=====	=====	=====	=====	=====	=====

7. Is your heating system automatic?

NO	YES
=====	=====

8. Is your home heated by:

WARM AIR FURNACE	STEAM OR HOT WATER	BUILT-IN ELECTRIC UNITS	SPACE HEATER	OTHER
=====	=====	=====	=====	=====

9. Do you have any air conditioning in your house?

How much?

NONE	1 UNIT	2 OR MORE UNITS	CENTRAL SYSTEM
=====	=====	=====	=====

10. How much dirt does your heating system make?

NONE	VERY LITTLE	SOME	MUCH
=====	=====	=====	=====

11. In how many rooms (including baths) was some care given yesterday?

0	1	2	3	4	5	6	7	8	9+
=====	=====	=====	=====	=====	=====	=====	=====	=====	=====

12. Were any of the following used yesterday?

NO	YES	
=====	=====	carpet sweeper &/or electric broom
=====	=====	vacuum cleaner
=====	=====	kitchen exhaust fan
=====	=====	indoor incinerator &/or garbage disposer
=====	=====	fireplace (indoor)
=====	=====	rug shampooer &/or floor scrubber
=====	=====	floor polisher

paid help with cleaning

NONE	1 HR.	2 HRS.	3 HRS.	4 HRS.	5 HRS.	6 HRS.	7 HRS.	8+ HRS.	DON'T USE
=====	=====	=====	=====	=====	=====	=====	=====	=====	=====

13. About what year was your home built?

DON'T KNOW	BEFORE 1900	1900–1919	1920–1939	1940–1959	AFTER 1960
=====	=====	=====	=====	=====	=====

14. How many cats and/or dogs does your family have as house pets?

0	1	2	3	4	5	6	7	8	9+
=====	=====	=====	=====	=====	=====	=====	=====	=====	=====

15. In how many rooms (including baths) was some care given yesterday?

0	1	2	3	4	5	6	7	8	9+
=====	=====	=====	=====	=====	=====	=====	=====	=====	=====

16. Were any of the following used yesterday?

NO	YES	
=====	=====	carpet sweeper &/or electric broom
=====	=====	vacuum cleaner
=====	=====	kitchen exhaust fan
=====	=====	indoor incinerator &/or garbage disposer
=====	=====	fireplace (indoor)
=====	=====	rug shampooer &/or floor scrubber
=====	=====	floor polisher

paid help with cleaning

NONE	1 HR.	2 HRS.	3 HRS.	4 HRS.	5 HRS.	6 HRS.	7 HRS.	8+ HRS.
=====	=====	=====	=====	=====	=====	=====	=====	=====

17. On about how many of the last 7 days were the following used?

0	1	2	3	4	5	6	7	
=====	=====	=====	=====	=====	=====	=====	=====	carpet sweeper/ electric broom
=====	=====	=====	=====	=====	=====	=====	=====	vacuum cleaner
=====	=====	=====	=====	=====	=====	=====	=====	kitchen exhaust fan
=====	=====	=====	=====	=====	=====	=====	=====	incinerator/garbage disposer
=====	=====	=====	=====	=====	=====	=====	=====	fireplace (indoor)
=====	=====	=====	=====	=====	=====	=====	=====	floor scrubber / rug shampooer
=====	=====	=====	=====	=====	=====	=====	=====	floor polisher
=====	=====	=====	=====	=====	=====	=====	=====	hired cleaning help
=====	=====	=====	=====	=====	=====	=====	=====	commercial cleaning services/equip. rental

18. On how many of the last 7 days was general cleaning done?

0	1	2	3	4	5	6	7
=====	=====	=====	=====	=====	=====	=====	=====

19. In how many rooms was some care given in the past 7 days?

0	1	2	3	4	5	6	7	8	9+
=====	=====	=====	=====	=====	=====	=====	=====	=====	=====

20. How many rooms were not used in the past 7 days?

0	1	2	3	4	5	6	7	8	9+
=====	=====	=====	=====	=====	=====	=====	=====	=====	=====

The letters DO NOT THAVE appear vertically in the middle column between questions 12 and 16.

```
 0    10    20    30    40       50    60    70    80    90   Deck   0     1     2     3     4        5     6     7     8     9
====  ====  ====  ====  ====     ====  ====  ====  ====  ====   No.  ====  ====  ====  ====  ====      ====  ====  ====  ====  ====
 0    10    20    30    40       50    60    70    80    90   Study  0     1     2     3     4        5     6     7     8     9
====  ====  ====  ====  ====     ====  ====  ====  ====  ====   No.  ====  ====  ====  ====  ====      ====  ====  ====  ====  ====
```

Record No. _____

The House and Its Care (2)

000	100	200	300	400		500	600	700	800	900		00	10	20	30	40		50	60	70	80	90
0	1	2	3	4		5	6	7	8	9	Record	000	100	200	300	400		500	600	700	800	900
00	10	20	30	40		50	60	70	80	90	No.	0	1	2	3	4		5	6	7	8	9

21. Do you have available work space in your kitchen

NO YES at right of sink

NO YES at left of sink

NO YES beside surface units (range or built-in)

NO YES beside oven (range or built-in)

NO YES adjacent to latch side of refrigerator

NO YES 36" or more counter frontage for preparing food

NO YES 72" or more of total counter frontage

22. Do you have

NO YES 72" or more of wall cabinet frontage

NO YES 72" or more of base cabinet frontage

NO YES some storage space beside range

NO YES some storage space beside sink

NO YES some storage space beside refrigerator

23. Do you have

NO YES dishwasher

NO YES disposer

NO YES 0° F. freezer unit or freezer

24. How satisfactory do you find your kitchen for meal preparation?

UNSATISFACTORY			SATISFACTORY		
1	2	3	4	5	6
VERY	FAIRLY	UNSATIS-FACTORY	SATIS-FACTORY	FAIRLY	VERY

25. How satisfactory do you find your kitchen for after-meal cleanup?

UNSATISFACTORY			SATISFACTORY		
1	2	3	4	5	6
VERY	FAIRLY	UNSATIS-FACTORY	SATIS-FACTORY	FAIRLY	VERY

26. Were any of the following used yesterday?

NO YES electric fry-pan, griddle or deep fat fryer

NO YES pressure cooker

NO YES electric mixer or blender

NO YES oven (for other than broiling)

NO YES broiler (separate or in oven)

NO YES outdoor fireplace or grill

D
O
N
O
T
H
A
V
E

27. Were any of the following used yesterday?

NO YES electric fry pan, griddle or deep fat fryer

NO YES pressure cooker

NO YES electric mixer or blender

NO YES oven (for other than broiling)

NO YES broiler (separate or in oven)

NO YES outdoor fireplace or grill

28. On how many of the last 7 days were the following used?

0	1	2	3	4	5	6	7	
0	1	2	3	4	5	6	7	dishwasher
0	1	2	3	4	5	6	7	disposer
0	1	2	3	4	5	6	7	food from 0° F. freezer
0	1	2	3	4	5	6	7	elec. frypan/griddle/deep fat fryer
0	1	2	3	4	5	6	7	oven
0	1	2	3	4	5	6	7	broiler
0	1	2	3	4	5	6	7	pressure cooker
0	1	2	3	4	5	6	7	elec. mixer/blender
0	1	2	3	4	5	6	7	outdoor fireplace/grill

29. Did any of the following increase time required for cleaning your home in the last 7 days?

NO YES inadequate storage space

NO YES extra dirt from drive, walk, yard

NO YES neighborhood construction

NO YES weather condition (rain, snow, mud)

NO YES entertaining family or friends

NO YES room arrangement of house

30. Were any of the following done in the last 7 days to reduce cleaning time in your home?

NO YES use of mats at entrance

NO YES use of special entrance or mud room

NO YES frequent cleaning of entrance areas

NO YES changing shoes/work or playclothes near entrance

| 00 | 10 | 20 | 30 | 40 | | 50 | 60 | 70 | 80 | 90 | Deck No. | 0 | 1 | 2 | 3 | 4 | | 5 | 6 | 7 | 8 | 9 |
| 00 | 10 | 20 | 30 | 40 | | 50 | 60 | 70 | 80 | 90 | Study No. | 0 | 1 | 2 | 3 | 4 | | 5 | 6 | 7 | 8 | 9 |

IBM H95323

Record No. _____

House, Yard, and Car Care

000	100	200	300	400		500	600	700	800	900		00	10	20	30	40		50	60	70	80	90
0	I	2	3	4		5	6	7	8	9	Record No.	000	100	200	300	400		500	600	700	800	900
00	10	20	30	40		50	60	70	80	90		0	I	2	3	4		5	6	7	8	9

1. Is your family responsible for?

NO YES care of drive &/or walks
NO YES care of lawn
NO YES care of shrubs & trees
NO YES care of flower beds or garden
NO YES care of vegetable garden
NO YES outside maintenance of house &/or equipment

2. If your family is responsible for any of the above, how many square feet is the lot?

NOT RESPONSIBLE | UNDER 6,000 | 6,000 TO 9,999 | 10,000 TO 19,999 | OVER 20,000

3. Were the following used in the last 12 months?

NO YES power lawn mower
NO YES hired help for lawn mowing
NO YES snow blower or snowplow
NO YES hired help for snow removal
NO YES hired help for outside maintenance of house
NO YES hired help for yard & garden care

4. How many cars are regularly used in your family? (Count company car &/or truck)

0 I 2 3 MORE

5. NO YES Do you drive?

6. How many drivers are in your family?

0 I 2 3 4 5

7. How often does your family do the following?

DON'T DO | WEEKLY | SEMI-MONTHLY | MONTHLY | OCCASIONALLY | ANNUALLY wash car at home
DON'T DO | WEEKLY | SEMI-MONTHLY | MONTHLY | OCCASIONALLY | ANNUALLY take car to car wash
DON'T DO | WEEKLY | SEMI-MONTHLY | MONTHLY | OCCASIONALLY | ANNUALLY wax car
DON'T DO | WEEKLY | SEMI-MONTHLY | MONTHLY | OCCASIONALLY | ANNUALLY service car at home

8. Which family members used the following yesterday?

NO ONE	H	W	H/W	P/C		H/C	W/C	C	
NO ONE	H	W	H/W	P/C		H/C	W/C	C	family car
NO ONE	H	W	H/W	P/C		H/C	W/C	C	bus
NO ONE	H	W	H/W	P/C		H/C	W/C	C	taxi
NO ONE	H	W	H/W	P/C		H/C	W/C	C	car pool

9. Were the following done yesterday?

NO YES care of walks &/or drive
NO YES care of lawn &/or garden
NO YES maintenance of house &/or equipment
NO YES special house cleaning
NO YES making household furnishings
NO YES care of car
NO YES care of garbage & trash

10. Were any of the following done yesterday?

NO YES care of walks &/or drive
NO YES care of lawn &/or garden
NO YES maintenance of house &/or equipment
NO YES special house cleaning
NO YES making household furnishings
NO YES care of car
NO YES care of garbage & trash

11. Which family members used the following yesterday?

NO ONE	H	W	H/W	P/C		H/C	W/C	C	family car
NO ONE	H	W	H/W	P/C		H/C	W/C	C	bus
NO ONE	H	W	H/W	P/C		H/C	W/C	C	taxi
NO ONE	H	W	H/W	P/C		H/C	W/C	C	car pool

12. On how many of the last 7 days were any of the following done?

0	I	2	3	4		5	6	7	lawn/garden care
0	I	2	3	4		5	6	7	walk/drive care
0	I	2	3	4		5	6	7	house maintenance
0	I	2	3	4		5	6	7	special house-cleaning
0	I	2	3	4		5	6	7	household furnishings made
0	I	2	3	4		5	6	7	car care

13. Which family members used the following in the last 7 days?

NO ONE	H	W	H/W	P/C		H/C	W/C	C	family car
NO ONE	H	W	H/W	P/C		H/C	W/C	C	bus
NO ONE	H	W	H/W	P/C		H/C	W/C	C	taxi
NO ONE	H	W	H/W	P/C		H/C	W/C	C	car pool

00	10	20	30	40		50	60	70	80	90	Deck No.	0	I	2	3	4		5	6	7	8	9
00	10	20	30	40		50	60	70	80	90	Study No.	0	I	2	3	4		5	6	7	8	9

Record No. _____ - _____

Recall date:	Meal 1	Meal 2	Meal 3	Meal 4	Meal 5	Meal 6	Meal 7	Meal 8	Meal 9	Meal 10
Number of persons served this meal at the same time										
Meal prepared by (use symbols from time record)										
Approximate time meal preparation started										

1. Was there anything unusual about the day's meals? If yes, for which meal and what was it?

Meal 1: _____   Meal 6: _____

Meal 2: _____   Meal 7: _____

Meal 3: _____   Meal 8: _____

Meal 4: _____   Meal 9: _____

Meal 5: _____   Meal 10: _____

Record date:	Meal 1	Meal 2	Meal 3	Meal 4	Meal 5	Meal 6	Meal 7	Meal 8	Meal 9	Meal 10
Number of persons served this meal at the same time										
Meal prepared by (use symbols from time record)										
Approximate time meal preparation started										

1. Was there anything unusual about the day's meals? If yes, for which meal and what was it:

Meal 1: _____   Meal 6: _____

Meal 2: _____   Meal 7: _____

Meal 3: _____   Meal 8: _____

Meal 4: _____   Meal 9: _____

Meal 5: _____   Meal 10: _____

Record No. ___ - ___

(1) No. of meal*	(2) Description of food prepared List dishes served (on indented line list major ingredients)	(3) Coded form of food**	None	To single ingredient	To combine ingredients	To finish dish	Total	None	Heat, boil, toast	Roast, bake	Broil, fry	Total	Preserving (Slice, chill, garnish, season, etc.) Total
			a	b	c	d	e	f	g	h	i	j	k

(Column group headers: Number of operations — Non-cooking (clean, form changes, measure, combine, manipulate) covers a–e; Cooking covers f–k)

* Beginning with first meal prepared.

**Form before preparation:
    1. Fresh; 2. Canned; 3. Frozen; 4. Dried; 5. Ready-to-serve; 6. Ready-to-bake;
    7. Ready-to-mix; 8. Home prepared; 9. Leftovers: (a) ready-to-serve; (b) reheated;
                                              (c) completely changed.

Care of Clothing

Record No. _____

000	100	200	300	400		500	600	700	800	900		00	10	20	30	40		50	60	70	80	90

0	1	2	3	4		5	6	7	8	9	Record No.	000	100	200	300	400		500	600	700	800	900

00	10	20	30	40		50	60	70	80	90		0	1	2	3	4		5	6	7	8	9

1. Were any of the following used yesterday?

NO YES		NO YES	
automatic washer		commercial laundry (other than coin laundry)	
nonautomatic washer		diaper service	
dryer		coin operated drycleaning	
combination washer-dryer		commercial drycleaner	
iron		paid laundry help (specify_____)	
sewing equipment			

2. How many loads of clothes were machine washed yesterday?

3. Where was this washer? — AT HOME / IN COIN LAUNDRY / ELSEWHERE

4. How large was the machine used? — VERY SMALL / AVERAGE / ABOVE AVERAGE / VERY LARGE / VARIETY OF SIZES

0	1	2	3	4		5	6	7	8	9			0	1	2	3	4		5	6	7	8	9

5. About how many pieces of clothing (adult/children) were hand washed yesterday?

0	10	20	30	40		50	60	70	80	90		0	1	2	3	4		5	6	7	8	9

6. About how many pieces of household textiles were washed by hand yesterday?

0	10	20	30	40		50	60	70	80	90		0	1	2	3	4		5	6	7	8	9

7. About how many pieces of clothing (adult/children) were ironed in your home yesterday?

0	10	20	30	40		50	60	70	80	90		0	1	2	3	4		5	6	7	8	9

8. About how many pieces of household textiles were ironed in your home yesterday?

0	10	20	30	40		50	60	70	80	90		0	1	2	3	4		5	6	7	8	9

9. Were any of the following used yesterday?

NO YES		NO YES	
automatic washer		commercial laundry (other than coin laundry)	
nonautomatic washer		diaper service	
dryer		coin operated drycleaning	
combination washer-dryer		commercial drycleaners	
iron		paid laundry help (specify_____)	
sewing equipment			

10. How many loads of clothes were machine washed yesterday?

11. Where was this washer? — AT HOME / IN COIN LAUNDRY / ELSEWHERE

12. How large was the machine used? — VERY SMALL / AVERAGE / ABOVE AVERAGE / VERY LARGE / VARIETY OF SIZES

0	1	2	3	4		5	6	7	8	9		0	1	2	3	4		5	6	7	8	9

13. About how many pieces of clothing (adult/children) were hand washed yesterday?

0	10	20	30	40		50	60	70	80	90		0	1	2	3	4		5	6	7	8	9

14. About how many pieces of household textiles were washed by hand yesterday?

0	10	20	30	40		50	60	70	80	90		0	1	2	3	4		5	6	7	8	9

15. About how many pieces of clothing (adult/children) were ironed in your home yesterday?

0	10	20	30	40		50	60	70	80	90		0	1	2	3	4		5	6	7	8	9

16. About how many pieces of household textiles were ironed in your home yesterday?

0	10	20	30	40		50	60	70	80	90		0	1	2	3	4		5	6	7	8	9

17. On how many of the last 7 days did someone:

0	1	2	3	4		5	6	7		0	1	2	3	4		5	6	7	
								sew or mend										wash at coin laundry
								wash by hand										use commercial laundry
								wash with automatic washer										iron clothing
								wash with non-automatic washer										iron household textiles

18. How many average size loads of clothes were washed by your family in the last 7 days?

0	10	20	30	40		50	60	70	80[1]	90		0	1	2	3	4		5	6	7	8	9

0	10	20	30	40		50	60	70	80	90	Deck No.	0	1	2	3	4		5	6	7	8	9

0	10	20	30	40		50	60	70	80	90	Study No.	0	1	2	3	4		5	6	7	8	9

IBM H95327

Care of Family Members

Record No. _____

```
000   100   200   300   400      500   600   700   800   900         00   10   20   30   40       50   60   70   80   90
 0     1     2     3     4         5     6     7     8     9    Record 000  100  200  300  400      500  600  700  800  900
00    10    20    30    40        50    60    70    80    90    No.     0    1    2    3    4        5    6    7    8    9
```

1. Was any time given for physical care of the following yesterday?

NO YES   a baby (under 2 years)

NO YES   one or more 2-5 year olds

NO YES   one or more 6-11 year olds

NO YES   one or more 12-17 year olds

NO YES   adult

2. Was any time given for other care of the following yesterday?

NO YES   a baby (under 2 years)

NO YES   one or more 2-5 year olds

NO YES   one or more 6-11 year olds

NO YES   one or more 12-17 year olds

NO YES   adult

NO YES   pet

3. Were any of the family ill in bed yesterday?

NO YES   a baby (under 2 years)

NO YES   one or more 2-5 year olds

NO YES   one or more 6-11 year olds

NO YES   one or more 12-17 year olds

NO YES   adult

4. If you have a pet, was extra time given for its care yesterday?

NO   PET—NO   PET—
PET   EXTRA TIME   EXTRA TIME

5. On how many of the last 7 days was some physical care given?

0 1 2 3 4   5 6 7 a baby

0 1 2 3 4   5 6 7 2-5 year olds

0 1 2 3 4   5 6 7 6-11 year olds

0 1 2 3 4   5 6 7 12-17 year olds

0 1 2 3 4   5 6 7 adult

6. Was any time given for physical care of the following yesterday?

NO YES   a baby (under 2 years)

NO YES   one or more 2-5 year olds

NO YES   one or more 6-11 year olds

NO YES   one or more 12-17 year olds

NO YES   adult

7. Was any time given for other care of the following yesterday?

NO YES   a baby (under 2 years)

NO YES   one or more 2-5 year olds

NO YES   one or more 6-11 year olds

NO YES   one or more 12-17 year olds

NO YES   adult

NO YES   pet

8. Were any of the family ill in bed yesterday?

NO YES   a baby (under 2 years)

NO YES   one or more 2-5 year olds

NO YES   one or more 6-11 year olds

NO YES   one or more 12-17 year olds

NO YES   adult

9. If you have a pet, was extra time given for its care yesterday?

NO   PET—NO   PET—
PET   EXTRA TIME   EXTRA TIME

10. On how many of the last 7 days was some time given for other care of family members?

0 1 2 3 4   5 6 7 a baby

0 1 2 3 4   5 6 7 2-5 year olds

0 1 2 3 4   5 6 7 6-11 year olds

0 1 2 3 4   5 6 7 12-17 year olds

0 1 2 3 4   5 6 7 adult

0 1 2 3 4   5 6 7 pet

```
0   10   20   30   40      50   60   70   80   90   Deck   0   1   2   3   4      5   6   7   8   9
0   10   20   30   40      50   60   70   80   90   No.
                                                   Study  0   1   2   3   4      5   6   7   8   9
                                                   No.
```

IBM H95326

Marketing and Chauffeuring   Record No. _____

000	100	200	300	400	500	600	700	800	900		00	10	20	30	40	50	60	70	80	90
0	1	2	3	4	5	6	7	8	9	Record No.	000	100	200	300	400	500	600	700	800	900
00	10	20	30	40	50	60	70	80	90		0	1	2	3	4	5	6	7	8	9

---

1. Yesterday, was any shopping done for the following and who was the primary shopper?

	NO	YES		NONE DONE	HUSBAND	WIFE	CHILD	OTHER	COMB.
	NO	YES	food &/or household supplies	NONE DONE	HUSBAND	WIFE	CHILD	OTHER	COMB.
	NO	YES	household equip. &/or furnishings	NONE DONE	H	W	C	O	COMB.
	NO	YES	clothing	NONE DONE	H	W	C	O	COMB.
	NO	YES	other (specify)	NONE DONE	H	W	C	O	COMB.

---

2. Did you do any conscious planning for shopping yesterday?

NO   YES

If so, what ways were used?

NO SHOPPING	WRITTEN LIST	"IN THE HEAD"	COMBINED

3. How often is the major food shopping done for your household?

NO SET PATTERN	DAILY	BI-WEEKLY	WEEKLY	SEMI-MONTHLY	MONTHLY

8. On how many of the last 7 days was chauffeuring done for these purposes?

0	1	2	3	4	5	6	7	shopping
0	1	2	3	4	5	6	7	transporting helper
0	1	2	3	4	5	6	7	taking a family member to or from work/school
0	1	2	3	4	5	6	7	chauff. f. m. for physical care
0	1	2	3	4	5	6	7	chauff. for social & educ. activities of family members

---

4. Was any chauffeuring done yesterday?   Which family member did the driving for the activity listed?

	NO	YES		NO ONE	WIFE	HUSBAND	TEEN-AGER	OTHER
	NO	YES	taking family members shopping	NO ONE	W	H	TEEN-AGER	OTHER
	NO	YES	chauff. helpers other than family	NO ONE	W	H	TEEN-AGER	OTHER
	NO	YES	chauff. family members to/from work/school	NO ONE	W	H	TEEN-AGER	OTHER
	NO	YES	chauff. family members for physical care	NO ONE	W	H	TEEN-AGER	OTHER
	NO	YES	chauff. family members to/from soc. &/or educ. activities	NO ONE	W	H	TEEN-AGER	OTHER

---

5. Yesterday, was any shopping done for the following and who was the primary shopper?

	NO	YES		NONE DONE	HUSBAND	WIFE	CHILD	OTHER	COMB.
	NO	YES	food &/or household supplies	NONE DONE	HUSBAND	WIFE	CHILD	OTHER	COMB.
	NO	YES	household equip. &/or furnishings	NONE DONE	H	W	C	O	COMB.
	NO	YES	clothing	NONE DONE	H	W	C	O	COMB.
	NO	YES	other (specify)	NONE DONE	H	W	C	O	COMB.

---

6. Was any chauffeuring done yesterday?   Which family member did the driving for the activity listed?

	NO	YES		NO ONE	WIFE	HUSBAND	TEEN-AGER	OTHER
	NO	YES	taking family members shopping	NO ONE	WIFE	HUSBAND	TEEN-AGER	OTHER
	NO	YES	chauff. helpers other than family	NO ONE	W	H	TEEN-AGER	OTHER
	NO	YES	chauff. family to &/or from work/school	NO ONE	W	H	TEEN-AGER	OTHER
	NO	YES	chauff. family members for physical care	NO ONE	W	H	TEEN-AGER	OTHER
	NO	YES	chauff. family members to/from soc. &/or educ. activities	NO ONE	W	H	TEEN-AGER	OTHER

---

7. How many trips were made during the last 7 days for food &/or household supplies for your family?

By whom were the trips made?

0	10	20	30		00	01	02	03	04	05	06	07	08	09
0	10	20	30	wife	00	01	02	03	04	05	06	07	08	09
0	10	20	30	husband	00	01	02	03	04	05	06	07	08	09
0	10	20	30	children	00	01	02	03	04	05	06	07	08	09
0	10	20	30	more than one at a time	00	01	02	03	04	05	06	07	08	09
0	10	20	30	other	00	01	02	03	04	05	06	07	08	09

| 0 | 10 | 20 | 30 | 40 | 50 | 60 | 70 | 80 | 90 | Deck No. | 0 | 1 | 2 | 3 | 4 | 5 | 6 | 7 | 8 | 9 |
| 0 | 10 | 20 | 30 | 40 | 50 | 60 | 70 | 80 | 90 | Study No. | 0 | 1 | 2 | 3 | 4 | 5 | 6 | 7 | 8 | 9 |

IBM H95325

Management and Record Keeping   Record No. _____

000	100	200	300	400		500	600	700	800	900			00	10	20	30	40		50	60	70	80	90
0	1	2	3	4		5	6	7	8	9	Record No.	000	100	200	300	400		500	600	700	800	900
00	10	20	30	40		50	60	70	80	90		0	1	2	3	4		5	6	7	8	9

1. What determined the order of your activities yesterday?

2. What techniques do you use to help yourself organize your use of time?

NO YES conscious planning   NO YES "in the head" schedule

NO YES regular weekly routine   NO YES assignment of tasks to family members

NO YES daily routine   NO YES other (specify_____)

NO YES written schedule

3. Under "A" on the card, did any members of your family spend time doing any of these management activities yesterday?

If yes, which members did these things?

NO YES

| NO ONE | WIFE | HUSBAND | H. & W. | CH. |

4. Under "B" on the card, did any members of the family spend time yesterday on these activities?

If yes, which members did these things?

NO YES

| NO ONE | WIFE | HUSBAND | H. & W. | CH. |

5. What determined the order of your activities yesterday?

6. Under "A" on the card, did any members of your family spend time doing any of these management activities yesterday?

If yes, which members did these things?

NO YES

| NO ONE | WIFE | HUSBAND | H. & W. | CH. |

7. Under "B" on the card, did any members of the family spend time yesterday on these activities?

If yes, which members did these things?

NO YES

| NO ONE | WIFE | HUSBAND | H. & W. | CH. |

8. NO YES Do you consider yourself a good Manager?   Why?

9. Under "A" on the card, did any members of your family spend time doing any of these management activities in the last 7 days?

If yes, which family member was primarily responsible?

NO YES

| NO ONE | WIFE | HUSBAND | H.&W. | CH. |

10. Under "B" on the card, did any member of the family spend time in the last 7 days on these activities?

If yes, which family member was primarily responsible?

NO YES

| NO ONE | WIFE | HUSBAND | H. & W. | CH. |

| 0 | 10 | 20 | 30 | 40 | | 50 | 60 | 70 | 80 | 90 | Deck No. | 0 | 1 | 2 | 3 | 4 | | 5 | 6 | 7 | 8 | 9 |
| 0 | 10 | 20 | 30 | 40 | | 50 | 60 | 70 | 80 | 90 | Study No. | 0 | 1 | 2 | 3 | 4 | | 5 | 6 | 7 | 8 | 9 |

IBM H95324

Time at Home and Away   Record No. _____

000	100	200	300	400		500	600	700	800	900		00	10	20	30	40		50	60	70	80	90
0	1	2	3	4		5	6	7	8	9	Record	000	100	200	300	400		500	600	700	800	900
00	10	20	30	40		50	60	70	80	90	No.	0	1	2	3	4		5	6	7	8	9

1. Yesterday, about how many hours were you:

0	10	20	at home (total hours)	00	01	02	03	04	05	06	07	08	09
0	10	20	away from home because of paid employment	00	01	02	03	04	05	06	07	08	09
0	10	20	at home doing paid work	00	01	02	03	04	05	06	07	08	09
0	10	20	doing unpaid &/or volunteer work	00	01	02	03	04	05	06	07	08	09

2. Yesterday, about how many hours was your husband:

0	10	20	at home (total hours)	00	01	02	03	04	05	06	07	08	09
0	10	20	away from home because of paid employment	00	01	02	03	04	05	06	07	08	09
0	10	20	at home doing paid work	00	01	02	03	04	05	06	07	08	09
0	10	20	doing unpaid &/or volunteer work	00	01	02	03	04	05	06	07	08	09

3. Yesterday, about how many hours were your children at home?

0	10	20	c_1	NO CHILD	00	01	02	03	04	05	06	07	08	09
0	10	20	c_2	NO CHILD	00	01	02	03	04	05	06	07	08	09
0	10	20	c_3	NO CHILD	00	01	02	03	04	05	06	07	08	09
0	10	20	c_4	NO CHILD	00	01	02	03	04	05	06	07	08	09
0	10	20	c_5	NO CHILD	00	01	02	03	04	05	06	07	08	09
0	10	20	c_6	NO CHILD	00	01	02	03	04	05	06	07	08	09

4. Yesterday, about how many hours was each child under supervision of someone other than family members? (Church, school, work, etc.)

0	10	20	c_1	NO CHILD	00	01	02	03	04	05	06	07	08	09
0	10	20	c_2	NO CHILD	00	01	02	03	04	05	06	07	08	09
0	10	20	c_3	NO CHILD	00	01	02	03	04	05	06	07	08	09
0	10	20	c_4	NO CHILD	00	01	02	03	04	05	06	07	08	09
0	10	20	c_5	NO CHILD	00	01	02	03	04	05	06	07	08	09
0	10	20	c_6	NO CHILD	00	01	02	03	04	05	06	07	08	09

5. Yesterday, about how many hours were you:

0	10	20	at home (total hours)	00	01	02	03	04	05	06	07	08	09
0	10	20	away from home because of paid employment	00	01	02	03	04	05	06	07	08	09
0	10	20	at home doing paid work	00	01	02	03	04	05	06	07	08	09
0	10	20	doing unpaid &/or volunteer work	00	01	02	03	04	05	06	07	08	09

6. Yesterday, about how many hours was your husband:

0	10	20	at home (total hours)	00	01	02	03	04	05	06	07	08	09
0	10	20	away from home because of paid employment	00	01	02	03	04	05	06	07	08	09
0	10	20	at home doing paid work	00	01	02	03	04	05	06	07	08	09
0	10	20	doing unpaid &/or volunteer work	00	01	02	03	04	05	06	07	08	09

0	10	20	30	40		50	60	70	80	90	Deck No.	0	1	2	3	4		5	6	7	8	9
0	10	20	30	40		50	60	70	80	90	Study No.	0	1	2	3	4		5	6	7	8	9

ITEM H95329

Time at Home and Away
(Record Day)

Record No. _____

000	100	200	300	400	500	600	700	800	900	Record No.	00	10	20	30	40	50	60	70	80	90
0	1	2	3	4	5	6	7	8	9		000	100	200	300	400	500	600	700	800	900
00	10	20	30	40	50	60	70	80	90		0	1	2	3	4	5	6	7	8	9

---

7. Yesterday, about how many hours were your children at home?

0	10	20	c_1	NO CHILD	00	01	02	03	04	05	06	07	08	09
0	10	20	c_2	NO CHILD	00	01	02	03	04	05	06	07	08	09
0	10	20	c_3	NO CHILD	00	01	02	03	04	05	06	07	08	09
0	10	20	c_4	NO CHILD	00	01	02	03	04	05	06	07	08	09
0	10	20	c_5	NO CHILD	00	01	02	03	04	05	06	07	08	09
0	10	20	c_6	NO CHILD	00	01	02	03	04	05	06	07	08	09

8. Yesterday, about how many hours was each child under supervision of someone other than family members (church, school, work, etc.)?

0	10	20	c_1	NO CHILD	00	01	02	03	04	05	06	07	08	09
0	10	20	c_2	NO CHILD	00	01	02	03	04	05	06	07	08	09
0	10	20	c_3	NO CHILD	00	01	02	03	04	05	06	07	08	09
0	10	20	c_4	NO CHILD	00	01	02	03	04	05	06	07	08	09
0	10	20	c_5	NO CHILD	00	01	02	03	04	05	06	07	08	09
0	10	20	c_6	NO CHILD	00	01	02	03	04	05	06	07	08	09

---

9. How much do you like or dislike each of the activities for which you have recorded some time? Rate each on a 6-point scale.

DON'T DO	DISLIKE VERY MUCH	DISLIKE	DISLIKE SOMEWHAT	LIKE SOMEWHAT	LIKE	LIKE VERY MUCH	
0	1	2	3	4	5	6	meal preparation
0	1	2	3	4	5	6	special food preparation
0	1	2	3	4	5	6	after meal cleanup
0	1	2	3	4	5	6	regular housecare
0	1	2	3	4	5	6	special housecare
0	1	2	3	4	5	6	care of yard
0	1	2	3	4	5	6	washing by machine
0	1	2	3	4	5	6	ironing
0	1	2	3	4	5	6	other care of clothing
0	1	2	3	4	5	6	physical care of family members
0	1	2	3	4	5	6	other care of family members
0	1	2	3	4	5	6	marketing or shopping
0	1	2	3	4	5	6	management
0	1	2	3	4	5	6	record keeping
0	1	2	3	4	5	6	care of car
0	1	2	3	4	5	6	volunteer work
0	1	2	3	4	5	6	paid work

0	10	20	30	40	50	60	70	80	90	Deck No.	0	1	2	3	4	5	6	7	8	9
0	10	20	30	40	50	60	70	80	90	Study No.	0	1	2	3	4	5	6	7	8	9

IBM H95331

Record No. _____ - _____

1. Did you do any work for pay last week? Yes ___ No ___ (If no, skip to Q2)

    How many hours did you work during the last 7 days (at all paid jobs)?   ____ hours

    For whom did you work? _____

    What kind of business or industry is this? _____

    What kind of work were you doing? _____

    _____

    How did you get to work?

    drive own car ___   bus   ___   walk only   ___
    car pool   ___   bicycle ___   other means   ___
    taxicab   ___   train   ___   worked at home ___

2. How many hours did your husband work for pay during the last 7 days?   ____ hours

    For whom did he work? _____

    What kind of business or industry is this? _____

    What kind of work was he doing? _____

    _____

    How did he get to work?

    drive own car ___   bus   ___   walk only   ___
    car pool   ___   bicycle ___   other means   ___
    taxicab   ___   train   ___   worked at home ___

3. Did any of your children work for pay during the last 7 days?
    Yes _____   No _____

    Which child? _____   For how many hours?   _____

    Doing what kind of work? _____

    Which child? _____   For how many hours?   _____

    Doing what kind of work? _____

4. What is the highest grade in school completed by your husband _____

                                          by wife _____

Record No. ___ - _____

	Data reported for day of week and date		Date interview taken	Name of interviewer
Recall day				
Record day				

Interviewer: Please note any circumstances that made the days reported different from other days:

1. Unusual weather conditions on recall day _____

   record day _____

   during last 7 days _____

2. Unusual home conditions on recall day _____

   record day _____

   during last 7 days _____

3. Unusual family activities on recall day _____

   record day _____

   during last 7 days _____

4. Special situations in home, such as chronically ill or handicapped person _____

   _____

Office Record   Date   By Whom

Interview validated   _____   _____

Time record completed	H	W	C-1	C-2	C-3	C-4	C-5	C-6	Checked with questionnaire
Recall day									
Record day									

Appendix C

List of References on Household Time Study in the United States

1915 Bailey, I. A study of management of farm homes. *Journal of Home Economics,* 1915, *7,* 348.
Carruth, E. F. A time study in dishwashing. *Journal of Home Economics,* 1915, *7,* 37-38.

1917 Rowe, M. Time necessary to do the work in a seven room house for a family of three. *Journal of Home Economics,* 1917, *9,* 569-573.

1918 Woodbury, M. Time required for housework in a family of five with small children. *Journal of Home Economics,* 1918, *10,* 226-230.

1921 Bailey, I. A survey of farm homes. *Journal of Home Economics,* 1921, *13,* 346-356.

1925 Rust, L. O. A time study of infant care. Unpublished master's thesis, Kansas State Agricultural College, 1925.

1926 Brossard, L. C. Study of time in care of babies. *Journal of Home Economics,* 1926, *18,* 123-127.

1927 Crawford, I. Z. *The Use of Time by Farm Women.* University of Idaho Agricultural Experiment Station Bulletin No. 146, 1927.

1928 Kneeland, H. Women on farms average 63 hours' work weekly, survey of 700 homes. In U.S. Department of Agriculture *Yearbook 1928.* Washington, D.C.: U.S. Government Printing Office, 1929.
Rankin, J. O. *The Use of Time In Farm Homes.* Nebraska Agricultural Experiment Station Bulletin No. 230, 1928.

1929 Arnquist, I. F., and Roberts, E. H. *The Present Use of Work Time of Farm Homemakers.* Washington State College Agricultural Experiment Station Bulletin No. 234, 1929.
Kneeland, H. Is the modern housewife a lady of leisure? *Survey Graphic,* June 1, 1929, 301-302.
Kneeland, H. Women's economic contribution in the home. *Annals of the American Academy, 143,* 1929, 33-40.
Whittemore, M., and Neil, B. *Time Factors in the Business of Home Making in Rural Rhode Island.* Rhode Island State College Agricultural Experiment Station Bulletin No. 221, 1929.
Wilson, M. *Use of Time by Oregon Farm Homemakers.* Oregon Agricultural Experiment Station Bulletin No. 256, 1929.

1930 Brossard, L. C. A study of the time spent in the care of infants one year of age and under. Unpublished master's thesis, University of Chicago, 1930.
Clark, R., and Gray, G. *The Routine and Seasonal Work of Nebraska Farm Women.* Nebraska Agricultural Experiment Station Bulletin No. 238, 1930.
Cushman, E. M. A study of time spent in dishwashing. *Journal of Home Economics,* 1930, *22,* 295-297.
Frayser, M. E. *The Use of Leisure in Selected Rural Areas of South Carolina.* South Carolina Agricultural Experiment Station Bulletin No. 263, 1930.
Wasson, J. *The Use of Time by South Dakota Farm Homemakers.* South Dakota Agricultural Experiment Station Bulletin No. 247, 1930.
Wilson, M. Studies of rural homemakers' time—How can they influence extension programs? Paper read at Extension Department of American Home Economics Association, Denver, June 27, 1930. (Mimeographed)

Wilson, M. Laundry time costs. *Journal of Home Economics,* 1930, *22,* 735-740.

Wilson, M. Studies of rural homemakers' time. *Journal of Home Economics,* 1930, *22,* 832.

Wilson, M. Time costs of children. *Journal of Home Economics,* 1930, *22,* 836-837.

Wilson, M. *Time Used in the Operation of Representative Oregon Households.* A preliminary report. School of Home Economics, Oregon State Agricultural College, 1930.

Wilson, M. *Time Spent in Meal Preparation.* A preliminary report. School of Home Economics, Oregon State Agricultural College, 1930.

Wilson, M. *Time Given to Clearing Away Meals.* A preliminary report. School of Home Economics, Oregon State Agricultural College, 1930.

1932   Kneeland, H. Leisure of homemakers studied for light on standards of living. In U.S. Department of Agriculture *Yearbook of Agriculture.* Washington, D.C.: U.S. Government Printing Office, 1932.

Monroe, D., with Macleod, S. J., Kneeland, H., Davison, E., and Atwater, H. W. Determination of standards for the establishment of household budgets for the expenditure of money, time, and energy. *Journal of Home Economics,* 1932, *24,* 1047-1052; 1933, *25,* 9-12, 109-114.

Wilson, M. Time spent in meal preparation in private households. *Journal of Home Economics,* 1932, *24,* 10-16.

1933   Richardson, J. E. *The Use of Time by Rural Homemakers in Montana.* Montana State College Agricultural Experiment Station Bulletin No. 271, 1933.

Swartz, V. *The Human Energy Cost of Certain Household Tasks.* State College of Washington Agricultural Experiment Station Bulletin No. 282, 1933.

1934   Carpenter, R. S. *The Share of Family Members in Work and Leisure.* (U.S. Department of Agriculture Extension Service, Division of Cooperative Extension, Washington, D.C., Oct. 31, 1934). (Mimeographed)

Kneeland, H. Homemaking in this modern age. *Journal of Association of American University Women,* January 1934, 75-79.

1935   Moser, A. M. *Food Consumption and Use of Time for Food Work Among Farm Families in the South Carolina Piedmont.* South Carolina Agricultural Experiment Station of Clemson Agricultural College, Bulletin No. 300, 1935.

1936   Morey, N. B. The energy requirement of farm women. *Journal of Home Economics,* 1936, *28,* 38-44.

Runnals, M. E. *Planning the Leisure Hours.* University of Nebraska Agricultural Extension Service Circular No. 1188, 1936.

1938   Britton, V. Gainfully employed homemakers. *Journal of Home Economics,* 1938, *30,* 467-469.

Kuschke, B. M. *Allocation of Time by Employed Married Women in Rhode Island.* Rhode Island State College Agricultural Experiment Station Bulletin No. 267, 1938.

Warren J. Use of time in its relation to home management. Unpublished doctoral dissertation, Cornell University, 1938.

1940   Smith, R. E. Testing a measure of household work for use in studying work load and labor efficiency. Unpublished master's thesis, Cornell University, 1940.

Warren, J. *Use of Time in Its Relation to Home Management.* Cornell University Agricultural Experiment Station Bulletin No. 734, 1940.

1943   Hansl, E. V. *Part-time Employment of Women in Wartime.* U.S. Department of Labor, Women's Bureau, Special Bulletin No. 13, July 1943.

1944   U.S. Department of Agriculture, Bureau of Human Nutrition and Home Economics. *The Time Costs of Homemaking—A Study of 1,500 Rural and Urban Households, 1944.* (Mimeographed report of data collected from 1924 to 1931).

1945   Dickins, D. *Time Activities in Homemaking.* Mississippi Agricultural Experiment Station Bulletin No. 424, 1945.

Dickins, D. *Changing Patterns of Food Preparation of Small Town Families.* Mississippi Agricultural Experiment Station Bulletin No. 415, 1945.

Perkins, N. L., Beyer, W., and Bane, L. *A Survey of Some Fatigue Problems of Rural Homemakers.* University of Illinois Agricultural Experiment Station Bulletin No. 514, 1945.

1946 Muse, M. *Time Expenditures on Homemaking Activities in 183 Vermont Farm Homes.* University of Vermont Agricultural Experiment Station Bulletin No. 530, 1946.

1948 Aiken, A. *Family Laundry Practices and Costs.* Cornell University Agricultural Experiment Station Bulletin No. 847, 1948.

1950 Leevy, J. R. Leisure time of the American housewife. *Sociology and Social Research,* 1950, *35,* 97-105.

Snow, C. B. A study of the development of a technique for determining the amount of time and types of activities family members share. Unpublished master's thesis, University of Georgia, 1950.

1952 General Electric Co. The homemaking habits of the working wife. General Electric Co., Public Relations Dept., New York, N.Y. November 1952, 17 pp. (Mimeographed).

1953 Wiegand, E. Comparative use of time of farm and city full-time homemakers and homemakers in the labor force in relation to home management. Doctoral dissertation, Cornell University, 1953.

1954 Thomas, V. F. Time management practices of 47 professionally employed Negro homemakers, Tyler, Texas, 1953-54. Unpublished master's thesis, Ohio State University, 1954.

VanBortel, D., and Gross, I. H. *A Comparison of Home Management in Two Socio-Economic Groups.* Michigan State University Agricultural Experiment Station Technical Bulletin No. 240, 1954.

Weiss, G. S. Time and money costs of meals using home- and prekitchen-prepared foods. *Journal of Home Economics,* 1954, *46,* 98-100.

Wiegand, E. *Use of Time by Full-time and Part-time Homemakers in Relation to Home Management.* Cornell University Agricultural Experiment Station Memoir No. 330, 1954.

1955 Cowles, M., Dietz, R., and Marty, M. Chart use of time by farm homemakers. In *What's New in Farm Science.* Madison: University of Wisconsin Agricultural Experiment Station, 1955.

Gross, I. H. *Home Management of Working and Non-working Homemakers with Young Children.* Michigan Agricultural Experiment Station Quarterly Bulletin, Vol. 37, February 1955.

Thorpe, A., and Gross, I. *How Homes Are Used on Farms and in Small Cities.* Michigan Agricultural Experiment Station Technical Bulletin No. 254, 1955.

Walker, K. E. *Homemaking Work Units for New York State Households.* (Doctoral dissertation, Cornell University) Ann Arbor, Mich.: University Microfilms, 1955, No. 15,437.

1956 Brew, M., and others. Money savings and time costs of homemade children's dresses. In *Rural Family Living.* Washington, D.C.: U.S. Department of Agriculture, 1956.

Broman, E. A. A time and cost study of shopping practices and meals on three levels of preparation. Unpublished master's thesis, University of Texas, 1956.

Cowles, M. L., and Dietz, R. P. Time spent in homemaking activities by a selected group of Wisconsin farm homemakers. *Journal of Home Economics,* 1956, *48,* 29-35.

Knarr, C. A. Management problems of a selected group of employed farm homemakers in Pendleton County, Kentucky, 1956. Unpublished master's thesis, Ohio State University, 1956.

1957 Asp, E. I., and Clark, F. Pilot study of money and time spent in preparing baked products from individual and premixed ingredients. *Journal of Home Economics,* 1957, *49,* 717-719.

Dailey, H. Georgia homemaking work units in meal preparation and dishwashing. Unpublished master's thesis, Cornell University, 1957.

Johannis, T. B. Participation by fathers, mothers and teenage sons and daughters in selected child care and control activities. *Family Life Coordinator,* 1957, *6,* 31-32.

Phillips, S. S. Participation in household tasks by children from 4-12 years of age. Unpublished master's thesis, Cornell University, 1957.

Thorpe, A. C. *Patterns of Family Interaction in Farm and Town Homes.* Michigan State University Agricultural Experiment Station Technical Bulletin No. 260, 1957.

Walker, K. E. *Homemaking Work Units for New York State Households.* Cornell University Agricultural Experiment Station Memoir No. 353, 1957.

1958   Brew, M. L., and Jaeger, C. M. *Exploratory Studies of Measuring Money Savings and Time Costs of Homemade Clothing.* (U.S. Department of Agriculture, Research Service, ARS 62-8).

Dickins, D. *Food Use and Gainful Employment of the Wife.* Mississippi Agricultural Experiment Station Bulletin No. 558, 1958.

Johannis, T. B. Participation by fathers, mothers and teenage sons and daughters in selected household tasks. *Family Life Coordinator,* 1958, *6,* 61-62.

Ross, J. E., and Bostian, L. R. *Time Use Patterns and Communications Activities of Wisconsin Farm Families in Wintertime.* University of Wisconsin, Department of Agricultural Journalism Bulletin No. 28, 1958.

O'Brien, O. J. A study of time use in relation to selected homemaking activities carried on by full-time and employed rural homemakers in Sevier County, Tennessee. Unpublished master's thesis, University of Tennessee, 1958.

Steidl, R. E. Use of time during family meal preparation and cleanup. *Journal of Home Economics,* 1958, *50,* 447-450.

Walker, K. E. *New York State Homemaking Work Units.* Cornell University Miscellaneous Bulletin No. 28, 1958.

Wiegand, E., and Gross, I. H. *Fatigue of Homemakers with Young Children.* Michigan State University Agricultural Experiment Station Technical Bulletin No. 265, 1958.

1959   Foote, N. N., and Meyersohn, R. Allocations of Time Among Family Activities. Paper presented at Fourth World Congress of Sociology, Stresa, Italy, 1959.

McCandless, B. J. Kinds of tasks performed and time used in day-to-day care of the house. Unpublished master's thesis, Cornell University, 1959.

Northeastern Farm Housing Technical Committee. *Farmhouse Planning Guides: Household Activity Data and Space Needs Related to Design.* Ithaca, N.Y.: Cornell University Agricultural Experiment Station and New York State College of Home Economics, 1959.

Smith, R. H., Beyer, G., Klinck, M.S., and Grady, E. *Farmhouse Planning Guides, Household Activity Data and Space Needs Related to Design.* Ithaca, N.Y.: Cornell University Agricultural Experiment Station, 1959. (A Northeastern Regional Research Publication.)

1960   Anderson, E. S., and Fitzsimmons, C. Use of time and money by employed homemakers. *Journal of Home Economics,* 1960, *52,* 452-455.

Deacon, R. E. *Family Laundering at Home and with Commercial Services.* Ohio Agricultural Experiment Station Research Bulletin No. 869, 1960.

Gage, M. G. *The Work Load and Its Value for 50 Homemakers, Tompkins County, New York.* (Doctoral dissertation, Cornell University) Ann Arbor, Mich.: University Microfilms, 1960, No. 61-1440.

Wyskiel, E. W. Time and money management of married students. Unpublished master's thesis, Cornell University, 1960.

1961   Belshaw, B. M. Time spent at household activities. Unpublished master's thesis, Cornell University, 1961.

deGrazia, S. The uses of time. In R.W. Kleemeier (Ed.), *Aging and Leisure.* New York: Oxford Press, 1961.

Dickins, D. *Food Purchases and Use Practices of Families of Gainfully Employed Homemakers.* Mississippi Agricultural Experiment Station Bulletin No. 620, 1961.

Smith, R. H., Gerhold, M., and Kivlin, L. *Family Activity Patterns Basic to Farm Home Planning.* Pennsylvania State University Agricultural Experiment Station Bulletin No. 678, 1961.

Suneson, D. I. Use of time for family food shopping activities. Unpublished master's thesis, Cornell University, 1961.

1962   Bailey, B. W. *Food Management Practices of Employed and Nonemployed Homemaker Families.* Georgia Agricultural Experiment Station Bulletin N.S. 98, 1962.

deGrazia, S. *Of Time, Work and Leisure.* New York: Twentieth Century Fund, 1962, 11-33.

Meyersohn, R. Applying a basic discovery in the recording of behavior. Paper read at the 57th Annual Meeting of the American Sociological Association devoted to the Uses of Sociology, August 31, 1962.

Tasker, G. E. Case studies of homemakers' organization. Unpublished master's thesis, Cornell University, 1962.

1963   Hook, N. C. Use of time in regular care of the house in selected Indiana families. Unpublished master's thesis, Purdue University, 1963.

Steidl, R. E. *Continuity of Household Work.* Cornell University Agricultural Experiment Station Memoir No. 383, 1963.

1964   daFonseca, D. M. Analysis of dishwashing time in selected Indiana families. Unpublished master's thesis, Purdue University, 1964.

Kranz, P. Product innovation through research in the use of time. Report presented at General Electric Marketing Research Seminar, Louisville, Ky., November 18, 1964.

1965   Chapin, F. S., Jr., and Hightower, H. C. Household activity patterns and land use. *Journal of American Institute of Planners,* August 1965, *31,* 222-231.

Goetz, H. M. *Examination of Selected Social and Economic Influences on the Performance of Certain Household Tasks.* (Doctoral dissertation, Purdue University) Ann Arbor, Mich.: University Microfilms, 1965, No. 66-2264.

Purcell, C. E. Development of an Indiana homemaking work unit for washing

clothes. Unpublished master's thesis, Purdue University, 1965.

1966   Chapin, F. S., Jr., and Hightower, H. C. *Household Activity Systems—A Pilot Investigation.* Published by Center for Urban and Regional Studies, Institute for Research in Social Science, University of North Carolina, Chapel Hill, May 1966.

Goetz, H. M., and others. *Quantity and Quality Measures for Homemaking Work Units.* Purdue University Agricultural Experiment Station Research Progress Report No. 217, 1966.

*Hoppen, K. K. Teenage contribution to the work of the home in 28 families, Baldwin, New York. Unpublished master's thesis, Cornell University, 1966.

Morgan, J. N., Sirageldin, I., and Baerwaldt, N. *Productive Americans: A Study of How Individuals Contribute to Economic Progress.* Ann Arbor: University of Michigan, Survey Research Center, Monograph No. 43, 1966.

Robinson, J. P., and Converse, P. E. *66 Basic Tables of Time Budget Research Data for the United States.* Ann Arbor: University of Michigan, Survey Research Center, 1966.

Szalai, A. The multinational comparative time budget research project: A venture in international research cooperation. *The American Behavioral Scientist,* December 1966, *10,* 1-30.

1967   Alcaro, H. D. Analysis of time spent in physical care of children in selected Indiana families. Unpublished master's thesis, Purdue University, 1967.

1968   Chapin, F. S., Jr. Activity systems and urban structure: A working schema. *Journal of the American Institute of Planners,* 1968, *34,* 11-18.

Manning, S. L. *Time Use in Household Tasks by Indiana Families.* Purdue University Agricultural Experiment Station Research Bulletin No. 837, 1968.

*Walker, K. E. Time use for homemaking work. Paper prepared for XIV CIOSTA Congress, Helsinki, Finland, July 1968. (Mimeographed)

---

*Report from Cornell project.

1969 Chapin, F. S., Jr., and Brail, R. K. Human activity systems in the metropolitan United States. *Environment and Behavior*, 1969, *1*, 107-130.

Chapin, F. S., Jr., and Logan, T. H. Patterns of time and space use. In H. S. Perloff (Ed.), *The Quality of the Urban Environment*. Baltimore: The Johns Hopkins Press, 1969.

*Lyerly, B. K. Time used for work in female-headed single-parent families as compared with two-parent families. Unpublished master's thesis, Cornell University, 1969.

*Walker, K. E. Time spent in household work by homemakers. *Family Economics Review* ARS September 1969, 5-6.

*Walker, K. E. Homemaking still takes time. *Journal of Home Economics,* 1969, *61*, 621-624.

1970 Hall, F. T., and Schroeder, M. P. Effects of family and housing characteristics on time spent on household tasks. *Journal of Home Economics,* 1970, *62*, 23-29.

Thrall, C. Household technology and the division of labor in families. Unpublished doctoral dissertation, Harvard University, 1970.

*Walker, K. E. Time-use patterns for household work related to homemakers' employment. Paper read at the 1970 National Agricultural Outlook Conference, Washington, D.C., February 18, 1970.

*Walker, K. E. Time spent by husbands in household work. *Family Economics Review* ARS June 1970, 8-11.

*Walker, K. E. How much help for working mothers? The children's role. *Human Ecology Forum,* 1970, *1*, 13-15.

*"Watcha Doin' Mama?" — Two 30-minute black and white videotapes in four popular technical formats. Produced by ETV Center, New York State College of Human Ecology, Cornell University, Ithaca, N.Y., 1970.

1971 Davey, A. J. *Relationship of Family Interaction to Family Environment.* (Doctoral dissertation, Michigan State University) Fall 1971.

Donnalley, A. E. An investigation of meal management practices of college educated homemakers. Unpublished master's thesis, Cornell University, 1971.

*Walker, K. E. *Time Used for Household Work.* (U.S. Department of Agriculture Research Service, ARS Summary Report, June 15, 1971.)

1972 *Gitobu, J. K. Use of time for household activities by employed and non-employed rural homemakers. Unpublished master's thesis, Cornell University, 1972.

*Jarmon, C. G. Relationship between homemakers' attitudes toward specific household tasks and family composition, other situational variables and time allocation. Unpublished master's thesis, Cornell University, 1972.

Leibowitz, A. Education and the allocation of women's time. New York: National Bureau of Economic Research, 261 Madison Avenue, N.Y. 1972. (Mimeographed).

Szalai, A. (Ed.) *The Use of Time: Daily Activities of Urban and Suburban Populations in Twelve Countries.* The Hague, Paris: Mouton, 1972.

*Walker, K. E., and Woods, M. E. Time use for care of family members. Working paper prepared September 1972. (Mimeographed)

*Whitman, F. The market value of a housewife. Unpublished master's thesis, Cornell University, 1972.

1973 *Gauger, W. H. The potential contribution to the GNP of valuing household work. Paper prepared for Family Economics-Home Management Section of the American Home Economics Association meeting in Atlantic City, N.J., June 26, 1973.

*Gauger, W. H. Household work: Can we add it to the GNP? *Journal of Home Economics,* October 1973, *65*, 12-15.

Vanek, J. *Keeping Busy: Time Spent in Housework, United States, 1920-1970.* (Doctoral dissertation, The University of Michigan) Ann Arbor, Mich.: University Microfilms, 1973, No. 74-3741.

*Walker, K. E., and Gauger, W. H. *The Dollar Value of Household Work.* Information Bulletin No. 60, New York State College of Human Ecology, Cornell University, 1973.

*Report from Cornell project.

*Walker, K. E. Effects of family composition on time contributed for household work by various members. Paper prepared for Family Economics-Home Management Section of the American Home Economics Association meeting in Atlantic City, N.J., June 26, 1973.

*Walker, K. E. Statement of the American Home Economics Association: National Income Accounting of Household Work. *Economic Problems of Women, Hearings before the Joint Economic Committee,* Congress of the United States, Ninety-Third Congress, First Session, Part 3, Statement for the Record. Washington, D.C.: U.S. Government Printing Office, Aug. 13, 1973, 472-476.

*Walker, K. E. Commentary on Women's lib, sex role development, and children's play by Richard A. Gardner. *Medical Aspects of Human Sexuality,* August 1973, *7,* 69.

*Walker, K. E. Household work time: Its implications for family decisions. *Journal of Home Economics,* October 1973, *65,* 7-11.

*Walker, K. E. Economic discrimination and household work. *Human Ecology Forum,* Autumn 1973, *4,* 21-23.

*Walker, K. E., and Gauger, W. H. Time and its dollar value in household work. *Family Economics Review* ARS 62-5, Fall 1973, 8-13.

1974   Chapin, F. S., Jr. *Human Activity Patterns*

in the City: Things People Do in Time and in Space. New York: John Wiley, 1974.

Lindert, P. H. Family inputs and inequality among children. Discussion papers for Institute for Research on Poverty, University of Wisconsin, Madison, October 1974.

*Walker, K. E. Is household production nonwork? Paper prepared for presentation at Conference of the Wisconsin Commission on the Status of Women in Milwaukee, Sept. 19, 1974.

1975   Lindert, P. H. *Fertility and Scarcity in America.* N.J.: Princeton University Press, Princeton (Forthcoming)

*Lynch, M. C. Participation in household work by children 6-17 years of age. Unpublished master's thesis, Cornell University, 1975.

*Lynch, M. C. Sex role stereotype: Household work of children. *Human Ecology Forum,* Winter 1975, *5,* 22-26.

Szalai, A. *The Situation of Women in the Light of the Contemporary Time-Budget Research.* (United Nations, World Conference of the International Women's Year, Mexico City, June 19-July 2, 1975.) E/CONF. 66/BP/6, April 15, 1975.

*Walker, K. E. Who shares in the family work? *American Vocational Journal,* February 1975, *50,* 52-56.

*Report from Cornell project.

Index

Index of Names

Subject Index